ECONOMIC AND SOCIAL COMMISSION FOR ASIA AND THE PACIFIC

Greater Mekong Subregion Business Handbook

UNITED NATIONS
New York, 2002

ESCAP WORKS TOWARDS REDUCING POVERTY AND MANAGING GLOBALIZATION

ST/ESCAP/2183

UNITED NATIONS PUBLICATION
Sales No. E.02.II.F.49
Copyright © United Nations 2002
ISBN: 92-1-120113-6   ISSN: 1020-3516

This manuscript has been prepared by The Brooker Group Public Company Limited, Bangkok, for the International Trade and Industry Division of the Economic and Social Commission for Asia and the Pacific. It may not be reproduced or reprinted without the express permission of the United Nations.

The opinions, figures and estimates contained in this publication are those of the authors, and should not necessarily be considered as reflecting the views or carrying the endorsement of the United Nations or of any particular organization or company.

The designations employed and the presentation of the material in this publication do not imply the expression of any opinion whatsoever on the part of the Secretariat of the United Nations concerning the legal status of any country, territory, city or area, or its authorities, or concerning the delimitation of its frontiers or boundaries. Mention of names of firms and commercial products does not imply the endorsement of the United Nations.

FOREWORD

The Economic and Social Commission for Asia and the Pacific (ESCAP) has been working to enhance private sector development in the Greater Mekong Subregion (GMS) by implementing a comprehensive programme in the subregion. To this end, one of the most recent initiatives of ESCAP is the Hi-Fi Plan, which comprises four main strategies:

- H – human resources development at the enterprise level, including a series of targeted management training initiatives
- i – institutional capacity-building of private sector associations and chambers of commerce and industry, advisory services to exporters, and the creation of a GMS Business Support Centre
- F – facilitation measures, especially in the areas of trade and related procedures
- i – investment promotion through increased interface between foreign and domestic business communities and the creation of a stronger enabling environment for investment.

As part of the investment promotion aspect of the Hi-Fi Plan, ESCAP commissioned the preparation of the *Greater Mekong Subregion Business Handbook*. The Handbook is designed to stimulate interest in and attract investors to the Greater Mekong Subregion by compiling comprehensive information on numerous facets of the Subregion, including background on GMS arrangements, country profiles, projects, investment climate and opportunities, foreign investment procedures and customs, regulatory frameworks, support networks, travel and accommodations, and more. Numerous individual country business handbooks and investor guides are available from public and private agencies, but this Handbook compiles business and investment information from all six economies in the Subregion and places the information in the context of regional opportunities and strategies as opposed to merely an individual country. Not only does the Handbook facilitate new foreign investors in the Subregion, it also provides useful information for those investors already there.

In addition, as a result of the Asian economic crisis, a reassessment of the overall business and investment climate in the Subregion is needed so that investors and business persons there can comprehend the changes that have occurred in the region since the onset of the crisis and adjust their business strategies accordingly. The economic crisis has heightened awareness of the need for global competitiveness, and therefore the last chapter of the Handbook explores the key concepts of competitiveness and how firms in the Subregion should respond to the emerging business challenges and trends.

It is hoped that this Handbook will promote a more positive image of the Greater Mekong Subregion and demonstrate that, with a proper understanding of the business environment, the Subregion offers viable investment opportunities as Asia's next frontier.

CONTENTS

CONTENTS *(continued)*

CONTENTS *(continued)*

LIST OF FIGURES

CONTENTS *(continued)*

I. THE GMS STORY

A. Introduction to the GMS

The Greater Mekong Subregion (GMS) Programme is a subregional initiative designed to promote closer economic ties and economic cooperation among its six members – Cambodia, the Lao People's Democratic Republic, Myanmar, Thailand, Viet Nam, and Yunnan Province, China – all of whom share the Mekong River, the world's twelfth longest river at 4,200 kilometres. The GMS was established in 1992 with the support of the Asian Development Bank (ADB), but the GMS has also benefited greatly over the years from additional contributions and involvement by the United Nations Economic and Social Commission for Asia and the Pacific (ESCAP).

The Mekong region contains approximately 250 million people and covers a land area of 2.3 million square kilometres. The gross domestic product (GDP) of the subregion totaled US$ 212 billion in 1997 and is estimated to grow to US$ 863 billion by the year 2010. The average per capita GDP in the GMS is US$ 2,700. The GMS economies are predominantly based on subsistence agriculture, but they are gradually diversifying into several modern economic sectors and rooted in a more transparent, market-based system.

Overall, the GMS is well-endowed with resources. Along with its strong agricultural base, the GMS contains vast amounts of timber, fisheries resources, a wide variety of minerals, petroleum, natural gas, coal, and some of Asia's best potential for hydropower projects. The human resource base is also considered a potential asset because of its large size and affordable labour. Furthermore, with the relatively young population and above average population growth rates, the GMS offers a significantly large pool of future workers and a substantial consumer market.

Five of the six GMS economies are still undergoing a transition to a market-based economy and opening their sectors to foreign participation. With the exception of Thailand, which has had a free market economy for decades, the GMS economies were previously centrally planned and characterized by state-owned means of production. Low levels of productivity, inadequate amounts of goods, and severe economic problems compelled the Governments in five of the GMS countries to reduce the state's productive role in the economy and allow the business sector to take a greater role in developing the countries both economically and socially. The structural reform process is not complete, but the private sector now functions openly and in most cases has surpassed the state-owned portion of the economy.

The willingness to open up their economies paved the way for subregional economic cooperation, but equally important was the reduction in political and security tensions that plagued peninsular South-East Asia throughout the 1970s and 1980s. The end of the Cold War brought about an improved political and security climate in the region, and at the same time the eventual GMS members recognized that their future well-being depended on economic and social cooperation.

The GMS members share other similarities as well. Although Thailand is more developed economically, all of them have extensive needs in hard and soft infrastructure, education, private sector development (particularly small to medium size enterprises), technology, human resource development, a heavy reliance on subsistence agriculture, and other issues. Many of these matters, such as telecommunications, transportation networks, and energy, are more effectively conducted in a regional setting compared to each country developing on its own. Thus, one of the core objectives of the GMS programme is to link these economies together in the hope of stimulating faster growth and eventually global competitiveness.

Among the key objectives for the GMS, as identified by the Asian Development Bank, are:

- Facilitating subregional trade and investment
- Facilitating subregional development opportunities, particularly for energy, tourism, and other projects
- Facilitating the resolution of transborder issues, such as disease and environmental degradation
- Fulfilling common resource or other needs

These main objectives are meant to improve employment opportunities, generate higher living standards, reduce poverty, and modernize the various economic sectors.

The GMS is not a highly structured regional grouping like the Association of South-East Asian Nations (ASEAN), although all of the GMS members except for Yunnan are now a part of ASEAN. In contrast to ASEAN, the GMS functions with minimal institutional arrangements and is guided by only a general set of principles. The GMS Ministerial Conferences serve as the forums for outlining the agenda, discussing key issues, and deciding on general areas of concentration. Thus far there have been nine Ministerial Conferences, with the most recent one held in January 2000. The GMS also has various forums and working groups in nine areas: transport, electric power, telecommunications, environment, human resource development, trade facilitation, investment, tourism, and the private sector. Other steering groups and similar arrangements are established on an as needed basis.

The intention is not to create a trade bloc, nor do all GMS projects have to involve all six members. Bilateral arrangements are also considered to be vital building blocks of multilateral cooperation and are therefore encouraged within the GMS.

B. The early years of the GMS

Although the GMS officially began in 1992, it was not until 1994 at the Third Conference on Subregional Economic Cooperation in Hanoi that the GMS got its feet on the ground. The Third Conference represents the transition from merely consultation and background studies to feasibility assessments and implementation. The early focus of the GMS centred on seven priority sectors: transport, telecommunications, energy, environment and natural resources management, human resource development, trade and investment, and tourism. A set of project profiles was developed for each of these sectors, and in some cases as many as 34 projects were identified for one sector. A brief summary of the sectors is as follows:

1. Transport

The framework for transport intends to create a subregional transport sector that would facilitate trade. The plans included road, railway, water, and air transportation projects, but road projects were given the highest priority, especially the Bangkok-Phnom Penh-Ho Chi Minh-Vung Tau road and the East-West Corridor running from Viet Nam to the Thai-Myanmar border.

2. Telecommunications

Several of the GMS members did not have direct telecommunication links between them, and so these connections became a priority objective. Plans were also made to upgrade existing infrastructure to fiber optic lines, digitize the national networks, expand facilities, create common standards and technology, and adjust regulations, policies, and tariffs.

3. Energy

The energy projects sought to mobilize the GMS's vast potential in hydropower, coal, and hydrocarbon energy. With such an abundance of resources, it was assumed that energy costs would be low for the members once they harnessed this potential. Projects identified included power generation and transmission, natural gas transmission, institution building, and environmental collaboration. A major goal was to shift energy programmes from isolated, single country projects to cross-border cooperation and complementarity, in particular exporting energy to other members of the GMS.

4. Environment and natural resources management

The Mekong River basin contains numerous watersheds dispersed across boundaries, and this interconnectedness requires cooperation in watershed management, forest management, pollution control, and maintaining bio-diversity. The 11 projects initially identified for this sector revolve around institution building, management of waste and hazardous substances, and management of natural resources.

5. Human resource development

The GMS has a large workforce, over half of the total population of 250 million, but it is underutilized due to unemployment, underemployment, and a shortage of appropriate skills for modern economic activities. The majority of the 11 initial projects identified in this sector focused on education, skills training, and training the trainers, but other projects dealt with health issues such as HIV/AIDS prevention and malaria control.

6. Trade and investment

The GMS members face common problems related to trade and investment. Among these problems are structural adjustment issues arising from the transition to a market economy, underdeveloped legal and regulatory frameworks, limited financial markets, and an inexperienced private sector. The GMS members decided to embark on a series of projects to facilitate trade and investment within the subregion and outside it as well. The eight original project profiles in this sector fell into four categories: facilitating and enhancing trade flows, improving investment climates, building a strong science and technology base, and increasing the role of the private sector in economic development.

7. Tourism

The GMS countries contain rich cultural heritage and a wide variety of geographic features that create considerable tourism potential. The benefits of tourism for economic development made the sector an obvious choice for initiating regional economic cooperation. The GMS governments endorsed six priority projects related to subregional tourism promotion, long-term planning, capacity building, and linkages and networking.

Despite identifying the seven sets of projects, several problems arose in the mid-1990s that slowed the pace of economic cooperation. First, with such a wide variety of projects identified, along with each country's own national planning, duplication of projects and activities occurred because of insufficient coordination. Second, bureaucratic inertia held back many of the projects, and this was compounded by what appears to have been overly ambitious expectations for implementing projects. In most instances, the relevant agencies and ministries in the Governments of the Subregion had a severe shortage of personnel with the requisite skills to implement many of the technical projects. Moreover, bureaucrats and government officials were not always committed to fostering subregional cooperation.

A third set of problems related to political controversies in some of the member countries. Instability in the Government of Cambodia and the ongoing civil war clearly hindered the country's full participation in the GMS framework. The boycott levied by several Western States against Myanmar inhibited multilateral lending and investment, again making it difficult to fully realize many of the projects envisaged for the GMS.

Fourth, and perhaps the most devastating problem, was the advent of the East Asian economic crisis that erupted in mid-1997 in Thailand. The fallout from the crisis brought subregional economic cooperation to a standstill, as countries all across East Asia concentrated on restoring domestic financial and economic stability. Thailand, the GMS's most developed and prosperous member, faced severe economic challenges that forced it to turn inward at least temporarily, but Thailand's problems also created spillovers for others in the GMS, especially the Lao People's Democratic Republic, which relied heavily on trade and investment from Thailand.

C. 2000 and beyond: the GMS on the roll again

Towards the end of 1999, the GMS began to regain momentum as the immediate impact of the crisis began to subside and other factors converged. Among these additional factors were progress in the ADB's "corridor approach" to development, a series of GMS forums bringing together public and private sector representatives, the Ninth Ministerial Conference, and an increased recognition of the need to involve the private sector in the overall GMS strategy.

The two main economic corridors, the East-West Corridor and the North-South Corridor, are an attempt to devise a more holistic approach to development and cooperation in the GMS (see section G). According to ADB, an economic corridor "is a well-defined area where infrastructure improvements are linked with production, trade and other development opportunities in order to promote economic development and cooperation among contiguous regions or countries." In the past, infrastructure projects in the GMS were often conducted in isolation from population centres, markets, access to raw materials, and social and economic services. The aim is to generate investment, employment, and higher income with infrastructure development along key economic channels.

Several GMS forums have been held since late 1999 that helped reinvigorate interest in the GMS as a potential investment area. A special GMS session held in conjunction with the World Economic Forum in October 1999 in Singapore brought together public and private sector representatives from all over the world. The year ended in a flurry of GMS activities, most notably a series of ADB meetings from November to December. No less than five consequential meetings were hosted by the ADB in Thailand, the Lao People's Democratic Republic, and the Philippines:

- Inception Meeting of the Subregional Trade Facilitation Working Group (Bangkok, November 1999)
- Fifth Meeting of the Subregional Transport Forum (Thailand, November 1999)
- Tenth Meeting of the Working Group on Tourism (Vientiane, November 1999)
- Fourth Mekong Tourism Forum (Vientiane, November 1999)
- Sixth Meeting of the Working Group on Environment (Manila, December 1999)

The Ninth GMS Ministerial Conference, held in Manila in January 2000, represents a watershed in the development of the GMS. The theme of the conference, "opening borders," encapsulates the renewed emphasis on software issues designed to increase the flow of people, goods, and investment across the GMS. The first manifestation of this commitment to opening borders was the promulgation of the "Agreement on Commercial Navigation on the Lancang-Mekong River," which was signed in April 2000 by the Governments of China, the Lao People's Democratic Republic, Myanmar, and Thailand. The agreement, which comes into effect in June 2001, will promote trade and tourism, strengthen cooperation in commercial navigation, and help attract greater investment along the upper portion of the river.

Also instrumental in reviving the GMS concept was the "GMS Business Sector Meeting" in February 2000, sponsored by ESCAP and ADB. Soon afterwards, Thailand's Board of Investment (BOI) hosted the "GMS Business Workshops." A significant step was taken in October 2000 with the launch of the GMS Business Forum, which brings together the business community throughout the GMS via the national chambers of commerce (see section F on the evolution of the GMS business sector).

Although initially sidelined from much of the GMS process, the private sector is receiving its deserved attention from Governments of the Subregion and the major multilateral institutions. In addition to the formation of the GMS Business Forum, several programmes are under way for enhancing the private sector throughout the subregion. ESCAP devised its "Hi-Fi Plan" for private sector development in the GMS, which focuses on human resources development, institutional capacity-building, trade facilitation measures, and investment promotion.

ESCAP launched three key projects of the Hi-Fi Plan in 1999 and 2000: a management training course for private sector entrepreneurs in Myanmar, the GMS Business Handbook, and the GMS Business Support Centre. Additional management projects are scheduled in 2001 and 2002 for Cambodia, the Lao People's Democratic Republic, Viet Nam, and Yunnan. Also, ESCAP will commence with its GMS Chambers of Commerce Strengthening project in 2001 to build up the service capacities of the chambers' staff.

D. Old and new problems for the GMS

Despite the unprecedented progress and recent flurry of activities for the GMS, the subregion is still beset by several lingering problems and the onset of more recent ones. Five of the six GMS members are continuing their transitions to a more open and market-based economy, but progress has been slow and incremental at best and, at times, even regressive. Some of the economic reforms have either not been launched by the governments or have been rescinded, creating an uncertain environment which deters many investors. The "one step forward, two steps back" approach to opening the economy has caused some investors to pull out of the GMS and relocate their investments elsewhere. Moreover, the legal and regulatory frameworks in many of the GMS countries are still below internationally-accepted standards.

A second issue hampering the progress of the GMS is that, despite repeated calls for greater involvement of the business sector, the GMS programme still relies heavily on the multilateral agencies and the Governments. A combination of a weak private sector in most GMS economies, regulatory obstacles to the private sector, and insufficient interface between the private sector on one hand and the major GMS multilateral agencies and Governments on the other. A consensus has emerged all over the world that the private sector must be the driving force in economic development, with the Government playing a facilitating role. However, in some of the GMS economies the state-owned enterprise sector still dominates and inhibits the growth of the private sector.

Third, while the crisis-hit countries of East Asia have made important steps towards economic recovery, there are still several fundamental political and economic issues that need to be addressed:

(a)   While the economic philosophies have changed in the GMS to market-oriented economies, the bureaucracies contain many of the same people who were formerly guiding the centrally-planned economies. The shortage of government officials trained in market economic principles is clearly an obstacle for five of the six GMS countries.

(b)   The Governments tend to utilize control-oriented approaches to economic management. Slight reforms or openings are made, but often times the Government maintains strict control over business activities and in particular over policy-making.

(c)   Bureaucracies in many of the GMS economies are designed to prevent abuse as opposed to being efficient. Foreign investors frequently complain about the large amount of red tape involved in setting up and operating a business, importing and exporting, and other related activities.

(d)   The private sector is still viewed with suspicion by many of the GMS Governments. Although they proclaim to be committed to market-style economics, strict limits are set on competition (particularly with state-owned enterprises), the formation of business associations, labour unions, foreign ownership, and the movement of labour.

Other fundamental weaknesses in the GMS compound the aforementioned problems. The educational systems in the GMS are still weak in terms of the quality of education and levels of enrolment and retention. Also, the labour force in the GMS is in desperate need of upgrading its skills, but training programmes are limited and there is typically a dearth of modern technology. Another barrier to development includes the financial systems in all of the GMS economies, which were epitomized by the near collapse of the financial system in Thailand in 1997 and 1998. The lesser developed GMS members have much smaller financial systems than Thailand, and credit is extremely limited at present. Investors' confidence in the GMS economies has diminished over the past few years because of these problems, but the underdeveloped legal and regulatory frameworks throughout the GMS are still a major barrier in attracting foreign investors. The Governments will need to continue making reforms for opening the economy and put in place the necessary legislation and regulations to create an environment conducive to business.

The GMS has been fortunate in terminating international hostilities in the region, but certain ongoing political issues will likely impede economic progress. For instance, some of the major multilateral agencies are prohibited by their stakeholders from extending loans or grants to Myanmar, and some Western donor countries have also refused to give loans or allow full trade and investment relations between their private sectors and Myanmar.

Additionally, an imposing challenge for the GMS is the inability to match the current economic and business needs for a modern economy. Shortages of trained workers, low levels of technology, few managers capable of operating modern factories, and a lack of entrepreneurship render some of the GMS countries uncompetitive in the regional and global economies. The subregion must address these and other fundamental issues if it intends to spur growth and prosperity.

E.   The GMS: the emerging frontier in Asia?

Like other developing regions, the GMS has its fair share of obstacles to overcome. Yet at the same time, it offers exciting opportunities for business activities. One of the GMS's greatest assets is its strategic location. Lying at the crossroads of the world's two most populous countries, China and India, the GMS provides a strategic foothold for accessing those two markets. Even the domestic market of the GMS is substantial, with approximately 250 million people who are gradually becoming more interconnected and increasing their purchasing power. Furthermore, the GMS, via Thailand, aspires to be South-East Asia's regional transportation and services hub, along with one of Asia's primary energy producers because of the hydropower potential in the Lao People's Democratic Republic, Myanmar, Yunnan, and to a lesser extent, Cambodia.

The GMS is also well-endowed with vast tracts of fertile land. For instance, in Myanmar 9 million hectares are currently under cultivation, representing only 13 per cent of the total land area of the country. The Ministry of Agriculture and Irrigation estimates that another 9 million acres can be sown in fallow and cultivatable unused land. With the agricultural base already established, the GMS is a perfect opportunity for many agro-based industries such as food production, processing, and packaging.

The rich natural resources found in the GMS are also enticing investment opportunities. A wide variety of resources such as timber, minerals, gems, coal, oil, natural gas, and metals abound in the subregion and, in many cases, are only beginning to be exploited. In Cambodia, the north-east area contains a wide variety of minerals, coal, and other valuable resources, but almost no extractive activities are being undertaken. In fact, the exploration phase is still only in the preliminary stages, yet dozens of mines and deposits have already been discovered.

Likewise, the energy sector is operating at a small fraction of its total capacity – a little more than two per cent of the full potential. Several sites have been identified for hydropower projects in the Lao People's Democratic Republic, Myanmar, and Yunnan, but only a few are in the construction process or already on-line. An inventory of hydropower in the GMS estimates that the subregion has the potential for 1,090 TWh per annum, while the energy demand in the GMS by the year 2020 is expected to reach only 600 TWh per year, leaving a substantial amount available for exporting out of the region.

Some of the GMS countries are considered among the least developed in the world and therefore receive special trade preferences from several industrialized countries. Cambodia and the Lao People's Democratic Republic, for instance, received Generalized System of Preferences (GSP) status on selected goods. Although these favorable terms will eventually be phased out under World Trade Organization (WTO) rules and replaced with a collective system of concessions yet to be determined, they are expected to remain in place for several years to come.

The skill level of the GMS labour force is typically seen as a drawback for the region in attracting attention from foreign investors. Although the overall level of education and skill is below other parts of Asia, the GMS offers a large, low cost, and ambitious labour force. Viet Nam, for instance, is reputed to have one of the most disciplined and hard working populations in Asia and, along with the other GMS members, its workforce is eager for training and is highly adaptable. Thailand's large labour pool provides an excellent combination of intermediate and advanced skills with competitive wages.

These aforementioned general attractions and advantages of the GMS are accompanied by specific sectoral opportunities for investors. The details of the key sectors are discussed in the country chapters of the Handbook, but a brief overview is presented here.

Infrastructure is one of the most appealing sectors in the GMS because of the ambitious network plans and projects identified for roads, rail, seaports, telecommunications, and aviation. Although several projects have already been completed or are under construction, there are numerous opportunities for investors in some of ADB's priority projects, especially taking the ADB-funded network projects a step further by connecting them to villages, households, and industrial sites.

Agro-industries are an obvious investment opportunity in the GMS because of the well-established agricultural base in all six GMS economies. With land available throughout the subregion, an experienced pool of farm workers, and a climate and topography that enable a wide variety of crops to be cultivated, the GMS is an ideal base for agriculture and agro-processing industries.

Investment in the education sector is also emerging as the demand for educational opportunities outstrips the available seats. Courses offered by private schools or companies providing educational services for English, computers and programming, and business are extremely popular in the GMS and the demand is expected to grow.

Tourism has become one of the GMS's most important sectors. The natural beauty and diversified landscapes are accented by the colourful mix of cultural groups, including various hilltribes in every GMS country. The combination of beautiful physical attractions and intriguing cultural experiences is making the GMS a favourite destination for travelers looking for a unique holiday. Whether in the capital cities, beach areas, or trekking in the mountains, opportunities abound for tour agents, hotel and resort developers, and attraction operators.

As noted earlier, the GMS contains extensive amounts of minerals and other natural resources, many of which are only beginning to be harnessed. The Governments of the Subregion offer private firms various types of concessions for resource exploitation, depending on the type of resource and other factors. Furthermore, the processing of resources is typically conducted outside of the GMS, but the conditions are increasingly favorable for establishing processing plants and refineries within the subregion.

As a result of rising wages in the more developed countries of Asia, companies are increasingly shifting their light assembly and manufacturing operations to the GMS. The GMS's competitive wages, surplus of employable people, and increasingly skilled labour force have attracted investment from multinational companies such as Nike, Proctor and Gamble, Toyota, Isuzu, Unilever, and many others. Electronics assembly is rapidly expanding throughout the GMS, as well as automotive assembly and consumer products. Furthermore, companies are beginning to realize the market potential in the whole GMS compared to the typical perception of individual small markets.

Likewise, garments and textiles continue to be a popular industry in the GMS for many of the same reasons as assembly and manufacturing. Also, some of the GMS members receive preferential trade and tariff treatment by the wealthy Western countries for garments and textiles, which allows foreign invested garment and textile firms in Cambodia and the Lao People's Democratic Republic, for example, to gain greater market access to Europe and the United States.

F. The evolution of business sector cooperation in the GMS

The prevailing perception of the GMS among foreign business people is that it is still a highly underdeveloped area with low purchasing power, state domination of the economies, and weak capacities of the indigenous business sector. To a certain extent this perception is still valid in some of the GMS economies, except Thailand, but the other five GMS economies are gradually opening up and putting in place the requisite components for a solid business and economic foundation. One of the most often overlooked developments is the growing indigenous business sector in the GMS.

The business sector in much of the GMS is still in a nascent stage of development as a result of the relatively late transition to market economic principles. The transition from a command economy to a private sector in some GMS countries is less than 15 years old as in the case of Myanmar. Initiatives for developing the business sector as a whole throughout the GMS are even more recent, essentially dating back to 1994-1995.

The first major focus on private sector development in the Greater Mekong Subregion came under the umbrella of the ADB-supported Greater Mekong Subregion Economic Cooperation Project. The Third Ministerial Meeting for GMS subregional cooperation in Hanoi in April 1994 called for the creation of a "Subregional Growth Zone through Constructive Business Facilitation," explicitly recognizing the importance of the business community.

In the original set of trade and investment cooperation projects presented at the Third Conference on Subregional Economic Cooperation in Hanoi from 20 to 23 April 1994, the Conference generally endorsed the further study of strengthening the private sector and small and medium-size enterprise (SME) development through the creation of a Network of Chambers of Commerce and Industry within the subregion.

At the GMS Ministerial Meeting in Manila in November 1995, the Ministers called for greater efforts in exploring mechanisms to enhance the involvement of the private sector, both domestic and foreign, in the economic cooperation process. Subsequently, a 1996 report by ADB noted progress in subregional economic cooperation among the private sector and also confirmed the subregion's recognition that private sector finance, expertise, management skills, and technology will be a key to the dynamism of all GMS countries. The report noted that business representatives have been increasingly involved in trade and investment activities of the respective countries, and that the chambers of commerce have become more active in international forums such as the World Economic Forum and similar activities.

The support for the business sector has been evident in other initiatives as well. In February 1995 at the ministerial meeting of the Forum for the Comprehensive Development of Indo-China, the participants agreed in principle to set up an advisory group under the auspices of ESCAP to absorb views and opinions of the private sector on the role of development assistance to promote private sector activities in the Indo-China subregion. The first meeting of the Private Sector Advisory Group was held in Bangkok on 5 March 1996, and it was agreed to examine in more detail the role of the private sector and official development assistance in the Indo-China countries. Accordingly, a study on private sector development in Cambodia, the Lao People's Democratic Republic, and Viet Nam provided members of the Private Sector Advisory Group with detailed analysis concerning the current status of private sector development in the three countries, along with recommendations for reforms to remove existing impediments to private sector development.

As a part of disseminating the findings of the study prepared for the Private Sector Advisory Group, the first meeting of the GMS Chambers of Commerce and Industry was convened in Ho Chi Minh City in September 1996. The meeting, which was attended by representatives of the private sector from all GMS countries, concluded that significant scope exists for cooperation between the GMS Chambers of Commerce and Industry in the following areas:

(1) Information exchange
(2) Institutional strengthening
(3) Exchange meetings and fact-finding visits
(4) Coordinating private sector activities in the GMS.

Following the meeting, a number of follow-up activities were undertaken, including: training programmes coordinated by the Thai Chamber of Commerce through the University of the Thai Chamber of Commerce; further discussions with the ASEAN Chamber of Commerce and Industry regarding the new ASEAN members; and the Private Sector Salute to ASEAN in December 1997.

At the Seventh Conference on Greater Mekong Subregion Economic Cooperation in April 1997, representatives from the GMS Chambers of Commerce and Industry held a coordination meeting. This activity marked a significant step forward with regard to involving the GMS business community in the GMS economic cooperation process. In particular, the GMS ministers agreed to endorse the establishment of a GMS Business Forum that will report to the GMS Ministerial Conference and to support enhanced private sector participation in meetings of GMS working groups and forums.

The ESCAP-supported project mentioned above explicitly examined the potential for enhancing the interface between the business sectors in Cambodia, the Lao People's Democratic Republic, Myanmar, and Viet Nam and their partners in ASEAN. The practical experiences with the three workshops (entitled *Maximizing Benefits from ASEAN on Economic Cooperation and Trade Facilitation* held in close cooperation with the chambers of commerce in the Lao People's Democratic Republic, Myanmar, and Viet Nam) and interviews in Cambodia confirmed that the business community would benefit from greater activities of the chambers of commerce in their respective countries.

The 1997 Asian economic crisis disrupted the momentum for business sector cooperation in the GMS, as many countries in the region focused on resolving domestic macroeconomic problems and even questioned moves to economic liberalization. By mid-1999, however, steps were taken towards resuming subregional economic cooperation.

A critical milestone in the re-emergence of GMS economic cooperation from the perspective of the business sector occurred in September 1999 in Kunming, Yunnan with the second meeting of the Subregional Investment Working Group (SIWG). In particular, the SIWG designated "Support for the GMS Business Forum" as its third prioritized project, with ESCAP as the coordinating agency. An earlier ministerial mandate gave the ADB authority to activate the GMS Business Forum, but various reasons delayed its launch.

The report from the second meeting of the SIWG delineated the scope of the GMS Business Forum:

- Review of key needs and existing initiatives supporting business chambers in the GMS (e.g., through ESCAP), focusing specifically on their role in GMS investment promotion, and on strengthening investment facilitation and regulation as related to subregional projects.
- Evaluation of linkages with investment-related government agencies in the context of GMS-related activities.
- Development of a programme to support linkages (e.g., information) among the chambers focused on mobilizing their contribution to formulating and implementing a promotional strategy for the GMS, and for ensuring their continuing contribution to improvements related to subregional investment facilitation and regulation.
- Design a roadmap for a network of private sector activities and GMS country institutions.
- Integrating the financial and business services sectors into the investment network.

As the region began to recover from the economic crisis in the second half of 1999, a renewed commitment to GMS cooperation was launched during the GMS Networking Luncheon at the WEF Summit in October 1999. Thailand's Deputy Prime Minister Supachai Panitchpakdi called for greater involvement of the GMS business sector, and ESCAP responded by introducing its Hi-Fi Plan – a comprehensive approach to the business sector and linkage development in the GMS.

Private sector activities in 2000 kicked off with the "GMS Business Sector Meeting" sponsored by ESCAP and ADB, which brought in several representatives from the GMS chambers of commerce and served as a precursor to the GMS Business Forum. The chambers of commerce discussed with ADB and ESCAP representatives the ongoing GMS programmes sponsored by the two multilateral agencies. The participants also prepared an action plan for moving the GMS business sector forward in its development. The action plan contained six main elements: 1) management training; 2) strengthening business associations; 3) establishing the GMS Business Centre; 4) greater business sector involvement in the GMS economic cooperation initiatives; 5) creating a GMS business sector priority matrix and tracking mechanism; and 6) implementing the GMS Business Forum.

The Business Sector Meeting concluded with a draft of the "Bangkok Blueprint for Business Sector Development in the GMS." The blueprint contained a set of cooperation commitments to be undertaken by the GMS business associations and several key objectives to advance their development. The final version of the Bangkok Blueprint was signed by all of the participating business associations within a couple of months.

Following the ESCAP event, Thailand's Board of Investment (BOI) hosted the "GMS Business Workshops" in February 2000 as a part of its "BOI Fair 2000." This important event brought together prospective foreign and domestic investors and existing businesspeople in the GMS with senior government and multilateral officials. The "GMS Business Workshops" explored the current economic and business conditions in the GMS, reviewed the key legal and regulatory changes, highlighted the main investment opportunities available, and facilitated the crucial public-private sector interface that had been lacking in the past.

The launch of the GMS Business Forum in October 2000 is a key milestone in the development of the business sector. The GMS Business Forum is an independent, non-government body formed by the national chambers of commerce and industry in the six GMS economies, with assistance from ADB and ESCAP. It aims to promote business activities and investment in the area by building up the capacity of the local private sector, creating stronger linkages between local firms and foreign firms, and enhancing the public-private sector interface in the GMS, including the major multilateral agencies. The Business Forum represents an important step in cementing the private sector's role in the overall GMS scheme and will ensure a greater voice for the business community's interests and concerns. One of the weaknesses of the GMS arrangement has been the lack of involvement of the business sector, and thus the GMS Business Forum should help overcome this constraint.

A small institutional structure is emerging for the Business Forum in the form of a Secretariat, which is scheduled to officially open in June 2000. Efforts are under way to expand the membership of the GMS Business Forum by inviting the foreign chambers of commerce to participate as affiliate members. Over time the Business Forum will articulate both the domestic GMS business perspectives and the foreign sector as well.

G. GMS growth areas

The GMS countries adopted an important strategic change at the Eighth Ministerial Conference in October 1998 with the endorsement of the "economic corridor" approach. The expectation is that these corridors will stimulate nodes of economic activity, such as special production and trade zones, from the existing opportunities and endowments along the routes.

Presently four economic corridors are featured in the GMS. The East-West Corridor, the pilot project for the approach, will link Mawlamyine (Myanmar) with Da Nang (Viet Nam) via north-central and north-east Thailand and Savannakhet (Lao People's Democratic Republic). The second connection is the North-South Corridor linking Kunming (Yunnan, China) and Chiang Rai (Thailand) through north-western Lao People's Democratic Republic. The third corridor will extend from Bangkok to Phnom Penh (Cambodia) to Ho Chi Minh City and Vung Tau (Viet Nam). The last planned corridor will run from Kunming to Hanoi to Haiphong (Viet Nam).

The East-West Corridor is the priority corridor project, and ADB approved the project in December 1999 for approximately US$ 740 million. Approximately 90 per cent of Route 9, the road network along the corridor connecting Myanmar to Viet Nam, will be complete by 2003. The road link will span nearly 1,500 kilometres, with ports on both ends at Mawlamyine and Da Nang. The East-West Corridor is expected to improve access to raw materials, stimulate trade and exports, bring together many of the inherent factors of production found throughout the region, and create higher growth rates for many of the secondary cities and towns along the route.

The various studies and sectoral reports for the East-West Corridor identified 63 project initiatives for the public sector. Projects are grouped into seven categories: spatial planning (road network), physical infrastructure, policy and procedural reform (especially for reducing trade barriers), supporting programmes, skills development, capital and financing (for SMEs), and institutional development. Of course, there are seemingly limitless opportunities for private sector projects stemming from and complementing these public sector initiatives.

For the North-South Corridor, the three countries are in the process of upgrading their respective roads. Problems with the concession in the Lao People's Democratic Republic caused a delay in the Lao portion of the network, but ADB and other sources will put up the finance to complete the road rehabilitation.

The Kunming-Hanoi-Haiphong Corridor is expected to commence with technical assistance to China and Viet Nam in 2001. Also, ADB will extend US$ 60 million worth of loans to Viet Nam in 2002 for financing part of the corridor.

H. GMS in ASEAN

All of the members of the GMS except for Yunnan are concurrently members of the Association of South-East Asian Nations (ASEAN). ASEAN was formed in 1967 by Indonesia, Malaysia, the Philippines, Singapore, and Thailand, and then later welcomed Brunei Darussalam in 1984. ASEAN originally proclaimed that its intention was to foster economic and social cooperation, but the organization implicitly focused on political and security matters for the first few decades.

Although the goal since ASEAN's formation in 1967 was to encompass all 10 South-East Asian countries, the political and economic complexities in the region kept the ASEAN members apart from their other neighbours until the mid-1990s, when the remaining South-East Asian countries gradually became members. Viet Nam joined in 1995, followed by the Lao People's Democratic Republic and Myanmar in 1997. Cambodia's domestic turmoil postponed its membership until 1999, and after 32 years ASEAN finally became complete. As the political landscape in South-East Asia changed in the 1990s, as well as ASEAN's membership, there has been a noticeable shift in ASEAN's goals. Nowadays, the association focuses on economic cooperation such as the ASEAN Free Trade Area (AFTA), cultural and social cooperation (women, health, poverty eradication, and other issues), and the environment.

ASEAN does not compete with GMS, nor is it contrary to the GMS's goals and strategies. In fact, ASEAN and GMS are highly complementary and work towards the same goals, only with slightly different arrangements. ASEAN has an explicit focus on raising the standard of living and closing the gap between the original members and the newer (and poorer) members. As early as 1996, ASEAN devised its "Basic Framework of ASEAN-Mekong Basin Development Cooperation," which provided the foundation for the ASEAN Mekong Basin Development Scheme. The seven members of ASEAN at that time formed a "core group" for the Mekong Basin scheme that included Cambodia, the Lao People's Democratic Republic, and China.

The framework laid out the objectives and principles for cooperation, and also identified priority sectors: infrastructure, trade and investment activities, agriculture, forestry and minerals, industry, tourism, human resource development, and science and technology. It also recognized the role of the other Mekong-related multilateral institutions in the development process and sought to complement their activities.

Of particular interest to the local and foreign business communities are the various economic cooperation programmes that the newest members of ASEAN will benefit from, and even Yunnan is likely to benefit at least indirectly. The most ambitious economic programme is AFTA, which aims to reduce tariffs in most product categories. ASEAN agreed on the AFTA framework in 1992, but it has been amended several times as a result of the new members and other circumstances.

Under the Common Effective Preferential Tariff (CEPT) for AFTA, many manufactured products will have tariffs at 0-5 per cent by 2003 (the original schedule was 2008). A 1999 agreement allows the member states to phase in tariff reductions on sensitive and highly sensitive products. Brunei Darussalam, Indonesia, Malaysia, the Philippines, Singapore, and Thailand must phase in the 0-5 per cent tariff on sensitive products by January 1, 2001 or at least by January 2003, with full implementation complete by January 1, 2010. For highly sensitive products, such as rice and other agricultural goods, the end tariff rates are flexible but will likely be around 20 per cent. These will be phased in beginning in January 2001 or by 2005, with full implementation by January 2010.

The newer members of ASEAN were granted extensions on sensitive products as shown in table 1:

Table 1. New ASEAN members' timetable for sensitive products tariff reductions

Country	Sensitive products	
	Start phase-in	Completion
Cambodia	2008-2010	2017
Lao People's Democratic Republic	2006-2008	2010
Myanmar	2006-2008	2010
Viet Nam	2004-2006	2013

AFTA also includes a schedule for eliminating quantitative restrictions between 2010 and 2017, depending on the agreement made by each state.

The five GMS members who are also a part of ASEAN are participating in the ASEAN Industrial Cooperation Scheme (AICO), which was created in 1996. AICO promotes joint manufacturing industrial activities involving two or more companies from two or more ASEAN states. The objective is to promote investment in technology-based industries and enhance value added activities among the members. Firms participating in AICO receive special tariff and non-tariff incentives.

Another ASEAN economic cooperation scheme is the ASEAN Investment Area (AIA). The agreement, reached in 1998, intends to promote investment from within and outside of ASEAN. AIA's main objectives/ benefits are to coordinate investment facilitation programmes; open industries for investment; and grant national treatment to firms that qualify.

I. What's next for the GMS?

The development and prosperity of the GMS will be a function of how well it can meet the business challenges of the twenty first century. Overcoming the challenges requires that the countries address the critical needs for the business sector and economy, and adopt the available "tools" to lift them into the realm of newly industrialized states. The development process need not take several decades like in the case of East Asia's dragons (Singapore, Hong Kong, China, Taiwan Province of China, and the Republic of Korea) because of the lessons available from their experiences and the ability to leapfrog – making large gains in a short span of time. Although some people might argue that many of the GMS economies are further behind now than when the Asian dragons began their industrialization, the less developed countries nowadays have the advantage of information technology (IT). By harnessing all that IT has to offer, countries in the GMS can cut years, if not decades, off their development process compared their more advanced neighbours.

The key is to embrace IT and put it to work; however, some of the GMS countries are still skeptical about IT because of the perceived negative effects it could have on their societies. A decision to keep IT at arm's length or to strictly control it will almost certainly prolong the poverty and slow economic growth in the region. The application of IT could very well be the decisive factor in whether the GMS becomes the emerging economic frontier that many people believe is possible or if most of its members will remain among the poorest countries in Asia.

Another important factor is how quickly and how well the GMS countries can develop their human resources. The educational systems in all of the GMS countries are in dire need of updating curricula, providing even basic facilities, teacher training, and administrative modernization, but the funding from Governments is insufficient to meet the multitude of needs. Also, the GMS is still beset by low enrollment rates, high dropout and repetition rates, and old fashioned attitudes about education.

The transfer of technology is another critical variable in the development equation. At present the level of technology throughout the GMS is generally antiquated with only small pockets of fairly modern technology. The GMS countries must provide the conditions that will encourage technology transfer from abroad as they continually strive to create a semblance of a domestic technology base.

A variety of tools are widely used nowadays to enhance the competitiveness of a country's firms. One tool to gauge where firms stand vis-à-vis their counterparts in other countries is international benchmarking. Firms are able to measure their own performance and compare it with competitors elsewhere to gain an understanding of international best practice and how they can improve their performance. More and more benchmarking exercises are being undertaken in developing countries, and the GMS ought to commence with such an activity to build its competitiveness.

Another important element of competitiveness is the development of value chains/supply chains. In general, GMS firms are engaged in basic commodity production, export, or very low levels of value added activities. By focusing on exporting raw commodities, the GMS countries are essentially giving away their potential wealth to others who process them into higher value added products. This occurs because of the low levels of technology available in the GMS and a dearth of skilled labour. Exacerbating the problem is the fact that value chains and supply chains are not well developed either domestically or perhaps more importantly internationally. In a related matter, subcontracting is not widely practised in much of the GMS, and therefore linkages among firms are not as widespread as they should be. In order for the GMS countries to become more prosperous, their firms must adopt more sophisticated processing activities that will move them up the value chain and establish supplier linkages with other firms around the world. Naturally this will require improved management skills, labour skills, and modern technology, all three of which are currently in short supply around the GMS.

Policymakers and private firms in many developing countries often react to recommendations for moving into more sophisticated production activities by saying the country is not ready yet in terms of technology and skilled labour. However, developing countries have stores of knowledge and experiences from other countries at their disposal, which enables them to leapfrog into higher wealth-generating business activities without the long development phases, which characterized the industrialized countries' progression. Part of the battle, then, is to change firms' mentality about their potential capabilities.

Another factor that could improve the prospects for developing the business environment in the GMS is the formation of clusters. Clusters are geographic concentrations of related companies and institutions that link together suppliers, producers, and supporting industries in a particular field. The benefits of clusters are well documented, and the acceptance that clusters can play a vital role in increasing a domestic industry's competitiveness is spreading over the globe. However, the concept of clusters is either very new or simply unheard of by the local businesses and Governments of the GMS, and its introduction will probably require a stimulus from multilateral agencies.

The GMS must also rectify the low levels of public and private sector interface. Because of the relatively recent introduction of the private sector in much of the GMS and the tendency for central planning, the business sector has few opportunities to articulate its needs and concerns to policy makers. Compounding the problem are the restrictions on the formation and functioning of business associations in five of the six GMS economies, with the exception being Thailand. Business associations play a critical role in public-private sector interface in the developed countries, but the limits they face in the developing world result in ineffective policies for business (or their complete absence) and hidden barriers to business-to-business linkages. In parts of the GMS, the private sector is still looked upon with suspicion by the Governments and seen as something to be controlled as opposed to being encouraged. This lack of public-private sector interface is certainly one of the biggest obstacles to a flourishing business sector in the GMS and simultaneously one of the most difficult to overcome.

Some of the coolness of Governments in the Subregion towards the private sector raises the issue of transparency and openness, and this is equally relevant in places such as Thailand and Cambodia that have made a serious commitment to the private sector. The absence of openness and transparency is inherent in many countries all over the world, but it is imperative that the GMS members rectify this problem and change their image, particularly among the foreign business community. Capital, technology transfer, skill development, and other benefits of foreign investment will not accumulate in the GMS if investors continue to perceive the Governments of the Subregion, rightly or wrongly, as unfriendly towards business, corrupt, and non-transparent.

Will the GMS become Asia's newest group of economic dragons? The answer to this question will be determined by the aforementioned success factors and how the Governments and business communities respond to them. Many of the inherent factors are present in the GMS for the subregion to emerge as the next economic frontier in Asia, but there are also extensive challenges to overcome. However, it is important to put the current situation in the proper perspective. Undeniably, there are obstacles to business in the region, but the GMS has made substantial progress in opening its economies and adopting market principles in a rather short period of time. The economic reform processes commenced as early as the 1980s, but essentially the changes and subsequent opportunities were not manifest until the 1990s. As recently as the early to mid 1990s, some of the GMS countries did not even have a semblance of a legal framework for business. The legal and regulatory frameworks are being put into place, and more government officials, particularly the younger generation, are acquiring the knowledge and skills to better serve the business community.

It appears that the economic reforms embarked upon over the past two decades are irreversible, and that the business environment throughout the GMS will continue to improve and at even greater speed than before. Excellent opportunities exist for foreign and domestic business people as long as they are aware that the immediate returns might not be high, but in the medium term their efforts and patience will begin to bear fruit.

II. CAMBODIA

A. Basic operating environment

1. Geography and climate

Cambodia covers an area of 181,035 square kilometres in the south-western part of mainland South-East Asia, sharing borders with Thailand, the Lao People's Democratic Republic, and Viet Nam. Cambodia also has a coastline of 803 kilometres along the Gulf of Thailand.

An estimated 20 per cent of land is used for agriculture and 5 per cent consists of rivers and lakes. Prominent features of the Cambodian landscape are the large Tonle Sap (Great Lake), the Bassac River systems, and the Mekong River. The Tonle Sap is linked to Phnom Penh, the capital city, by a 100-kilometre long river.

Cambodia is composed of 20 provinces, 3 of which have maritime boundaries, 2 municipalities, 172 districts, and 1,547 communes.

Cambodia's climate, like the rest of South-East Asia, is dominated by the monsoons. The cooler, dry monsoon season runs from November to February; the hot season lasts from March to May; and the rainy season lasts from June to October.

2. History

Cambodia's roots can be traced back to the first century, when the Indianized State of Funan took hold and lasted until the sixth century. Cambodia had one of the world's greatest ancient civilizations during the Angkor Empire, which was established in 802 by King Jayavarman II. Angkor, symbolized by the famed Angkor Wat, became South-East Asia's most powerful empire and represents the pinnacle of Khmer civilization in terms of culture, engineering, and administration.

The country's modern history is in stark contrast to the glorious Angkor Kingdom and is characterized by conflict and tragedy. After becoming a French protectorate in the nineteenth century, Cambodians struggled for their independence in the first half of the twentieth century, finally obtaining it in 1953. The charismatic King Norodom Sihanouk abdicated his thrown in 1955 in order to enter politics, and Cambodia functioned as a multiparty democracy in the 1950s and 1960s. The pressures of the war in Viet Nam and the Lao People's Democratic Republic inevitably affected Cambodia, and in 1970 General Lon Nol overthrew Prince Sihanouk.

The Lon Nol regime was short-lived, as the communist Khmer Rouge took control in 1975. The Khmer Rouge years were Cambodia's darkest time, as 1.7 million people died. In early 1979 the Khmer Rouge were overthrown and replaced by a Vietnamese-backed Government.

The Vietnamese withdrew in 1989, but the country continued to be plagued by civil strife. Finally, in 1991 a political settlement paved the way for a peacekeeping mission called the United Nations Transitional Authority in Cambodia (UNTAC). Elections were held in 1993 under the authority of UNTAC, marking Cambodia's transition to a newly emerging multi-party democracy. Cambodia is now a constitutional monarchy under King Sihanouk, who returned as head of State as part of the settlement.

In April 1999 Cambodia became a full member of ASEAN, which fulfilled the long-awaited goal of having all 10 South-East Asian countries join the regional grouping.

3. Population

Cambodia's population is approximately 11 million, with over 1 million people living in the capital, Phnom Penh. The population is relatively homogeneous with over 90 per cent being ethnic Khmer. Other groups include the Chinese (1 per cent), Vietnamese (1 per cent), Cham Muslims, and a small number of indigenous minorities.

Approximately one quarter of Cambodia's population is in the 10-14-year-old age bracket, and nearly 45 per cent is under the age of 14, providing the potential for a strong labour force in the coming years. One of the challenges, however, is to overcome the high level of poverty and illiteracy so that this future labour force can be utilized to its maximum potential.

4. Languages

The official language of Cambodia is Khmer, which is spoken throughout the country with very few regional variations. Some of the older generation still speak French, but English is now widely used in business, government, and especially by the younger generation. Chinese is also fairly common. The hill tribes have their own local languages.

5. Economy

The Cambodian economy was decimated by the decades of war, which officially ended in the late 1990s. As a result, the economy has only had a chance to develop fully over the past few years. Compounding matters is the legacy of the Khmer Rouge years, when the economy was completely dismantled in an attempt to build an agrarian society.

In light of these setbacks, Cambodia's economy has made tremendous achievements in a very short time. Starting in 1993, the Government moved towards restoring fiscal and monetary discipline and establishing good working relations with international financial institutions.

Cambodia now has one of the most liberal economies in Asia and some of the most generous investment incentives. Foreign investors are warmly welcomed in almost any sector, and unlike other countries in the region, Cambodia does not have the burden of a large state-owned economic sector. Several multinational firms operate in Cambodia to take advantage of the business opportunities and natural resources, and local businesses are springing up throughout the country.

In order to spur investment, the Government in January 1999 unveiled a reform programme that commits to "strengthening the institutions responsible for promoting investments, notably in order to improve the approval procedures for investment applications, to strictly enforce the rules in effect and banish illegal activities and corruption".

Cambodia remains, however, a major recipient of foreign assistance and aid from multilateral agencies such as the International Monetary Fund, Asian Development Bank, and the United Nations, but it also receives assistance from bilateral donors around the world.

6. Government

The new constitution was adopted in September 1993, establishing the Kingdom of Cambodia as a constitutional monarchy with King Sihanouk as the head of Government. The National Assembly contains 120 members, with elections to be held every 5 years. The current Prime Minister is Hun Sen, and the President of the National Assembly is Prince Ranariddh, King Sihanouk's son. The most recent elections were held in 1998.

Cambodia has 21 government ministries. The country is divided into 21 administrative units: 20 provinces and the capital, Phnom Penh.

B. Macroeconomic business climate

1. Gross domestic product and other macro indicators

The Cambodian economy grew rapidly in the mid-1990s, with GDP growth rates exceeding 7 per cent. However, political instability in 1997 and 1998 slowed growth to a trickle. Now that domestic political order has been restored, the economy is once again moving ahead at rates of 4-5.5 per cent annually (see figure 1) and, according to the International Monetary Fund, is expected to grow at 6 per cent or more over the next few years.

16

Figure 1. Annual GDP growth rates
(percentage)

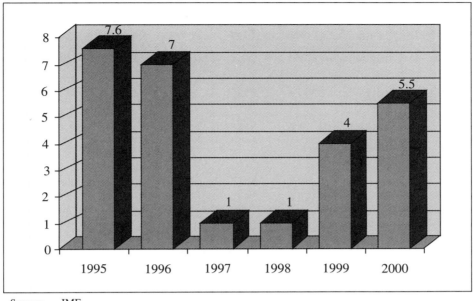

Source: IMF

Cambodia's economic growth relies heavily on a good harvest (and correspondingly, on good weather) because over half of GDP derives from the agriculture sector. Figure 2 shows the composition of Cambodia's GDP for 1998. The manufacturing base is still small but growing, and services account for over 34 per cent of GDP.

Figure 2. Composition of GDP, 1998

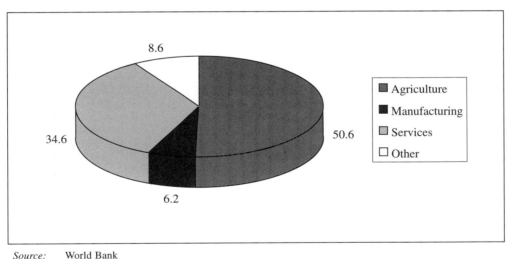

Source: World Bank

Table 2 presents IMF macroeconomic data and forecasts for Cambodia.

Table 2. Cambodia macroeconomic data, 1996-2000

	Unit	1996	1997	1998	1999	2000[t]	2001[t]	2002[t]
GDP Current Price	Billion riel	8,251	9,100	10,750	11,900	13,000	14,331	15,799
GDP Constant 1989 Price	Billion riel	349.8	353.3	356.8	371.1	391.5	415.0	439.9
Growth Rate	per cent	7.0	1.0	1.0	4.0	5.5	6.0	6.0
Government Budget	Billion riel							
Revenue		749.1	881.0	917.9	1,318.0	1,469	1,705.4	2,038.1
Expenditure		1,342.8	1,267.8	1,342.1	1,791.0	2,041	2,436.3	2,843.8
Overall Balance		-593.7	-386.8	-424.2	-473.0	-572.0	-730.9	-805.7
M1		328.9	384.8	543.3	531.9	n.a.	n.a.	n.a.
M2		911.6	1,062.9	1,230.0	1,442.0	n.a.	n.a.	n.a.
Interest Rates (End of Period)								
Deposit Rate	per cent	8.8	8.0	7.8	7.3	n.a.	n.a.	n.a.
Lending Rate	per cent	18.8	18.4	18.3	17.6	n.a.	n.a.	n.a.
Trade Balance	US$ Million	-476.0	-265.0	-223.0	-350.0	-397.0	-438.0	-456.0
Current Account[2]	US$ Million	-493.0	-254.0	-261.0	-386.0	-448.0	-490.0	-509.0
Capital Account	US$ Million	123.0	-46.0	-38.0	77.0	95.0	230.0	249.0
Balance of Payments	US$ Million	-70.0	-90.0	-105.0	-102.0	-136.0	-36.0	-29.0
Gross Official Reserves*	US$ Million	234.0	262.0	390.0	426.0	486.0	556.0	626.0
Import Cover	Months	2.1	2.4	3.6	3.5	3.5	3.7	3.9
External Debt**	US$ Million	624.0	2,056.0	2,146	n.a.	n.a.	n.a.	n.a.
Debt-Service Ratio	per cent	29.5	17.8	16.5	17.7	5.3	5.9	5.6
Foreign Investment Approvals	US$ Million	803.0	759.0	414.7	247.0	n.a.	n.a.	n.a.
Official Exchange Rate	Riel/US$	2,713	3,460	3,780	3,800	3,820	3,800	n.a.

Source: International Monetary Fund (IMF)

Notes: [t] = IMF target

[1] = excludes re-exports

n.a. = not available

[2] = excludes official transfers

** Starting in 1997, includes $ 1,346 million owed to countries of the former Council of Mutual Economic Assistance.

Inflation has fluctuated widely since 1995, from as low as 1 per cent in 1995 to nearly 15 per cent in 1998 (see figure 3). Inflation in 1998 rose to 14.7 per cent as a result of the depreciation of Cambodia's currency, the riel, and also because poor weather caused higher prices for agriculture goods.

Figure 3. Annual inflation rate, 1995-1998

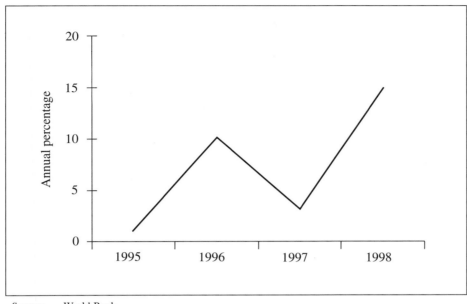

Source:　World Bank

2. Main economic sectors

(a)　*Agriculture sector*

The Cambodian economy remains largely based on agriculture, with over 50 per cent of GDP deriving from the agriculture sector. Moreover, 85-90 per cent of the labour force is involved in agriculture. Unfortunately, the agriculture sector is beset by several problems, in particular alternating periods of floods and draught. As a result, the annual growth rate of agriculture has declined sharply the past few years. Figure 4 shows that growth fell from around 6.5 per cent in 1995 to less than 1 per cent in 1998.

Figure 4. Agriculture sector annual growth

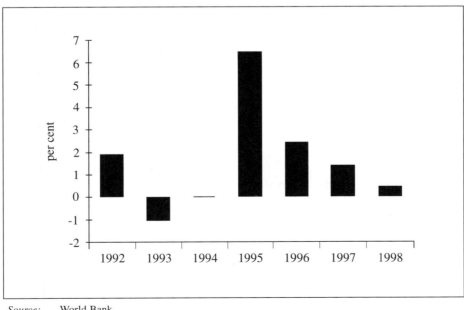

Source:　World Bank

With an average population growth rate in the 1990s of 2.7 per cent, it is imperative for the agriculture sector to resume high annual growth rates.

The main staple food is rice, which is grown in over 90 per cent of the farmed areas. Rice constitutes about 13 per cent of total GDP, and the Government is promoting foreign investment to boost rice production. The best rice growing regions are in Siem Reap, Banteay Meanchey, and Battambang Provinces. Due to insufficient irrigation and other inputs, Cambodia's yield is low by regional standards. Other food crops include maize, soybeans, root crops, vegetables, and fruit trees. Livestock is another major contributor, accounting for almost one-third of the total agricultural output.

(b) *Service sector*

The service sector contributes nearly 35 per cent to GDP. This sector experienced rapid growth in the mid-1990s, especially in the tourism industry, but like other sectors the growth rates slowed in 1997 and 1998 (see figure 5).

Figure 5. Services sector annual growth

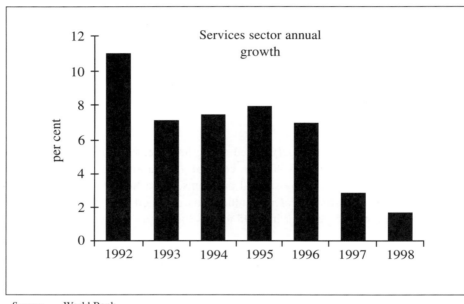

Source: World Bank

The tourism industry is expected to remain one of the driving forces in Cambodia's development for many years because of the large number of visitors and the related support industries that tourism requires. Foreign arrivals peaked in 1996 at 260,489, but declined gradually to 186,333 arrivals in 1998 because of the domestic political situation. Arrivals have since picked up 41.1 per cent to 262,907 in 1999 and are expected to increase even further.

Wholesale and retail trading is another key activity in the services sector and makes up nearly 40 per cent of services' share of GDP. Hotels and restaurants and transportation and communication are the next leading segments of the services industry.

(c) *Manufacturing sector*

Manufacturing makes up less than 7 per cent of the country's GDP, but with the under-utilization of Cambodia's natural resources, manufacturing has great potential for expansion. Currently, the leading industries include rice milling, cigarettes, beer and soft drinks, wood and wood products, rubber, garments, and textiles. The manufacturing sector has experienced some of the highest sectoral growth rates over the past few years. As seen in figure 6, growth rates in manufacturing were between 6.5 and 13.5 per cent between 1995 and 1998.

Figure 6. Manufacturing sector annual growth

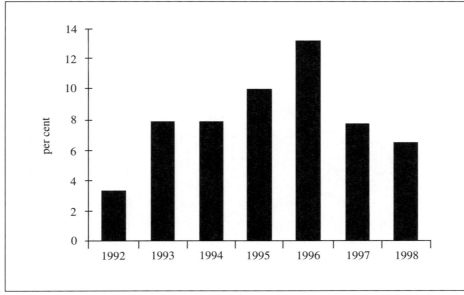

Source: World Bank

The garment industry has grown tremendously, especially with the Generalized System of Preferences (GSP) privileges in the EU market which helped boost exports by 60 per cent to US$ 600 million in 1999. However, the United States has imposed new quota restrictions on Cambodia's garment exports for three years from January 1, 1999 to December 31, 2001. Of the total workforce of 5.54 million, an estimated 100,000 work in the garment industry in about 200 factories.

Construction materials is becoming a fast growing sector as several companies are now operating in this field. Cambodia received its first consumer electronics factor in 1998.

3. International trade

In the 1970s and 1980s Cambodia's trade was oriented toward the former Union of Soviet Socialist Republics and other communist States, with much of it conducted on a barter basis. In the early 1990s, Cambodia began hard-currency trading and concentrated on its Asian neighbours. Cambodia is now a fully integrated member of the international community, and its burgeoning international trade reflects this commitment to participating on the regional and global economies. Cambodia holds observer status in the WTO and will apply for full membership in the near future. Cambodia is still considered one of the poorest countries in Asia and as a result receives GSP and Most Favored Nation (MNF) status from 28 countries, including Australia, Canada, Japan, the United States and the European Union.

Through its membership in ASEAN, Cambodia and its ASEAN neighbours are establishing the ASEAN Free Trade Area (AFTA). AFTA will eventually lower most tariff rates within ASEAN to 0-5 per cent. With its strategic location between Thailand and Viet Nam, Cambodia is expected to benefit greatly from free trade in the region.

(a) *Exports*

Cambodia's exports grew rapidly in 1994 and 1995 before dropping off in 1996 (see figure 7). Exports have remained relatively steady since 1997 at US$ 700-800 million, including the preliminary figure for 1999 of US$ 770 million. The Asian economic crisis certainly had an impact on Cambodia even though the country was not as directly affected as others.

Figure 7. Merchandise exports

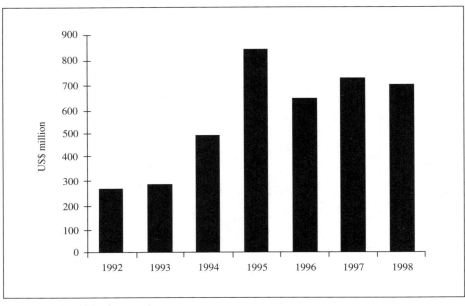

Source: World Bank

Before 1996, primary products made up most of Cambodia's exports, especially timber. The ban on logging the previous year and the subsequent development of other industries led to manufactured goods and processed food surpassing primary products in 1997.

Garments, re-exported products, wood products, and footwear continue to be the major exports from Cambodia (see figure 8). The garment industry is far and away the largest sector, accounting for US$ 597 million in exports in 1999, which was 69 per cent of Cambodia's total exports that year. Roughly 75 per cent of Cambodian garment exports go to the United States, with the remainder going to Europe.

Figure 8. Major export items, 1998
(millions of US dollars)

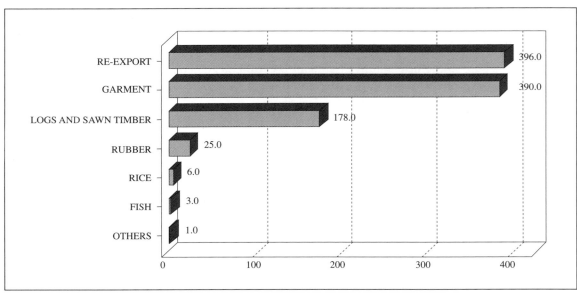

Source: IMF Staff Country Report, "Cambodia: Statistical Annex", April 1999 (from EXIM Bank web site)

Note: Including estimates for unrecorded illegal exports

The main export markets are usually Viet Nam, Thailand, United States, Singapore, China, United Kingdom, and Germany.

(b) *Imports*

Cambodia remains highly dependent on imports because of its limited manufacturing base. Throughout the 1990s, Cambodia imported more goods each year than it exported. The annual changes in imports closely resemble Cambodia's export patterns in that import levels peaked in 1995 and have subsequently leveled off for the past four years. Figure 9 shows merchandise imports from 1992-1998. The preliminary figure for 1999 is US$ 1,104 million worth of imports, which is less than one per cent increase from the previous year.

Figure 9. Merchandise imports

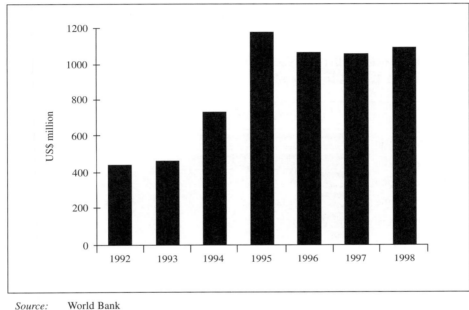

Source: World Bank

The major imports are cigarettes, petroleum products, capital goods, and vehicles (including motorcycles), but consumer goods are increasing their share of imports. Figure 10 shows the main imported items for 1998.

**Figure 10. Major import items, 1998
(millions of US dollars)**

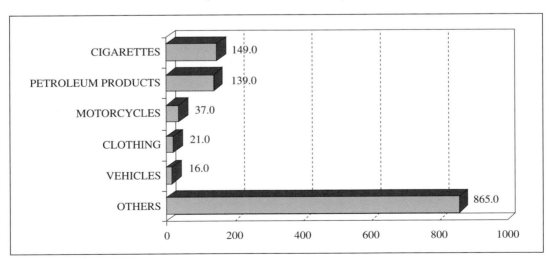

Source: IMF Staff Country Report, "Cambodia: Statistical Annex", April 1999 (from EXIM Bank web site)

23

The main sources of imports are Thailand, Viet Nam, Japan, China, France, Germany, and the United States.

4. Foreign investment

Since the promulgation of Cambodia's new investment law in August 1994, more than US$ 4.27 billion worth of foreign direct investment (FDI) has been approved by the Council for the Development of Cambodia (CDC). As of 1999, there were over 700 foreign projects approved. Foreign investment began its surge in 1995 with 146 projects approved worth nearly US$ 2 billion. The number of projects approved increased the next two years, peaking in 1997 at 192 projects. However, the annual dollar values between 1996 and 1998 did not match the huge amount of 1995, ranging from US$ 592-622 million.

Most foreign direct investment (FDI) into Cambodia over the past few years has been from South-East Asia. In 1999, China and Taiwan Province of China were the main foreign investors but, as figure 11 shows, Malaysia has also played a significant role during the period between 1994 and 1999.

Figure 11. Foreign direct investment in Cambodia classified by countries*
(August 1, 1994 to December 31, 1999, in millions of US dollars)

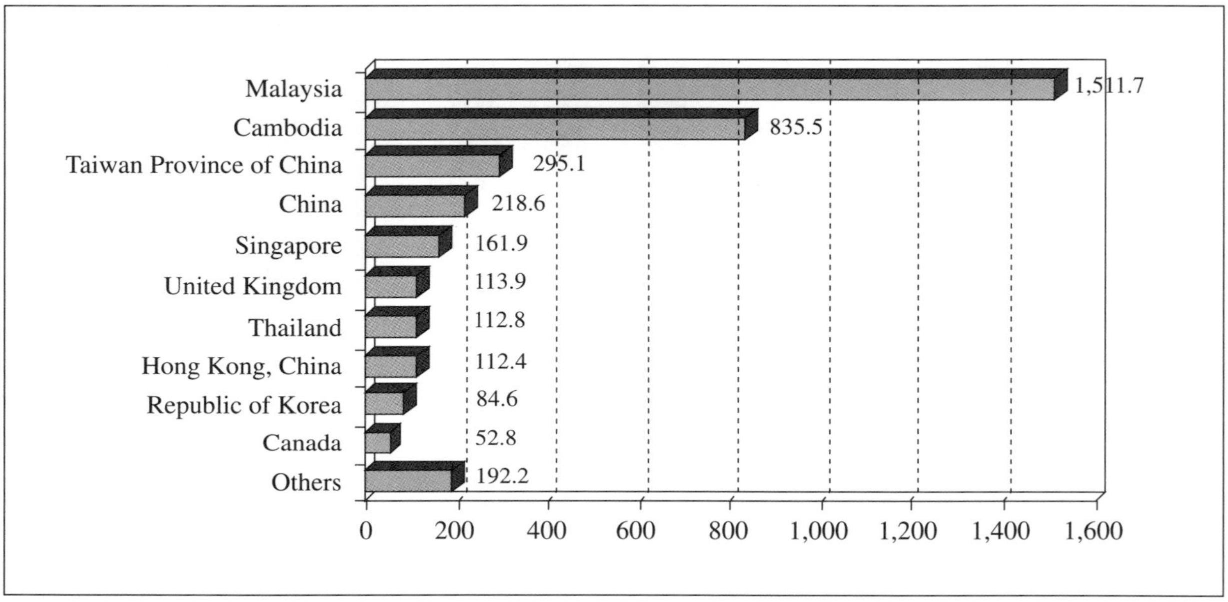

Source: The Cambodia Investment Board (from EXIM Bank web site)

* Including joint ventures

Hotels and tourism is the most popular choice for foreign investors, making up nearly 45 per cent of all foreign investment projects. Figure 12 shows the leading industries for foreign investment.

24

Figure 12. Foreign direct investment in Cambodia classified by industry*
(August 1, 1994 to December 31, 1999)

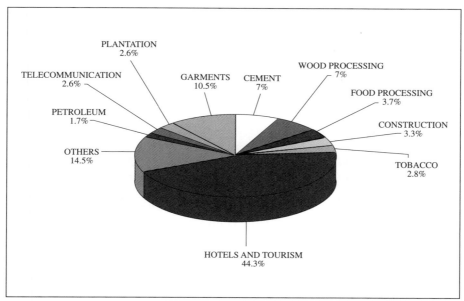

Source: The Cambodia Investment Board (from EXIM Bank web site)
* Including joint ventures.

C. Institutional and support network: public and private sector organizations

1. Government organizations and agencies

The Council for the Development of Cambodia (CDC)

The Council for the Development of Cambodia was established in 1994 and is comprised of the Cambodian Investment Board (CIB) and the Cambodian Rehabilitation and Development Board (CRDB). One of its core responsibilities is to promote and facilitate foreign and domestic investment. CDC is the highest authority on investment and is chaired by the Prime Minister. Other senior ministers also sit on the Council.

CIB is designed to be a one-stop private investment service centre, while CRDB deals with infrastructure planning and all public sector projects. CRDB is also responsible for liaison with aid organizations and non-governmental organizations (NGOs).

Contact address:
Government Palace, Sisowath Quay
Wat Phnom, Phnom Penh
Tel: (855-23) 981-154, 981-156
Fax: (855-23) 428-426, 428-953-4
Email: CDC.CIB@bigpond.com.kh

Contact information for other key government agencies is as follows:

Ministry of Economy and Finance
Street 92, Sangkat Wat Phnom
Khan Daun Penh, Phnom Penh
Tel/fax: (855-23) 277-798
Fax: (855-23) 426-396

Ministry of Commerce
No. 20 A-B, Preah Norodom Blvd.
Phnom Penh
Tel: (855-23) 427-358

Ministry of Industry, Mines, and Energy
45 Preah Norodom Blvd.
Khan Daun Penh, Phnom Penh
Tel/fax: (855-23) 428-263

Ministry of Tourism
No. 3, Preah Monivong Blvd.
Phnom Penh
Tel: 855 426107/427130

2. Chambers of commerce and other business associations

Phnom Penh Chamber of Commerce

The Phnom Penh Chamber of Commerce was established in July 1995 as a public institution under the provisions of the Law on Chamber of Commerce.

The mission of the Phnom Penh Chamber of Commerce is to protect the rights and interests of its members and develop the business environment through three specific actions:

- Support the business community: assistance in establishing new ventures, legal and fiscal advice, information on external markets and partnership opportunities, arbitration of commercial disputes
- Advise the Government and local authorities in the area of economic and commercial legislation and regulation
- Promote capacity-building for the corporate management and training of business staff

Contact address:
Phnom Penh Chamber of Commerce
Villa No. 22, Kramuon Sar St.
Sangkat Phsar Thmei II
Daun Penh District, Phnom Penh
Tel: (855-23) 212-265
Fax: (855-23) 212-270

International Business Club

The International Business Club (IBC) is the largest business association in Cambodia. IBC was founded in 1993 in recognition of the need for discussion among international investors. Its main objective is to foster a closer relationship among the Government of Cambodia, the business community, and international organizations to ensure that sound economic policies and laws encouraging foreign investment are implemented.

Its members invest an estimated US$ 400 million in the economy and employ nearly 4,000 people. Its membership currently consists of 33 international companies.

Contact address:
P.O. Box 2323
Phnom Penh
Tel: (855-12) 800-422
Fax: (855-23) 430-171
E-mail: 012800422@mobitel.com.kh
http://www.bigpond.com/kh/ibc

3. Law, accounting and consulting firms

(a) *Law firms*

Tilleke & Gibbins & Associates Ltd.
No. 56 Samdech Sothearos Boulevard
Khan Daun Penh, Phnom Penh
Tel: (855-23) 362-670, 725-153
Fax: (855-23) 362-671
TGA@bigpond.com.kh

Dirksen, Flipse, Doran & Le
45 Suramit Boulevard
Phnom Penh
Tel: (855-23) 428-726
Fax: (855-23) 428-227

Cambodia International Law Firm
21 BEO, Street 178
Phnom Penh
Tel: (855-23) 212-966
Fax: (855-23) 219-077
cilf@bigpond.com.kh

Phnom Penh International Law Group
No. 142, Street 51, Street Corner 302
Phnom Penh
Tel: (855-23) 219-128
Fax: (855-23) 219-228

(b) *Accounting firms*

PriceWaterhouseCoopers
No. 41 Norodom St.
Phnom Penh
Tel: (855-23) 218-086
Fax: (855-23) 211-594

KPMG
No. 312E, Monivong (St. 93)
Phnom Penh
Tel: (855-23) 216-899
Fax: (855-23) 428-279
kpmg@bigpond.com.kh

KAK and Associes
No. 74B, Street 360
Phnom Penh
Tel: (855-23) 218-994
Fax: (855-23) 218-993
kakcpa@worldmail.com.kh

Kimari Nitha
No. 12 Senei Vanna Vaut Oum (St. 254)
Phnom Penh
Tel: (855-23) 211-438
Fax: (855-23) 362-580
kimari@bigpond.com.kh

(c) *Consulting firms*

IMIC
216 Norodom Blvd.
Phnom Penh
P.O. Box 629 PHN1
Tel: (855-23) 721-755, 362-392
Fax: (855-23) 721-756
imic@bigpond.com.kh

PriceWaterhouseCoopers
No. 41 Norodom St.
Phnom Penh
Tel: (855-23) 218-086
Fax: (855-23) 211-594

Kimari Nitha
No. 12 Senei Vanna Vaut Oum (St. 254)
Phnom Penh
Tel: (855-23) 211-438
Fax: (855-23) 362-580
kimari@bigpond.com.kh

KPMG
No. 312E, Monivong (St. 93)
Phnom Penh
Tel: (855-23) 216-899
Fax: (855-23) 428-279
kpmg@bigpond.com.kh

Seng Business Consultant
Phnom Penh
Tel: (855-12) 853-754
Fax: (855-23) 216-654

Tilleke and Gibbins and Associates
No. 56 Sothearos (St. 3)
Phnom Penh
Tel: (855-23) 362-670, 210-225
Fax: (855-23) 362-671
TGA@bigpond.com.kh

4. Financial institutions

The National Bank of Cambodia (NBC) is Cambodia's central bank. It is responsible for supervising and regulating all the financial institutions in Cambodia. It is also responsible for managing money transactions, credit, domestic, international settlements and foreign exchange.

The commercial banking sector is undergoing major changes. In 1999 the National Assembly passed strict new laws boosting the minimum capital requirements for commercial banks in an effort to strengthen the country's financial sector. The minimum capital requirements were raised from US$ 5 million to US$ 13 million. Although the new laws intended to shore up the financial sector, one result is that several commercial banks have shut down because of their inability or unwillingness to meet the higher capital requirements. Eleven banks have already been closed down since the new legislation took effect. Fifteen additional banks have until the end of 2001 to increase their capital to US$ 13 million, and because of the high requirements, further consolidation of the sector is likely to occur.

Of the 30 previous commercial banks, only 4 have had their licenses renewed as of December 2000: May Bank, Cambodia Public Bank, Standard Chartered Bank, and First Commercial Bank. Before the reform of the financial sector, Cambodia's banking industry had a mix of state-owned banks, joint ventures, private domestic banks, and wholly foreign-owned banks.

Below is the contact information of 30 commercial banks in operation before the capital requirement was raised. However, because of the ongoing consolidation of the financial sector, some of the information in this chart will not be valid.

Agriculture & Commercial Bank
of Cambodia
No. 49, 214 Samdach Pann St.

Bangkok Bank Ltd.
(Phnom Penh Branch)
No. 26, Norodom Boulevard
Tel: (855-23) 725-398
Fax: 426-593

The Bank of National Wealth
Cambodia Ltd.
No. 15, Street 214

Cambodia Asia Bank Ltd.
No. 252, Monivong Boulevard
Tel: (855-23) 363-111
Fax: 426-628

Cambodia Commercial Bank
No. 6, Monivong Boulevard

Cambodia Development Bank
No. 26, Monivong Boulevard

Cambodia Farmers Bank Ltd.
No. 4, Kampuchea-Vietnam Rd.

Cambodia International Bank Ltd.
No. 21, Road 12 107

Cambodia Mekong Bank
No. 1, Kramuon Sar
Tel: (855-23) 217-112
Fax: 217-122

Cambodia Public Bank
No. 23, Street 114
Tel: (855-23) 723-664
Fax: 426-068

Canadia Bank Ltd.
No. 265, Ang Duong
Tel: (855-23) 215-284
Fax: 427-064

Chansavanwonk Bank Co., Ltd.
No. 145a, Street 154
Tel: (855-23) 982-456
Fax: 427-464

Credit Agricole Indosuez
(Phnom Penh Branch)
No. 70, Norodom Boulevard
Tel: (855-23) 428-112
Fax: 214-481

Emperor International Bank
No. 230-232 Monivong
Tel: (855-23) 428-585
Fax: 426-417

First Commercial Bank
No. 263, Ang Duong
Tel: (855-23) 210-026
Fax: 210-029

First Overseas Bank Ltd.
No. 20FE-Eo, Kramuon Sar
Tel: (855-23) 213-023
Fax: 427-439

Foreign Trade Bank
No. 24, Norodom Boulevard
Tel: (855-23) 723-866
Fax: 426-108

Global Commercial Bank Ltd.
No. 337, Monivong Street
Tel: (855-23) 364-258
Fax: 426-612

Great International Bank Ltd.
No. 320 A-B, Monivong
Tel: (855-23) 427-282
Fax: 427-878

Krung Thai Branch Ltd.
No. 149, Street 215
Tel/Fax: (855-23) 366-005

May bank Phnom Penh Branch
No. 2, Norodom Boulevard
Tel: (855-23) 217-590
Fax: 217-594

Municipal Bank
No. 18, Ang Eng Street

Pacific Commercial Bank Ltd.
No. 175, Mao Tse Toung
Tel/Fax: (855-23) 982-909

Phnom Penh City Bank Ltd.
No. 101, Norodom
Tel/Fax: (855-23) 362-885

Royal Cambodia Bank No. 94, Norodom Blvd.	Siam City Bank (Phnom Penh Branch) No. 79, Kampuchea Vietnam Street	Singapore Banking Corporation No. 68, Street 214 Tel: (855-23) 427-555 Fax: 427-277
Standard Chartered Bank No. 95A, Norodom Blvd. Tel: (855-23) 212-726 Fax: 216-687	Thai Farmers Bank (Phnom Penh Branch) No. 335, Monivong Tel: (855-23) 426-536 Fax: 426-548	Union Commercial Bank Ltd. No. 61, Street 130 Tel: (855-23) 427-995 Fax: 427-997

5. Transportation

(a)   *Road network*

There are over 3,200 kilometres of national roads, 31,000 kilometres of provincial roads and about 28,000 kilometres of tertiary roads in Cambodia. Only 7.5 per cent of the roads were paved as of 1998. The main road network links Phnom Penh, the capital, with the provincial capitals.

(b)   *Air transport*

Cambodia has 11 airports throughout the country, including 2 international airports in Phnom Penh and Siem Reap. The domestic airports are located in Siem Reap, Krong Preah Sihanouk, Kampong Chnang, Koh Kong, Battambang, Ratana Kiri, Stung Treng, Mondol Kiri, Preah Vihear, and Kratie.

(c)   *Railways*

Cambodia has two main railway lines at present. The first line runs from Phnom Penh to Battambang to Sisophon. The second line runs from Phnom Penh to Kampot to the port at Sihanoukville.

6. Communications

The capital, Phnom Penh, has most of the telecommunication network facilities. The telecommunications system is comprised of a mixture of wireless systems, cellular mobile systems, old local networks and a few (1,500) newly installed IDD lines.

In 1997-1998, there were an estimated 23,000 telephone subscribers, of whom 6,500 were cable landlines and the rest made up largely of mobile telephone subscribers.

7. Other infrastructure

(a)   *International ports*

Sihanoukville port on the south-west coast is the principal and only deep water maritime port in Cambodia. It can accommodate ships of 10,000-15,000 tons deadweight. There are two other important ports in Phnom Penh and Koh Kong. Phnom Penh port, a traditional river port, is accessible to vessels from South China through Viet Nam. Koh Kong port is made up of three smaller ports and acts as a docking bay for vessels from Singapore, Malaysia, and Thailand entering Cambodia.

D.   Legal and regulatory frameworks for trade and investment

1. Foreign investment

(a)   *Overall investment climate*

The CDC is targeting a wide range of pioneer and high-tech industries, in particular those that create jobs for Cambodians, export-orientated industries, tourism, agro-industries and processing, light electronic assembly, transport and infrastructure, and energy sectors for foreign investment. In addition, it encourages industries enhancing provincial and rural development, as well as environmental protection.

Under the 1994 Foreign Investment Law, all sectors of the economy are open to foreign investment. There are no performance requirements, and foreign investors are granted the same treatment as domestic firms in all sectors.

However, an August 1999 sub-decree places some restrictions on foreign investment in a limited number of activities. Publishing, printing, radio and television activities are limited to 49 per cent foreign equity, and there must be an unspecified amount of local equity in gemstone exploitation, brick making, rice milling, wood and stone carving, manufacturing, and silk weaving. While other sectors are eligible for 100 per cent foreign investment, investment incentives vary according to the nature of the investment project.

Investment guarantees include:

- Investors are treated in a non-discriminatory manner except for land ownership. Only Khmer legal entities and citizens of Khmer nationality have the right to own land. However, renewable leases of up to 70 years are available.
- The Government will not undertake a nationalization policy that adversely affects the private property of investors.
- The Government will not impose price controls on the products or services of an investor who has received prior approval from the Government.
- The Government allows investors to purchase foreign currencies through the banking system and to remit abroad such currency as payments for imports, repayments on loans, payments of royalties and management fees, profit remittances, and repatriation of capital.

As for expropriation, the Cambodian constitution states that "the state's right to confiscate properties from any person shall be exercised only in the public interest as provided for under the law and shall require fair and just compensation in advance".

The Investment Law offers the following incentives:

- Nine per cent corporate income tax
- Tax holidays of up to eight years
- Full import duty exemptions for export-oriented projects
- Free repatriation of profits
- No withholding tax on dividends
- Five year loss carried forward

(b) Foreign investment law

The Foreign Investment Law came into effect in 1994. The full text is shown below.

Chapter 1: General provisions

Article 1: This law governs all investment projects made by investors who are Cambodian citizens and/ or foreigners within the Kingdom of Cambodia.

Article 2: Investor can be either a natural person or a legal entity.

Chapter 2: Council for the Development of Cambodia

Article 3: The Council for the Development of Cambodia is the sole and one-stop service organization responsible for rehabilitation, development, and the oversight of investment activities. The Council for the Development of Cambodia is the Royal Government's "Etat-Major" responsible for the evaluation and the decision-making on all rehabilitation, development, and investment project activities.

Article 4: The Council for the Development of Cambodia comprises the following two operational boards:

1. The Cambodian Rehabilitation and Development Board
2. The Cambodian Investment Board

Article 5: The organization and functioning of the Council for the Development of Cambodia shall be specified by Sub-Decree.

Chapter 3: Investment procedures

Article 6: Investors have to submit investment applications to the Council for the Development of Cambodia for review and decision.

Article 7: The Council for the Development of Cambodia shall provide a response as to its decision to all investors/applicants within a period of a maximum forty five (45) days following the date of submission of the complete investment application.

Any government officials who without proper justification refuse to review and respond to investors' application past the above mentioned period of time shall be punished by law.

Chapter 4: Investment guarantees

Article 8: Investors shall be treated in a non-discriminatory manner as set by law, except for ownership of land as set forth in the Constitution of the Kingdom of Cambodia.

Article 9: The Royal Government shall not undertake nationalization policy which shall adversely affect the private properties of investors in the Kingdom of Cambodia.

Article 10: The Royal Government shall not impose price controls on the products or services of investors who have received prior approval from the Government.

Article 11: In accordance with the relevant laws and regulations issued and published to the public by the National Bank of Cambodia, the Royal Government shall permit investors with investments in Cambodia to purchase foreign currencies through the banking system and to remit abroad these currencies for the discharge of financial obligations incurred in connection with their investments. This covers the following payments:

(1) Payment for imports and repayment of principal and interest on international loans.
(2) Payment of royalties and management fees.
(3) Remittance of profits.
(4) Repatriation of invested capital in compliance with Chapter 8.

Chapter 5: Investment incentives

Article 12: The Royal Government shall make available incentives to encourage investments in such important fields as:

(1) Pioneer and/or high technology industries
(2) Job creation
(3) Export-oriented
(4) Tourism industry
(5) Agro-industry and processing industry
(6) Physical infrastructure and energy
(7) Provincial and rural development
(8) Environmental protection
(9) Investments in a Special Promotion Zone (SPZ) as shall be created by law

Article 13: Incentives and privileges shall include the exemption, in whole or in part, of customs duties and taxes.

Article 14: Incentives shall consist of the following:

1. A corporate tax rate of nine per cent exempt tax rate on the exploration and exploitation of natural resources, timber, oil, mines, gold, and precious stones which shall be set in separate laws.

2. A corporate tax exemption of up to eight years, depending on the characteristics of the project and the priority of the government which shall be mentioned in a Sub-Decree. Corporate tax exemption shall take effect beginning from the year the project derives its first profit. A five-year loss carried forward shall be allowed. In the event profits are being reinvested in the country, such profits shall be exempted from all corporate tax.

3. Non-taxation on the distribution of dividends or profits or proceeds of investments, whether transferred abroad or distributed in the country.

4. 100 per cent import duties exemption on construction materials, means of production, equipment, intermediate goods, raw materials, and spare parts used by:

   (a) An export-oriented project with a minimum of 80 per cent of the production set apart for export, and
   (b) Located in a designated Special Promotion Zone (SPZ) listed in a development priority list issued by the Council
   (c) Tourism industry
   (d) Labour-intensive industry, processing industry, agro-industry
   (e) Physical infrastructure and energy industry

These 100 per cent exemptions of duties and taxes mentioned above shall be in effect according to the terms of the agreement or specification document of the investment projects which will produce goods for export in a minimum of 80 per cent of overall productivities as stipulated in the above point (4a) and for the investment projects that will be located in a Special Promotion Zone (SPZ) as in 4b.

Besides the kinds of investment projects mentioned in the above points (4a) and (4b), the 100 per cent exemption of duties and taxes shall only be authorized for the construction of enterprises, factories, and buildings and the first year of operation of business production.

5. 100 per cent exemption of export tax, if any.
6. Permission to bring into the Kingdom of Cambodia foreign nationals who are:

   – Management personnel and experts
   – Technical personnel
   – Skilled workers

Spouses and dependents of the above persons as authorized by the Council for Development of Cambodia and in compliance with the immigration and labour laws.

Article 15: The approval and incentives granted by the Council for Development of Cambodia shall not be transferred or assigned to any third parties.

Chapter 6: Land ownership and use

Article 16: In accordance with the Constitution and relevant laws and regulations pertaining to the ownership and use of land:

1. Ownership of land for the purpose of carrying on promoted investment activities shall be vested only in natural persons holding Cambodian citizenship or in legal entities in which more than 51 per cent of the equity capital are directly owned by natural persons or legal entities holding Cambodian citizenship.

2. Use of land shall be permitted to investors, including long-term leases of up to a period of 70 years, renewable upon request. Upon such use may include the right of ownership of real and personal property situated on the land as may be permitted by law.

Chapter 7: Employment Practices

Article 17: Investors in the Kingdom of Cambodia shall be free to hire Cambodian nationals and foreign nationals of their choosing in compliance with the labour and immigration laws.

Article 18: The investors shall be allowed to hire foreign employees who are listed in Article 14 (6) provided that:

1. The qualification and expertise are not available in the Kingdom of Cambodia among the Cambodian populace. In the event of such hiring, appropriate documentation including photocopies of the employee's passport, certificate and/or degree, and a curriculum vitae shall be submitted to the Council.
2. Investors shall have the obligation to provide adequate and consistent training to Cambodian staff.
3. Promotion of Cambodian staff to senior positions will be made over time.

Article 19: Foreign employees shall be allowed to remit abroad their wages and salaries earned in the Kingdom, after payment of appropriate tax, in foreign currencies obtained through the banking system.

Chapter 8: Disputes and Dissolution

Article 20: Any dispute relating to a promoted investment established in the Kingdom by a Cambodian or a foreign national concerning its rights and obligations set forth in the Law shall be settled amicably as far as possible through consultation between the parties in dispute.

Should the parties fail to reach an amicable settlement within two months from the date of the first written request to enter such consultations, the dispute shall be brought by either party for:

- Conciliation before the Council which shall provide its opinion, or
- Refer the matter to the court of the Kingdom of Cambodia, or
- Refer to any international rules to settle the dispute as mutually agreed by the parties

Article 21: In the event a promoted company intends to end its activity in the Kingdom of Cambodia, it shall inform the Council through either a registered letter or a hand delivered letter stating the reasons for such a decision, which shall be signed by the investor or his attorney-in-fact.

Article 22: In the event of a proposal for a dissolution of a company without judicial procedures, the investor shall provide proof to the Council that the company has properly settled its potential creditors, complainants, and claims from the Ministry of Economy and Finance before the investor is allowed to officially dissolve his company or enterprise according to the applicable commercial law.

Article 23: Once the investor is allowed to officially dissolve his company, either within the judicial procedures or not, the investor can transfer the remaining proceeds of its assets overseas or use them in the Kingdom of Cambodia. However, in the event that the dissolving company had used machineries and equipment which were imported duty free for less than five years, the company shall have the obligations to pay the duties applicable to those machineries and equipment.

Chapter 9: Final Provisions

Article 24: Investments authorized under the previous "Law on Investment" of the State of Cambodia and its Sub-Decrees shall be subject to the same benefits and obligations as stated under this Law. This law is not retroactive.

Article 25: In the case where the promoted company violates or fails to comply with the conditions stipulated by the Council, the Council shall have the power to withdraw the privileges and incentives granted to him, in whole or in part.

Article 26: This Law shall be promulgated immediately.

(c)   *Investment procedure*

In 1997, the Government passed the "Sub-decree on the Implementation of the Law on Investment of the Kingdom of Cambodia". This sub-decree offers many details of the investment procedure, incentives, taxation, and other important matters, which are summarized in the following sections.

Investors are required to submit the following documents to the Cambodian Investment Board:

- Investment project application form CIB 01A
- Letter stating the intentions to invest along with a summary of investors, the project, objectives, and any requests made to the Council
- The Memorandum of Association or Articles of Association
- Financial and technical feasibility study of the project
- Details of the applicant's technical capacity, marketing capacity, human resources and managerial capacity, and financial capacity
- More recent annual report of the company
- US$ 100 application fee for investments less than or equal to US$ 1 million, and then US$ 500 upon investment approval; US$ 200 application fee for investments over US$ 1 million, and then US$ 1,000 upon investment approval

The Cambodian Investment Board will review the application and make a decision within 45 days.

See annex 1 for the complete investment application form.

The feasibility study should address the following points:

- Proposed market for the products
- Perceived demand, pricing techniques, and competition for the products
- Proposed techniques for manufacturing and production, including the use of domestic or imported raw materials
- Proposed import and export ratios
- Proposed employment ratios for Cambodian and foreign nationals
- Financial and technical analysis of the project, including the cost of production and proposed retail pricing
- Proposed earnings in local and foreign currency and the ability to satisfy foreign exchange needs
- An environmental impact study, including detailed plans for the treatment and disposal of all waste
- Proposed human resources development plan

(d)   *Investment incentives*

(i)   *Incentives*

Investors who wish to take advantage of investment incentives must submit an application to the Cambodian Investment Board (CIB), the division of the CDC charged with reviewing investment applications. Investors who do not wish to apply for investment incentives may establish their investment simply by registering corporate documents with the Ministry of Commerce.

Once the investor's application is complete and an application fee paid, the CDC is required by executive order to issue a decision on an investor's application within 45 days of submission. The CDC is billed as a one-stop shop, but some investors report that in practice licensing might involve visits to multiple government agencies. Once the CDC approves the project in principle, the investor must pay a second application fee, and deposit a performance guarantee of between 1.5 and 2 per cent of the total investment capital at the National Bank of Cambodia (depending on the level of total investment), and register the corporate entity at the Ministry of Commerce.

Once these steps have been taken, the investor will receive a formal investment license from the CDC requiring the investment to proceed within six months. Once the project is 30 per cent completed, the investor is eligible for a refund of the performance guarantee.

The Government has scaled back its investment incentives, which the World Bank has called "critical impediments to revenue mobilization". The Government is committed to review the law on investment before 2001, and further revision is likely.

The law on investment and subsequent decrees created the following incentives:

- A corporate tax rate of 9 per cent, compared to the standard corporate profit tax rate of 20 per cent for business enterprises not receiving CDC investment incentives. Natural resources companies, including timber and oil companies and companies mining gold and precious stones, are subject to a 30 per cent corporate profit tax rate.
- An exemption from the corporate profit tax of up to eight years, depending on the type and location of project.
- A five-year loss carried forward.
- Tax-free distribution of dividends, profits, and proceeds of investment.
- Tax-free repatriation of profits.
- 100 per cent exemption from import duties on construction materials, machinery and equipment, spare parts, raw materials and semi-finished products, and packaging materials for most projects for the construction period and first year of operation.
- The period of exemption from customs duties for the above items can be extended for export-oriented projects with a minimum of 80 per cent of production set aside for export and projects located in a special development zone, although these have not yet been specified.
- Employment of expatriates where qualified Cambodians are unavailable.

The list of sectors to which investment incentives apply, without regard to the amount of investment capital, includes: crop production; livestock production; fisheries; manufacture of transportation equipment; highway and street construction; exploitation of minerals, ore, coal, oil, and natural gas; production of consumption goods; hotel construction (three stars or higher); medical and educational facilities meeting international standards; vocational training centres; physical infrastructure to support the tourism and cultural sectors; and production and exploitation activities to protect the environment.

Investment incentives are available for manufacturing projects in the following sectors when investment capital exceeds US$ 500,000: rubber and miscellaneous plastics; leather and other products; electrical and electronic equipment; and manufacturing and processing of food and related products.

A minimum investment of US$ 1,000,000 applies when seeking incentives in the following three sectors: apparel and other textiles; furniture and fixtures; chemicals and allied products; textile mills; paper and allied products; fabricated metal products; and production of machinery and industrial equipment.

The following sectors are not eligible for investment incentives, although investment is permitted: all types of trading activities; all forms of transportation services; duty-free shops; restaurants, karaoke, massage parlors, and night clubs outside of international standard hotels; shopping malls; press related activities and media networks; retail and wholesale operations; and professional services.

(ii) *Special promotion zones*

Industrial zones are being developed in Phnom Penh and the main deep water port at Sihanoukville. Investment in these zones will qualify investors for additional incentives.

Cambodia is divided into four zones for the purpose of promoting disadvantaged areas. The zones are as follows:

- Zone 1: Phnom Penh, Kandal, Siem Reap, and Sihanoukville
- Zone 2: Kampong Cham, Kampong Chnang, Kampong Speu, Kampot, Prey Veng, Svay Rieng, and Takeo
- Zone 3: Battambang, Kampong Thom, and Pursat
- Zone 4: Banteay Mean Chey, Kratie, Koh Kong, Mondol Kiri, Preah Vihear, Ratana Kiri, and Stung Treng

(e)   *Types of investment forms*

Except for a few sectors as noted above, there are no restrictions placed on the level of foreign participation in Cambodian companies.   As a result, many investors choose to establish 100 per cent foreign-owned limited companies in Cambodia.   The legal forms of investment permitted include:

- Wholly-owned domestic capital
- Wholly-owned foreign capital
- Joint ventures
- Build-Operate-Transfer (BOT)
- Business Cooperation Contract (BCC)

The Ministry of Commerce allows several options for setting up a commercial entity.   The types of commercial entities allowed are:

- Joint stock company
- Limited liability company
- Sole proprietorship limited company
- Commercial partnership
- Representative office
- Branch office of a foreign company
- Subsidiary

See annex 2 for the company registration form.

(i)   *Joint stock company*

A joint stock company may be formed with at least 7 shareholders, and have a minimum issued capital of 100 million riels at a par value per share of at least 10,000 riels.

Capital contributions in a joint stock company require:

- For cash contribution, the par value of shares must be at least 25 per cent paid-in upon incorporation, with shares fully paid-up within three years;
- For non-cash contribution, payment of issued capital must be fully paid upon incorporation, and can only be sold after two years of ownership. The remaining capital must be paid within three years.

The Board of Directors of a joint stock company must be comprised of at least three directors who must be chosen from among the shareholders of the company.

(ii)   *Limited liability company*

A limited liability company is a company of persons and of capital in which the shareholders are not liable beyond their contributions and are not considered merchants.   Businesses employing large funds, such as financial institutions and insurance companies, may not incorporate as a limited liability company.

The maximum number of shareholders of a limited liability company is 30, and the minimum is 2.

Either shareholders or outsiders can be appointed as directors of a limited liability company.   The minimum issued and paid up capital is 20 million riels, at a par value per share of at least 20,000 riels.   The shares must be paid up in full and distributed.   Issued capital must be fully paid in cash or with non-cash items before the company is incorporated.

The transfer of shares in a limited liability company to third parties must have the prior written consent of a majority of the shareholders representing at least three quarters of the capital of the company.

(iii)   *Sole proprietorship limited company*

A sole proprietorship limited company is subject to the same requirements as a limited liability company with the exception that the sole shareholder must be a national person and may not be at another company. The management of the sole proprietorship can be performed by the shareholder or by an individual appointed by the shareholder.

(iv)   *Commercial partnership*

A commercial partnership is an agreement of association that joins two or more partners with a view to carrying on commercial operations under the same trade name. Each of the partners is deemed a merchant and is held personally and jointly liable for the debts of the partnership. The partnership shares are not transferable or assignable without the consent of all partners.

(v)   *Representative office*

A representative office may be established by an eligible foreign investor to facilitate the sourcing of local goods and services and to collect information for its parent company. The representative office also serves as a channel for promoting and marketing the home company's products and services in the host country. In Cambodia, the representative office is not considered a separate legal entity from its parent company. It is regarded as a cost centre and accordingly should derive no income from its activities. Therefore, it is not subject to Cambodian tax laws.

The representative office agent is under the management of one or more directors who may be appointed and removed by the principal enterprise. It may lease a premise for its office, employ local staff, advertise its products, and organize trade fairs to introduce their commercial products.

The representative office agent can enter into a contract with a local enterprise in Cambodia if the principal enterprise is so authorized. However, it may not purchase, sell, or conduct any services as its usual business nor can it conduct any production or construction activities within Cambodia.

The representative office agent is subject to commercial registration requirements of the Ministry of Commerce. The words "Representative Office Agent" shall be placed before or after the name of the principal enterprise.

(vi)   *Branch office of a foreign company*

A branch office is an office that is opened by a company of another foreign country for the purpose of conducting a particular commercial activity in Cambodia. Its management and control shall be under one or more directors who may be appointed and removed by the parent company.

The branch office can conduct the same activities as the representative office agent, but the difference is that the branch office may purchase, sell, or conduct regular professional services or other operations engaged in production or construction in Cambodia.

Liabilities with respect to losses and debts of a branch office are the joint liability of both the branch office and the parent company.

The branch office is subject to commercial registration requirements of the Ministry of Commerce. The word "Branch Office" shall be placed before or after the name of the parent company.

(vii)   *Subsidiary*

A subsidiary is a limited company formed in Cambodia with at least 51 per cent of its capital being held by a foreign company. Its formation, management, rights and other obligations shall be provided for in the memorandum and articles of association of the limited company.

Each subsidiary is subject to the commercial registration requirements of the Ministry of Commerce. The word "Subsidiary" shall be placed before or after the name of the parent company.

There are a few distinctions in the scope of commercial activities allowed for local and foreign-owned companies. A company is considered to have Cambodian nationality if its stated office is located in Cambodia, more than 51 per cent of its stated capital is held by Cambodian citizens or Cambodian legal entities, and more than 51 per cent of its financial interests in the profits and losses are held by Cambodian citizens or Cambodian legal entities. Only local companies are permitted to register corporate names that imply Cambodian nationality. Furthermore, only local companies are entitled to own land, and local companies are allowed to engage in import or export activities without limitations. The Chairman of the Board of Directors of a local company must be a Cambodian national, but other directors can be foreigners.

Foreign-owned enterprises have two limitations in the scope of their activities. They are eligible to engage in import/export activities only as required by their investment/production activities, not import/export for the sole purpose of re-selling without transformation. They are not allowed to own, sell, or buy land, or engage in real estate business outside their stated scope of activities.

(f) *Taxation*

(i) *Income tax*

Cambodia's personal income tax took effect in 1995 and was amended in 1997. It applies to services provided in Cambodia to a local or overseas employer regardless of whether or not the employer or employee actually resides in Cambodia. A resident is defined as an employer or person whose principle place of abode is in Cambodia or someone who is present for more than 182 days during a calendar year. Salaries earned from working outside of Cambodia are taxable if the person is a Cambodian resident.

Taxable income is usually comprised of wages and salary, overtime payments, loans and partial payments made by the employer that are netted off against any repayments due from the employee, and payments resulting from overseas expenses. Fringe benefits are taxed at the rate of 20 per cent of the total value of fringe benefits given to the employee.

Items that are exempt from personal income tax are (1) travelling allowances received in the course of employment; (2) superannuation payments deducted from an employee's income; (3) free or subsidized allowances for uniforms or facilities used in the course of employment.

The personal income tax rates are as follows:

Employers are required to withhold and pay the Tax on Salary to the Tax Department by the fifteenth of each month.

Payments made to a non-tax resident are subject to a 15 per cent withholding tax. Cambodia does not have a social security system, so there are no taxes in this category.

Income (in riels)	Tax rate (percentage)
0-500,000	0
500,001-1.25 million	5
1,250,001-8.5 million	10
8,500,001-12.5 million	15
over 12.5 million	20

Source: KPMG Cambodia Limited

(ii) *VAT and profit tax*

There are no local taxes in Cambodia, but the value added tax (VAT) is 10 per cent. Other taxes include a profit tax ranging from 0 to 20 per cent and a "minimum turnover tax" that is 1 per cent. All investment enterprises approved by the CDC, including those firms granted a Tax on Profit holiday, are obligated to file to the Tax Department monthly and annual tax declarations.

(iii) *Customs duties*

Customs duties are classified into four categories, with rates ranging from 7 to 50 per cent.

Items with a 50 per cent duty are luxury goods such as automobiles, wine, cigarettes, perfume, weapons, and cosmetics. Products with a 35 per cent duty are finished products such as televisions, radios, paint, and household furnishings. Machinery and equipment are taxed at 15 per cent. Raw materials such as cement, iron, and brick, along with basic daily items such as meat, fruit, vegetable oil, sugar, soap, shoes, and clothing carry a 7 per cent tariff.

The types of investment that are eligible for customs duty exemptions include:

- Investment in export-oriented projects with a minimum of 80 per cent of production designated for export
- Projects located in a Special Promotion Zone
- Tourism projects
- Projects in labour intensive industries, processing industries, and agro-industries
- Physical infrastructure and energy projects

The types of good that are exempt from customs duties include:

- Construction materials for the project
- Machinery used directly in the production process
- Other equipment used directly in the project other than administrative equipment, transportation and distribution equipment
- Spare parts for machinery and equipment used in the above-mentioned items
- Raw materials and intermediate goods used directly in the production process
- Packaging equipment

Finished products are also entitled to 100 per cent export tax exemptions.

(g)   *Foreign exchange*

According to the Law on Foreign Exchange (1997), as well as the regulations issued by the National Bank of Cambodia, foreign currencies can be freely purchased through the banking system. The Law on Foreign Exchange specifically states that there are no restrictions on foreign exchange operations, specifically including the purchase and sale of foreign exchange, and transfers and all other types of international settlements.

However, the Law on Foreign Exchange requires that only authorized intermediaries perform these transactions. These intermediaries are legally recognized banks in Cambodia, which are required to report to the National Bank of Cambodia transactions in excess of US$ 10,000. There is no requirement that the investor sending or receiving the funds make a report on the transaction. The burden rests solely on the bank as the authorized intermediary.

There are currently no restrictions on the repatriation of profit or capital derived from investments made in Cambodia, nor on most transfers of funds abroad. The Law on Investment guarantees that investors can freely remit foreign currencies abroad for the purposes of:

- Payment for imported goods and services and repayment of loans including interests and principals made by foreign banks or institutions
- Royalties and management fees
- Profits after discharge of obligations due and payment of all relevant taxes and royalties
- Repatriation of invested capital on dissolution of an investment project

(h)   *Labour issues*

(i)   *Overview*

In 1997, Cambodia replaced its communist-style labour code with a highly-detailed, progressive law which guarantees freedom of association and the right to strike, provides for the free registration of labour unions and collective bargaining, and sets a minimum age of employment.

The Ministry of Social Affairs, Labour and Youth Rehabilitation (MOSALVY) is responsible for issuing labour regulations, and MOSALVY's labour inspection department is responsible for enforcing the labour law. MOSALVY also chairs Cambodia's tripartite Labour Advisory Committee (LAC), which reviews labour laws, including the minimum wage. MOSALVY conducts frequent workplace inspections and mediates workplace disputes. However, the Government's enforcement efforts have been hampered by a lack of resources, little knowledge of the law by factory managers, and a lack of qualified labour inspectors.

However, in July 2000 the Ministry of Commerce and MOSALVY issued a joint declaration to improve enforcement of the labour law. The declaration created an inter-ministerial committee that will review labour-related complaints from various sources, and recommend penalties based on the severity of the violation. Penalties can include suspension of export privileges.

Although required under the Labour Law, there is still no labour court system.

Only a fraction of Cambodia's labour force is organized. Unionization of the work force is not significant outside the industrial sector, and within the sector it is highly concentrated in the garment industry. Only 16 out of 106 registered labour unions are in industries other than garments.

There were 76 strikes in Cambodia during 1999 and 35 in the first 7 months of 2000. Most of these were related to the lack of enforcement of the labour laws.

Given the severe disruption of the education system in the Khmer Rouge years, Cambodia's work force is largely unskilled. According to United Nations statistics, the adult literacy rate is about 37 per cent, but the youth literacy rate (15-24 year olds) is nearly 57 per cent. However, the desire to learn is keen and many adults and children enrol in supplementary educational programmes, including English and computer training. Workers with higher education or specialized skills are few and in high demand. Many investors bring in expatriate employees to fill skilled positions, and Cambodian immigration and investment regulations make this relatively easy.

(ii)   *Employment of local and foreign workers*

Foreign companies have virtually unrestricted access to Cambodia's labour force. However, for employment of foreigners, certain restrictions exist. For example, expatriate employment regulations require that the proportion of foreign experts to local workers shall be maintained at least at 1:10, i.e., employment of one foreign expert shall be accompanied by employment of at least 10 local workers. Investors are permitted to bring into Cambodia foreign nationals who are qualified managerial personnel, technical personnel, or skilled workers.

(iii)   *Wages*

Wages are set by market forces, except for civil servants, for whom wages are set by the government. MOSALVY has the right to set minimum wages for each sector of the economy based on recommendations by the Labour Advisory Committee.

MOSALVY formally exercised this authority for the first time in July 2000, when it approved a US$ 45/ month minimum wage for post-probation period workers in the garment and footwear sector. Workers who are in the probation period of one to three months receive a minimum monthly wage of US$ 40. Also, the garment and footwear sector is obligated to provide the following benefits to workers:

- An incentive of at least US$ 5 per month for full attendance
- Food allowance of 1,000 riels or one free meal for each worker who volunteers for overtime as requested by the employer
- A benefit of US$ 2-5 per month to acknowledge the seniority payment of workers
- Workers are allowed an annual leave of 18 days per year in line with the Labour Law

At present there is no minimum wage for any other industry.

(iv)   *Hours and overtime*

The Labour Law provides for a standard legal workweek of 48 hours, not to exceed 8 hours per day. The law stipulates time-and-a-half for overtime and double time if overtime occurs at night, on a Sunday, or on a holiday.

Fifteen is set as the minimum allowable age for a salary position, and 18 is the minimum allowable age for anyone engaged in work that may be hazardous, unhealthy, or unsafe.

There is no public social safety net for workers in Cambodia. MOSALVY has drafted legislation to create a national pension, an unemployment insurance system, and a workers' compensation scheme, but these have not been passed into law or implemented.

(i)   *Dispute settlement*

Cambodia's legal system is an amalgam of pre-1975 statutes modeled on French law, communist-era legislation dating from 1979-1991, statutes put in place by the United Nations Transitional Authority in Cambodia (UNTAC) during 1991-1993, and legislation passed by the government since 1993.

The legal system is still developing and thus foreign investors should not expect it to function as well as they are used to in their home countries. Many judges and lawyers are still not adequately familiarized with business law, and procedures such as arbitration of international commercial disputes are still in the process of being institutionalized. The government intends to become a member of the International Centre for the Settlement of Investment Disputes (ICSD).

The legal system favors mediation over adversarial conflict and adjudication, and compromise solutions are often preferred even when the law favors one party in a dispute. The courts are currently the only judicial forums in which to settle commercial disputes, but the system is fraught with difficulties. Judges are poorly paid and they often have limited access to published Cambodian law.

Cambodia has signed investment agreements with several countries, including China, France, Germany, Malaysia, Netherlands, Republic of Korea, Singapore, Switzerland, Thailand. These agreements provide reciprocal national treatment to investors, excluding benefits deriving from membership in future customs unions or free trade areas and agreements relating to taxation.

The agreements preclude expropriations except those that are undertaken for a lawful or public purpose, non-discriminatory, accompanied by prompt, adequate and effective compensation at the fair market value of the property prior to expropriation; guarantee repatriation of investments; and provide for settlement of investment disputes via arbitration.

(j)   *Capital market*

Cambodia currently has no capital markets. There is no stock or bond market, and no means to purchase equity in a company except by agreement with the existing owners. Most companies are privately held, the exception being multinational firms.

Domestic financing has traditionally not been difficult to obtain for foreign firms, but the recent consolidation of the banking sector might change the availability of credit. Most loans are secured by real property mortgages or deposits of cash or other liquid assets, as provided for in the existing contract law and land law.

Export/import financing is available from multinational banks through a variety of credit instruments. The United States Overseas Private Investment Corporation (OPIC), the International Finance Corporation (IFC), and the Multi-lateral Investment Guarantee Agency (MIGA) offer both investment guarantees and loans in Cambodia.

(k)   *Protection of property rights*

The 1992 Land Law provides a framework for real property security and a system for recording titles and ownership, but its effectiveness is limited because the majority of property owners have no documentation to prove their ownership.

As for intellectual property rights, protection is based on articles contained in the 1992 UNTAC Criminal Code. Cambodia acceded to the Paris Convention in 1998 and it is making progress on legislation such as drafting trademark, copyright, trade secrets, and patent laws. Cambodia ratified a bilateral agreement with the United States which establishes standards for intellectual property rights.

With no trademark law in force in Cambodia, owners of trademarks are unable to seek relief in court. Until the law is passed, complaints go to the Ministry of Commerce, which has responsibility for registering trademarks, but it does not have clear legal authority to conduct enforcement activities.

Responsibility for copyrights is split between the Ministry of Culture (phonograms, CDs, and other recordings) and the Ministry of Information (printed materials). The Ministry of Culture prepared a draft copyright law in 1998 which is under review.

As Cambodia has a very small industrial base, and infringement on patents and industrial designs is not yet commercially significant. The Ministry of Industry has prepared a draft of a comprehensive law on the protection of patents and industrial designs.

(l)   *Important legislation*

The National Assembly passed a law and associated decree regulating pharmaceuticals in June 1996, and giving administrative authority to the Ministry of Health. In May 2000, the National Assembly passed a law on the quality of goods and services, food safety, consumer protection, and product liability.

Food and product safety issues fall under the jurisdiction of the Cambodian standards authority, Camcontrol, which is under the Ministry of Commerce.

Camcontrol, the government's standards-setting arm, does not currently have a mechanism for industry participation in setting standards. There are currently no industry standards-setting organizations operating in Cambodia.

Cambodia's banks and financial institutions fall under the supervision of the National Bank of Cambodia (NBC), which is being advised by the International Monetary Fund.

In November 1999, Cambodia passed a new law on banking and financial institutions. This law, and subsequent regulations issued by NBC, superceded earlier legislation and regulations. An insurance law, which would give the Ministry of Economy and Finance regulatory authority over the insurance industry, is being drafted.

E. Main opportunities for investment

1. Energy

The growth in the commercial and industrial sector in Cambodia creates an opportunity for power generation. Currently, the demand for power is been met by a combination of the power utility Electricite du Cambodge and privately-owned generators. The Government of Cambodia is actively seeking investors for the energy sector as demand and industrialization continue to increase.

Cambodia's hydropower potential is still relatively untapped, although numerous sites on various rivers have been identified as suitable for hydropower generators. Most of the potential hydroelectric sites are located in the north-east and south-west regions of the country.

2. Transportation

(a)   *Land transportation*

Cambodia's land transportation infrastructure is not well developed. Much of the 34,100 kilometre road network is in need of repair and upgrading, and a great deal of new roads are required to link rural areas to towns and cities. Multilateral and bilateral donors, such as the World Bank, Asian Development Bank, and the

Japanese International Cooperation Agency (JICA), are contributing to Cambodia's Five-Year Master Plan for reconstruction and rehabilitation of the national road network. In addition to the public works, several private construction projects are either under way or currently being planned.

(b) *Water transportation*

Water transportation is an important means of moving goods and people throughout much of Cambodia because of the lengthy rivers and tributaries, but also because of the inadequate road network. The ports in Sihanoukville and Phnom Penh offer a huge potential for expanding regional trade but their berthing facilities and equipment are in need of substantial improvement, thus providing several opportunities for investment and services.

(c) *Air transportation*

The two international airports in Cambodia (Phnom Penh and Siem Reap) are in the process of being upgraded and expanded, with much of the financing coming from the Asian Development Bank. There are also several provincial airports or airfields that are no longer functioning but could serve as potential investments.

3. Construction and engineering

Now that the decades of civil war are over, Cambodia is embarking on an ambitious reconstruction phase to repair old and damaged infrastructure and put in place new, modern infrastructure for the twenty fist century. As a result, construction and engineering services are in high demand by both the public sector and private sector. With significant amounts of foreign aid and loans coming into the country, numerous opportunities are available for construction and engineering projects. Foreign firms are estimated to account for over 75 per cent of total sales in construction and engineering.

4. Agriculture

Cambodia has several regions suitable for a number of crops including rubber, soybean, sugar palm, coffee, pepper, cashew nuts, fruit trees, rice, and others. There are significant tracts of land available for livestock rearing. In addition to the cultivation of crops, the Government is encouraging increased yields through improved irrigation, new technology and equipment, and related support services.

5. Minerals

According to the Ministry of Industry, Mines, and Energy, Cambodia's mineral wealth is still undetermined because of the lack of studies conducted to assess the country's natural resources. Numerous minerals are known to be present, such as zircon, gold, base metals, gems, coal, dolomite, marble, and manganese, but the exact amounts are uncertain. Most of the known deposits are located in the northern half of the country, but a few areas in the south also contain deposits. Numerous opportunities are available for exploration of minerals. Furthermore, many of the known deposits are not being tapped because of the lack of roads and equipment.

6. Pharmaceuticals

Due to the high rate of illness and disease in this poverty-stricken country, Cambodia purchases significant amounts of pharmaceuticals from other countries. Pharmaceuticals is a multimillion dollar industry (in terms of sales) in Cambodia. Private sector pharmacies and clinics are springing up rapidly throughout the country, providing numerous outlets for pharmaceuticals.

7. Automotive industry

The demand for automobiles, particularly used cars and sport utility vehicles, and auto parts is increasing steadily in Cambodia. With numerous foreign aid agencies present in Cambodia and a rapidly expanding nouveau riche class, the automotive industry is becoming a lucrative sector.

8. Tourism

Cambodia's tourism industry is one of the fastest growing sectors of the economy. Numerous tour operators, hotels, and restaurants have opened since the mid-1990s, but as long as the number of tourist arrivals continues to increase, there is still plenty of opportunity for new investment. Also, the Government strongly encourages investment in the tourism sector, especially as more parts of the country are becoming accessible. Eco-tourism and cultural tourism (aside from Angkor Wat) are essentially just getting started in Cambodia, and the country's pristine forested and mountainous areas are seen as a new frontier in eco-tourism.

F. Tips for visitors

1. Passports and visas

A valid passport and visa are required of all foreigners visiting Cambodia. Cambodian consulates (or Consular section of Embassy) in Bangkok, Hanoi, Ho Chi Minh City, Vientiane, Moscow, and Washington, D.C. are able to issue visas. Visas are also available on arrival at the international airports.

Tourists on package tours will normally have their visas arranged by the tour operator. Business visas are obtainable through the Ministry of Foreign Affairs in Phnom Penh or an official invitation.

Application requirements: (a) Completed application form; (b) 2 passport-size photos; (c) photocopy of passport; (d) tour itinerary and fee; (e) business card, if applying for business visa.

The visa fee is US$ 20 and is usually valid for one month, although extensions may be granted by the Foreign Ministry in Phnom Penh.

2. Health

Regulations and requirements may be subject to change at short notice, and you are advised to contact your doctor well in advance of your intended date of departure. The numbers in the following chart are explained below.

[1]: Travelers arriving from infected areas require a yellow fever vaccination certificate.

[2]: A cholera vaccination certificate is no longer a condition of entry to Cambodia. However, cholera is a serious risk in this country and precautions are essential. Up-to-date advice should be sought before deciding whether these precautions should include vaccination as medical opinion is divided over its effectiveness.

Requirements	Special Precautions	Certificate Required
Yellow Fever	No	1
Cholera	Yes	2
Typhoid & Polio	Yes	–
Malaria	3	–
Food & Drink	4	–

[3]: Malaria risk exists all year throughout the country. The malignant *falciparum* strain predominates and is reported to be highly resistant to chloroquine and resistant to sulfadoxine/pyrimethamine. Resistance to mefloquine has been reported from the western provinces.

[4]: All water should be regarded as being potentially contaminated. Water for drinking, brushing teeth or making ice should first be boiled or otherwise sterilized. However, bottled water is increasingly available throughout the country. Milk is typically unpasteurized and should be boiled. Powdered or tinned milk is available and is advised, but make sure that it is reconstituted with pure water. Avoid dairy products which are likely to have been made from unboiled milk. Only eat well-cooked meat and fish, preferably served hot. Pork, salad and mayonnaise may carry increased risk. Vegetables should be cooked and fruit peeled.

Plague is present and vaccination is advised.

Poliomyelitis continues to be reported.

Bilharzia (schistosomiasis) is present. Avoid swimming and paddling in fresh water. Swimming pools which are well-chlorinated and maintained are safe.

Rabies is present.

Health insurance is absolutely essential and doctors and hospitals expect cash payments for any medical treatment.

3. Money

The *riel* is Cambodia's currency. However, the United States dollar is widely accepted and usually preferred by hotels, restaurants, and tourist sites. Travellers' cheques in United States dollars can be changed at most banks in Phnom Penh and Siem Reap. If you plan to travel to outskirts, it is advisable to use small change in United States dollars although the riel is acceptable. Credit card facilities are limited but some banks, hotels, and restaurants do accept them.

4. Travel to and within Cambodia

(a) *Air*

Twelve international airlines service direct flights to and from Cambodia, including Malaysia Airlines and Thai Airways International. There are 11 cities in Asia that have direct international flights to and from Cambodia, including Bangkok, Kuala Lumpur, Shanghai, and Singapore. Within Cambodia, four airlines (Siem Reap Airways, Royal Phnom Penh Airways, President Airlines, and Royal Air Cambodge) serve seven cities or towns throughout the country. The cities/towns with flights are Battambang, Koh Kong, Mondol Kiri, Phnom Penh, Ratana Kiri, Siem Reap, and Stung Treng.

(b) *Waterways*

Visitors can reach Cambodia by waterway at the two international ports at Sihanoukville and Phnom Penh. Sihanoukville receives cruise ships from around the world. Visitors arriving by water are required to have an entry visa for Cambodia in advance.

Ferries and boats are also used to travelling around Cambodia. Government-run ferries depart from the Psar Cha Ministry of Transport Ferry Landing between 102 and 104 Streets and go to Kompong Cham, Kratie, Stung Treng, Kampong Chnang and Phnom Krom.

(c) *Land*

    (i)   *Access from Viet Nam*

There is one international border checkpoint between Cambodia and Viet Nam, which is at Bovet (Cambodia) and Mocbay (Viet Nam). Most visitors travelling by land across this point are going between Ho Chi Minh City and Phnom Penh. At the border, there are many taxis on both sides, and a taxi to Phnom Penh costs around US$ 10 per person.

Visitors accessing Cambodia through this point are required to have an entry visa for Cambodia in advance, which can obtained from a Royal Cambodian Embassy or at Cambodian consulate in Ho Chi Minh City.

    (ii)   *Access from Thailand*

Currently there are two international land border points between Cambodia and Thailand. One is located between Poipet and Aranyaprathet, and this is commonly used for travelers going to Angkor Wat by land. Visitors can get an entry visa for Cambodia on arrival at a cost of US$ 20. Taxi also available there, especially for Siem Reap, and it costs around US$ 15 per person. The journey from the border to Siem Reap takes around seven hours.

The second land crossing is at Cham Yem in Koh Kong (Cambodia) and Trad (Thailand). To cross at this point visitors are required to have an entry visa for Cambodia, which can be obtained at the Royal Cambodian Embassy in Bangkok. From Koh Kong, visitors can continue their trip to Sihanoukville, the seaside paradise of Cambodia, by speedboat. The trip takes around 3 hours and cost US$ 20 (one way).

Other land crossings between Thailand and Cambodia are being discussed by the two Governments.

(iii)   *Land transport within Cambodia*

Buses to Phnom Penh suburbs are available from 182 Street. The bus station is open from 0530 to 1730.

Cruising taxis are not common in Cambodia. However, service taxis can be hired at various locations in Phnom Penh, including the international airport. Another location is Psar Chbam Pao Shared-Taxi Station between 367 Street and 369 Street. Cars can be hired easily from most major hotels in Phnom Penh and the other main cities.

There is a railway passenger service in the southern and northwestern regions of the country. Planning has commenced to provide international rail service between Poipet and Aranyaprathet, thereby creating a link between Phnom Penh and Bangkok.

5. Hotels

There are numerous hotels located in Phnom Penh. Below is a short list of the major foreign business and tourist hotels in the capital. The country and area code for Phnom Penh is 855-23.

City Central Hotel
Monivong Blvd. at Street 128
Tel: 722-022; Fax: 722-021

Hotel Cambodiana
No. 313, Sisowath
Tel: 426-288; Fax: 426-392

Hotel Inter-Continental
No. 296, Mao Tse Toung
Tel: 424-888; Fax: 424-885

Hotel Le Royal
92 Rukhak Vithei Daun Penh
Tel: 981-888; Fax: 981-168

Juliana Hotel
No. 16, Street 152
Tel: 366-070; Fax: 427-916

Royal Phnom Penh Hotel
No. 26, Sothearos
Tel: 982-673; Fax: 982-661

Sunway Hotel
No. 1, Daun Penh, Sangkat
Wat Phnom
Tel: 430-333; Fax: 430-339

Hotels also abound in Siem Reap. Below is a short list of the major foreign business-class/tourist hotels.

Angkor Hotel
Street 6, Phum Sala Kanseng
Tel: (63) 964-301
Fax: (63) 964-302

Grand Hotel d' Angkor
Vithaei Charles De Gaulle
Tel: (63) 963-888
Fax: (63) 963-168

Sofitel Royal Angkor
(opened in late 2000)

6. Embassies

There are 26 foreign embassies in Cambodia:

Embassy of Australia
No. 11, Street 254
Tel: 213-466; Fax: 213-413

Embassy of Brunei Darussalam
No. 237, Street 51
Tel: 211-457; Fax: 211-456

Embassy of Bulgaria
No. 227, Norodom Blvd.
Tel: 723-182; Fax: 426-491

Embassy of Canada
No. 11, Street 254
Tel: 213-470; Fax: 211-389

Embassy of Cuba
No. 96-98, Yougoslavie
Tel: 368-610; Fax: 217-428

Embassy of the Democratic
People's Republic of Korea
No. 39, Suramarith St.
Tel/Fax: 217-013

Embassy of France
No. 1, Monivong Blvd.
Tel: 430-020; Fax: 430-038

Embassy of Germany
No. 76, Yougoslavie
Tel: 216-193; Fax: 427-746

Embassy of India
No. 782, Monivong Blvd.
Tel: 210-912; Fax: 364-489

Embassy of Indonesia
No. 90, Norodom Blvd.
Tel: 216-148; Fax: 216-129

Embassy of Japan
No. 75, Norodom Blvd.
Tel: 217-161; Fax: 216-162

Embassy of the Lao People's
Democratic Republic
No. 15-17, Mao Tse Toung Blvd.
Tel: 982-632; Fax: 720-907

Embassy of Malaysia
No. 11, Street 254
Tel: 216-176; Fax: 216-004

Embassy of Myanmar
No. 181 Norodom
Tel: 213-664; Fax: 213-665

Embassy of the People's Republic
of China
No. 256, Mao Tse Toung Blvd.
Tel: 720-920; Fax: 210-861

Embassy of Philippines
No. 33, Street 294
Tel: 428-592; Fax: 428-048

Embassy of Poland
No. 767, Monivong Blvd.
Tel: 720-916; Fax: 720-918

Embassy of the Republic of Korea
No. 64, Samdech Pan
Tel: 211-901; Fax: 211-903

Embassy of the Republic of Malta
No. 10, Street 370
Tel/Fax: 368-184

Embassy of the Russian Federation
No. 213, Sothearos Blvd.
Tel: 210-931; Fax: 216-776

Embassy of Singapore
No. 92, Norodom Blvd.
Tel: 360-855; Fax: 360-850

Embassy of Sweden
No. 8, Street 352
Tel: 212-259; Fax: 212-867

Embassy of Thailand
196 Norodom Blvd.
Tel: 363-869; Fax: 810-860

Embassy of the United Kingdom
No. 27-29, Street 75
Tel: 427-124; Fax: 427-125

Embassy of the United States
of America
No. 27, Street 240
Tel: 216-436; Fax: 216-437

Embassy of Viet Nam
No. 436, Monivong Blvd.
Tel: 362-741; Fax: 362-314

G. Learning more

1. Related web sites

www.phnompenh.com
www.embassy.org

www.cambodia.org
www.tradeport.org/ts/countries/
cambodia/index.html

www.cambodia-web.net
www.camtour.org

Annex I
Investment Application Form

CIB 01A

CAMBODIAN INVESTMENT BOARD

INVESTMENT PROJECT APPLICATION

1.   **APPLICANT**

Project Description:

_____

_____

_____

Field of Activity (1):   Agriculture   Civil Works   Energy   Finance   Industry
                       Mining   Telecoms   Tourism   Transport   Others

Name and Surname: _____ Nationality: _____

Address: _____

_____

Telephone: _____ Fax: _____

The applicant is or will be acting as:

         o   A major shareholder

         o   A director

         o   A manager

Name, address, phone, and fax of the parent company:

_____

_____

_____

Regional headquarters address, phone and fax (if any):

_____

_____

Name, address, phone, and fax of the local company located or to be located in the Kingdom:

_____

_____

_____

Location of the factory/operation in Cambodia:

City: _____ Province: _____

CIB 01A

2. **FINANCIAL INFORMATION:**

United States dollars should be used as a reference.

Registered capital: _____

Paid-up capital: _____

Par value of the shares: _____

Shareholding percentage and amount

Foreign shareholding (in %): _____ Value: _____

Cambodian shareholding (in %): _____ Value: _____

Name(s) and breakdown of foreign shareholders (if any):

1. _____

_____

2. _____

_____

3. _____

_____

4. _____

_____

Name(s) and breakdown of Cambodian shareholders (if any):

1. _____

_____

2. _____

_____

3. _____

_____

4. _____

_____

FINANCING

Foreign loan: _____ Banks' name(s): _____

Domestic loan: _____ Banks' name(s): _____

Working capital:

_____

Debt/equity ratio at start-up:

_____

TOTAL FIXED ASSETS (1+2+3+4+5):

1. Land (if purchased): _____ Area (in square metre): _____
2. Factory: _____ Covering (in square metre): _____
3. Office: _____ Covering (in square metre): _____
4. Machineries and/or equipment: _____
5. Other fixed assets: _____

3.   PROJECT IMPLEMENTATION SCHEDULE

Construction start-up date:
Forecasted completion:
Date of machinery installation:
Date of factory start-up:

4.   LIST OF MAIN MACHINERY/EQUIPMENT TO BE USED IN THE PROJECT

1. _____

   _____

2. _____

   _____

3. _____

   _____

4. _____

   _____

5. _____

   _____

5.   MARKETING INFORMATION

	VOLUME (2)	AMOUNT
Local market potential		
Export market potential (if any)		
Current imports		
Other		

(2) Specify type of unit

	Company's sales target	
Year	Domestic Market	Export Market

Export Destinations:

_____

_____

6. MANPOWER REQUIREMENT

	Start-up		Start-up	
	Local	Foreign	Local	Foreign
Management Personnel				
Engineers				
Technicians				
Supervisors				
Office Staff/Clerical				
Skilled Workers				
Unskilled Workers				
Total				
Grand Total				

MANPOWER REQUIREMENT (Continued)

Foreign Staff		
Nationality	Position	Number

7. TRAINING PLAN OF LOCAL STAFF

	Number	Field
Management Personnel		
Engineers		
Technicians		
Supervisors		
Office Staff/Clerical		
Skilled Workers		
Unskilled Workers		

Local training duration in man-days:

_____

Overseas training duration in man-days and country:

_____

_____

CIB 01A

8. **PRODUCTION INFORMATION**
   (If Service Industry, please adapt output accordingly)

PRODUCT DESCRIPTION	Capacity (3)		Work Days/Years	
	Maximum	Minimum	Maximum	Minimum

CIB 01A

(3) in volume

PRODUCTION INFORMATION (Continued)
PRODUCTION FORECAST

Production Description	1st Year	2nd Year	3rd Year	4th Year

RAW MATERIALS NEEDED AT FULL CAPACITY

PRODUCT NAME	LOCAL SOURCING		FOREIGN SOURCING	
	VOLUME	AMOUNT	VOLUME	AMOUNT

CIB 01A

LOCAL INTEGRATION SCHEDULE

PERCENTAGE	YEAR	AMOUNT
_____	_____	_____
_____	_____	_____
_____	_____	_____
_____	_____	_____
_____	_____	_____

CIB 01R

COMPANY'S REGISTRATION

1. **Requested Company's Name**

   _____

2. **Capital**

   – **Registered Capital:** _____ **U.S. Dollars**

   – **Paid-up Capital (1):** _____ **U.S. Dollars**

   (1) **A minimum of 25% of the shares must be paid-up upon incorporation**

3. **Shareholders**

   – **Foreign:** _____ **%**

   – **Cambodian:** _____ **%**

   – **Names of Foreign and Cambodian shareholders:**

   _____

   _____

   _____

   _____

   _____

   _____

   _____

4. **Directors**

   – **Numbers of persons:** _____

   – **Names**   **Nationality**

   1. _____   _____

   2. _____   _____

   3. _____   _____

   4. _____   _____

   5. _____   _____

   6. _____   _____

   7. _____   _____

Particulars of each director need to be submitted with the present form, according to the format of Appendix CIB 01R-1 attached here.

5.   Authorized Directors

These are directors who can sign and bind the company. Please mention whether one director, any one director, any two directors, etc., will have the power to sign and bind.

Full Name(s) of Authorized Directors:

_____

_____

_____

6.   **Registered Head Office**

Please list the exact address with number, street name, building name, room number, floor number, district and province.

_____

_____

Also provide a photocopy of the certificate of ownership of the office or land or the lease agreement.

7.   **Accounting Year**

Starting Period: _____

Ending Period: _____

8.   **Banks**

1.   _____

2.   _____

9.   **Auditor**

Name: _____

License Number: _____

Yearly Remuneration: _____ **U.S. Dollars**

10.   **Memorandum and Articles of Association of the Company**

These two Articles must be submitted together with the current form.

INFORMATION ON DIRECTORS

1.   **Full Name (Underline surname)**

_____

2.   **Residential Address**

_____

_____

3.   **Identification Card or Passport Number**

_____

Please attach a photocopy of the Identification Card or Passport (on the pages of picture, personal data and passport number) duly signed and with the written mention "Certified true and correct".[1]

---

[1]   Appendix CIB-01R-1 should be filled up by each director on a separate sheet.

III. LAO PEOPLE'S DEMOCRATIC REPUBLIC

A. Basic operating environment

1. Geography

The Lao People's Democratic Republic is centrally located in South-East Asia with a land area of 236,800 square kilometres. With no coastline, it is bordered by China to the north (505 kilometres), Cambodia to the south (435 kilometres), Viet Nam to the east (2,069 kilometres), Myanmar to the north-west (236 kilometres), and by Thailand to the west (1,833 kilometres).

About 75 per cent of the country is mountainous, and the remaining 25 per cent is lowlands adjacent to the Mekong River, which runs for 1,800 kilometres along and within the western border. Geographically the country is located in a warm and humid zone with only two seasons a year. The rainy season, with an average temperature of 27.3 degrees Celsius (May to November), and the dry season, with an average temperature of 24.2 degrees Celsius (December to April).

The Mekong River provides the main transport artery between the north and south, as well as irrigating the fertile flood plains. The country is rich in flora and fauna. About 50 per cent of the primary forest is hardwood timber.

2. History and culture

(a) *History*

The first recorded history of the Lao People's Democratic Republic began with the unification of the country in 1353 by King Fa Ngum. Establishing his capital at Luang Prabang, King Fa Ngum ruled a kingdom called Lan Xang (literally, "Million Elephants") which covered much of what today is Thailand and the Lao People's Democratic Republic. His successors, especially King Setthathirat in the sixteenth century, established Buddhism as the predominant religion of the country.

In the eighteenth century, Lan Xang entered a period of decline caused by dynastic struggles and conflicts with Burma (Myanmar), Siam (Thailand), Viet Nam and the Khmer kingdom.

In the nineteenth century, the Siamese established hegemony over much of what is now the Lao People's Democratic Republic. Late in the century, the French supplanted the Siamese and integrated all of the country into the French Empire as directly ruled provinces, except for Luang Prabang, which was ruled as a protectorate.

The Franco-Siamese treaty of 1907 defined much of the present Lao People's Democratic Republic's boundary with Thailand.

During World War II, the Japanese occupied French Indo-China, including what is now the Lao People's Democratic Republic. King Sisavang Vong of Luang Prabang was induced to declare independence from France in 1945, just prior to Japan's surrender. In September 1945, Vientiane and Champassak united with Luang Prabang to form an independent Government under the Free Lao (Lao Issara) banner.

In 1946, French troops reoccupied the country and conferred limited autonomy following elections for a constituent assembly. France formally recognized the country's independence within the French Union in 1949, and it remained a member of the Union until 1953.

Pro-western Governments held power after the 1954 Geneva peace conference until 1957, when the first coalition government, led by Prince Souvanna Phouma, was formed. The coalition government collapsed in 1958 amid increased polarization of the political process. Rightist forces took over the Government and communist liberation movement (known as the Pathet Lao) resumed in 1959. In 1960, Kong Le seized Vientiane in a coup and demanded the formation of a neutralist Government to end the fighting.

This Government was led by Souvanna Phouma but was driven from power later that same year by rightist forces under General Phoumi Nosavan. In response, the neutralists allied themselves with the communist movement and began to receive support from the former Soviet Union. Phoumi Nosavan's rightist regime received support from the United States.

In 1972, the communist people's party renamed itself the Lao People's Revolutionary Party (LPRP) and went on to join a new coalition Government, but political struggle between the communists, neutralists and rightists continued. The communist victories in Saigon and Phnom Penh in 1975 hastened the decline of the coalition. On December 2, 1975, the king renounced his throne in the constitutional monarchy and entrusted his power to the Lao people. The LPRP dissolved the coalition cabinet and the communist Lao People's Democratic Republic was established.

The LPRP introduced socialist economic policies soon after taking control of the Government, but the economy never became completely socialized. For example, the party leaders initially encouraged the formation of cooperatives in the agriculture sector, but within three years they reversed the policy to allow farmers the option of joining a cooperative or not in the hope of reviving the agriculture sector. A series of economic setbacks in the 1980s eventually led the LPRP to alter its economic course and embark on the New Economic Mechanism (NEM) in 1986. The NEM entailed a shift towards limited market principles, essentially blending socialism with a modicum of a market economy.

Since the introduction of the NEM, the LPRP has pursued a gradual, but steady, move towards a modern market economy. The legal framework for the economy is still in the process of development, but the country has had a constitution since 1991 and one of the most liberal foreign investment laws in South-East Asia.

(b) *Culture*

The majority of the Lao population are Buddhists (60 per cent) which is regarded as the national religion. Laotian values and beliefs are, however, a blend of Buddhism and Hinduism. Several of the hill tribes practice animism, while Islam and Christianity can also be found in small numbers among the hill tribes and others. Many of the traditional values, costumes, and ways of living are still found throughout the country, which combine to create an enchanting and serene place to live.

3. Population

The population is estimated at 5.1 million people (July 1997), with a growth rate of 2.78 per cent. Despite its small size, the population of the country is extremely diverse. In total, the Lao People's Democratic Republic contains 68 ethnic groups based on their linguistic features, and many of the ethnic groups are hill tribes living in the mountain ranges.

The Lao People's Democratic Republic is also one of the least densely populated countries in Asia with around 20 people per square kilometre.

4. Land size

The Lao People's Democratic Republic has a total land area of 236,800 square kilometres, comprised largely of mountains, highlands and plateaus. Despite the assumption that the country is quite small because of its population, the actual land size is equivalent to the United Kingdom.

5. Languages

Linguistically, the population of the Lao People's Democratic Republic may be classified into six broad groups:

- Tai-Lao
  This consists of the Phutai, Tai Dam, Tai Jhao, Tai Deng, Tai Neua, Tai Lue, Phuan and Yuan. This group comprises two thirds of the total population and its oral and written languages are regarded as the official language.

- Mon-Khmer

  The Khmu, Lamed, Lavae, So and Makong belong to this group.
- Hmong-Yao

  This group consists of the Hmong Khao, Hmong-Lai, Yao, Lantan and Akha. They are scattered throughout the north and the higher altitudes of the central region.
- Tibeto-Burman

  The Kho, Khui, Sida, Lolo, Phu Noi and Musir belong to this group.
- Viet-Mon

  This group consists largely of the Mon, Tum, Slang, Tree and Nguan.
- Hau (Haw)

  This group consists only of the Hau tribe, who live in the northern provinces.

Other languages include French, English, and various ethnic languages.

6. Government structure

The Lao People's Democratic Republic is governed by the Lao People's Revolutionary Party (LPRP), which is under the direction of the Party Congress. Election of party leaders occurs every four or five years. The main decision-making body is the Political Bureau (Politburo), which is comprised of nine members and chosen by the Central Committee. The Central Committee contains 49 members.

The Lao People's Democratic Republic adopted its constitution in 1991. The following year elections were held for a new 85-seat National Assembly, with members elected by secret ballot to 5-year terms. The assembly, which expanded in 1997 to 99 members and meets once a year, approves all laws, although the executive branch retains the authority to issue binding decrees.

The National Assembly elects the President on the recommendation of the National Assembly Standing Committee. It also elects the Prime Minister and the Cabinet on the recommendation of the President. The Council of Government (Cabinet) is based on the 12 ministries. The next election for the National Assembly is scheduled for December 2002.

Other features of the government structure include a judicial branch comprised of district and provincial courts, and a national Supreme Court. The legal system is a mixture of traditional customary law, French legal norms, and socialist practices. The first legal code was not established until 1988, but the foundation of the legal system is the 1991 Constitution. Administratively, the Lao People's Democratic Republic is divided into 16 provinces, Vientiane prefecture, and one special zone.

B. Macroeconomic business climate

1. Gross domestic product and other macro-indicators

GDP growth, which had averaged 7 per cent for the past six years, slowed in 1998 to 4 per cent, the lowest rate since 1991. Although the Lao People's Democratic Republic has experienced positive GDP growth since the early days of reform in 1989, government efforts to diversify its narrow manufacturing base – most of which relies on imported inputs – have progressed slowly. Moreover, although both the industrial and service sectors' share of GDP continue to grow annually (by 8.5 per cent and 4.8 per cent, respectively, in 1998), more than 85 per cent of the Lao population remains engaged in subsistence agriculture.

The Lao economy is based primarily on agriculture, with 80 per cent of the population employed in agriculture, forestry, and fisheries. The country's GDP is thus heavily reliant upon a good harvest, but other key contributors to GDP are exports of hydro-electricity and garments. Agriculture accounted for 51 per cent of GDP in 1999, with industry comprising 22 per cent and services at 27 per cent. The Lao People's Democratic Republic's GDP grew at impressive rates in the mid-1990s until the Asian economic crisis slowed growth in 1998 to 4 per cent (see table 3). The 4 per cent growth rates of 1998 and 1999 were bolstered by strong performance in agriculture, which benefited from a major government irrigation programme and the rebound in garment production largely due to increased penetration of European markets. Like most countries in the region affected by the crisis, the projected growth rates are a modest 4.5-5 per cent for 2000 and 2001, and the Lao

People's Democratic Republic's economic recovery is naturally intertwined with its neighbours' recovery, particularly Thailand.

Table 3. Major economic indicators 1997-2001
(percentage)

Item	1997	1998	1999	2000*	2001*
GDP growth	6.9	4.0	4.0	4.5	5.0
Gross domestic investment/GDP	26.2	26.1	23.7	24.0	25.0
Gross savings/GDP	9.4	15.5	13.4	13.0	13.0
Inflation rate (consumer price index)[a]	26.6	142.0	86.7	30.0	10.0
Money supply (M2) growth	65.8	113.3	86.3	50.0	30.0
Fiscal balance/GDP[b]	-8.8	-13.9	-9.3	-8.5	-8.0
Merchandise exports growth	-1.2	7.7	2.9	5.0	6.0
Merchandise imports growth	-6.0	-14.7	-2.9	7.0	6.5
Current account balance/GDP[c]	-16.8	-10.6	-10.3	-11.0	-12.0
Debt service/exports	9.0	11.1	12.0	12.5	12.0

Sources: Bank of Lao People's Democratic Republic; IMF; Ministry of Finance; National Statistical Centre

Notes: figures for 1999 are preliminary estimates

   * Estimates for 2000 and 2001

   [a] End of period
   [b] On a fiscal year basis ending 30 September; exclude official transfers
   [c] Excludes official transfers

Services represent about 28 per cent of GDP and output in this sector grew by 4.8 per cent in 1998. The nascent tourism industry is among the fastest-growing areas in this sector, generating nearly US$ 80 million in revenue in 1998. The Lao government expected revenue to grow by 15 per cent in FY 1999-2000, when the country launched an official tourism promotion programme.

Industrial output grew by 8.5 per cent in 1998 and represented 21 per cent of GDP. Electricity generation, boosted by the completion of a 210 megawatt (MW) power plant, jumped by 63 per cent that year, while manufacturing went up by almost 10 per cent and mining by around 14 per cent. Construction on the other hand declined by 20 per cent during the year.

Agriculture, which accounts for 51 per cent of GDP, grew by nearly four per cent in 1998. Livestock production increased by more than 6 per cent, while rice production went up by 2.5 per cent. Timber production, in contrast, declined by more than 4 per cent for the year.

The country's fiscal performance improved in 1999 largely as a result of the Government's reduction in public investment from 14 per cent in 1998 to 9.3 per cent in 1999. Revenues also improved to about 11.3 per cent because of improvements in both tax and non-tax revenue collections. At the same period, the Government reduced current expenditure from 7.1 per cent in 1998 to 5.5 per cent in 1999.

After reaching manageable inflation rates of less than 10 per cent from 1992-1996, the Asian economic crisis and subsequent currency depreciation (especially due to the Thai baht) fueled inflation in 1998 to 142 per cent. The rate fell to around 87 per cent in 1999, but the forecast for 2000 and 2001 predicts a further drop to 30 per cent in 2000 and 10 per cent in 2001.

Both the current account and trade balance improved in 1998 largely due to the currency depreciation. Improvements in some macroeconomic indicators such as the current account balance continued in 1999, but with the heavy reliance on imports, the trade related indicators are not expected to improve in 2000 and 2001 (see table 3).

The Lao People's Democratic Republic relies heavily on official development assistance for meeting its budget expenditures. Foreign aid averages US$ 150 million a year (around 45 per cent of the annual budget), with around 70 per cent of this deriving from the major multinational agencies such as the Asian Development Bank, International Monetary Fund, United Nations Development Programme, UNICEF. Bilateral assistance is also an important component of the annual budget, and the Lao People's Democratic Republic received a major boost in 1995 when the United States lifted aid restrictions. The major bilateral donors are Japan, Australia, Sweden, France, Germany, and the United States. Foreign direct investment and official development assistance disbursements increased slightly in 1999 while the gross official reserves increased from US$ 112.8 million to US$ 115.9 million. As a result of the high levels of foreign aid and improved fiscal management, the Lao People's Democratic Republic has a low and manageable foreign debt.

As one of the world's poorest countries, the Lao People's Democratic Republic receives extensive foreign assistance (both loans and grants) from a range of multilateral and bilateral sources, amounting to 44 per cent of the national budget in 1997. In 1998, however, foreign aid, which had financed the budget deficit in previous years, declined from the previous year. In 1998, recorded disbursements of grants and loans were US$ 74 million and US$ 151 million respectively, compared with 1997 disbursements of US$ 98 million in grants and US$ 275 million in loans.

The Lao currency has had a floating exchange rate since 1995, when the exchange rate was 804 kip to the United States dollar. The currency declined sharply between June 1997 and June 1999 because of its close link with the Thai baht and ended up losing 87 per cent of its value (see table 4). As of November 2000, the currency stands around 7,900 kip to the United States dollar. The currency has remained steady at this level for much of 2000. Two positive outcomes of the currency depreciation are that it boosted exports and reduced imports.

Table 4. Average exchange rate of the Lao kip to US$
(1995 – first half of 1999)

Country	1995	1996	1997	1998	1999
Lao People's Democratic Republic	804.69	921.14	1,256.74	3,299.2	5,967.25

Source: ASEAN Secretariat, Statistics of Foreign Direct Investment in ASEAN, 1999

The forecast for 2000 and 2001 is generally optimistic. Growth in agriculture is expected to continue with the support of continued investment in irrigation, while export earnings from hydropower are expected to rise as Thailand's energy consumption returns to pre-crisis levels. Furthermore, inflation rates should continue to decline, as currencies become more stable in the region.

2. Main economic sectors

Since the economic reform movement commenced in the late 1980s, the Lao People's Democratic Republic's economy has made noticeable improvements in terms of growth rates and opportunities for a variety of commercial activities. However, overall the Lao economy remains heavily oriented towards agriculture and has a narrow manufacturing and services base despite attempts to promote industry. Agriculture continues to account for more than 50 per cent of GDP, and the heavy reliance on imported goods shows few signs of ending any time soon.

(a) *Agricultural*

The agricultural sector remains the most important sector for the Lao People's Democratic Republic's economy, and as a result the Government has paid much attention to upgrading its production technology, infrastructure network, and human resource development. Agriculture, which accounts for 51 per cent of GDP, grew by nearly 4 per cent in 1998. Also in that year, livestock production increased by more than 6 per cent. Glutinous rice is the primary crop grown throughout the country, but other important crops include maize, sugar cane, root crops, beans, tobacco, cotton, fruits, tea, and coffee.

(b) *Forestry*

Unlike many of its neighbours, the Lao People's Democratic Republic retains much of its virgin forest. Over two thirds of the country is still covered by forest, which renders timber and wood products a major industry and earner of foreign exchange. Wood products comprised nearly 35 per cent of Lao exports in 1997. Approximately 85 per cent of the country's wood products are exported to Thailand and Japan. In effort to preserve much of the natural forest cover, the Government restricts the amount of timber that can be felled each year. Also, unprocessed logs are forbidden for export.

(c) *Minerals*

The Lao People's Democratic Republic is blessed with a number of minerals, including gypsum, tin, copper, gold, coal, zinc, phosphorite, and iron ore. Much of the mineral wealth is still untapped, and thus the minerals sector will certainly increase its importance to the economy in the years to come. Oil exploration has also begun mainly in the southern part of the country.

(d) *Hydropower*

The Lao People's Democratic Republic is one of the world's greatest sources of hydropower potential. Currently the country has approximately 202 MW of installed capacity, but it has plans to increase to over 7,000 MW by 2009. Most of the electricity generated comes from the Nam Ngum dam near Vientiane, although over 20 power stations are in the process of being constructed or already on line. Electricity is exported solely to Thailand via high power lines across the Mekong River, and up until the drop in demand by Thailand during the crisis, electricity was one of the Lao People's Democratic Republic's major foreign exchange earners.

(e) *Tourism*

The Lao People's Democratic Republic possesses great natural beauty, with tracts of forests, mountains, and spectacular waterfalls. Together with its historical, cultural and artistic heritage, the country has much to offer to tourists. As a result, the tourism sector has become a promising industry for the Lao People's Democratic Republic and the supporting tourism infrastructure in terms of hotels, guesthouses, etc. is gradually emerging.

Since 1990, 34 projects worth over US$ 600 million have been approved in the tourism sector, averaging 50 per cent growth per year over that period. National revenue from tourism reached almost US$ 80 million in 1998, bypassing garments for the first time. The number of tourists increased tremendously during the 1990s. In 1991, a mere 14,400 tourists visited the country compared to 403,000 in 1996. 1999-2000 was been proclaimed as "Visit Laos Year" to further boost tourism, and the Government anticipated that over 780,000 visitors would arrive.

3. Trade

Since the Lao People's Democratic Republic adopted a new economic policy in 1986, economic relations with foreign countries have been widely expanded in line with the Government's policy of opening up the country.

The Lao People's Democratic Republic imports more than twice as much as it exports, relying upon its neighbours (primarily Thailand) for even basic consumer goods and some food supplies, giving the country a negative trade balance that represented 16.5 per cent of GDP in 1998. The Government is trying to diversify its trading and investment partners, especially among the other nations of the region. Following its admission to ASEAN in 1997, the Lao People's Democratic Republic applied for membership in the World Trade Organization (WTO) in 1998. Although the United States is the second largest source of foreign investment in the Lao People's Democratic Republic (following Thailand), bilateral trade remains limited due in part to the lack of normal trade relations (NTR) between the two nations. Imports from the United States for 1998 totaled US$ 4 million, with chemicals used in industrial processing the leading import item. Exports from the Lao People's Democratic Republic for the same year totaled US$ 21 million, with garments topping the list.

The country's leading exports, in descending order, are garments, wood and wood products, minerals such as tin and gypsum, hydroelectricity, and coffee. Electricity exports experienced the sharpest rise in 1998, increasing nearly 220 per cent, while coffee exports grew by 150 per cent. The range of goods manufactured for export is limited primarily to garments, wood and rattan products, and handicrafts. Fuel is the leading import item.

(a) **Exports**

Before the impact of the economic crisis, Lao exports had seen a steady increase throughout the 1990s (see table 3). In 1997, before the brunt of the crisis was felt, the Lao People's Democratic Republic exported nearly US$ 317 million. The value of exports fell the following year to US$ 251 million before rebounding in 1999 at US$ 271 million. As seen in table 5, garments, wood products, gold re-exports, and hydroelectricity are the leading export items. The growth in garments is a consequence of the substantial inflow of foreign investment in the garments sector. Investors in garments took advantage of the Generalized System of Preference (GSP) trade privileges with the European Union.

Table 5. Main exports, 1993-1997
(millions of US dollars)

Export Item	1993	1994	1995	1996	1997
Garments	49.0	58.2	76.7	64.0	90.5
Wood & wood products	65.8	96.1	88.3	125.0	89.7
Gold re-exports	4.2	18.8	21.9	15.2	41.5
Hydroelectric power	19.6	24.8	24.1	30.0	20.8
Coffee	4.1	3.1	21.3	25.0	19.2
Other manufactured goods	38.1	36.3	43.4	27.9	15.2
Total exports	**240.5**	**300.4**	**312.8**	**320.7**	**316.9**

Source: Economist Intelligence Unit and International Trade Centre UNCTAD/WTO September 1999

Figure 13 shows the leading export items for 1998. Wood products far surpassed other items, including garments, to become once again the leading export category.

Figure 13. Exports by commodity, 1998

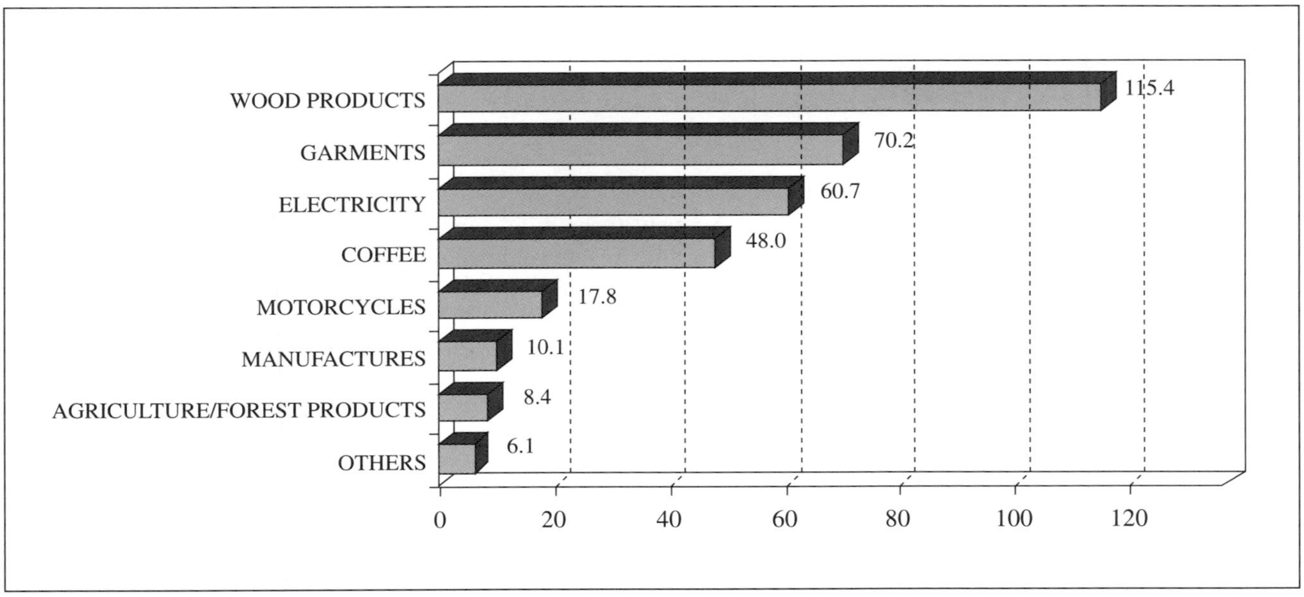

Source: EXIM Bank of Thailand

63

Currently, the Lao People's Democratic Republic has trading relations with more than 30 nations. Trade volume has increased by an average of 18.7 per cent a year. At present, the most important trading partners are mainly Asian and Pacific nations such as Thailand, Viet Nam, Japan and China. The United States has not yet extended NTR to the Lao People's Democratic Republic. The two countries signed a bilateral trade agreement that will take effect once NTR status has been granted by the United States Congress. The bilateral trade agreement was concluded in August 2000. Among the elements of the agreement are limitations on the use of non-tariff impediments to trade, specific commitments to market access in a broad range of service sectors, and comprehensive commitments to protect all forms of intellectual property, and enforcement requirements against intellectual property piracy.

On becoming a member of ASEAN in 1997, the Lao People's Democratic Republic committed to bringing all of its tariffs in line with its ASEAN Free Trade Area (AFTA) commitments by 2008. The following countries have granted Most Favored Nation status to the Lao People's Democratic Republic: China; Myanmar; Thailand; the European Union; and the Russian Federation. The Lao People's Democratic Republic has signed trade agreements with 14 countries, most recently with the United States.

Figure 14. Leading trade partners, 1997

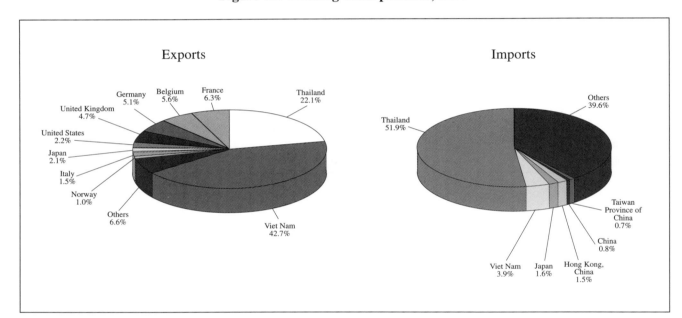

Source: EXIM Bank of Thailand

(b) *Imports*

The Lao People's Democratic Republic is heavily dependent on imported finished goods as a result of its small manufacturing base. Imports rose continuously throughout the 1990s until the Asian economic crisis struck in 1997 (see table 6), when a three-year decline in the value of imports began. From 1997 to 1998, imports fell from nearly US$ 648 million to US$ 596 million, and then dropped to US$ 497 million in 1999.

Major imports are consumer products, equipment and machinery for construction works and agriculture, material for the garment industry, electrical appliances, medicine, and fuels. Figure 15 shows the breakdown of imports for 1998.

Table 6. Main imports 1993-1997
(millions of US dollars)

Imports	1993	1994	1995	1996	1997
Consumer goods	224.7	276.5	283.8	308.0	267.7
Investment goods	113.8	146.1	189.3	277.0	226.8
Construction &					
Electrical equipment	48.9	67.7	78.8	101.2	82.8
Intermediate goods	77.7	90.8	79.6	82.0	98.6
Inputs for garment					
Industry	36.2	51.3	66.3	70.0	73.7
Motorcycle parts	27.0	34.6	13.3	12.0	24.9
Gold & Silver	12.9	46.8	29.5	18.8	50.4
Total Imports	**431.9**	**564.1**	**588.8**	**689.6**	**647.9**

Source: Economist Intelligence Unit (EIU)

Figure 15. Imports by commodity, 1998

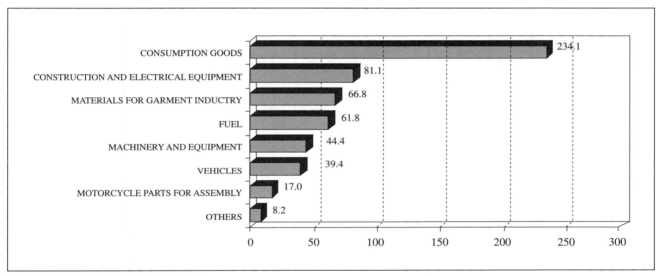

Source: EXIM Bank of Thailand

For years Thailand has been the principal supplier of imports to the Lao People's Democratic Republic, typically accounting for over half of all goods imported. Other main sources of imported goods are Singapore, China, Japan, Viet Nam, and Myanmar, but individually these countries comprise only a small share of Lao imports.

4. Foreign investment

The Lao People's Democratic Republic first opened to foreign investment in 1988. Foreign investment since the beginning has been dominated by Thailand both in terms of the number of projects and their monetary value. Table 7 shows the top 14 foreign investors between December 1988 and January 2000.

Table 7. Foreign investment in the Lao People's Democratic Republic by country/area of origin

Country/Area	Number of projects	Amount of capital (US$ million)
Thailand	257	2,932
United States of America	46	1,491
Republic of Korea	34	634
Malaysia	19	290
China	72	86
United Kingdom	18	69
Taiwan Province of China	35	67
Australia	44	42
France	90	38
Hong Kong, China	20	26
Singapore	17	20
Russian Federation	15	19
Japan	27	18
Viet Nam	20	14
Total* (including other countries)	**714**	**7,058**

Source: Foreign Investment Management Committee

* Includes Lao investment in joint ventures

The Lao People's Democratic Republic reached a bilateral investment guarantee treaty with the United States. The treaty, which is the first of its kind for the United States with a South-East Asian country, is pending the advice and consent of the United States Senate. The investment treaty guarantees investors of each country the right to invest in the other country on terms no less favourable than those accorded domestic or third-country investors in most sectors. It also guarantees the free transfer of capital, profits and royalties, freedom from performance requirements that distort trade and investment flows, access to international arbitration, and internationally recognized standards for expropriation and compensation.

Data on foreign investment by sector reveal that electric power is the by far the leading sector in terms of capital cost, accounting for nearly 64 per cent of the total amount of foreign investment. However, the services sector has attracted the largest number of projects from foreign investment (150). Table 6 shows the number of projects and amount invested by sector between December 1988 and January 2000.

Table 8. Foreign investment in the Lao People's Democratic Republic by sector, December 1998-January 2000

Country	Number of projects	Amount of capital (US$ million)
Agro-business	88	135
Textiles and garments	79	73
Industry and handicrafts	141	516
Wood industry	37	167
Mining and oil	33	139
Trading	117	69
Hotel and tourism	35	601
Banking and insurance	12	84
Consultancy	34	7
Services	150	63
Construction	39	65
Telecom. and transport	16	638
Electric power	7	4,500
Total	**788**	**7,058**

Source: Foreign Investment Management Committee

5. National economic policies and priorities

In 1986, the Government of the Lao People's Democratic Republic embarked on the "New Economic Mechanism" (NEM) in an attempt to transform the country into a market economy. The NEM represented the transformation of the economy from a state planning model to a market oriented economy. Subsequently, additional laws have been passed to support the NEM, including a business law in 1994 and a domestic investment law in 1995. The transformation of the economy is evidenced by the fact that approximately 90 per cent of state-owned enterprises have been converted to another system of management (many via leases) or liquidated. The old state planning legacy has not been entirely disbanded, however, as the Government still sets production targets for the agricultural sector, as well as for some other industries, and controls the price on a few essential goods such as cement and gasoline.

In an effort to reduce the country's import dependency and trade deficit, the Government is seeking ways to promote production for domestic consumption and for export, especially in targeted sectors such as agriculture, construction materials, and light industry. To achieve these objectives, the Government encourages import companies to also develop plans for increasing or initiating domestic production.

The economic reform process is ongoing in the Lao People's Democratic Republic, and thus as part of its aim to strengthen the macroeconomic fundamentals of the country, the Government intends to accomplish the following:

- Improvement of the banking sector performance by full interest rate liberalization, introduction of new monetary instruments, stabilization of exchange rates and inflation, enhancement of credit and saving mechanisms, and reinforcement of the Bank of Lao People's Democratic Republic's supervisory capacity.
- Enhance fiscal discipline by improving revenue collection and expenditure rationalization through the development of a multi-year integrated macroeconomic framework.
- Strengthen the government organizational structure to foster better coordination among the various layers of administration.
- Continue decentralization at the provincial and district levels while also strengthening their institutional development.
- Improve the legal and regulatory frameworks to enhance private sector development.
- Establish planning and evaluation departments in a number of major ministries.
- Participate more fully in ASEAN and ensure the timely implementation of ASEAN obligations such as the ASEAN Free Trade Area (AFTA).

In addition to the aforementioned policy priorities, the current Socio-Economic Development Plan (1996-2000) targets eight areas for reform and assistance:

1. Food production
2. Commercial production
3. Shifting cultivation stabilization
4. Rural development
5. Infrastructure development
6. External economic relations
7. Human resources development
8. Services development

C. Institutional and support network: public and private sector organizations

1. Government organizations and agencies

The Foreign Investment Management Committee (FIMC)

The FIMC is designed to serve as a "one-stop" centre for potential investors in the Lao People's Democratic Republic. The FIMC performs several duties on behalf of investors from the application stage to actual operations, such as assisting foreign investors, granting investment licenses, and monitoring foreign investment. Also included in its duties are the screening of investment applications, coordinating with other concerned ministries and provincial authorities, compiling statistics, and promoting investment in the country.

Contact Address:
Luang Prabang Road, Ban Sithantay, Sikhottabong District, Vientiane
Tel: (856) 21 414925   Fax: (856) 21 215491

Ministry of Commerce and Tourism

The Ministry of Commerce and Tourism is responsible for administering domestic and foreign trade policy and supervising trade activities. It also promotes Lao products and commodities in domestic and international markets, organizes trade fairs, and handles the registration of enterprises.

The Ministry of Commerce has a provincial trade service in each province along with a district trade office. The main duties of these provincial services and district offices are to implement trade policy and to manage and promote trade activities.

Contact Address:
Phonxay Road, P.O. Box 4107, Vientiane
Tel: (856) 21 412014   Fax: (856) 21 412434

Ministry of Finance (Customs Department)

The Customs Department is responsible for import-export tariff and customs matters.

Contact Address:
Thatluang Rd., Ban Phonxay, Xiansettha District, Vientiane
P.O. Box 46, Tel: (856) 21 412409   Fax: (856) 21 412250

Ministry of Industry and Handicrafts

Contact Address:
Nongbone Road, Ban Xiangyeune, Chanthabouly District, Vientiane, P.O. Box 4708
Tel: (856) 21 413002   Fax: (856) 21 414351

2. Chamber of commerce and industry associations

Established in 1989 under the guidance of the Ministry of Commerce and Tourism, the Lao National Chamber of Commerce and Industry aims to enhance cooperation among traders, farmers and manufacturers of major export or import products. Under the realm of the Lao National Chamber of Commerce and Industry are nine trade associations:

– The Lao People's Democratic Republic Coffee Export Association
– The Lao People's Democratic Republic Handicraft Group
– The Lao People's Democratic Republic Construction Material Group
– The Lao People's Democratic Republic Food Group
– The Lao People's Democratic Republic Garment and Textile Group
– The Lao People's Democratic Republic Vehicle and Spare Parts Group
– The Lao People's Democratic Republic Hotel Group
– The Lao People's Democratic Republic Construction Group
– The Lao People's Democratic Republic Petroleum Group

Although each trade association is a separate entity with regulations and practices of its own, it is a member of the Lao National Chamber of Commerce and Industry, which acts as a centre of coordination among and between associations, as well as with the Government. Coordination with the Government usually entails providing input on the rules and regulations governing the business sector.

Traders, farmers, or manufacturers, both local and foreign, can apply for membership directly with the related trade association. Members of the trade associations are automatically members of the Lao National Chamber of Commerce and Industry.

The main objectives of the trade associations are to enhance cooperation among members in the areas of production, trade and export/import. This is achieved through consolidating the supply of export products to increase bargaining power in the world market and prevent price-cutting, consolidating demand for imports to lessen processing costs and increase bargaining power; and providing members with the information on the world market situation, price trends, new technology, etc.

3. Consulting, accounting, and law firms

This section provides contact information for an assortment of consulting, accounting, and legal firms in the Lao People's Democratic Republic. However, the following information does not imply endorsement or recommendation.

(a) *Consulting/accounting firms*

International standard consulting and accounting firms are available in the Lao People's Democratic Republic, but these are essentially located in Vientiane.

PriceWaterhouseCoopers
Unit 1, Fourth Floor
Vientiane Commercial Building
33 Lan Xang Avenue P.O. Box 7003 Vientiane
Tel: (856 21) 222 718
Fax: (856 21) 222 723
E-mail: pwc-laos@loxinfo.co.th

Services provided:
Audit, assurance, and business advisory,
financial advisory, global tax services,
global human resource solutions,
management consulting

KPMG
Mark Jerome, Country Manager
Km. 2 Luang Prabang Rd., P.O. Box 6978 Vientiane
Tel: (856 21) 219 491-3
Fax: (856 21) 219 490
E-mail: kpmglaom@loxinfo.co.th

Services provided
Assurance, tax and legal, consulting
financial advisory

Vientiane International Consultants
234 Samsenthai Road
Vientiane
Tel: (856-21) 214-182
Fax: (856-21) 215-797
E-mail: vic@laonet.net; vic@pan-laos.net

(b) *Law firms*

Commercial law is a rather recent addition to the Lao legal system. One of the major problems for businesses is that few of the Lao laws have been translated into English and none has been officially translated.

Dirksen, Flipse, Doran, and Lee
Mekong Commerce Building #1
P.O. Box 2920
Luang Prabang Road, Vientiane
Tel: (856) 21 2169279
Fax: (856) 21 216919
E-mail: dfdllaos@loxinfo.co.th

KMPG Lao Ltd.
Luang Prabang Rd.
Ban Khouta Thong
P.O. Box 6978
Vientiane
Tel: (856-21) 222-042; 219-491
Fax: (856-21) 219-490

Services provided

Legal services in investment contacts, licensing negotiations with government and joint venture partners land purchasing, leasing and financing

Mr. Khamphay Bothapanith
106 Ban Wat Nak, Sisattanak District
Vientiane
Tel: (856-21) 312-397

Mr. Sabh Phommarath
191, Unit 17, Nongbouathong Tai
Vientiane
Tel: (856-21) 222-346

4. Financial institutions

The Central Bank of the Lao People's Democratic Republic is responsible for all the financial institutions in the country. It has 34 commercial banks and branches under its responsibility. In mid-1999, eight state-owned commercial banks were merged into four banks in order to strengthen the financial sector.

At present, the four state-owned banks are:

- **Banque pour le Commerce Exterieur Lao Ltd. (BCEL)**, the foreign trade bank, based in Vientiane.
- **Lan Xang Bank Ltd.**, a state-owned commercial bank, based in Luang Prabang. It is the result of a merger of three state-owned banks: Setthathirath Bank, Aroun Mai Bank and Lan Xang Bank.
- **Lao May Bank Ltd.**, a state-owned commercial bank based in Savannakhet. Three state-owned banks, Nakhoneluang Bank, Lao May Bank, and Phak Tai Bank, were merged into one.
- **The Agricultural Promotion Bank,** based in Vientiane.

There are other privately owned commercial banks which includes three joint venture banks, Thai bank branches, one foreign bank, and one representative office:

Joint venture banks

- Joint Development Bank: a joint venture between Thailand (70 per cent) and the Lao People's Democratic Republic (30 per cent)
- Vientiane Commercial Bank: a joint venture between Australia, Taiwan Province of China and Thailand (75 per cent) along with the Lao People's Democratic Republic (25 per cent)
- Lao-Viet Bank: a joint venture between BCEL of the Lao People's Democratic Republic and the Bank for Investment and Development of Viet Nam

Thai bank branches

- Bank of Ayuddhya Public Company Limited
- Bangkok Bank Public Company Limited
- Krung Thai Bank Public Company Limited
- Siam Commercial Bank Public Company Limited
- Thai Farmers Bank Public Company Limited
- Thai Military Bank Public Company Limited

Foreign bank branches

- Public Bank Berhard Public Company Limited (Malaysia)

Representative offices

- Standard Chartered Bank (United Kingdom)

Another important institution in the financial sector is the Mekong Project Development Facility (MPDF), which is an arm of the World Bank's International Finance Corporation. MPDF was established in 1997 and has offices in Vientiane and Viet Nam. MPDF provides companies with local and international assistance with financial engineering and business development. While it does not actually lend financing, it helps small and medium size firms (SMEs) with project development to access finance. For more information contact:

Mekong Project Development Facility
Nehru Road, Pathou Xay
P.O. Box 9690 Vientiane
Tel: (856-21) 450-017
Fax: (856-21) 450-020

Also of note is that an Overseas Private Investment Cooperation (OPIC) agreement was signed in 1996, and an agreement with the Multilateral Investment Guarantee Agency (MIGA) in 1998.

5. Transportation

The Lao People's Democratic Republic is strategically located to become the land transportation hub of South-East Asia, because it is the only country in the region that borders five countries. Unfortunately, the mountainous terrain is a hindrance to speedily developing the country's transportation infrastructure, and many of the mountainous areas are difficult and many of the mountainous areas are difficult to reach during the five-month rainy season (May-September). Infrastructure within the Lao People's Democratic Republic is inadequate at the moment but improving each year, especially the highway network.

There are currently about 22,000 kilometres of roadways in the country, less than half of which are paved, and many of which are in poor repair. Efforts to upgrade and extend the national road network are supported by bilateral or multilateral assistance funds such as the Government of Japan and the Asian Development Bank.

A summary of the six major routes is as follows:

Highway Route 1:	Runs from the Chinese-Lao border through Luang Prabang to Route 6 at Huaphanh
Highway Route 6:	Connects with Route 1 in Huaphanh.
Highway Route 13:	The main artery connecting the southern part of the country to the north. Runs from the Lao-Cambodian border in Champassak, through Vientiane and Luang Prabang, and connects to Oudomsay.
Highway Route 7:	Starts from Route 13 in Luang Prabang, through Xieng Khouang, to the Lao-Vietnamese border.
Highway Route 8:	Begins in Bolikhamxay at Route 13 and runs to the Lao-Vietnamese border.
Highway Route 9:	Runs from Savannakhet and then joins Route 13 to the Lao-Vietnamese border. Route 9 serves as the Lao People's Democratic Republic main link to the sea via Viet Nam's Danang port.

A significant undertaking for the GMS that stands to offer significant benefits to the Lao People's Democratic Republic is the East-West Corridor. This Asia Development Bank initiative entails the development of a 1,500 kilometre road link from Danang in Viet Nam, through Savannakhet in southern Lao People's Democratic Republic, and extending all the way via Thailand to Mawlamyine and Myamaddy in Myanmar.

Nineteen other major road and bridge projects are ongoing throughout the country, with many of them expected to be complete in the next few years. An important recent addition to the road infrastructure is the new bridge across the Mekong River at Pakse, which will facilitate the flow of goods and people between Thailand and Viet Nam. A second international bridge across the Mekong River at Savannakhet (joining with Thailand's Mukdahan Province) is underway and scheduled for completion in 2003. This bridge will complement the first international bridge (completed in 1994) between Vientiane and Thailand's Nong Khai Province.

(a) *Water transportation*

The waterway system consists of 4,587 kilometres of major rivers, notably the Mekong River and its tributaries. The Mekong River itself is over 1,800 kilometres and serves as the country's lifeblood for transportation, food, irrigation, and other vital needs. Smaller vessels can navigate an additional 2,897 kilometres of waterways.

In April 2000, the Lao People's Democratic Republic joined Myanmar, Thailand, and China in signing the Upper Lancang-Mekong River Commercial Navigation Agreement, which takes effect in mid-2001 and aims to facilitate the transportation of goods along the Mekong River.

(b) *Air transportation*

The Lao People's Democratic Republic has 14 airports, but most of them are rather small. The country's only international airport, Wattay, is located in Vientiane and is only a few minutes from the heart of the city. The airport in Luang Prabang is slated to become an international airport, but it is not offering international flights as of yet. International flights from Thailand, China, Viet Nam, and other countries arrive and depart daily to and from Wattay, but several of the inter-provincial flights are only a couple of times a week and the schedules change frequently without prior notification.

(c) *Railways*

As for railroads, the Lao People's Democratic Republic is one of the rare countries without any rail system. The mountainous terrain has prevented the establishment of a railroad, but the issue of a rail system is raised occasionally in the context of linking southwest China with Thailand and even Viet Nam.

6. Telecommunications

Telephone service to the general public is limited but improving. In 1993, the country installed a modern, but limited, telecommunications system that continues to develop through the Telecommunications Master Plan (1987-2010). Assistance from the World Bank and foreign donors is helping to expand the system gradually throughout the country. The system utilizes digital technology and satellites, but even by the end of the fifth phase of the Master Plan the country will still only have 340,000 telephone lines (an average of five lines per 100 people).

7. Other infrastructure

(a) *Electricity and Energy*

Only about 20 per cent of the population has access to electricity despite the country's vast potential for hydropower. While the electricity supply in Vientiane is fairly regular, other parts of the country have a limited number of hours per day in which electricity is available, and many other areas are without electricity altogether.

The Lao People's Democratic Republic has 13 tributaries that join the Mekong River and cover 1,500 kilometres. These provide the country with a total electricity generating capacity of not less than 17,000 megawatts. By 2009, the plan is to have over 7,000 MW of installed capacity. The Lao People's Democratic Republic is poised to become the focal point for an integrated regional power grid over the coming decade, and it already has a memorandum of understanding with Thailand for the sale of 1,500 MW of energy per year and has entered into talks with Cambodia as well.

D. Legal and regulatory frameworks for trade and investment

1. Foreign investment

(a) *Overall investment climate*

Since the implementation of the NEM in 1986, the Government of the Lao People's Democratic Republic has actively encouraged private investment, both foreign and domestic. The Foreign Investment Management Committee (FIMC), located in the Prime Minister's Office (PMO), administers the foreign investment system. To support and encourage investment, the Government offers various incentives to investors, including reduced corporate profit taxes, reduced duties and turnover taxes on imported capital equipment and inputs to production, and investment permissions and guarantees.

The legal and regulatory frameworks for investment are relatively new and still seen as developing. The initial foreign investment law was passed in 1989, but then revised in 1994. A major boost to investment and the business environment in general was the promulgation of the 1991 Constitution. In Chapter 2 of the Constitution, which deals with the socio-economic system, an explicit reference is made to the "goods [market] economy" and to the guarantee of protection of "private ownership of domestic capitalists and foreigners".

The Government welcomes foreign investment in "all fields of lawful economic activity, such as agriculture and forestry, manufacturing, energy, mineral extraction, handicrafts, communications and transport, construction, tourism, trade, services, and others".

Foreign investors, however, may not invest in enterprises that are "detrimental to national security, the natural environment, public health or the national culture, or which violate the laws and regulations of the Lao People's Democratic Republic".

The Lao People's Democratic Republic has no free trade zone, but the Ministry of Commerce has indicated its willingness to establish these in many areas of the country as an investment incentive on a case-by-case basis.

(b) *Foreign investment law*

The Lao People's Democratic Republic has one of the most liberal investment codes in the region, and gradually the supporting legal framework is taking shape to match it. The main laws governing the promotion of investment are the Law on the Promotion and Management of Foreign Investment (1994), the Business Law (1994), the Customs Law (1994), the Law on Domestic Investment (1995), and the Tax Law (1995). The initial investment law was issued in 1989, but it was revised and simplified by the 1994 legislation. See annex 1 for the full text of the foreign investment law.

The revised 1994 investment law allows for wholly-owned foreign firms, joint ventures, and foreign-owned branches. Investors are allowed full profit repatriation and, as noted above, guarantees are made against expropriation. The investment law also sets a flat profit tax rate of 20 per cent and standard import duty concessions. Moreover, the 1994 legislation simplifies and shortens the investment application procedures: the number of procedures fell from 18 to 10, and processing time was reduced from 90 days to 60 days.

The investment law allows two forms of foreign investment: 1) *wholly-owned foreign firms*, and 2) *joint ventures*. Foreign investment can be 100 per cent foreign owned and take the form of a new company or a branch or representative office of a foreign company. A foreign investment that is a branch or representative office of a foreign company must have Articles of Association consistent with the laws and regulations of the Lao People's Democratic Republic and subject to the approval of the FIMC.

Under the 1994 foreign investment law, a *business cooperation contract* (similar to a partnership) provides for the division of profits and liabilities between partners. In this case, the partners assume full liability as no separate legal entity is formed.

In joint ventures/licensing arrangements, the foreign partner must contribute at least 30 per cent of total equity in the investment. The foreign partner's equity may be foreign currency, plant and equipment, capital goods, technology, and/or skills and management. The domestic partner's share, whether a private firm or the Government, can comprise money, land, water rights, natural resources, and/or capital goods. The contributions of each partner are determined at international market rates but converted into Lao kip according to the exchange rate for the date of equity payment.

Other key points from the 1994 Foreign Investment Law include:

Landholding: Foreign investors may lease land within the Lao People's Democratic Republic and transfer their leasehold interests. They are allowed to own improvements on the land and moveable property, and to transfer the ownership of the improvements and moveable property.

Accounts: Foreign investors must open accounts both in Lao kip and in foreign convertible currency with a domestic or foreign bank established in the Lao People's Democratic Republic.

(c)   *Taxation*

Personal income tax: Foreign investors and their foreign personnel working within the Lao People's Democratic Republic pay a flat rate of 10 per cent of the income earned in the Lao People's Democratic Republic.

Corporate tax: Foreign investments must pay an annual profit tax at a uniform flat rate of 20 per cent. For foreign investments involving natural resources exploitation and energy generation, sector-specific taxes and royalties will vary, depending on the agreement entered into between the investors and Government of the Lao People's Democratic Republic.

Import duties: Foreign investments pay a 1 per cent import duty on equipment, means of production, spare parts and other materials used in the operation of their investment projects or in their productive enterprises (based on their imported value). Raw materials and intermediate components imported for the purpose of processing and then re-exported are exempt from import duties. Raw materials and intermediate components imported for the purpose of achieving import substitution are eligible for special duty reductions as determined by the Government.

All exported finished products are exempted from export duties.

(d)   *Investment licensing process (This section extracted from www.laopdr.com)*

To receive a foreign investment license (FI License) in all sectors, except mining, hydropower and forestry sectors, a foreign investor must submit the following to FIMC:

- completed application form (available from FIMC)
- projected assets and liabilities, pro forma income statement for five years
- biodata of the investor
- support of financial capacity of the investor to undertake the proposed investment
- application fee of $100-$200 depending on the size of the project
- four copies of all of the above

The Screening Division of the FIMC reviews the application form for completeness and accuracy. The investor is contacted to supply necessary additional information or to clarify issues arising from the application. The application is then forwarded to the line ministries concerned with the sector in which the investment project is to be made, to the Ministry of Finance and to the Bank of the Lao People's Democratic Republic. The ministries may come back to the FIMC with queries or requests for additional information.

When the ministries have formulated a position on the application, the application is brought before the Technical Committee at the FIMC on which the ministries have representatives. The decision of the Technical Committee is then forwarded to the Chairman of the FIMC for endorsement (either to approve or to reject the application). The Chairman of the FIMC then forwards the endorsed application to the PMO for a final decision.

If the PMO's decision is in accordance with that of the FIMC, either a FI License is issued by the FIMC or the investor is informed that the application has not been approved. If the PMO's viewpoint on the application is at variance with that of the FIMC, the FIMC resubmits the application for further study by the Technical Committee, for endorsement by the Chairman of the FIMC, and final decision by the PMO.

Under the FI Law, this process is required to take a maximum of 60 days. The government is currently studying proposals that would dramatically reduce the approval time for most applications and would radically change the procedures for vetting investment applications for most investments.

For applications in the hydropower, forestry, and mining sectors (and other sectors at the discretion of the FIMC), the investment approval process is significantly different. The application goes to the Mining and Hydropower Division of the FIMC for evaluation. If this evaluation is positive, a memorandum of understanding (MOU) is signed. Based on this MOU, the investor carries out a feasibility study and makes a detailed project proposal, including a thorough feasibility study and proposals for project financing. If the discussions and negotiations over this proposal are positive, a Project Development Agreement is signed and an investment license is issued.

Joint venture applications must also include an agreement on technology transfer and a joint venture agreement signed by both parties.

Within 90 days of receipt of the license, a company must register with the Ministry of Commerce and Tourism in order to obtain a business license, register with the Tax Department at the Ministry of Finance, and receive an industrial establishment authorization from the Department of Industry, Ministry of Industry and Handicrafts.

(e)   ***Setting up a business***

The Business Law regulates the formation, conduct of affairs, and liquidation of all companies. (The Bankruptcy Law of 1994 also deals with liquidations). All firms must register with the Ministry of Commerce and Tourism (MCT), Department of Enterprise Registration, for inclusion into the Company Register. Business operations can be established in a number of forms:

- Representative office
- Branch office
- Partnership
- Partnership
- Limited company
- Sole trader
- Public company
- Private-state mixed enterprise

(i)   *Representative and branch offices*

Unlike the Foreign Investment Law, the Business Law does not mention either representative offices or branch offices, and therefore their legal status is not properly defined. Investors must negotiate their status with the MCT on a case by case basis, but this does not present much of a barrier to establishing a business. Under the FIMC terms for a representative office, such an office is not allowed to conduct business within the country and instead can only refer interested parties to its main offices outside of the country.

For branch offices, the office is regarded as the same legal entity as its parent company and can be held liable for actions and conduct of the branch office with the Lao People's Democratic Republic.

(ii)   *Partnership*

As noted above, foreign firms can enter into joint ventures with domestic private firms or with the Government. The partnership can be managed by either or all of the partners or by a designated manager. All partners are jointly and severally liable for the liabilities of the partnership.

(iii)   *Limited liability company*

A limited liability company can comprise 1 to 20 shareholders, and the minimum capital requirement is 5 million kip, half of which must be paid up capital once the company is registered. The other half of the registered capital must be paid in full within two years of the company's registration. Shares within the company are transferable with the consent of two thirds of the shareholders. All limited liability companies must establish reserve funds based on 5 to 10 per cent from their net profits.

(iv)   *Sole trader enterprise*

The minimum registered capital requirements for a sole trader enterprise is 1 million kip.

(v)   *Public company*

The establishment of a public company requires a minimum of 7 shareholders and at least 50 million kip of registered capital. The maximum value of each share is 10,000 kip. A public company must have 5 to 17 members of a management team, including 1 or 2 workers' representatives. Although there is no stock market in the Lao People's Democratic Republic, shares of a public company can be sold outside the firm.

(vi)   *Private-state mixed enterprise*

This form of enterprise consists of the Government and a private business, with the State holding at least a 51 per cent stake in the firm. Mixed enterprises are regulated by the same rules as public companies but subject to the following exceptions:

- The Government determines the transfer of shares owned by the State while the private shares are managed as shares of a public company
- The share certificates are transferable
- The Chairman of the Board of Director is appointed by the Minister of Finance and the Vice-Chairman is selected by the private party and approved by the Minister of Finance
- The President of the Board of Directors has a casting vote.

Firms must register with the MCT and obtain an Enterprise Registration Certificate from the Department of Enterprise Registration. A company must submit the following documents to register:

- Application form
- Resume of the owner/manager
- Declaration of Sentencing No. 3 (issued by the Lao courts)
- Joint venture applications must also include an agreement on technology transfer and a joint venture agreement signed by both sides.
- Articles of Association
- Feasibility study
- Copy of passport (for foreign company)
- Eight 3 cm x 4 cm photos
- Certificate of Profession of the sectors concerned
- Construction License from the Committee of Planning Construction with Planning Details
- Foreign Investment License
- License from the Bank of the Lao People's Democratic Republic (for companies that operate in the financial sector)
- License from the Ministry of Public Health (for companies that are concerned with the medical sector)
- Notification of approval from the relevant ministry, as required
- Financial statement
- List of fixed assets along with a certificate of ownership which has been registered with a notary

Companies must also have written by-laws containing the following:

- Name, surname, occupation, nationality, and address of the investors
- Name, objectives, duration and location of the headquarters of the company
- Organization chart and management of the company
- Distribution of dividends and responsibility for losses
- Meeting and voting procedures
- Dissolution and liquidation provisions
- Settlement of dispute provisions

(f)   *Labour issues*

According to the Foreign Investment Law, foreign investors are required to give priority to Lao citizens in recruiting and hiring. However, foreign enterprises have the right to employ skilled and expert foreign personnel when necessary and with the approval of the Government of the Lao People's Democratic Republic.

The Foreign Investment Law also calls for foreign investors to upgrade the skills of their Lao employees through training within the Lao People's Democratic Republic or abroad.

(g)   *Investment incentives (This section extracted from www.laoembassy.com)*

The FIMC automatically awards all approved foreign investors an incentive tax rate of 20 per cent, compared to the general tax rate of 35 per cent. This is among the lowest tax rates in Asia. Unlike most other countries, this 20 per cent rate applies to foreign investment in all sectors of the economy and does not depend on company or performance. Accelerated depreciation and tax loss can be carried forward up to three years. The withholding tax on dividends, interest, royalties, and fees paid abroad is only 10 per cent. Foreign investors and their expatriate staff pay only a 10 per cent income tax. For large projects and others that are deemed to have a significant impact on the economic and social development of the country, tax holidays can be negotiated on a case-by-case basis. For companies that locate their projects outside major cities, the tax rate is reduced to 15 per cent if located in lowland areas and 10 per cent if located in mountainous and remote areas.

Additional incentives: The Government provides the following incentives to all foreign investors:

- Permission to bring in foreign nationals to undertake investment feasibility studies.
- Permission to bring in foreign technicians, experts, and managers if qualified Lao nationals are not available to work on investment projects.
- Permission to lease land for up to 20 years from a Lao national and up to 50 years from the Government.
- Permission to own all improvements and structures on the leased land, transfer leases to other entities, and permission to sell or remove improvements or structures.
- Facilitation of entry and exit visa facilities and work permits for expatriate personnel.

Repatriation of profits: There is no limitation on foreign investors transferring foreign currencies and their legal assets to their countries or to third countries for:

- Profits gained from business production activities
- Income from the transfer of technology and technical services
- Initial capital and interests from loans
- Capital stipulated in the agreement or the status of enterprises, including supplementary investments, salaries of foreign employees in units or enterprises with foreign shares.

(h)   *Intellectual property rights*

The protection of intellectual property rights (IPR) is gradually taking hold in the Lao People's Democratic Republic. One of the first steps towards IPR began with a decree from the Prime Minister in 1995 allowing for the registration of trademarks. The protection of IPR in the country is strengthened by its memberships in the World Intellectual Property Organization (WIPO) and the Paris Convention on the protection of industrial property. However, the Lao People's Democratic Republic has yet to sign the Berne Convention on copyrights.

WIPO has helped the Lao People's Democratic Republic in drafting legislation to protect patents, industrial designs, lay out designs, integrated circuits, specially bred plant species, and other relevant concerns. Also, additional legislation is being drafted in line with trade related aspects of intellectual property rights (TRIPS).

The Lao People's Democratic Republic is not perceived as a major violator of intellectual property rights. The United States Trade Representative has not placed the Lao People's Democratic Republic on its watch list of countries of concern for IPR violations.

Thailand and the Lao People's Democratic Republic signed a bilateral IPR agreement that ensures protection of patents that have been granted in Thailand.

2. Customs and trade procedures

(a)   *Imports and exports*

Firms seeking to import goods and other items are required to obtain an import license from the provincial trade authority where the importer is located. The license remains valid for three months. Importers must provide six types of documents for each shipment:

- A contract with the foreign supplier or a purchase order
- Import license
- Letter of credit or payment guarantee from a foreign exchange bank
- Transport documents
- Bill of lading
- Customs clearance report

After receiving permission to import, firms must establish a line of credit through a foreign exchange bank within the specified time period for importing, although it is possible to apply for an amendment to the line of credit if the completion time for the entire import transaction exceeds the original timeframe. The amount of the line of credit should not exceed the authorized amount, and it must be expressed in the same currency specified in the import authorization form.

For customs purposes, the importer must submit a report to the superintendent of the customs house. The customs clearance report can only be prepared by a consignee (importer), employing a certified customs specialist or a certified customs clearance corporation.

Exporters are required to submit the following documents when applying for an export declaration:

- Application for export declaration
- Permission to export from the provincial trading authority
- Invoice
- Packing list
- Certificate of country of origin and generalized system of preferences certificate of origin (if applicable)
- Phytosanitary certificate for food exports
- Industrial products certification for industrial products

Exporters are recommended to have the appropriate authorities review the items for export after receiving a letter of credit from the importer but before obtaining export permission. This is to ensure that the goods to be exported are not on the Government's list of restricted products for export.

Each export transaction requires permission from the provincial trade authorities, and thus exporters have to submit the export permission application and the other required documents each time. Goods are sometimes inspected prior to shipment by the customs house, depending on the type of goods.

Temporary goods, that is those brought in for processing and assembly into finished products and re-exported, and those for trans-shipment, are not subject to import or export taxes. However, the trans-shipment of goods requires all the necessary documents for importing and exporting, along with submitting an annual trans-shipment plan to the appropriate ministry and receiving permission for each shipment.

The importing or exporting of pharmaceuticals, food, and chemical products requires a license issued by the Food and Drug Control Import Division in the Ministry of Public Health.

(b)   *Tariffs*

All capital equipment, means of production, spare parts, and other materials used in operation of investment projects are subject to only a 1 per cent duty on import and no turnover tax or excise tax. Raw materials and intermediate components imported for the purpose of processing and re-export are exempt from import duties and taxes. There is no minimum percentage of output for exports in order to receive these incentives. Raw materials and intermediate components imported for the purpose of import substitution also receive duty reductions at negotiated rates.

The Government has simplified its tariff structure, although some non-tariff barriers, such as a quota on the import of automobiles, still exist. The Lao People's Democratic Republic uses two types of customs valuations:

(1)   Valuation based on the transaction value of the imported item, which is usually based on the shipping invoice.

(2)   Valuation based on certification by an embassy of the Lao People's Democratic Republic or a reputable organization having expertise on price and fair market value, such as the Chamber of Commerce of the country of origin.

If the importers cannot provide such documents, the customs valuation is based on domestic price minus 15 per cent. The importers must employ a certified customs specialist or certified customs clearance corporation to complete the report.

There are six rates of import tariffs:

- Five per cent for promoted goods such as heavy equipment and machine tools
- 10 per cent for some medicines and some materials used in light industry such as fabrics and chemicals
- 20 per cent for some food products, such as frozen fish
- 30 per cent for certain kinds of fruit and vegetables
- 40 per cent for automobiles.

In addition to the import tariff, the Government also imposes an excise tax on a certain products, with the steepest assessed on automobiles (72-104 per cent, depending on engine size), alcohol (60 per cent), and motorcycles, beer and cigarettes (50 per cent).

In addition to the excise tax, importers may also face a turnover tax of 5-10 per cent on most goods. Most goods are assessed at the higher 10 per cent rate, while goods considered essential to domestic production (such as agricultural equipment, power tools, construction equipment, fabric, and cotton thread) are assessed at 5 per cent. Tax-exempt goods include rice, fertilizer and animal feed, along with others.

The Government is expected to introduce a value added tax, which will replace the turnover tax, by 2002.

E. Main opportunities for investment

The Lao People's Democratic Republic provides numerous opportunities for investment because of its strategic location in South-East Asia and proximity to China, abundant and untapped natural resources, and vast tracts of available land. Other important factors to consider are the following:

- A stable political environment for the past 25 years
- Extremely low labour costs
- Simple and generous tax regimen
- 100 per cent foreign ownership allowed
- Opportunity to take advantage of the various ASEAN economic cooperation schemes such as the ASEAN Free Trade Area (AFTA), ASEAN Investment Area (AIA), and the ASEAN Industrial Cooperation programme (AICO).

In terms of the main sectors for investment opportunity, six sectors are seen as the most enticing to investors: energy (namely hydropower), minerals and mining, agro-business, timber processing, light manufacturing, and eco-cultural tourism.

1. Energy

As noted earlier, the Lao People's Democratic Republic has some of the best and largest hydropower potential in the world. The Mekong River and its numerous tributaries in the country are only beginning to be tapped for energy generation. The Lao People's Democratic Republic possesses an estimated potential of over 18,000 MW installed capacity for hydropower, of which only about two per cent has been developed to date.

The Government promotes the development of hydropower projects through foreign Build-Operate-Own-Transfer and Build-Operate-Transfer projects in many locations throughout the country. Firms from Asia, Europe, and North America are involved in several dam and energy projects, but there is much more room for additional projects as the Lao People's Democratic Republic strives toward becoming the region's main energy supplier. The aim is to bring on line over 7,000 MW by 2009. The key export market at the moment is Thailand, but Viet Nam will soon become a major importer of Lao electricity. The Lao People's Democratic Republic signed an agreement with Viet Nam to supply 1,500-2,000 MW of power by 2010.

An additional attractive feature of the energy sector is that because of the Lao People's Democratic Republic's status as a least developed country, low interest rates are often available for financing these major projects through international development finance institutions like the World Bank and the Asian Development Bank.

2. Mining

The Lao People's Democratic Republic has substantial potential for mineral ore production. Numerous minerals have been identified in many parts of the country, including gold, tin, iron, lead, zinc, precious stones, coal, lignite, limestone and gypsum. The Government has awarded concession areas to foreign investors to explore for oil and natural gas, and although it is not known whether these resources exist, there is a strong possibility that reserves may be found.

The 1997 Mining Law created a legal framework for new investors. Fiscal regulations, such as royalty rates, corporate income tax rates, and other financial incentives in the mining sector are widely recognized to be competitive by international standards.

3. Agro-business

The economic growth of the Lao People's Democratic Republic depends to a large extent on the performance of its agricultural sector as it contributes over half of the country's GDP. The Lao People's Democratic Republic has large tracts of unused fertile land and favourable climatic conditions, particularly on the Boloven Plateau. The combination of good soil, extensive areas of uncultivated land, and highly suitable climate conditions provide tremendous potential for land-intensive agriculture and agro-processing industries for export.

A wide variety of crops can be cultivated throughout the country as a result of the differences in climate between the plateaus and mountainous areas. Among the major crops are rice, palm oil, coffee, cotton, sugarcane, tobacco, fruits, vegetables, groundnuts, and flowers. The country's extensive river network also presents a great of potential for establishing irrigation networks.

Livestock rearing and processing is also a potentially lucrative investment sector because of the vast tracts of open land.

4. Forestry

The Lao People's Democratic Republic is endowed with bountiful forest resources, giving it the highest ratio of forest area to total land area of any country in Asia. Forest covers between 40-50 per cent of the entire country, including highly sought tropical hardwoods such as teak, mahogany, and rosewood. Wood products, including lumber, are therefore one of the country's main export earners.

In an effort to preserve the country's environment and slow deforestation, the Government grants commercial forestry licenses through a system of provincial quotas. However, government regulations do not permit foreign wood processing firms, but foreign investment is permitted for the export of processed wood such as plywood, parquet flooring, and furniture. Firms seeking to engage in exporting wood products must receive a license.

5. Garments and textiles

The Lao People's Democratic Republic is quickly becoming an important investment market for garment manufacturing and textiles in Asia. One of the main attractions is that the European Union reinstated Generalized System of Preferences (GSP) status to the Lao People's Democratic Republic from 1999 to the end of 2001. Several regional manufacturers have established plants in the Lao People's Democratic Republic to take advantage of the favorable export terms that the country receives for garments and textiles from the industrialized countries.

6. Other light industries

Light manufacturing industries other than garments and textiles include wood-based products, semi-finished and finished leather products, and agriculture-based and mineral-based products can be produced for export using the inexpensive electricity, low-cost labour force, and the abundant agricultural products and minerals available.

7. Transportation infrastructure

Although much progress has been made, the transportation infrastructure needs further development. The state of the road system continues to be a major impediment to trade, cooperation, the development of the rich natural resources and agricultural lands, and the many tourist sites.

The Government welcomes investment in infrastructure projects. Transportation infrastructure projects are often arranged with the assistance of multilateral and bilateral assistance organizations. This situation can give investors access to low-cost financing and thereby reduce capital costs for investors.

8. Tourism

The Lao People's Democratic Republic has made great strides over the past several years in opening up towards the rest of the world, and nowhere is this more evident than in the tourism sector. National revenue from tourism reached almost US$ 80 million in 1998, bypassing garments for the first time. Gone are the days when budget travelers were frowned upon in favour of high-priced packaged tours, and thus numerous opportunities await investors in the tourism industry. Most of the country's historical, cultural, and natural attractions are underdeveloped, despite the immense potential for tourism. A range of investment opportunities are available to foreign investors, including hotels and guesthouses, restaurants, air, ground, and water transportation, and other services.

9. Consulting services

As a result of the significant levels of multilateral and bilateral assistance, consulting services are potentially lucrative investment opportunity. Local consultants are needed for the numerous projects funded by the World Bank, Asian Development Bank, United Nations agencies, and bilateral donors in a number of fields covering agriculture, environmental issues, human resource development, and economic development. Between 1997 and 2000, the major multilateral agencies earmarked over US$ 675 million in grants and loans for the Lao People's Democratic Republic.

F. Tips for visitors

1. Getting there

The most common way to enter the Lao People's Democratic Republic is via Wattay International Airport in Vientiane, which has regularly scheduled flights from/to Bangkok, Chiang Mai, Phnom Penh, Hanoi, Ho Chi Minh City and Kunming. Land crossings with the Lao People's Democratic Republic's neighbours are permitted in many areas, but some of these are only for local residents. The major international land crossings are from Nong Khai, Thailand to Vientiane via the Friendship Bridge and at Thailand's Chong Mek (Ubon Ratchathani Province) to Champassak. Several bus routes also run between Viet Nam and the Lao People's Democratic Republic.

2. Passports and visas

A passport and visa are required of all foreigners visiting Lao People's Democratic Republic, except for citizens of countries that have a visa exemption agreement: Viet Nam, China, Cambodia, Democratic People's Republic of Korea, the Russian Federation, Eastern European countries, Malaysia, and Thailand (exemption only for diplomats, but border passes can be obtained).

Tourism visas are available on arrival at Wattay International Airport, the Lao-Thai Friendship Bridge, Luang Prabang Airport, and Ban Muang Kao. All other international checkpoints require a visa in advance of arrival.

Validity period of visa:

- For businesspeople collecting information or contacting local businesses, the visa is good for one month and can be extended
- For tourists, the visa is valid for one month
- For foreign invested companies' employees and their families, visas are typically granted for the duration of the investment projects

3. Health

The following immunizations are normally recommended for all travellers to Lao People's Democratic Republic, and other countries in South-East Asia.

- Hepatitis A
- Typhoid
- Diptheria and Tetanus
- Hepatitis B
- Polio

Other vaccines are recommended, depending on where one is located in the country.

4. Currency

The unit of currency in the Lao People's Democratic Republic is the kip, which is available in 5,000, 2,000, 1,000, 500, 100 and 50 kip notes. In major towns, Thai baht and United States dollars are readily accepted in markets, hotels and restaurants.

Travellers cheques can be changed in major banks in Vientiane but are of limited use elsewhere. Credit cards can be used in major hotels in Vientiane but are also limited to a few areas of the country.

5. Embassies

In total there are 19 embassies in the Lao People's Democratic Republic:

Australia
Nehru Street, Vat Phonsay Area
Tel: 41-3610, 41-3805, 41-3602

China
Vat Nak Street, Sisattanak Area
Tel: 31-5103, 31-5100, 31-5101

Bulgaria
Sisangvone Area
Tel: 41-110

Cuba Cambodia
Saphathong Nua Area
Tel: 31-4902

India
Saphathong Nua Area
Tel: 31-4952
Fax: 31-2584

That Luang Road
Vat Phonsay Area
Tel: 41-3802

Indonesia
Phon Kheng Road
Tel: 41-3910, 41-3909
        41-3907, 41-3914

Japan
Sisangvone Road
Tel: 21-2623, 41-4400-2
        41-4406
Fax: 41-4403

Russian Federation
Tel: 31-2219, 31-222

Democratic People's
Republic of Korea
Vat Nak Street, Sisattanak
Tel: 31-5261, 31-5260

Malaysia
That Luang Street
Vat Phonsay Area
Tel: 41-4205

Sweden
Sokpaluang Street, Vat Nak
Tel: 31-5018, 31-5000
        31-3772
Fax: 31-5003

Myanmar
Sokpaluang Street
Sisattanak Area
Tel: 31-2439, 31-4910

Poland
Thadeua Road, Km 3
Tel: 31-2219, 31-2085

Thailand
Phonekheng Road
Tel: 21-4581-3, 21-4585

Viet Nam
That Luang Road
Tel: 41-3400, 41-3409
        41-3403

United States
That Dam
Tel: 21-2580-2, 31-2609
Fax: 21-2584

France
Setthathirath Road
Tel: 21-5258, 21-5259
Fax: 21-5255

Germany
26 Sokpaluang Road
Tel: 31-2111, 31-2110

6. Hotel accommodations

Numerous hotels can be found throughout Vientiane, and the other major areas such as Luang Prabang and Pakse are offering a wider variety of accommodations each year. Most business travellers to Vientiane stay in the following hotels:

Asian Pavilion Hotel, Lan Xang Hotel, Tai-Pan Hotel, Novotel Belvedere Vientiane, New Apollo Hotel, and the Lao Plaza Hotel.

Rates vary widely depending on the type of room, but start as low as US$ 20 for a standard room.

7. In-country travelling

Among the country's key attractions are the following:

That Luang (Vientiane)
That Luang is the national symbol of the Lao People's Democratic Republic and is the country's most important Buddhist monument. Built in 1566 by King Say Settathirath, it symbolizes the Buddhist religion and Lao sovereignty.

Wat Si Saket (Vientiane)

Wat Si Saket is the oldest standing temple in Vientiane. Built in 1818, this famous temple has its walls inlaid with over 2,000 silver and ceramic Buddha images.

Morning Market (Vientiane)

Morning Market (Talat Sao) is the city's major marketplace and offers a variety of goods including clothing, electronics, jewelry, traditional textiles, and souvenirs.

Buddha Park (Vientiane)

Also known by its real name Xieng Khouang, this spacious park contains numerous Buddhist and Hindu sculptures, many of which are extremely large.

Luang Prabang

Luang Prabang is the old royal capital but also contains some of the country's most stunning Buddhist temples. This beautiful city is situated 500 kilometres from Vientiane along the Mekong River and nestled between scenic mountains. The main attractions are the historic temples, the Royal Palace Museum, Wat Xieng Thong and Wat Wisunlat. On the outskirts of Luang Prabang are the Pak-Ou caves (inhabitant to thousands of Buddha statues), Ban Phanom- a weaver's village, and the Khoung Sy Waterfalls.

Plain of Jars (Xieng Khouang)

The Plain of Jars is famous for its ancient stone jars, which remain one of South-East Asia's great mysteries. The origins and purpose of the huge stone jars that cover the plain are still unknown.

Khone Phapheng Falls (Champassak)

These virtually unknown waterfalls are among the largest in South-East Asia. Located near the Lao-Cambodian border, the Khone Phapheng Falls and the surrounding Si Phan Done area is one of the Lao People's Democratic Republic's most scenic regions.

G. Learning more

1. Related web sites

www.investlao.com

www.jps.net.laos

www.laoembassy.com

www.laopdr.com

www.hotelstravel.com/laos.html

www.visitlao.com

www.global.lao.net

2. Recommended readings

- *Laos (Culture Shock! Guides)* by Stephen Mansfield. Written for people moving to the Lao People's Democratic Republic, this book gives an excellent insight into Lao lifestyle from a western perspective.
- *Lonely Planet Laos, 3rd Edition* by Joe Cummings. One of the most complete travel books on the Lao People's Democratic Republic.
- *Lonely Planet Lao Phrasebook* by Joe Cummings. Contains useful expressions and vocabulary for beginners.

Annex III
Foreign Investment Law (1994)

Law No. 1 on the promotion and management of foreign investment adopted by the National Assembly on 14 March 1994.

(a)   ***Section One: General provisions***

Article 1: The Government of the Lao People's Democratic Republic encourages foreign persons, either individuals or legal entities, to invest capital in the Lao People's Democratic Republic on the basis of mutual benefit and observance of the laws and regulations of the Lao People's Democratic Republic. Such persons hereinafter shall be referred to as "foreign investors".

Article 2: Foreign investors may invest in and operate enterprises in all fields of lawful economic activity such as agriculture and forestry, manufacturing, energy, mineral extraction, handicrafts, communications and transport, construction, tourism, trade, services and others. Foreign investors may not invest in or operate enterprises which are detrimental to national security, the natural environment, public health or the national culture, or which violate the laws and regulations of the Lao People's Democratic Republic.

Article 3: The property and investments in the Lao People's Democratic Republic of foreign investors shall be fully protected by the laws and regulations of the Lao People's Democratic Republic. Such property and investments may not be requisitioned, confiscated or nationalized except for a public purpose and upon payment of prompt, adequate and effective compensation.

(b)   ***Section Two: Forms of foreign investment***

Article 4: Foreign investors may invest in the Lao People's Democratic Republic in either of two forms:

(1)   A Joint Venture with one or more domestic investors, or
(2)   A Wholly Foreign-Owned Enterprise.

Article 5: A Joint Venture is a foreign investment established and registered under the laws and regulations of the Lao People's Democratic Republic which is jointly owned and operated by one or more foreign investors and by one or more domestic investors. The organization management and activities of the Joint Venture and the relationship between its parties shall be governed by the contract between its parties and the Joint Venture's Articles of Association, in accordance with the laws and regulations of the Lao People's Democratic Republic.

Article 6: Foreign investors who invest in a joint venture must contribute a minimum portion of thirty per cent (30 per cent) of the total equity investment in that venture. The contribution of the venture's foreign party or parties shall be converted in accordance with the laws and regulation of the Lao People's Democratic Republic into Lao currency at the exchange rate prevailing on the date of the equity payment(s), as quoted by the Bank of the Lao People's Democratic Republic.

Article 7: A wholly Foreign-Owned Enterprise is a foreign investment registered under the laws and regulations of the Lao People's Democratic Republic by one or more foreign investors without the participation of domestic investors. The Enterprise established in the Lao People's Democratic Republic may be either a new company or a branch or representative office of a foreign company.

Article 8: A foreign investment, which is a branch or representative office of a foreign company in the Lao People's Democratic Republic, shall have Articles of Association consistent with the laws and regulations of the Lao People's Democratic Republic and subject to the approval of the Foreign Investment Management Committee of the Lao People's Democratic Republic.

Article 9: The incorporation and registration of a foreign investment shall be in conformity with the Enterprise Decree of the Lao People's Democratic Republic.

(c)   *Section Three: Benefits, rights and obligations of foreign investors*

Article 10: The Government of the Lao People's Democratic Republic shall protect foreign investments and the property of foreign investors in accordance with the laws and regulations of the Lao People's Democratic Republic.

Foreign investors may lease land within the Lao People's Democratic Republic and transfer their leasehold interests and they may own improvements on land and other moveable property and transfer those ownership interests.

Foreign investors shall be free to operate their enterprises within the limits of the laws and regulations of the Lao People's Democratic Republic. The Government shall not interfere in the business management of those enterprises.

Article 11: Foreign investors shall give priority to Lao citizens in recruiting and hiring their employees. However, such enterprises have the right to employ skilled and expert foreign personnel when necessary and with the approval of the competent authority of the Government of the Lao People's Democratic Republic.

Foreign investors have an obligation to upgrade the skills of their Lao employees, through such techniques as training within the Lao People's Democratic Republic or abroad.

Article 12: The Government of the Lao People's Democratic Republic shall facilitate the entry into, travel within, stay within, and exit from People's Democratic Republic territory of foreign investors, their foreign personnel, and the immediate family members of those investors and those personnel. All such persons are subject to and must obey the laws and regulations of the Lao People's Democratic Republic while they are on the Lao People's Democratic Republic territory.

Foreign investors and their foreign personnel working within the Lao People's Democratic Republic shall pay to the Lao government personal income tax at a flat rate of ten per cent of their income earned in the Lao People's Democratic Republic.

Article 13: Foreign investors shall open accounts both in the currency of the Lao People's Democratic Republic and in foreign convertible currency with a domestic or foreign bank established in the Lao People's Democratic Republic.

Article 14: In the management of their enterprises, foreign investors shall utilize the national system of financial accounting of the Lao People's Democratic Republic. Their accounts shall be subject to periodic audit by the Government's financial authorities in conformity with the applicable Lao accounting regulations.

Article 15: In conformity with the law and regulations governing the management of foreign exchange and precious metals, foreign investors may repatriate earnings and capital from their foreign investments to their own home countries or to third countries through a domestic or foreign bank established in the Lao People's Democratic Republic at the exchange rate prevailing on the date of repatriation, as quoted by the Bank of the Lao People's Democratic Republic. Foreign personnel of foreign investments may also repatriate their earnings after payment of Lao personal income taxes and all other taxes due.

Article 16: Foreign investments subject to this law shall pay a Lao People's Democratic Republic annual profit tax at a uniform flat rate of twenty per cent (20 per cent), calculated in accordance with the provisions of the applicable laws and regulations of the Lao People's Democratic Republic.

Other domestic taxes, duties and fees shall be payable in accordance with the applicable laws and regulations of the Lao People's Democratic Republic.

For foreign investments involving natural resources exploitation and energy generation, sector-specific taxes and royalties shall be prescribed in project agreements entered into between the investors and Lao People's Democratic Republic Government.

Article 17: Foreign investments shall pay a Lao People's Democratic Republic import duty on equipment, means of production, spare parts and other materials used in the operation of their investment projects or in their productive enterprises as a uniform flat rate of one per cent (1 per cent) of their imported value.

Raw materials and intermediate components imported for the purpose of processing and then re-exported shall be exempt from such import duties. All exported finished products shall also be exempted from export duties.

Raw materials and intermediate components imported for the purpose of achieving import substitution shall be eligible for special duty reductions in accordance with the Government's incentive policies.

Article 18: In highly exceptional cases and by specific decision of the Government of the Lao People's Democratic Republic, foreign investors may be granted special privileges and benefits which may possibly include a reduction in or exemption from the profit tax rate prescribed by Article 16 and/or a reduction in or exemption from the import duty rate prescribed by Article 17, because of the large size of their investments and the significant positive impact which those investments are expected to have upon the socio-economic development of the Lao People's Democratic Republic.

In the event of the establishment of one or more Free Zones or Investment Promotion Zones, the Government shall issue area-specific or general regulations or resolutions.

Article 19: After payment of its annual profit tax, a foreign investor shall devote a portion of its profit each year to various reserve funds necessary for the operation and development of the enterprise in order to continuously improve the enterprise's efficiency, in accordance with the policy and the Articles of Association of the Enterprise.

Article 20: Foreign investments approved under this law shall at all times be operated in accordance with the laws and regulations of the Lao People's Democratic Republic. In particular foreign investors shall take all measures necessary and appropriate to ensure that their investments facilities, factories and activities protect the natural environment and the health and safety of the workers and the public at large, and that their investments contribute to the social insurance and welfare programmes for their workers in conformity with the policy and the laws and regulations of the Lao People's Democratic Republic.

Article 21: In the event of disputes between foreign parties within a foreign investment, or between foreign investors and Lao parties, the disputants should first seek to settle their differences through consultation or mediation.

In the event that they fail to resolve the matter, they shall then submit their dispute to the economic arbitration authority of the Lao People's Democratic Republic or to any other mechanism for dispute resolution of the Lao People's Democratic Republic, a foreign country or an appropriate international organization which the disputants can agree upon.

(d) *Section Four: The organization of foreign investment management*

Article 22: The Government of the Lao People's Democratic Republic has established a state organization to promote and to manage foreign investment within the Lao People's Democratic Republic titled the Foreign Investment Management Committee (hereinafter called "the FIMC").

The FIMC is responsible for administration of this law and for the protection and promotion of foreign investment within the Lao People's Democratic Republic.

Article 23: All foreign investments established within the Lao People's Democratic Republic shall be assisted, licensed and monitored through the "1-stop-service" of the FIMC, acting as the central focal point for all Government interactions with the investors, with the collaboration of the concerned ministries and the relevant provincial authorities.

Article 24: A foreign investment shall be considered to be legally established within the Lao People's Democratic Republic only upon the investment's receipt of a written foreign investment license granted by the FIMC.

Article 25: A foreign investor which seeks a license for a foreign investment shall submit to the FIMC an application and such supporting documentation as the FIMC may prescribe by regulation. The FIMC may grant preliminary approval-in-principle for investment projects being specially promoted by the Government.

Article 26: Upon receipt of a completed application and supporting documentation, the FIMC shall screen them, take a foreign-investment licensing decision and notify the applicant of the decision within 60 days of the application's submission date.

Within the same overall 60-day period, concerned ministries and provincial authorities consulted by the FIMC for their views shall have a maximum of 20 days in which to reply.

Article 27: Within 90 days of receiving its foreign investment license from the FIMC, a foreign investor shall register that license and commence operation of its investment in conformity with the implementation schedule contained in the investment's feasibility study and with the terms and conditions of the license granted by the FIMC, and in accordance with the laws and regulations of the Lao People's Democratic Republic.

Article 28: The FIMC has responsibility to coordinate with other concerned ministries and provincial authorities in monitoring and enforcing the implementation of a foreign investment in conformity with the investment's feasibility study and with the terms and conditions of the investment license, and in accordance with the laws and regulations of the Lao People's Democratic Republic.

The concerned ministries and provincial authorities have the responsibility to perform their respective monitoring and enforcement obligations.

Article 29: If a foreign investor violates the agreement and the terms and conditions of its foreign investment license or the laws and regulations of the Lao People's Democratic Republic, the investor shall be notified of the detected violation and shall be instructed to promptly desist. In the event the investor fails to desist or in case of a serious violation, the investor's foreign investment license may be suspended or revoked and the investor may additionally be subject to other sanctions under the applicable laws and regulations of the Lao People's Democratic Republic.

(e)   *Section Five: Final provisions*

Article 30: This law shall come into force 60 days after its ratification. Upon the entry into force of the present law, the foreign investment law of the Lao People's Democratic Republic No. 07/PSA dated 19 April 1988 shall cease to have effect, without prejudice to the rights and privileges granted to, and the obligations imposed upon, foreign investments under the law No. 07/PSA

Notwithstanding this provision, a foreign investor which received its license under the prior law may elect to petition the FIMC in writing, within 120 days of the coming into force of this law, to become subject to the terms of this law. The FIMC may grant such petitions at its discretion.

For a foreign investor whose petition is granted, the right and benefits previously granted, and the obligations previously imposed under the law No. 07/PSA shall thereafter prospectively cease to have effect.

Article 31: The Government of the Lao People's Democratic Republic shall, by decree, issue detailed regulations for the implementation of this law.

IV. MYANMAR

A. Basic operating environment

1. Geography and climate

Myanmar spans 676,578 square kilometres. It is nestled between China, the Lao People's Democratic Republic, Bangladesh, India, and Thailand. The Bay of Bengal and the Andaman Sea form the 2,832-kilometre southern boundary from the Kra Isthmus (with Thailand) to the border with Bangladesh. The country is generally divided into seven main regions: the Northern Hills, the Western Hills, the Rakhine Coast in the southwest, the Shan Plateau in the east, the Central Belt, the Lower Ayeyarwady Delta, and the Tanintharyi Coast in the south. Administratively, Myanmar contains 14 states and divisions. States are designated for the main ethnic groups, while the divisions correspond to the majority Bamar people.

The terrain varies extensively throughout the country, with snow-capped mountains in the north to the vast flatlands in the central region. Most of the country's perimeter is comprised of mountains and hills, which often make travel and communication in those regions extremely difficult. The three main mountain ranges found in the western, central, and eastern regions all run in a north-south direction, and as a result the extensive river system in the country tends to follow a similar longitudinal pattern. The country's longest river is the Ayeyarwady, which stretches 2,170 kilometres.

Myanmar is a tropical country with three distinct seasons, although some regional variations do occur. The dry season runs from mid-February to mid-May, but in the central region the dry season often extends into what is for the rest of the country the rainy period. The wet season begins in mid-May and lasts until mid-October, when the cool season commences. Rainfall varies widely throughout Myanmar, with an average of 250 centimetres annually in the coastal and delta regions compared to only 70 centimetres in the central area.

2. History and culture

Myanmar civilization traces its roots back as early as the fifth century. The first major Myanmar kingdom was Bagan, founded in the eleventh century and lasting until the Mongol invasion in the late thirteenth century. Bagan represents the pinnacle of ancient Myanmar civilization in a number of ways, including engineering, science, Buddhism, and architecture. The legacy of Bagan can be seen today in the thousands of pagodas that still stand.

Several kingdoms followed Bagan such as Bago and Ava (near Mandalay) until the British consolidated their control and abolished the monarchy in 1885. From that point until World War II, Myanmar was ruled as a part of the British Indian Empire.

In the early decades of the twentieth century a strong nationalist movement emerged in Myanmar led by General Aung San. During World War II, the nationalists sent a group known as the Thirty Comrades to Japan for training and returned in 1942 with the invading Japanese army to lead the Myanmar Independence Army. Not long after the Japanese occupation began, the Thirty Comrades formed the Anti-Fascist People's Freedom League (AFPFL) to resist the Japanese and eventually secure the country's independence in 1948.

Myanmar had a democratic Government between 1948 and 1962, but throughout this period a number of rebellions by communist and ethnic groups broke out. After being invited by Prime Minister U Nu to serve as a temporary caretaker Government between 1958 and 1960, the military enacted a coup d'état in 1962 as the country was on the verge of collapse from the rebellions.

General Ne Win led the military government for nearly three decades and instituted a socialist State. The Burma Socialist Programme Party administered the State through its ideology known as the Burmese Way to Socialism.

In 1988 socialist policies were abandoned when a new military regime called the State Law and Order Restoration Council (SLORC) took over the Government. The military leaders renamed SLORC as the State Peace and Development Council in 1997.

Myanmar has a rich and diverse culture that is still well preserved. Traditional clothing, dance, and music are common throughout the country, and the people of Myanmar have not lost their deep Buddhist beliefs which play an integral part of daily life. Pagodas can be seen throughout the country, from Yangon's commercial district to the most remote mountain sides upcountry.

3. Population

Myanmar contains a diverse population of over 48 million people and 135 different ethnic groups. Over 69 per cent of the population is ethnic Bamar, and these people tend to inhabit the lowlands. Many of the ethnic groups live in highlands around the perimeter of the country and bordering Bangladesh, China, India, the Lao People's Democratic Republic, and Thailand. The major ethnic groups are Kachin, Kayah, Kayin (Karen), Chin, Mon, Rakhine, and Shan. Over 75 per cent of the population live in rural areas.

Myanmar is predominantly a Buddhist country (85 per cent of the population), but certain ethnic groups, most notably along the border with Bangladesh, are Muslim. Christianity is also present among both the majority Bamar and some minorities such as the Chin and Kachin, while the Indian population tends to be Muslim or Hindu.

The central language of Myanmar is used in business and administration, but with so many ethnic groups in the country, dozens of languages can be heard throughout the country. English is also widely spoken because of the British colonial legacy and its increasing use in Myanmar's schools.

4. Languages

Due to its diverse population, numerous languages are spoken throughout Myanmar. The principal, and national language, is Myanmar, but English is also widely used in business and administration. At the local level the numerous ethnic groups tend to have their own languages.

5. Economy

From 1962 to 1988 Myanmar had a socialist economy. Elements of modern socialism in Myanmar date back to the 1930s, but a socialist form of economic system took shape in the early 1960s when the military, led by General Ne Win, assumed political and administrative control. The socialist era featured state-owned enterprises and Government initiated cooperatives with an orientation towards import substitution. The private sector continued to function during this period, albeit under many restrictions. As a result of the socialist policies and the country's overall isolation from international matters, private manufacturers did not produce for export, except for a few industries.

Once considered one of the wealthiest South-East Asian countries, Myanmar's economic problems hit rock bottom in 1987. The country was designated as one of the least developed nations by the United Nations General Assembly. By the late 1980s Myanmar's economy was in tatters due to the low productivity and inefficiency of state-owned enterprises, low levels of skill, and a shortage of capital and technology.

In response to the severe economic crisis and domestic unrest, the State Law and Order Restoration Council (SLORC) took the reins of Government in 1988 and embarked on a new course for the economy. SLORC reversed many of the socialist era policies and implemented several economic reforms, including new laws, regulations, operating methods, and reorganization of government agencies in an effort to utilize market principles to jumpstart the sluggish economy.

The reform programme since 1988 has had a major impact on most sectors of the economy. The new economic environment enabled entrepreneurs to start up their own businesses instead of working for state-owned enterprises or cooperatives. However, the structure of Myanmar's present economy has changed very little compared to the pre-independence years (before 1948). Agriculture dominated the economy and employed over 66 per cent of the workforce in 1931, but by the late 1990s, the percentage of workers in the agriculture sector had dropped to around 56 per cent. Agriculture is considered the base of the economy around which other sectors are expected to develop, but the Government is also trying to promote a variety of industries such as tourism, mining, construction, and forestry.

6. Government

Myanmar has had a federal union structure since independence in 1948, although the type of Government has changed on a few occasions. Myanmar had multiparty democracy after independence until the country nearly collapsed from civil war in the 1950s. After a brief interlude in which the military was invited to serve as a caretaker in the late 1950s, civil strife resumed until the military decided to take control in 1962. Under the leadership of General Ne Win, the military established an isolated, single-party socialist State led by the Burma Socialist Programme Party (BSPP), which held power until 1988.

With the economy in turmoil, the State Law and Order Restoration Council took on the responsibility of the government in late 1988. The new leadership abolished many of the socialist policies and began Myanmar reintegration into the rest of the world. In 1997, SLORC changed its name to the State Peace and Development Council (SPDC), which is comprised of 19 top military leaders. The current Government has 31 ministries with 36 ministers.

The judicial system is based on the common law system inherited from British colonial era, but it also contains elements of a civil system as well.

7. Natural resources

Myanmar is richly endowed with a wide variety of natural resources. Forests are one of its most precious resources, particularly teak trees, and altogether the country has over 2,300 species of trees. Forests cover approximately half of Myanmar, making it one of the country's most important economic sectors. Myanmar possesses around 80 per cent of the world's teak forests, with over 15 million acres of the highly sought after hardwood. Annual teak production capacity can reach 0.6 million cubic meters, but typically nearly 29,000 tons are produced annually.

Numerous minerals are found in Myanmar such as gold, copper, zinc, granite, iron, nickel, and several types of gems. The Ministry of Mines oversees all mining activities, and investors are required to enter into joint ventures with the Ministry's state-owned enterprises.

Oil and natural gas are also present in the Andaman Sea and have attracted several international oil and gas companies. The major gas field, Yadana, has a pipeline connecting with Thailand. Myanmar is estimated to have 1.2 trillion cubic feet of natural gas.

8. Human resources

Myanmar had 22.5 million people in the workforce in 1997-1998. Nearly 14 million were men and 8.6 million were women. Between 55 and 60 per cent of the workers are employed in the agriculture sector, followed by nearly 16 per cent in the retail, restaurant, and hotel sectors. Manufacturing is the third largest employer, taking in over 11 per cent of all workers. Eighty-five per cent of the population over 15 years old is literate, but the education system in Myanmar has not been working optimally for many years, particularly at the higher education level. Nonetheless, the people of Myanmar exhibit a thirst for learning and acquiring new skills, and possess many similar characteristics similar to the famed Vietnamese workforce such as a willingness to work hard, acquire new skills quickly, and discipline.

B. Macroeconomic business climate

1. Gross domestic product

Myanmar's economy recorded high growth rates through most of the 1990s. As seen in figure 16, GDP growth rates after 1991-1992 ranged between 5.7 and 9.7 per cent, an average of nearly 6 per cent growth annually.

Figure 16. GDP growth rates, 1991/1992-1998/1999

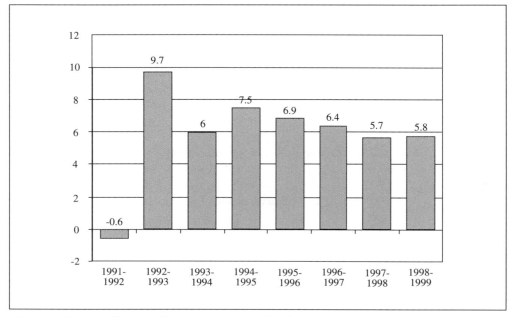

Source: Ministry of National Planning and Economic Development

Table 9 shows the annual GDP growth rates by sector. For the latest three fiscal years in which data are available (1996/1997-1998/1999), the three fastest growing sectors were mining (average of 16.37 per cent annual growth), construction (average of 13.57 per cent annual growth), and livestock and fisheries (average of 9.43 per cent annual growth).

Table 9. GDP growth rates by sector, 1992/1993-1998/1999
(percentage)

	1992-1993	1993-1994	1994-1995	1995-1996	1996-1997	1997-1998	1998-1999
Goods	11	6	6.9	6.7	6.4	5.1	4.9
Agriculture	12.4	4.7	6.7	5.5	3.8	3	3.5
Livestock/Fisheries	4.5	4.8	6	3	11.9	7.1	9.3
Manufacturing	10.8	9.4	8.5	7.6	4.6	5	6.2
Mining	32	13.8	21.3	18.5	12.4	29.7	7
Power	31.1	24.4	4.8	6.6	12.8	17.8	- 5.4
Construction	11.2	11.7	15.7	27.2	24.6	9.8	6.3
Services	6.1	8	10	9.3	8.3	8.8	7.8
Trade Sector	8.9	4.6	7	5.7	5	5	6.3

Source: Ministry of National Planning and Economic Development

Myanmar's GDP is still comprised mainly of goods, as seen in figure 17. Goods accounted for approximately 60 per cent of GDP in 1998-1999, while trade and services contributed 21 and 19 per cent, respectively.

Figure 17. General composition of GDP as of 1998-1999

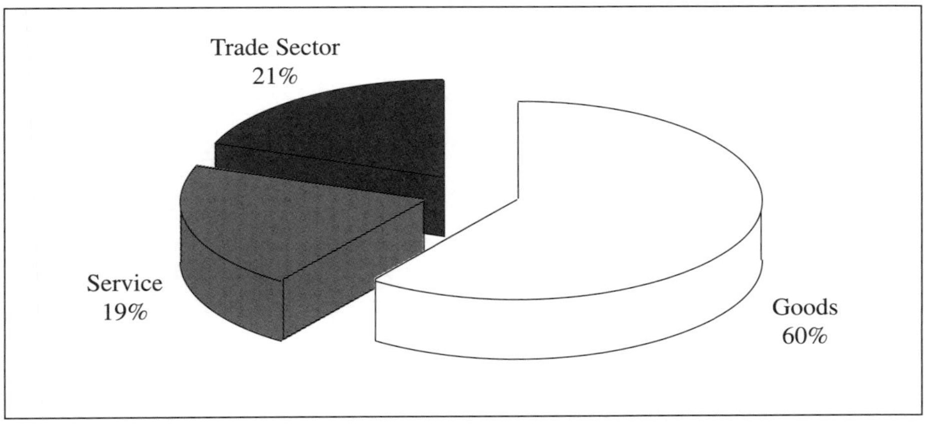

Source: Ministry of National Planning and Economic Development

2. Main economic sectors

(a) *Agriculture*

Myanmar's economy is still heavily reliant on agriculture. Agriculture accounted for 34.4 per cent of GDP in 1999-2000. No other sector comes close to matching agriculture's contributions to the national economy. The next largest sectors, manufacturing and livestock/fisheries, comprised 9.1 per cent and 7.5 per cent of GDP in 1998-1999.

With such a large percentage of the country's GDP and employment (see below) hinging on agriculture, steady growth in the sector is crucial if Myanmar's economy is going to improve. Myanmar's overall GDP has recorded some impressive gains since the mid-1990s, but the growth rates for agriculture are somewhat disappointing over the past few years. Table 10 shows a comparison of GDP growth and agriculture growth between 1994-1995 and 1998-1999.

Table 10. Real growth of GDP and agriculture, 1994/1995-1998/1999
(percentage)

	1994-1995	1995-1996	1996-1997	1997-1998	1998-1999
GDP	7.5	6.9	6.4	5.7	5.8
Agriculture	6.7	5.5	3.8	3.0	3.5

Source: Ministry of National Planning and Economic Development

Equally important is agriculture's contribution to employment. Sixty-three per cent of the labour force is engaged in the agriculture sector, indicating that agriculture will be a key sector in the economy for some time to come. Also notable is the percentage of manufacturing firms related to agriculture. Over 58 per cent of all manufacturing firms are in the food and beverage industry.

Rice is the staple crop and the second largest export commodity, after teak. Other important crops are sugar cane, groundnuts, sesame, wheat, maize, millet, jute, cotton, beans, pulses and oilseeds, vegetables, rubber, toddy palm, tobacco, spices and other edible produce.

(b)   *Manufacturing*

The manufacturing and processing sector accounts for nine per cent of the country's GDP. Manufacturing's contribution to GDP remained steady at 9.1 per cent between 1996/1997 and 1998/1999. Annual growth in the manufacturing sector is shown in table 11.

Table 11. Annual growth rates in manufacturing and processing sector, 1992/1993-1998/1999

	1992-1993	**1993-1994**	**1994-1995**	**1995-1996**	**1996-1997**	**1997-1998**	**1998-1999**
Manufacturing	10.8	9.4	8.5	7.6	4.6	5.0	6.2

Source: Ministry of National Planning and Economic Development

The principal industrial activities relate to agriculture, such as food processing and tobacco products, but other important industries include wood-based industries, beverages, clothing, jewelry, metal, pharmaceutical and household goods, paper and chemical, cement, animal feed, and iron and steel products.

(c)   *Livestock and fisheries*

With much available land and a lengthy coastline, livestock and fisheries is the third most important sector in terms of GDP. Livestock and fisheries contributed between 6.8 and 7.5 per cent of GDP from 1992/1993 to 1998/1999. Growth rates in this sector over the past four fiscal years (1995/1996-1998/1999) averaged 7.8 per cent. A variety of fish, shrimps, and other aquatic creatures are harvested from the ocean and rivers, while typical livestock such as cattle, pigs, and chicken are raised throughout the country.

3. International trade

Myanmar has bilateral trade agreements with several countries, including Bangladesh, China, India, Lao People's Democratic Republic, Pakistan, Thailand, Viet Nam, and seven countries in Eastern Europe. It also intends to develop more border trade with Bangladesh, China, India, Lao People's Democratic Republic and Thailand. Trade with regional neighbours is facilitated through Myanmar's memberships in various regional groupings such as the Association of South-East Asian Nations (ASEAN) and the Bangladesh, India, Myanmar, Sri Lanka, Thailand Economic Cooperation (BIMST-EC). Myanmar's ASEAN membership provides numerous trade benefits with the ASEAN Free Trade Area (AFTA), which is making rapid progress in lowering and eventually removing tariffs for intra-ASEAN trade. The less well-known BIMST-EC, formed in 1997, has plans for a preferential trade area and eventually a free trade area.

However, one result of Myanmar's reintegration into the global economy has been an increasing trade deficit. Part of the trade deficit is due to climatic conditions that periodically hurt rice exports and the overall decline in global market prices for agriculture commodities. Figure 18 shows Myanmar's trade deficit from 1995/1996 to 1998/1999.

Figure 18. Myanmar's trade deficit, 1995/1996-1998/1999

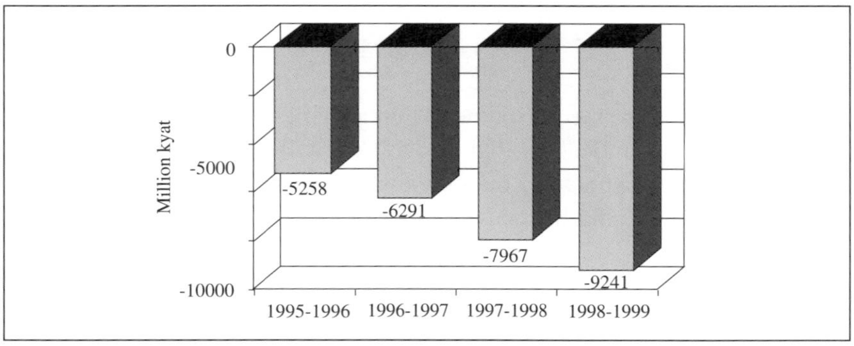

Source: Ministry of National Planning and Economic Development

94

(a)   *Exports*

Myanmar's exports have risen steadily over the past four fiscal years. Table 12 shows export values from 1995/1996 to 1998/1999.

Table 12. Myanmar export value, 1995/1996-1998/1999
(millions of kyat)

	1995/1996	1996/1997	1997/1998	1998/1999
Exports	5,044	5,488	6,290	7,700

Source: Ministry of National Planning and Economic Development

Figure 19 demonstrates the main export items for fiscal year 1998-1999. Pulses and beans were the leading export item, far surpassing rice and other agriculture commodities. As seen in figure 19, the main exports are essentially raw commodities as opposed to manufactured goods.

Figure 19. Main exports, FY 1998-1999
(millions of kyat)

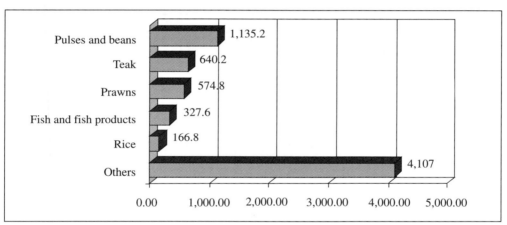

Source: Central Statistical Organization, Ministry of National Planning and Economic Development

Poor weather conditions resulted in reduced rice exports in 1995-1996, and the export levels have not reached their full potential ever since. However, growth in other export products, especially hardwoods, pulses, and fisheries, has helped boost export growth despite the fall in rice.

Myanmar's main export markets are its giant neighbours to the north and west. China and India combined for over 26 per cent of Myanmar's exports in 1998/1999 (see figure 20). This high percentage of exports to China and India indicates that Myanmar traders are taking advantage of their strategic proximity to the world's two largest markets.

In terms of border trade, Myanmar and China have a robust partnership that accounted for 71 per cent of Myanmar's total cross-border exports and 82 per cent of its total cross-border imports in 1998-1999. Thailand is the second largest border trade partner, followed by Bangladesh and then India.

(b)   *Imports*

Imported products continue to outpace exports despite measures since 1998 to reduce the need for imported goods. Myanmar continues to rely on imports of machinery, vehicles and parts, edible oils, and other categories of goods, as seen in figure 21. The opening up of more border checkpoints along the borders with Thailand and China has resulted in a large influx of consumer products as well.

Figure 20. Exports by country of destination, 1998/1999

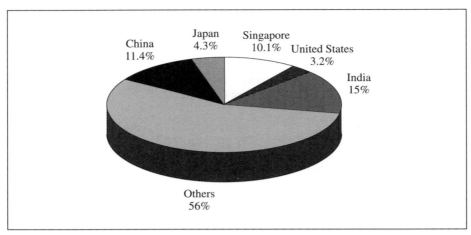

Source: Central Statistical Organization, Ministry of National Planning and Economic Development

**Figure 21. Main imports, FY 1998-1999
(millions of kyat)**

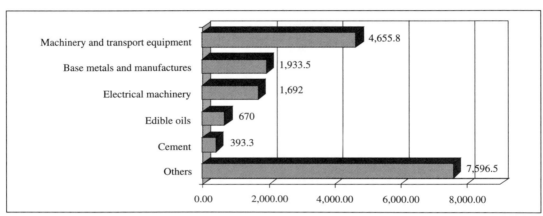

Source: Central Statistical Organization, Ministry of National Planning and Economic Development

Singapore is Myanmar's largest source of goods, comprising over 30 per cent of total imports in 1998-1999, followed by Japan, China, and then Indonesia (see figure 22).

Figure 22. Imports by country of origin, 1998/1999

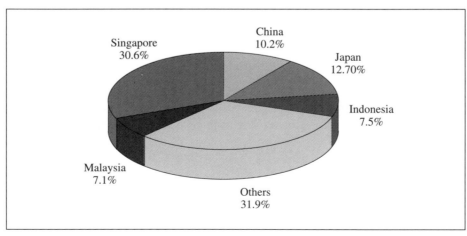

Source: Central Statistical Organization, Ministry of National Planning and Economic Development

4. Investment

Myanmar experienced a surge in foreign direct investment (FDI) soon after opening up its economy in the late 1980s and early 1990s. As of mid-2000, FDI surpassed US$ 7.2 billion from 337 investment projects. Table 13 shows that the oil and gas sector accounts for the largest amount of FDI in terms of dollar value, although manufacturing has the most projects. Hotels and other forms of real estate were particularly popular with investors in the early and mid 1990s in anticipation of a high demand for international business quality hotels and offices.

Table 13. Foreign investment in Myanmar as of 30 June 2000
(millions of US dollars)

Sector	No. of projects	Approved amount
Oil and gas	51	2,356
Manufacturing	131	1,514
Hotel and tourism	42	1,054
Real estate	18	997
Mining	50	523
Livestock and fisheries	20	283
Transport and communication	13	281
Industrial estates	3	193
Construction	1	17
Agriculture	3	14
Other services	5	14
Total	**337**	**7,246**

Source: Ministry of National Planning and Economic Development

The main source of FDI in Myanmar is from ASEAN countries, which account for three of the top four top investors (see table 14). In total, five ASEAN countries (Indonesia, Malaysia, Philippines, Singapore, and Thailand) collectively pledged 155 projects worth US$ 3,757 million. These projects account for over half of the total FDI flows to Myanmar. The European Union (EU) has 47 projects worth over US$ 2,181 million.

Table 14. Main foreign investors by country, as of June 2000
(millions of US dollars)

Country	No. of projects	Approved amount
Singapore	69	1,510
United Kingdom	35	1,372
Thailand	47	1,264
Malaysia	27	597
United States	16	582
France	3	470
Netherlands	5	239
Indonesia	10	239
Japan	22	233
China (incl. Hong Kong)	35	169
Philippines	2	147

Source: Ministry of National Planning and Economic Development

Domestic investment is seen in table 15. Real estate and manufacturing are the top sectors in terms of kyat, while manufacturing and mining have the largest number of projects.

Table 15. Domestic investment as of June 2000
(millions of kyat)

Sector	No. of projects	Approved amount
Real estate development	22	27,176
Manufacturing	288	18,214
Construction	5	5,316
Transport	5	4,368
Livestock and fisheries	21	1,876
Hotel and tourism	13	1,104
Industrial estate	1	1,013
Mining	31	788
Agriculture	5	548
Others	10	1,255
Total	**401**	**61,959**

Source: Ministry of National Planning and Economic Development

C. Institutional and support network: public and private sector organizations

1. Government organizations and agencies

The Myanmar Investment Commission (MIC) is the main government body for foreign investments. MIC performs many duties, including investment promotion; screening, negotiating, and approving foreign and domestic investment applications; licensing; and monitoring investments. All prospective foreign investments are channeled through this organization, but in most cases the prospective investor must also deal with the respective ministry for that economic activity. For example, investors in the hotel and tourism sector will submit proposals and other requirements to the Ministry of Hotels and Tourism, and then go through the MIC's approval procedures. One of Myanmar's investment constraints is that it has not established any semblance of a one-stop service centre for prospective investors.

Contact information:
Myanmar Investment Commission
653/691 Merchant Street
Yangon
Tel: 951-282-101
Fax: 951-282-101

The *Ministry of Commerce* implements policies and regulations related to trade and commerce. Its main objectives are to (1) support internal and external trade activities; (2) facilitate commercial efficiency; and (3) promote export activities.

Contact information:
Ministry of Commerce
228-240 Strand Road
Yangon
Tel: 951-284-299; 284-184
Fax: 951-289-578; 284-823

Other useful contact information for government agencies is as follows:

Ministry of Agriculture
Thirimingala Ln., Kaba Aye Pagoda Rd.
Yankin Township
Yangon
Tel: (951) 665-587

Ministry of Finance and Revenue
26 A, Setmu Road
Yankin Township
Yangon
Tel: (951) 543-745

Ministry of Electric Power
Theinbyu Road
Botataung Township
Yangon
Tel: (951) 220-923

Ministry of Energy
23 Pyay Road
Lanmadaw Township
Yangon
Tel: (951) 221-116

Ministry of Industry 1
192 Kaba Aye Road
Bahan Township
Yangon
Tel: (951) 566-066

Ministry Industry 2
56 Kaba Aye Pagoda Road
Yankin Township
Yangon
Tel: (951) 666-134

Ministry of Labour
Minister's Office, Theinbyu St.
Botataung Township
Yangon
Tel: (951) 280-586

Ministry of Transport
363/421 Merchant Street
Botataung Township
Yangon
Tel: (951) 296-815

Ministry of Hotels and Tourism
77-91 Sule Pagoda Road
Kyauktada Township
Yangon
Tel: (951) 254-098

2. Chambers of commerce and other business associations

The largest and most dominant non-government agency responsible for the private sector in Myanmar is the *Union of Myanmar Federation of Chambers of Commerce and Industry* (UMFCCI). It was established as the Burmese Chamber of Commerce in 1919 but became dormant during the socialist years when virtually all private enterprises were shut. The Union of Myanmar Chamber of Commerce was re-established in 1989 as a part of SLORC's first series of economic reforms, and then renamed once again in 1999 to its current form.

UMFCCI maintains four working committees: industry, agriculture, commerce, and administration/ finance. Currently it has over 8,527 members comprising local and foreign firms and individuals. There are also 15 state and division chambers of commerce and industry under its umbrella and 17 business associations.

UMFCCI performs a wide array of activities and offers numerous services for its members and the private sector in general. Among its main activities are the following:

- Articulate business news and views to the government and the public
- Providing training courses on personnel, marketing, finance, and production management
- Advising members about business opportunities at home and abroad
- Sponsoring dispute settlement (arbitration)
- Participation in government boards, councils, and committees
- Interaction on day to day operations or on an ad-hoc basis to address issues affecting the private sector
- Issuing commercial documents and certificate of origin for goods to be exported
- Publishing newsletters, business directories, and trade inquiries
- Organizing activities such as seminars, conferences, workshops, talks, and forums

The UMFCCI acts as the umbrella organization for all of Myanmar's business associations. The other 16 associations are:

1. Myanmar Rice Millers Association
2. Myanmar Rice and Paddy Wholesalers Association
3. Myanmar Edible Oil Dealers Association
4. Myanmar Forest Products and Timber Merchants Association
5. Myanmar Pulses, Beans and Sesame Seeds Merchants Association
6. Myanmar Fisheries Federation
7. Myanmar Industries Association
8. Myanmar Printers and Publishers Association
9. Myanmar Customs Clearing Agents Association
10. Myanmar Women Entrepreneurs Association
11. Myanmar Garment Manufacturers Association
12. Myanmar Mercantile Marine Development Association
13. Myanmar Computer Industry Association
14. Myanmar Pharmaceutical and Medical Equipment Entrepreneurs Association
15. Myanmar Construction Entrepreneurs Association
16. Myanmar Banks Association
I7. Myanmar Livestock Federation

3. Consulting, accounting, and law firms

This section provides contact information for an assortment of consulting, accounting, and legal firms in Myanmar. However, the following information does not imply endorsement or recommendation.

As of 1999, there were 151 accounting firms, 104 business consulting firms, and 26 law firms in Myanmar, most of which are located in Yangon.

Consulting firms

Coopers & Lybrand
Room #209, International Business Centre
Pyay Road, 61/2 mile
Yangon
Tel: (951) 664-993
Fax: (951) 665-209

SGV-Winthin Consulting Ltd.
Room #910 FMI Centre
Bogyoke Aung San Street
Yangon
Tel: (951) 240-265, 240-400 Ext. 1910
Fax: (951) 246-867

Daw Khine Khine
No. 299, Maha Bandoola Street
Botataung P.O.
Yangon
Tel: (951) 245-876, 566-315

EDA Myanmar
Kandawgyi Palace Hotel
Kan Yeik Tha Road
Yangon
Tel: (951) 242-623
Fax: (951) 280-412

Law firms

Russin & Vecchi
No. 22 Wingaba Road, Bahan P.O.
Yangon
Tel: (951) 541794/540995
Fax: (951) 548835

LWA Consultants Ltd.
The Strand
92, Strand Road, Kyauktada P.O.
Tel: (951) 254816/254817
Fax: (951) 254818

Daw Khine Khine Advocate and Notary Public
No. 55, Maha Bandoola Garden St.
Yangon
Tel: (951) 286706

U Mya Thein, Central Court Advocate
and Notary Public
No. 52, Maha Bandoola Garden St.
Yangon
Tel: (951) 277930

4. Financial institutions

The legal and regulatory framework for Myanmar's banking and finance sector is contained in the Financial Institution of Myanmar Law. This law covers all financial institutions, including commercial banks, development and investment banks, finance companies, and credit associations.

Myanmar has four state-owned banks, 20 private banks, and 38 representative offices of foreign banks. Aside from the central bank, the state owned banks are set up to provide specialized services. The Myanmar Economic Bank offers conventional domestic banking services. The Myanmar Investment and Commercial Bank engages in domestic and foreign exchange transactions, while a third bank, the Myanmar Foreign Trade Bank, primarily handles foreign exchange transactions. The fourth bank is the Myanmar Agricultural and Rural Development Bank, which extends seasonal and term-loans for the agriculture and livestock sectors. Only the state-owned banks are allowed to deal in foreign exchange.

(a)   *Central Bank of Myanmar*

(b)   *State-owned commercial banks*

- Myanma Agriculture and Rural Development Bank
- Myanma Economic Bank
- Myanma Foreign Trade Bank
- Myanma Investment and Commercial Bank.

(c)   *Private commercial banks*

    (i)   *Domestic banks (16)*

- Asia Wealth Bank Ltd.
- Asia Yangon International Bank Ltd.
- Co-operative Farmers Bank Ltd.
- Co-operative Promoters Bank Ltd.
- First Private Bank Ltd.
- Innwa Bank Ltd.
- Kanbawza Bank Ltd.
- Myama Industrial Development Bank Ltd.
- Myanmar Livestock and Fisheries Development Bank Ltd.
- Myanmar May Flower Bank Ltd.
- Myanmar Oriental Bank Ltd.
- Myanmar Universal Bank Ltd.
- Sibin Tharyar Yay Bank Ltd.
- Tun Foundation Bank Ltd.
- Yadanabon Bank Ltd. (Mandalay)
- Yoma Bank Ltd.

    (ii)   *Joint venture banks*

- Myawady Bank Ltd.
- Myanma Citizens Bank Ltd.
- Yangon City Bank Ltd.
- Co-operative Bank Ltd.

    (iii)   *Representative offices (38)*

- ABN-AMRO Bank N.V.
- Arab Bangladesh Bank Ltd.
- Bangkok Bank Plc.
- Bank of Commerce (M) Berhad

- Bank of Tokyo-Mitsubishi Ltd.
- Banque Francaise du Commerce Exterieur
- Banque Nationale de Paris
- Brunei Investment Bank (BIB)
- Credit Agricole Indesuez
- Credit Lyonnaise
- Daewoo Bank (Hungary) Ltd.
- Dai-Ichi Kangyo Bank Ltd.
- Deutsche Bank Aktiengesellschaft
- Development Bank of Singapore Ltd.
- First Commercial Bank, Singapore Branch
- First Overseas Bank Ltd.
- Global Commercial Bank
- Hana Bank
- Hong Kong and Shanghai Banking Corp. Ltd.
- ING Bank
- Keppel Bank of Singapore Ltd.
- Korea Long Term Credit Bank
- Korea Exchange Bank
- Krung Thai Bank Plc.
- Malayan Banking Berhad
- National Bank Ltd.
- Natexis Banque
- Overseas Union Bank Ltd.
- Overseas-Chinese Banking Corp. Ltd.
- Panin Bank International Inc., Nauru
- Public Bank Berhad
- RHB Bank Berhad
- Societe Generale
- Standard Chartered Bank
- Sanwa Bank Ltd.
- Sumitomo Bank Ltd.
- The Tokai Bank Ltd.
- United Overseas Bank Ltd.

Myanmar does not yet have a capital market, although some preliminary steps have been taken to explore the possibility of such a market.

With effect from March 1998, only two of the state-owned banks are allowed to engage in foreign exchange. Since the inception of the Foreign Investment Law in 1988, the official exchange rate has remained constant at 6 kyat to the United States dollar for some business activities.

An important point about the financial sector in Myanmar is that in addition to the main currency, kyat, Myanmar also uses Foreign Exchange Certificates (FECs). FECs came into use in February 1993 and are exchangeable with United States dollars, pound sterling, or travellers' cheques.

5. Transport

(a) *Road network*

Myanmar has over 27,800 kilometres of roads, but the quality of roads varies tremendously throughout the country. The major urban areas such as Yangon and Mandalay have suitable roads, but in many other parts of the country the roads are need of upgrading. However, numerous bridges are sprouting up in every region of the country to facilitate intra and international trade.

(b) *Air transportation*

Myanmar has 4 international airports located in Yangon, Mandalay, Bagan, and Heho. Altogether there are 67 airfields/airports in the country. Myanmar Airways and Air Mandalay serve most of the domestic routes, and for international flights there are 15 carriers.

(c) *Railways*

There is an extensive rail network in Myanmar. The 5,514-kilometre network links all of the major towns in Myanmar. The state-owned Myanmar Railways operates all passenger and cargo rail services through its fleet of 262 diesel locomotives, 42 steam engines, and thousands of coaches and wagons.

(d) *Waterways and ports*

The country's extensive river network, which generally traverses in a north-south direction, enables large amounts of cargo and passengers to travel via the waterways. The main obstacle, though, is that many of the main rivers are not navigable through their entirety. The state-owned Inland Water Transport Company is the major carrier, but private companies also operate cargo and passenger transportation.

Yangon's port handles 90 per cent of the country's cargo, but there are eight other ports as well in various parts of Myanmar. The others are located in the Rakhine State (3), Ayeyarwady Division (1), Mon State (1), and Tanintharyi (3). Aside from Yangon Port, only two other ports (one in Rakhine State and the other in Ayeyarwady Division) handle international cargo. All of the ports are under the authority of the Myanmar Port Authority.

Myanmar does not offer direct overseas shipping to the United States and Canada, but transshipment arrangements can be made with the Nippon Liner Service of Japan. In addition to the state-owned Myanmar Five Star Line, four foreign shipping lines enter Myanmar's ports.

6. Telecommunications

The telecommunication system in Myanmar is still under-developed. As of 1999, Myanmar had 190,600 telephones, 82 telegraph offices, and only 1,600 fax machines, but it does offer international direct dialing.

Mobile telephones are not yet widely available. Likewise, the Ministry of Telecommunications, Post, and Telegraph offers e-mail service, but the Internet is still not available anywhere in the country.

D. Legal and regulatory frameworks for trade and investment

1. Foreign investment

(a) *Overall investment climate*

The Government of Myanmar has taken measures to encourage foreign investment, most notably with the promulgation of the Foreign Investment Law in November 1988. In an effort to dispel any concerns about the country's prior history of socialism and nationalization, the investment law guarantees against the nationalization and expropriation of foreign investments. In 1994, Myanmar furthered the scope of the FIL by promulgating the Myanmar Citizens Investment Law. The goal of this law was essentially to promote internal investment. Generally, the law dictated a national desire to increase technology, education, employment opportunities, private sector presence, import substitution, and export expansion. The method of achieving these goals was similar to the FIL, i.e. through tax exemptions as well as protection against nationalization.

The Government is responsible for ensuring that the country at large acquires some of the benefits of foreign investment, and therefore some of the seemingly disadvantageous policies (from the perspective of foreign investors) can be legitimized. However, the Government of Myanmar faces a monumental task in overcoming the reluctance of many foreign firms to investment in Myanmar, particularly the ones in Western Europe and the United States.

Rectifying the situation will not be easy. Western European and American firms face extreme pressure not to invest in Myanmar, despite their desire to take advantage of the available natural resources, because of political differences between the Government of Myanmar on the one hand and many Western Governments and activist organizations on the other. In some cases American firms have been penalized for business activities in Myanmar, and even though most of those laws have been struck down by the United States' courts as unconstitutional, consumer boycotts and other forms of pressure dissuade firms from entering Myanmar's market.

Another major obstacle obstructing the flow of foreign investment is the overall legal and regulatory framework. Myanmar has made great strides in the past 13 years towards building a market economy, but numerous regulations remain on the books that seriously impede foreign investment. One of the most evident examples is the exchange rate system. The dual and sometimes triple exchange rates raise valid concerns among foreign investors who insist on a rational and consistent exchange rate system for conducting their activities. The wide disparity in the formal and informal exchange rates creates a multitude of problems for finance managers and bookkeepers. Difficulties in accessing foreign exchange within Myanmar is also a hindrance to investors, as only state-owned banks are allowed to deal in foreign exchange.

(b) *Foreign investment law and procedures*

Investors should acquire copies of the full text of the investment laws, procedures, and regulations. The "package" of legislation and regulations includes:

- The Union of Myanmar Foreign Investment Law (FIL) (1988)
- Procedures Relating to the Union of Myanmar Foreign Investment Law (1988)
- Form for the Proposal of the Promoter to Make Foreign Investment in the Union of Myanmar
- Types of Economic Activities Allowed for Foreign Investment (1989)

(i) *Form of organization*

Foreign investors can set up a business in two different ways. First, the enterprise can be 100 per cent foreign owned, whereby the foreign company brings in the total amount of capital to establish the branch office. The second version is the joint venture with domestic companies, individuals, government enterprises, cooperatives, or a combination acting as the partner. In this case, the foreign partner must assume at least 35 per cent of total equity capital. A foreign investor can enter into a partnership with his local counterpart or set up a limited liability company with shares held by local investors.

The minimum amount of capital to be eligible under the FIL is US\$ 500,000 for industry and US\$ 300,000 service organization.

(ii) *Eligible sectors*

The State-Owned Economic Enterprise Law (SOEE) originally reserved 12 specific sectors for state-owned enterprises (SOEs):

- Extraction of teak and sale of the same in the country and abroad
- Cultivation and conservation of forest plantation, with the exception of village-owned firewood plantations cultivated by the villagers for their personal use
- Exploration, extraction, and sale of petroleum and natural gas and the production of the same
- Exploration and extraction of pearls, jade and precious stones and their export
- Breeding and production of fish and prawns in fisheries which have been reserved by the government
- Postal and telecommunication services
- Air transport and railway transport services
- Banking and insurance services
- Broadcasting and television services
- Exploration and extraction of metals and their export
- Electricity generating other than those permitted by law to private and cooperative electricity generating service

- Manufacturing of products relating to security and defense which the Government has prescribed by notification

However, the Government has liberalized most of these areas and allows at least joint ventures with the Government in a majority of the cases. Investors need to acquire permission to enter these sectors under Section 4 of the State-Owned Economic Enterprises Law.

(iii) *Incentives*

Various incentives are offered to foreign investors, but because these can change regularly it is important to contact the MIC for the current package. All firms investing through the Foreign Investment Law are subject to a 30 per cent tax on gross profit, but typically a three-year tax holiday is offered once the firm begins commercial activities.

A foreign investor who invests and operates under the Foreign Investment Law has the right to enjoy appropriate economic benefits particularly in the form of tax incentives. Some investment incentives include:

- Exemption from income taxes for up to three years (renewable)
- Accelerated depreciation of assets
- A reduction of up to 50 per cent on income taxes due on product exports from Myanmar
- Exemption from customs duty on machinery and other capital goods imported as part of operation
- Government guarantees against nationalism
- Repatriation of profits and invested capital
- Losses carried forward for up to three years
- Exemption from customs duties on imported raw materials for the first three years of operation

(iv) *Foreign investment application procedure* (portions extracted from www.myanmar.com)

Submitting a proposal:

A promoter must submit a proposal in the prescribed form to the Myanmar Investment Commission enclosing the following documents:

- Documents in support of the investor's financial credibility (audited final accounts from the most recent year of the person or firm intending to make investment).
- Bank recommendation regarding the business standing.
- Detailed calculation relating to economic justification of the proposed project indicating, inter alia, estimated annual net profit; estimated annual foreign exchange earnings or savings as well as foreign exchange requirement for the operation; length of time to recoup investment; prospects of new employment; prospects of increased national income; local and foreign market conditions and distribution.

If it is a 100 per cent foreign investment, the investor must submit a draft contract to be executed with the organization determined by the Ministry concerned. If it is a firm, limited company or joint venture of any kind, a draft contract to be entered into between the foreign investor and local counterpart must be submitted. If it is a limited company or a joint venture in the form of a limited company, the investor must include in the application materials the draft Memorandum and Articles of Association.

Additional information must also be supplied, and thus investors should see Appendix 1 "Proposal of the Promoter to Make Foreign Investment in the Union of Myanmar".

Appraisal of the Proposal:

The Myanmar Investment Commission will scrutinize the proposal from the technical, financial, commercial, economic and social aspects within the framework of the policy objectives. Additional information may be requested by the MIC. Also, the Myanmar Foreign Commercial Bank will make inquiries with foreign banks regarding the business standing of the prospective investor.

The MIC scrutinizes the application based on the following criteria:

1. estimated annual net profit
2. estimated annual foreign exchange earnings and requirements
3. recoupment period
4. prospects of new employment
5. prospects of increased national income
6. local and foreign market conditions
7. requirements for local consumption
8. prospects of foreign exchange savings

Upon approval by the Commission, a permit is issued to carry out the business specifying the terms and conditions as required according to the type of business.

Application for a Permit to Trade from the Ministry of National Planning and Economic Development at the time of incorporation of the enterprise with the Registrar of Companies:

Essentially any enterprise which has obtained a permit from the MIC can start its business constituting itself as a sole proprietorship, a partnership or a limited company, or a branch office of a foreign company. A limited company which brings one hundred per cent foreign capital, forms a joint-venture limited company, or a branch company is deemed as a foreign company under section 27 A of the Myanmar Companies Act, and accordingly it is required to obtain a Permit to Trade by applying to the Registrar of the Companies Registration Office of the Directorate of Investment and Company Administration of the Ministry of National Planning and Economic Development. However, a limited company that is a joint venture with a state-owned economic enterprise formed under Special Company Act 1950 is exempted from obtaining a Permit to Trade.

The application must also include the following documents:

- Required particulars entered in Form A of the Myanmar Companies Regulation, 1957
- The Company's drafts Memorandum of Association, Articles of Association or other instruments defining the constitution of the company
- Duly completed questionnaire form prescribed by the Capital Structure Committee of the Ministry of National Planning and Economic Development
- List of economic activities intended to be performed in Myanmar (including permission from the relevant ministry, if any)
- Estimated expenditures to be incurred in Myanmar for the first year operations

In the case of a foreign branch the following shall be furnished in addition to the above mentioned documents:

- A copy of the head office's Memorandum and Articles of Association or of the Charter, Statute or other instruments constituting or defining the constitution of the company duly notarized by the Myanmar Embassy in the country where the company is incorporated
- Copies of the head office balance sheet and profit and loss accounts for the last two financial years
- Where the Memorandum of Association Articles of Association and other relevant documents are not originally in English, then the investor must provide authentication of the translation into English

The Ministry of National Planning and Economic Development will issue the Permit to Trade after considering the recommendation of the Capital Structure Committee. In the case of a company that has received a permit from the Myanmar Investment Commission, the terms and validity of the Permit to Trade shall be the same.

Registration of Business Organizations:

- A sole proprietorship is not required to register at the Companies Registration Office.
- A partnership firm may be registered, but registration is not compulsory.

- A company limited by shares is required to register under the Myanmar Companies Act at the Office of Registrar of Companies Registration.
- A company with share contribution of the State shall be registered under the Special Company Act of 1950 and the Myanmar Companies Act as a "special company" in Myanmar on behalf of the company (for a branch office of a foreign company).
- A company which comes under the definition of foreign company shall apply and obtain a permit from the Ministry of National Planning and Economic Development before registration.

In applying for registration of a company or branch office of a foreign company, the following papers and documents shall be submitted:

- Two sets of Memorandum of Association and Articles of Association duly stamped and printed both in Myanmar and English
- Declaration of registration
- Declaration of legal and official version of the documents
- Declaration of the situation of registered office
- Translation certificate by a competent translator
- List of Directors and Myanmar for a company incorporated in Myanmar
- List of person(s) authorized to accept services of process and notice

For a public company the following additional documents shall be submitted before commencing the business:

- List of persons to act as directors
- List of persons who have consented to act as directors
- Agreement to take qualification shares

Registration Fees:

For a partnership firm the registration fee is fixed at 45 kyat. For a company limited by shares, the registration fee ranges from a minimum of 600 kyat to a maximum of 15,000 kyat, depending upon the authorized capital of the company. It is calculated according to Table "B" of the Myanmar Companies Act.

(c) *Taxation*

Myanmar has 15 types of taxes and duties in four categories: 1) taxes on domestic production and public consumption; 2) taxes on income and ownership; 3) customs duties; and 4) taxes on the utility of state-owned property. The relevant tax legislation derives from several laws and related acts, namely the Income Tax Law (1974), the Profit Tax Law (1976), the Commercial Tax Law (1990) and its amendment in 1991, the Myanmar Stamp Act (1935), and the Court Fee Act (1937). The Internal Revenue Department under the Ministry of Finance and Revenue administers the tax legislation. The fiscal year begins on April 1 and ends on March 31 of the following year.

(i) *Personal income tax*

Income tax on salaries for foreigners range from 3 to 50 per cent, but tax on foreigners employed on government projects receive a rate of 20 per cent. For the rates, see Table 16. The employer must deduct the income tax from the salaries and send it to the Township Revenue Office.

Table 16. Tax rates on income

Income level (in kyat)	Tax rate (per cent)
1 - 5,000	3
5,001 - 10,000	10
10,001 - 15,000	15
15,001 - 20,000	20
20,001 - 30,000	25
30,001 - 40,000	30
40,001 - 50,000	35
50,001 - 70,000	40
70,001 - 100,000	45
100,001 - 150,000	48
Over 150,001	50

Source: UMFCCI, 1999 Myanmar Business Directory

Table 17. Withholding tax rates
(percentage)

Type of income	For resident foreigners	For non-resident foreigners
Interest	15	20
Royalties for use of license, trade-mark, patents, copy right	15	20
Payment on contracts with state agencies	3	3.5
Payment on work done for foreign contractors	2.5	3

Source: UMFCCI, 1999 Myanmar Business Directory

Allowances are given for a spouse (2,500 kyat) and for children according to their age, with the latter rates ranging from 500 kyat to 1,000 kyat. The basic allowance is 20 per cent of total income but maximum basic allowance is 6,000 kyat.

Several exemptions are available for foreign firms. The following items are among the most common exemptions, but investors should consult with the MIC for additional categories and for the ones for which they qualify:

1. Minimum three consecutive years tax holiday, starting from commencement of production or services
2. Exemption or relief on half of profits put back into the company within one year
3. Depreciation of capital assets
4. 50 per cent relief on income tax on profits from export of goods produced by the firm
5. Allowances for research and development
6. Carry forward and offset losses for up to three consecutive years from first year of loss
7. Deduct income tax paid to the state on behalf of foreign employee from the assessable income of the enterprise
8. Exemption or relief on customs duties on machinery, components, spare parts, and other items imported during the construction period
9. Exemption or relief on raw materials imported during first three of production after completion of construction

Exemptions on income and allowable expenses include:

1. Dividends received and share profits
2. Expenses incurred in the production of income
3. Statutory contributions to the provident fund recognized by the Myanmar Income Tax Act

Other exemptions include donations to religious or charitable organizations but not exceeding 25 per cent of the income and depreciation and amortization of capital assets.

(ii) *Business taxes*

The Commercial Tax Law 1990 and its amendment in 1991 apply to the turnover of goods and services produced within Myanmar or imported from abroad. The commercial tax is an ad valorem tax on the point of sale except for the tax paid on imported goods, which is collected by the Customs Department. The tax levels vary from 0 to 200 per cent and are listed in the various tax schedules contained in the legislation.

Myanmar also has a commercial tax of 10 per cent on hotel and restaurant services and for goods and services that go to the government.

(iii) *Capital gains tax*

The capital gains tax is determined by deducting the following items from the full value of the sales proceed of capital good:

1. The net remaining after deducting the total depreciation allowed under the Myanmar Income Tax Act from the total of the original cost to the assessee and any expenditure of a capital nature incurred for making any additions
2. Expenditures incurred in procuring the asset and in its sale, exchange, or transfer
3. Application of a flat rate of 10 per cent on capital gains for resident foreign companies, but 40 per cent for non-resident foreign companies
4. No tax is applied to the capital gains if the amount is less 50,000 kyat within one year

(d) *Foreign remittances*

Regarding foreign remittance, Section 26 of the Union of Myanmar Foreign Investment Law stipulates that the following shall be transferable abroad in relevant foreign currency through the bank prescribed by the commission (Myanmar Investment and Commercial Bank and Myanmar Foreign Trade Bank) at the prevailing official rate of exchange:

- Foreign currency entitled to by the person who has brought in foreign capital
- Foreign currency permitted for withdrawal by the Commission to the person who has brought in foreign capital
- Net profits after deducting from the annual profits received by the person who has brought in foreign capital, all taxes and the prescribed funds
- Legitimate balance, after causing payment to be made in respect of taxes and after deducting in the manner prescribed, living expenses incurred for himself and his family out of the salary, and lawful income obtained by the foreign personnel during performance of service in the State

(e) *Labour issues*

Labour issues in Myanmar are covered by several pieces of legislation dating back to the 1920s. Employers should familiarize themselves with the following laws:

- Employment Restriction Act, 1959
- Employment Statistics Act, 1948
- Employment and Training Act, 1950
- Factories Act, 1951
- Minimum Wages Act, 1949

- Payment of Wages Act, 1936
- Shops and Establishments Act, 1951
- Social Security Act, 1954
- The Leave and Holidays Act, 1951
- Trade Disputes Act, 1929
- Workmen's Compensation Act, 1923

Enterprises seeking five or more workers must apply to the Township Labour Office, which prepares a list of candidates with the requisite qualifications. The company can then choose workers from the township's list of eligible names. However, it is also possible in certain circumstances to recruit workers through employment agencies or by posting public notifications.

Wages and salaries vary according to the private enterprise. Myanmar does not have a standardized minimum wage, but in some industrial estates the wages may be predetermined.

Myanmar has had a Social Security scheme since 1954. Private firms with five or more employees must contribute two per cent of their insured wages to Social Security, and the employee contributes 1.5 per cent of his or her wages. The scheme entitles workers to sickness cash benefits, funeral grants, disability benefits, and a survivor's pension. Myanmar's Workmen's Compensation Act covers workers not under the Social Security system and who are injured or killed during their work duties.

The typical working hours in Myanmar are based on the type of business activity. For companies, retail shops, services, and entertainment, the usual working hours are eight hours per day and 48 hours per week. In factories, oil fields, and above ground mines, the hours are 8 per day and 44 hours per week. Factories involved in continuous production will have a maximum of 48 hours per week. Lastly, underground mining has a limit of eight hours per day and 40 hours per week.

People employed by private enterprises are entitled each year to six days of casual leave, 30 days of medical leave, 10 days earned leave, and 21 public holidays with wages. By law women are entitled to a paid maternity leave.

(f) *Land*

Foreigners seeking to acquire land have to apply to the Central Committee (which governs the allocation of land for agriculture) through the MIC. Once the right to use land has been granted, it cannot be mortgaged, sold, or transferred without the approval of the Central Committee. Leases are limited to 30 years, but they can be extended.

Individuals and firms, whether foreign or domestic, that desire to invest in commercial agro-enterprises will be allowed to use the land as follows:

1)   Agriculture

    a)   Plantation crops   5,000 acres
    b)   Orchards   3,000 acres
    c)   Seasonal crops   1,000 acres

2)   Livestock, poultry farming and aquaculture

    a)   Aquaculture   2,000 acres
    b)   Livestock and Poultry Farming
        i)   Buffalo, cattle, horses   5,000 acres
        ii)   Sheep, goats   1,000 acres
        iii) Poultry, pigs   500 acres

Rent for agricultural land per acre is as follows:

- Perennial crop cultivation on fallow land US$ 8-15
- Crop cultivation on deep water area US$ 8-20
- Crop cultivation on fallow land in dry zone US$ 15-40

2. Customs and trade procedures

(a) *Exporting*

Firms under the Foreign Investment Law that will conduct trade activities must register as an exporter-importer with the Export Import Registration Office, Directorate of Trade, Ministry of Commerce.

The export procedures are detailed in the UMFCCI's *1999 Myanmar Business Directory*. The following selection is extracted from that publication:

1. A registered exporter must obtain an export license...laid down by the Directorate of Trade. No fee is charged for the issuance of an export license.
2. In applying for an export license, the application shall have attached a sales contract or agreement and/or pro forma invoice mentioning detailed specifications with regard to grade, quantity, price, name of buyer and country, method of payment, shipment period, and destination.
3. An irrevocable letter of credit has to be opened at the Myanmar Foreign Trade Bank by the buyer through correspondent or an acceptable bank.
4. The vessel on which the cargo is to be shipped has to be nominated by the buyer.
5. The Myanmar Port Authority has to be contacted for the shipment of cargo on F.O.B. basis.
6. Pre-shipment inspection will be conducted by Inspection and Agency Services.
7. Details of the cargo, such as shipping bills, other shipping documents, and customs pass must be presented to the Bank.

As for the documentation required for exporting goods, a firm will need to submit the following:

a) Export license/permit
b) Invoice
c) Packing list
d) Sales contract
e) Shipping instructions
f) Letter of credit or General Remittance Exemption Certificate
g) Payment advice for the Inward Telegraphic Transfer Private Number/Inward Telegraphic Transfer Government Number
h) Sample of the goods

Additional documents may be required for certain types of goods.

The customs duty on exports is 10 per cent on export earning, comprising:

a) 8 per cent commercial tax
b) 2 per cent income tax

Only a few items are forbidden from export by private firms or face restrictions. Currently these include logs and rice, but the government does occasionally place restrictions on certain goods.

Credit is also a key issue for traders. Export activities must be self-financed in most cases, as lines of credit from banks in Myanmar essentially require that trader have the required amount in hand already.

(b) *Importing*

The procedure for imports is outlined once again in the UMFCCI's *1999 Myanmar Business Directory:*

1. A registered importer is required to open a foreign exchange account at a bank in order to apply for an import license from the Directorate of Trade.
2. In applying for an import license, the applicant shall attach the sales contract and/or pro forma invoice mentioning detailed specifications, mode of packing, and delivery phasing.
3. Import license fees payable on the C.I.F. (Yangon) value of the goods imported from abroad.
4. An irrevocable letter of credit has to be opened by the importer at the bank.
5. If the purchase is made on F.O.B. basis, the importer has to secure insurance from Myanmar Insurance and freight booking from Myanmar Five Star Line.
6. After receiving shipment advice from the suppliers, the importer has to arrange for the clearance of the goods.

Imports are subjected to an import license fee, which ranges from a minimum of 250 kyat to a maximum of 50,000 kyat.

Certain goods are exempted under the following terms for foreign investment enterprises:

1. Machinery, components, spare parts, and materials used during the construction phase and imported as foreign capital.
2. Raw materials and packing materials imported during the first three years of commercial production after completion of construction.
3. Medicine and selected pharmaceutical raw materials used in the manufacturing of medicines or for improving the public health.

State-owned enterprises receive additional import license fee exemptions.

As for the documentation required for importing goods, a firm will need to submit the following for customs clearance:

a) Import license/permit
b) Invoice
c) Bill of lading or air consignment note
d) Packing list
e) Other documents as required

Customs duties on imports were reduced in 1996 from the extremely high rates first enacted in 1992 under the Tariff Law. Customs duties now range from a low of 0.5 per cent to a high of 40 per cent, depending on the classification in the tariff schedule.

E. Main opportunities for investment

1. Energy

The country's abundance of hydroelectric potential stands at the forefront of investment opportunities in this sector. Although 41 per cent of current electricity originates from hydroelectric plants, only one per cent of hydroelectric potential is being utilized. Myanmar's natural gas deposits constitute other potentially successful investment opportunities.

Myanmar also has a blossoming oil and natural gas industry, with the latter considered to have extremely high potential.

2. Infrastructure

In order to meet the demand and qualifications of increased economic growth and attract foreign investment, its infrastructure needs tremendous expansion and further development. Under the current five-year economic plan, roads, bridges, and rail systems have been given priority. The Road Construction Plan dictates that along with the upgrading of existing roads, 3,500 miles of new roads will be constructed. In order to facilitate this enormous undertaking, the government has considered opening up bidding for major projects under a Build-Operate-Transfer scheme. This type of joint venture will allow a private contractor to build and operate the new road as well as collect tolls for a set period of time. At the conclusion of that stipulated period, the road will then be transferred over to the government.

Other investment opportunities in infrastructure include industrial estates.

3. Agriculture, fisheries, and livestock

The potential for agriculture FDI remains strong. Currently the agricultural sector attracts less than 0.2 per cent of total FDI. As only about 13 per cent of the land is cultivated, opportunities in this sector abound. However, export of rice is confined to the Government for the time being. Other crops such as beans and pulses, sugar cane, groundnuts, and maize retain high export potential but are still under-produced in the country.

Myanmar's coastline is one of the longest and cleanest in South-East Asia. The abundance of marine life has remained relatively untapped, although recent private sector activity has surged as a result of the dissolving of a government-run monopoly in this sector in 1994. Livestock is another potentially lucrative, but yet untapped, market.

With some of the most abundant and under-utilized resources, Myanmar's forests remain an import prospect for economic subsistence. The country contains about 80 per cent of the world's teak reserves and currently supplies about 90 per cent of the world market. However, forestry only accounts for 1 per cent of total GDP. Since 1994, the harvesting of and export of teak wood has remained a government monopoly, but opportunities exist for value-added exports of forest products.

4. Manufacturing

Manufacturing is one of Myanmar's most untapped sectors. Industries that exploit comparative advantage, such as teak manufacturing and export, hydroelectric power generation, mining, foodstuff, and light industry, have excellent potential as exports.

5. Services

As in other countries, the hotel and tourism sector is considered to be a lucrative earner of foreign exchange. The 199,359 visitors in the year up to March 2000 generated approximately US$ 34 million in foreign exchange, while foreign investment in the hotel industry, through licensed foreign investment hotels, joint-venture hotels and local private-owned hotels up to April 2000 was US$ 605 million. It should be noted that the arrival figures are more than doubled – to 477,962 – when one includes border visitors, including day visitors.

After a large boom in the construction of hotels during the early to mid-1990s, the recent economic difficulties have left most of these hotels either half-built or severely under capacity. Further, the dismal power situation leaves many of these hotels, as well as other service industries, relying on diesel power generators that increase the cost of business by ten to 20 per cent. Yet Myanmar's tourism sector is almost certain to grow as more people discover its "undiscovered" treasures and look for new and exotic vacation destinations.

Myanmar has a relatively new insurance industry with most of the legislation and regulations coming into effect since 1993. The Myanmar Insurance Law was enacted in 1993, followed by the Insurance Business Law in 1996, and the Insurance Business Rules of 1997. As Myanmar continues to reform its economy and interact with the outside world, the insurance industry will likely be an important sector in the near future.

F. Tips for visitors

1. Getting there

Tourist visas for Myanmar are valid for 28 days and can usually be issued the same day when applied for from any embassy or consulate of Myanmar worldwide. Three types of visas are available: foreign individual tourists, business, and package tour. *Foreign individual tourists and business visa holders* are required to purchase US$ 300 worth of Foreign Exchange Certificates (FEC) upon arrival in Myanmar (FEC 1 = US$ 1), while holders of package tour visas do not need to purchase FEC. However, a confirmation letter of one's booking through a tour operator is required when applying for a package tour visa. Tourist visas cost US$ 20, while business visas cost US$ 32.

By air: Myanmar is served internationally by Myanma Airways International, Thai Airways International, Indian Airlines International, Silk Air, Malaysia Airlines, Air China, Mandarin Airlines, Uni Air, Biman Bangladesh Airlines, and Air Mandalay. Generally, these flights run well below capacity. For the month of April 2000, there were 281 flights to Yangon International Airport with a seat capacity of 48,104. The utilization rate was only 14,593 seats – or 30.34 per cent. However, in the winter months of October to April, the Bangkok-Yangon route in particular is heavily booked.

Air travel within Myanmar is served by Air Mandalay, Yangon Airways, and Myanmar Airways en route to Mandalay, Bagan, Thandwe, Heho, Sittway, Tachiliek, Myiek and Kawthaung.

By sea: Cruise ships call at Yangon Port with visas on arrival granted on prior arrangement.

Overland: Overland entry with a border pass is permitted at the following checkpoints: Kyuukoke, Namkhan, and Muse on the Myanmar-Yunnan (China) border; and Tachileik, Myawaddy, and Kawthaung on the Myanmar-Thailand border. Note that these points can be closed without notice, and thus it is advisable to check in advance.

2. Hotel accommodations

Up to March 2000, the country had 512 hotels, motels and guesthouses, with a total of 14,541 rooms. One hundred and fifty nine of these establishments are in Yangon. Twenty one of the hotels involve foreign investment.

3. Places of interest

The diverse geography of the country offers a host of attractions – natural, anthropological, religious, cultural and ecological. With a long coastline of nearly 1,800 kilometres, Myanmar is rich in marine biodiversity. Unpolluted by industry and oilspills and unspoiled by over-development, its seas still remain an idyllic habitat of marine life.

For security reasons, the Government does not allow free travel to all parts of the country, especially the Golden Triangle area in the north. The standard destinations are the capital Yangon, Mandalay, Bagan, Inle Lake, and the Taunggyi quadrangle. For other areas one generally needs a permit and/or a guide, if one is allowed to go at all.

Yangon

Yangon lies in the fertile delta country of southern Myanmar on the Yangon River about 30 kilometres from the sea. It has a population of approximately 4 million people. Yangon's most celebrated attraction is the gold-plated Shwedagon Pagoda, which dominates the city. The present monument was built in the eighteenth century and is surrounded by statues, temples, shrines, images and pavilions. Other sights include the colonial architecture of the Strand Hotel, the giant reclining Buddha in Chaukhtatgyi Pagoda and the peaceful Kandawgyi and Inya Lakes.

Mandalay

The sprawling city was the last capital of Myanmar before the British took over and is the country's second-largest city. Highlights of Mandalay include Shwenandaw Kyaung, the sole remaining building of the once extravagant moated palace; Mandalay Hill, with its spiraling stairways, temples and views; and the ancient Rakhine Buddha image at Mahamuni Paya. Several markets and handicraft shops are found throughout Mandalay.

Bagan

Bagan represents the pinnacle of Myanmar culture with its multitude of stunning pagodas and temples on the banks of the Ayeyarwady. Along with the ruins of Angkor Wat in Cambodia, Bagan is one of the ancient wonders of Asia with its more than 5,000 temples. Bagan's heyday was in the eleventh to the thirteenth centuries.

Bago

During the Mon dynasty, Bago was a fabulous city, a major seaport and capital of lower Myanmar. The city was destroyed in 1757 but partially restored in the early nineteenth century. When the Bago River changed its course and cut the city off from the sea, Bago failed to return to its previous grandeur. Sights include the Shwemawdaw Pagoda which dominates the town, the Hintha Gone Pagoda and the 55 m (180 ft) long, reclining Shwethalyaung Buddha.

Beaches

Tourist authorities are placing increased emphasis on beach holidays. To date, some of the main areas include:

- Ngapali Beach, on the Rakhine coast, is an hour's flight from Yangon. It is an unspoiled beach stretching over three kilometres. There is an 18-hole golf course nearby.
- Chaung-tha Beach is 40 kilometres to the west of Pathein in Ayeyarwady Division, a five-hour drive from Yangon. It has three beach hotels.
- Kanthaya Beach is on the Rakhine coast and about 290 kilometres from Yangon.
- Maung-ma-gan Beach is a long shallow unspoiled area only a 75-minute flight from Yangon.

4. Embassies

There are 26 foreign embassies in Myanmar and they are:

Australia
88, Strand Road
Kyauktada Tsp., Yangon
Tel: (951) 251810
        251797, 251809
Fax: (951) 246159

Bangladesh
56, Kaba Aye Pagoda
Bahan Tsp., Yangon
Tel: (951) 549556, 549557
Fax: (951) 546745

Brunei Darussalam
98-A, Kaba Aye Pagoda
Bahan Tsp., Yangon
Tel: (951) 549152, 540377
Fax: (951) 549338

China
1, Pyidaungsu Yeiktha Rd.
Dagon Tsp., Yangon
Tel: (951) 221280, 221281
Fax: (951) 227019

Egypt
81 Pyidaungsu Yeiktha Rd.
Dagon Tsp., Yangon
Tel: (951) 222886, 222887
Fax: (951) 222865

France
102, Pyidaungsu Yeiktha Rd.
Dagon Tsp., Yangon
Tel: (951) 282122, 282418
Fax: (951) 287759

Germany
32, Natmauk Street
Bahan Tsp., Yangon
Tel: (951) 548951, 548952
Fax: (951) 548899

India
545-547, Merchant Street
Kyauktada Tsp., Yangon
Tel: (951) 282550, 282551
Fax: (951) 254086

Indonesia
100, Pyidaungsu Yeiktha Rd.
Dagon Tsp., Yangon
Tel: (951) 281714, 281358
Fax: (951) 282675

Israel
49, Pyay Road
Dagon Tsp., Yangon
Tel: (951) 282550, 282551
Fax: (951) 254086

Italy
3, Inya Myaing Road
Golden Valley, Bahan Tsp.
Yangon
Tel: (951) 527100, 527101
Fax: (951) 533670

Japan
100, Natmauk Road
Bahan Tsp., Yangon
Tel: (951) 549644, 549645
Fax: (951) 549643

Republic of Korea
97, University Avenue
Bahan Tsp., Yangon
Tel: (951) 527142, 527143
Fax: (951) 513286

Lao People's
Democratic Republic
A-1, Diplomatic Quarters
Tawwin St., Dagon Tsp.
Yangon
Tel: (951) 222482
Fax: (951) 227446

Malaysia
82, Pyidaungsu Yeiktha Rd.
Dagon Tsp., Yangon
Tel: (951) 220248, 220249
Fax: (951) 221840

Nepal
16, Natmauka Yeiktha Lane
Tawne Tsp., Yangon
Tel: (951) 550633, 553168
Fax: (951) 549803

Pakistan
A-4 Diplomatic Quarters
Pyay Road, Dagon Tsp.
Yangon, P.O. Box 581
Tel: (951) 222881, 222882
Fax: (951) 221147

Philippines
50, Pyay Road, 6 $^1/_2$ Mile
Hlaing Tsp., Yangon
Tel: (951) 525688, 525700
Fax: (951) 524084

Russian Federation
38, Sagawa Road
Dagon Tsp., Yangon
Tel: (951) 241955, 254161
Fax: (951) 241953

Singapore
326, Pyay Road
Sangyoung Tsp., Yangon
Tel: (951) 525688, 525700
Fax: (951) 525734

Sri Lanka
34 Tawwin Street
Dagon Tsp., Yangon
Tel: (951) 222812
Fax: (951) 221509

Thailand
45, Pyay Road, 6 $^1/_2$ Mile
Hlaing Tsp., Yangon
Tel: (951) 525670, 533082
Fax: (951) 527792

United Kingdom
80, Kan-na Road
Kyauktada Tsp.
Yangon
Tel: (951) 281700, 281702
Fax: (951) 289566

United States
581, Merchant Street
Kyauktada Tsp., Yangon
Tel: (951) 282055, 282056
Fax: (951) 280409

Viet Nam
36, Wingaba Road
Bahan Tsp., Yangon
Tel: (951) 548905, 549302
Fax: (951) 548329

Yugoslavia
114 A, Inya Road
Kamayut Tsp., Yangon
Tel: (951) 532655, 532822
Fax: (951) 532831

G. Learning more

1. Related web sites

www.myanmar.com

www.myanmar-shafu.com

www.myanmar-travel.com

www.myanmar-tourism.com
www.myanmaryellowpages.com

www.myanmardotcom.com
www.myanmar-hotels.com

www.asiatravel.com

V. THAILAND

A. Basic operating environment

1. Geography and climate

Thailand covers a total land area of 513,115 square kilometres. It shares boundaries with Myanmar on the west and north-west frontiers, the Lao People's Democratic Republic on the east and north-east, Cambodia on the south-east, and Malaysia to the south. The Gulf of Thailand is located south of Bangkok and east of the southern peninsula, and the Andaman Sea lies to the south-west. Its total coastline is approximately 2,700 kilometres.

Thailand is divided into four natural regions: North, Central Plains, or Chao Phraya River Basin, North-east, or the Korat Plateau and the South, or Southern Peninsula. The North is a mountainous region comprised of natural forest, ridges, and deep, narrow alluvial valleys. The North-east region is an arid region characterized by a rolling surface and undulating hills. Central Thailand is a lush, fertile valley – the richest and most extensive rice-producing area in the country. The southern region is hilly, thick in forests, and rich deposits of minerals and iron ores. This region is the centre for the production of rubber and the cultivation of other topical crops.

Thailand lies within the humid tropics and remains hot throughout the year. Average temperatures are about 29°C, ranging in Bangkok from 35°C in April to 17°C in December. There are three seasons: the cool season (November to February), the hot season (April to May), and the rainy season (June to October), though downpours rarely last more than a couple of hours.

2. History

Formerly known as Siam, Thailand means *"land of the free,"* and throughout its 800-year history, Thailand can boast the distinction of being the only country in South-East Asia never to have been colonized. Early in its history, the territory of what is modern-day Thailand was strongly influenced by ancient Indian civilization, which laid the ground for kingship, art, administration, and language that lasted several centuries. The great Khmer civilization of the seventh through thirteenth centuries also had a strong influence on the early States of Thailand and controlled virtually all of what is now Thailand.

The first Thai State, Nan Chao, was established in 650 A.D. and lasted until 1250. Located in southern China, a great number of people from Nan Chao migrated south as far as the Chao Phraya Basin and settled down over the Central Plains under the sovereignty of the Khmer Empire, whose culture they probably accepted.

The Thai people eventually founded their independent State of Sukhothai around 1238. Sukhothai, considered the golden era of Thai history, religion, and culture, lasted until 1378, when it was annexed by the Ayutthaya Kingdom.

Ayutthaya flourished from 1350 until 1767. An invasion from a Burmese kingdom destroyed Ayutthaya and forced the Thais to settle in the area of present day Bangkok.

Thailand traces its modern history to 1782, when Chao Phraya Chakri became the first king of the Chakri Dynasty. Since that time, nine kings have ascended the throne. The most famous of these is King Chulalongkorn, also known as Rama V (1869-1910), who is credited with the modernization of Thailand (then known as Siam) and for his skill in retaining Siam's freedom when all around him countries were succumbing to European colonialism.

During the reign of King Prajadhipok, Rama VII (1925-1935), Siam changed from an absolute monarchy to a constitutional monarchy. The country's name was changed from Siam to Thailand with the advent of a democratic government in 1939.

The present monarch, King Bhumibol Adulyadej, is King Rama IX of the Chakri Dynasty and is currently the world's longest reigning monarch (since 1946).

3. Population

Thailand has a population of about 60 million people. Ethnic Thais form the majority, though the area has historically been a migratory crossroads, and thus strains of Mon, Khmer, Myanmar, Lao, Malay, Indian and most strongly, Chinese stock produce a degree of ethnic diversity. However, the highly successful integration of most ethnic groups over the centuries has created a generally unified population.

Thailand also has about 10-20 hill tribes, depending on how they are categorized. The hill tribe population is estimated at 550,000. The hill tribes live primarily in the mountainous regions of the northern part of Thailand, and several of them still retain semi-nomadic lifestyles.

4. Language and culture

The official national language is Thai. Unlike Western languages, Thai is tonal, meaning that the pitch given to a particular syllable determines its meaning. With five tones, the same syllable can be spoken in five different ways, all of which have a different meaning. Most polysyllabic words in the vocabulary have been borrowed, mainly from Khmer, Pali and Sanskrit. Dialects are spoken in rural areas, with the most well-known being *Isan*, which is a form of Lao in the north-east region. Other languages are Chinese and Malay, along with the various hill tribe languages. English, a compulsory subject in public schools, is widely spoken and understood, particularly in Bangkok and other major cities.

Buddhism, the national religion, is the professed faith of 85-90 per cent of the population. Islam, Christianity, Hinduism, and other creeds comprise the remaining percentage.

The urbanized areas of Thailand have infused several aspects of modern Western culture into traditional Thai culture. The more rural areas and mountainous areas still retain much of their traditional culture, including music, dance, and rural lifestyle.

5. Economy

Between the mid-1980s and 1995 Thailand set the standard for economic development with its record-breaking growth rates. With annual growth in that period averaging over 8 per cent, Thailand appeared to have perfected the formula for industrialization. Thailand served as a model for other developing countries because of its success and due to the fact that its achievements were essentially led by the private sector, which is a sharp contrast to the heavily state-guided models of the Republic of Korea, Japan, Taiwan Province of China, and Singapore.

However, after these years of rapid economic growth and industrialization, Thailand's runaway economy came to an abrupt halt in mid-1997, with the onset of what developed into the Asian economic crisis. Years of high annual growth rates, at times exceeding 10 per cent, gave way to a severe recession that saw Thailand experience declining growth in 1997 of 1 per cent and a contraction of 10.2 per cent in 1998. While not alone in suffering from a major reversal, Thailand has been forced to confront the structural deficiencies that underlie its economy and political system. Many of the factors that enabled it to achieve unprecedented growth rates and achievements also sowed the seeds for the rapid decline.

Signs of an economic slowdown appeared in 1996, when Thailand's exports declined 1.9 per cent, its current account deficit rose to 8 per cent of GDP, and the country's foreign debt amounted to US$ 90.5 billion. Of this US$ 90.5 billion, nearly $ 74 billion was private sector debt. By 1997 the economy began to unravel. The stock market continued its plunge from over 1,200 points in mid-1996 to 370 at the end of 1997 and as low as 253 by the third quarter of 1998. The Thai currency, the baht, faced increasing pressure as speculators began to attack what had become a vulnerable and over-valued currency, forcing the Bank of Thailand (BOT) to expend billions of dollars in foreign reserves defending its pegged value of 25 baht to a basket of currencies dominated by the United States dollar.

With foreign reserves nearly depleted at US$ 800 million, the Government of Thailand decided on July 2, 1997 to float the value of the baht. Thailand's currency immediately depreciated, which in turn opened up a Pandora's Box of other problems, including triggering a regional currency crisis. The baht began a downward spiral, made worse by the eventual depreciation of other currencies in the region, and hit an all-time low of 56.2 to the United States dollar in January 1998.

The heavily indebted private sector could no longer afford to repay short-term debt to foreign institutions and domestic lending institutions, thereby setting off a financial and banking crisis in Thailand. The early stages of the crisis exposed the irregular practices of Thailand's financial and banking institutions and the inadequate regulatory framework and supervision by the Government. The end result was the closure of 56 finance firms by the end of 1997 and the nationalization of 6 commercial banks in 1998.

Other sectors of the economy, such as manufacturing and agriculture, also faced severe setbacks as they were confronted with falling world prices, fierce export competition from other crisis-struck countries, low domestic demand, tight liquidity, and high interest rates.

There were various causes of the crisis, and all of them were complex and highly interrelated, but at the core of Thailand's problems was the one factor that led to the country's exceptional growth: financial liberalization. When Thailand liberalized its financial structure in the 1980s, huge sums of foreign capital flowed into the country, but the eventual problem was that this capital inflow was unchecked and poorly managed, both on the part of the public and private sectors. The more specific causes of the crisis can be categorized as excessive investment in high-risk sectors; over-borrowing and over-lending; an unsound financial sector, including the regulatory framework; higher wages without a corresponding climb in the value chain, and a rigid pegged exchange rate of the Thai baht.

The Government of Thailand recognized the challenge of regaining macroeconomic stability in mid-1997, and so it reached an agreement for a US$ 17.2 billion assistance package with the International Monetary Fund (IMF) on August 20 of that year. Thailand's policy makers committed to a set of comprehensive measures to rehabilitate and restructure the economy. The reform package was prepared with assistance from the IMF, the World Bank, and the Asian Development Bank.

The Government of Thailand willingly accepted the conditions of the IMF assistance package, including the economic and political reforms required under the loan. The original terms of the deal in August 1997 called for the Government to reduce its current account deficit, raise taxes, reduce government spending to produce a budget surplus of 1 per cent of GDP in 1998, privatize selected state enterprises, and reform various components of the economic and political sectors.

The comprehensive rehabilitation plan encompassed five main areas: financial sector reform; monetary and fiscal policies; bureaucratic reforms and privatization; industrial and agriculture restructuring; and social and environmental agendas.

While Thailand has not fully emerged from the economic crisis and its causes, the reform process is clearly paying dividends. Exports and foreign investment are rising, the growth rate appears to have achieved the forecasted 4.5 per cent for 2000, and the non-performing loans are gradually falling. Clearly Thailand's continued recovery is a function of the health of the regional and global economies, but there is also widespread recognition that Thailand needs to get its house in order to achieve sustainable development.

6. Government

Thailand is a constitutional monarchy with a parliamentary system of government. In December 1932, King Prajadhipok signed Thailand's first constitution and thus ended 800 years of Thailand's absolute monarchy. Despite the number of successive constitutions that followed in the span of just over half a century, the basic concepts of constitutional government and monarchy laid down in the original 1932 constitution have remained unaltered. The king, currently King Bhumibol Adulyadej, is the Head of State, and the Prime Minister is the Head of Government. The king's role is not to handle day to day administration, but rather serve the people in other capacities, including signing bills into law and being the head patron of Buddhism.

From the 1930s until as recently as 1991, Thailand has experienced numerous coups d'état. The military controlled the Government for much of the twentieth century, and were last in power in 1992. However, democratic regimes frequently alternated with military-controlled Governments.

The 1997 Constitution, Thailand's sixteenth since 1932, made modifications to the political system, but most noteworthy are its more democratic aspects and making Government more transparent and accountable to the people. Thailand still retains a bicameral legislature, known as the National Assembly, which consists of the House of Representatives and the Senate. Unlike previous constitutions, the 1997 Constitution requires that the Senate be directly elected by the people. The Cabinet is the executive branch of the Government, led by the Prime Minister, who is formally appointed by the King upon nomination by the House of Representatives.

The most recent elections occurred in 2000 for the Senate and January 2001 for the House of Representatives.

The new constitution and subsequent legislation have also revamped the judicial system, making it more independent and less influenced by politics.

Thailand has 14 ministries, including the Office of the Prime Minister. The 76 provinces are subdivided into several levels that have corresponding governmental authorities.

7. Resources

Thailand is fortunate to have bountiful resources, both in terms of natural resources and human resources. Spanning over 513,000 square kilometres, 40 per cent of Thailand is devoted to farmland. Many parts of the country have excellent soil for agriculture, and the climate allows a variety of crops to be grown. The most fertile soils are found in the central region, which serves as the "rice bowl" of the country. Like most industrializing countries, forest coverage is declining in Thailand. However, approximately 23 per cent of the country is still covered by forests, and several pieces of environmental legislation passed in the early 1990s aim at maintaining a proper percentage of forest-covered land.

The southern region contains rich deposits of minerals and ore. Over 30 different minerals lie beneath the soil, including tin, gypsum, lignite, and fluorite. Minerals often rank in the top five foreign exchange earners for Thailand, yet there is enormous potential for more growth. Only 0.3 per cent of Thailand's total land area has been assigned for mineral concessions, meaning that there are likely plenty of untapped sources. Gems are also plentiful in Thailand and have enabled a domestic jewellery industry to flourish.

Thailand has only recently begun to tap its carbon-based resources, particularly natural gas in the Gulf of Thailand. Over 8,463 billion cubic feet of natural gas are estimated to lie beneath the Gulf, along with hundreds of millions of barrels worth of crude oil. Despite a growing domestic petroleum industry, Thailand imports approximately 75 per cent of its petroleum products. The Government aims to reduce the country's foreign dependence on energy imports to less than 50 per cent in the next few years.

Thailand is fortunate to have extensive maritime resources to provide a well-balanced natural resource base. The oceans surrounding Thailand contain vast stocks of aquatic life. As a result, the Thai fishing industry is one of the world's leading producers and exporters of shrimp, tuna, squid, and other seafood.

Human resources are equally impressive with a labour force of approximately 33 million. Thailand's literacy rate of 93 per cent is one of the highest in the region. Its well-educated population possesses the capacity to engage in sophisticated industries and can adapt quickly to the latest technology. Enrolment in education in the kingdom is nearly universal, and the secondary level and higher education systems are continually expanding. The 1999 National Education Bill ensures the rights of all citizens to receive free basic education from the State for at least 12 years.

B. Macroeconomic business climate

1. Gross domestic product and other macro-indicators

Thailand's economy expanded continuously during the 1980s up until 1997, when the economy contracted -1.7 per cent. Table 18 displays the GDP growth rates for the 1990s and projections for 2000. The first full year of the crisis, 1998, led to an even greater downturn of -10.2 per cent.

From 1987 until 1996 the manufacturing sector increased its contribution to GDP between 7 and 18 per cent per year, while services grew annually at a rate of 6 to 13 per cent. The economic growth in the 1980s and 1990s was fuelled by the expansion of Thailand's manufacturing and services.

Before the crisis, construction achieved some of the highest sector growth rates, such as 22 per cent in 1990, but its overall percentage of GDP remained much smaller than manufacturing and services. Agriculture performed erratically over the same period with contractions or no growth in 1987, 1990, and 1993, but interspersed among growth of 3-10 per cent in other years. Table 19 shows the performance of the major sectors of the economy from 1990 to 1999.

Table 18. Thailand's GDP growth, 1990-2000

Year	GDP (% change)
1990	11.2
1991	8.6
1992	8.1
1993	8.5
1994	8.9
1995	8.8
1996	5.5
1997	-1.7
1998	-10.2
1999p	4.2
2000p	4.5-5.0

Sources: Bank of Thailand and National Economic and Social Development Board
Note: p indicates projection

Table 19. Growth of real GDP by sector, 1990-1999
(percentage)

Sector	1990	1991	1992	1993	1994	1995	1996	1997	1998p	1999p*
Agriculture	-4.6	6.5	6	-1.9	5.5	3	3	-0.13	-0.43	-1.9
Industry	15.7	11.7	11.3	11.1	9.3	11	10	2.96	-9.73	17
Construction	22	13.6	4.7	9.5	13.8	10.7	8.2	-22.2	-37.7	10.3
Trade, services, other	12.7	6.6	7.3	9.1	8.6	8.2	7.5	-1.13	-8.08	3

Source: National Economic and Social Development Board
Notes: p indicates projection
* comparison between 1998 Q3 and 1999 Q3

Manufacturing accounted for only 16 per cent of GDP in 1970, but by 1998 it comprised approximately 36 per cent of GDP (see figure 23). Agriculture, the dominant sector in terms of employment, has seen a gradual decline in its contribution to GDP. In 1998, agriculture made up 12 per cent of GDP. Services are currently the dominant sector in terms of percentage of GDP, totaling over 48 per cent.

Despite the sharp drop in the value of the baht since the outbreak of the crisis, inflation has remained manageable. Over the past five years, only in 1998 did inflation rise above 6 per cent. Figure 24 shows the annual inflation rate change.

Figure 23. Percentage of GDP by sector, 1998

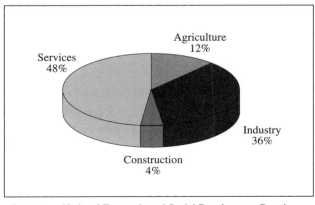

Source: National Economic and Social Development Board

121

Figure 24. Annual inflation rate change
(percentage)

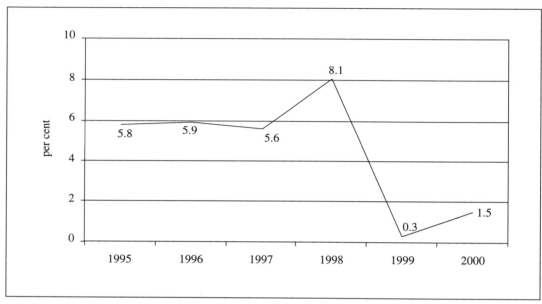

Source: Bank of Thailand

2. Main economic sectors

Diversification is a continuous theme for Thailand's economy. Extensive structural changes have occurred in the economy between the 1960s and 1990s, as seen in the progressive development from a predominantly agricultural economy in the 1960s, to simple manufacturing in the 1970s and 1980s, to the current movement towards more sophisticated industries, such as petrochemicals, high-tech electronics, and computer components. These newer high tech industries are also spurring the growth of numerous support industries and services.

(a)   *Agriculture and fishing*

Formerly the mainstay of the Thai economy, agriculture remains one of the key sectors in the economy in terms of employment and its contributions to GDP. Agriculture employs over 45 per cent of the Thai workforce and generates 12 per cent of the national income. Thailand is one of the world's top five overall food producers and is the number one rice exporter. Thailand is among the world's leading producers in several other categories as well, such as seafood production, tapioca, chicken exports, and rubber.

Thailand's top five agricultural products are rice, rubber, sugar cane, cassava, and maize (see table 20). Rice is the principal crop, and paddy production utilizes nearly half of the cultivated land in Thailand. Other major agriculture commodities include shrimp, coconut, and soybeans. Thailand's agriculture sector is expected to remain an important contributor to GDP due to an expanding range of value added activities in the processing of frozen seafood, poultry, fruits, and vegetables.

(b)   *Manufacturing and industry*

Up until the 1960s, Thailand's manufacturing sector was closely related to the agricultural industry, centred on rice and sugar mills, tobacco plants, and other food processing activities. However, the roles have been reversed, as agriculture now constitutes 25 per cent of the activities in the manufacturing sector. Thailand's manufacturing and industrial sector averaged 10-11 per cent annual growth throughout the late 1980s-mid-1990s and has bloomed into a diverse and productive sector that makes up the largest percentage of Thailand's exports. It also employs approximately 20 per cent of the labour force.

Table 20. Thailand's leading crop production, 1990-1998
(thousands of metric tons)

Crop	1990	1991	1992	1993	1994	1995	1996	1997	1998
Paddy[1]	17,026	19,809	20,184	19,098	20,125.5	20,678.6	22,069	23,088.8	22,999
Rubber[2]	1,250.0	1,340.0	1,500.0	1,553.0	1,737.0	1,810.0	1,937.0	2,032.7	2,100.0
Maize	3,800.0	3,600.0	3,400.0	3,300.0	3,900.0	4,060.0	3,970.0	3,831.6	4,986.4
Tapioca roots	19,705.0	20,356.0	20,203.0	19,091.0	15,374.0	17,387.8	18,087.9	15,590.6	16,506.6
Sugar cane	40,563.0	47,430.0	34,711.7	37,568.6	50,458.9	57,693.4	56,190.0	42,270.0	52,839.1
Mungbean	303.0	304.0	261.0	231.0	255.5	234.0	237.9	199.9	233.1
Groundnuts	161.0	157.0	137.0	136.0	150.3	147.0	151.6	126.5	146.4
Soybeans	500.0	436.0	435.0	513.0	527.6	386.0	352.3	337.8	334.9
Sesame	29.2	32.0	31.5	32.8	31.8	33.5	34.3	34.7	36.0
Coconut[3]	1,426.0	1,379.0	1,411.0	1,462.0	1,476.0	1,412.6	1,410.0	1,419.0	1,372.0
Castor beans	23.0	28.0	12.0	10.0	7.0	5.7	5.6	6.0	7.1
Cotton	97.0	129.0	99.0	67.0	77.9	80.7	75.1	51.4	42.6
Jute and Kenaf	191.0	139.1	151.0	144.0	126.8	79.0	109.3	96.6	51.4
Tobacco leaves	66.8	85.4	93.6	50.8	48.8	59.8	72.4	74.3	79.3

Source: Office of Agricultural Economics, Ministry of Agricultural and Co-operatives
Notes: p = preliminary
[1] Paddy production in year t includes the first crop in year t/t+1 and the second crop in year t
[2] Rubber Research Institute, Ministry of Agriculture and Co-operatives
[3] Production converted at 1.25 kg per nut

Thailand's manufacturing base centred mainly on textiles, plastics, and footwear early in the drive towards industrialization, but now the sector consists of numerous business activities utilizing higher technology and value added products. Several industries that began in the 1980s, such as electronics, computers and components, integrated circuits, automobiles and parts, are now major industrial activities.

Textiles, cement, and electronics are still major products, but Thailand is rapidly becoming one of the world's largest manufacturers of automobiles and trucks. At present, Thailand is the second leading manufacturer of pick-up trucks. Several of the big auto companies have established factories in Thailand's Eastern Seaboard, including Ford, GM, Honda, Mazda, and Toyota. Heavy industries, including steel and petrochemicals, are also increasing their contributions to the economy. A burgeoning petrochemical industry is developing alongside the oil refining activities, and both upstream and downstream activities are being undertaken.

(c)   *Services*

As Thailand's economy became more focused on manufacturing, there was a corresponding increase in the services necessary to support a modern industrial economy. In 1998, services comprised over 48 per cent of GDP and employed over 4.1 million people. Among the expanding services available to businesses, both local and foreign, are consulting firms, corporate legal offices, convention and exhibition halls, and transportation companies.

Thailand's famed tourism industry is one of the leading sources of income. Over 7.76 million tourists arrived in 1998 to enjoy Thailand's world-renowned beaches and cultural attractions, bringing in nearly US$ 8 billion. Several complementary service industries sprung up to support the tourism sector, such as hotels, restaurants, handicrafts, and travel agencies, all of which contribute to one of the most reputable travel service industries in the world.

3. International trade

(a)   *Overview*

Dating back to the 1400s, Thailand has been actively involved in the international economy. In recent times, Thailand's Governments since the 1970s made a conscious decision to tie into the global economy by adopting an export-led growth strategy. Thailand's expanding overseas market shares during the past few decades and its own liberal domestic market have fully integrated Thailand into the regional and global economies.

Fuelled by rising incomes in the 1980s, Thailand's imports outpaced exports and led to increasingly larger trade deficits. However, since the economic crisis the demand for imports has declined and Thailand now enjoys a trade surplus. In 1998 Thailand had a positive balance of trade of US$ 12.1 billion. Exports for that year topped US$ 54.5 billion and imports stood at US$ 42.4 billion.

The pattern of exports has shifted greatly between 1980 and the late 1990s. In 1980 agricultural products accounted for nearly 47 per cent of Thailand's exports, with manufacturing taking up only a 32 per cent share. Currently, manufactured goods comprise 82 per cent of Thailand's exports and agriculture has seen its share of exports drop to 11 per cent. The United States and Japan rank as Thailand's top export markets, while in the region Singapore, Hong Kong, China, Malaysia, and Taiwan Province of China are the major destinations for Thai goods.

Other important export markets include Germany, the United Kingdom, and the Netherlands. As for imports, Japan, the United States, Singapore, and Germany are the leading sources of goods brought into Thailand.

Figure 25 indicates the pace at which Thailand's trade with the rest of the world has expanded, with two exceptions. Thailand has registered a trade deficit every year since 1987; however, the bulk of its imports have been used in productive investment.

**Figure 25. Thailand's trade with the world
(millions of baht)**

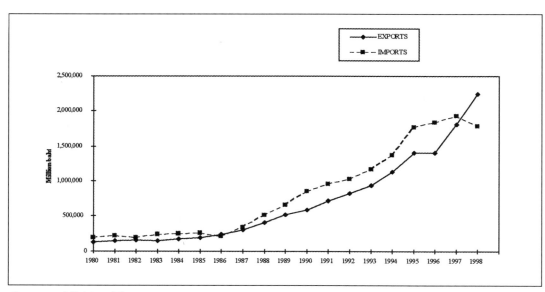

Source: Ministry of Commerce

(b) *Exports*

Thailand has been extremely successful in expanding its exports, with growth rates between 14 per cent and 28 per cent per year from 1990 until 1998. Compared to the structure of exports in the 1970s or even the 1980s, the structure of Thailand's exports in the 1990s has clearly diversified into a wide variety of products. Table 21 shows the breakdown of exports by sector.

Exports continued to be the main factor preventing the Thai economy from contracting. In 1998, export volume grew by 8.1 per cent during the first half of the year. Exports which showed substantial volume increases were manufacturing exports using high technology, including electronics and automobile products, and

Table 21. Breakdown of exports by sector, 1990-1998

Sector	1990	1992	1994	1995	1996	1997	1998	1999 (Jan.-Oct.)
Manufactured products	74.7	77.0	81.1	81.9	81.5	82.4	82.3	84.5
Agricultural products	16.9	15.0	11.4	11.4	11.8	10.2	9.4	8.3
Fishery products	5.5	5.9	6.0	5.1	4.5	4.0	4.0	3.6
Others	2.9	2.1	1.5	1.7	2.1	3.4	4.3	3.8
Total exports (value in billions of baht)	**590**	**825**	**1,138**	**1,406**	**1,412**	**1,807**	**2,248**	**1,795**

Source: Bank of Thailand

agricultural exports, such as rice and canned fish. Nevertheless, total export value decreased by 6.8 per cent, resulting from the slowdown of the world economy and financial crises in Asian countries. The value decline was caused mainly by the 13.8 per cent reduction in export prices following intense price competition among Thailand's major competitors, whose currencies also depreciated substantially, while the export volume increased at a lower rate than in the previous year.

Looking at Thailand's major export markets, the North American Free Trade Area (NAFTA) countries, especially the United States, are the largest export market with the export share rising from 21 per cent in 1997 to 24 per cent in 1998 (see table 22). This is partly due to the baht's depreciation and Thailand's ability to retain market share. The second largest market is the European Union (EU) with the export share rising to 17.8 per cent. Japan remains Thailand's largest single market. Meanwhile, the export value to the Asian and Pacific region (comprising ASEAN, GMS, China, Taiwan Province of China, Hong Kong, China, and the Republic of Korea) declined by 18.6 per cent.

Table 22. Thailand's major export markets by geographic region
(billions of baht)

Region	Value in 1996	Value in 1997	Value in 1998	Growth 1997	Growth 1998	Share in 1997	Share in 1998
NAFTA	270.7	379.1	537.4	40%	42%	21%	24%
EU	224.9	290.4	401.4	29%	38%	16%	18%
ASEAN[1]	296.3	380.8	396.7	29%	4%	21%	18%
Japan	237.5	270.8	308.5	14%	14%	15%	14%
NIEs[2]	143.8	187.7	212.3	31%	13%	10%	9%
Middle East	54.7	62.3	77.5	14%	25%	3%	3%
China	47.4	55.5	72.9	17%	31%	3%	3%
GMS[3]	41.1	51.0	66.2	24%	30%	3%	3%
Former Soviet Union	5.4	4.9	3.6	-9%	-27%	1%	1%
Eastern Europe	12.3	14.6	13.0	18%	-11%	1%	1%
Others	76.9	156.2	159.3	103%	2%	8%	7%
Total	1,411.0	1,806.7	2,248.8	28%	25%	100%	100%

Source: Bank of Thailand
Notes: [1] includes Myanmar, Viet Nam, and Lao People's Democratic Republic.
　　　　[2] includes Taiwan Province of China, Hong Kong, China, and the Republic of Korea.
　　　　[3] Myanmar, Viet Nam, Lao People's Democratic Republic, and Cambodia, excluding Yunnan. Figures may not sum due to rounding.

(c) *Imports*

Generally, imports are examined by looking at the economic purpose and the major import products. In terms of purpose of imported goods, it is clear that more than three-quarters of Thai imports are capital goods, intermediate products, and raw materials. These types of goods and materials are used in expanding industrial capacity and supply inputs into many of Thailand's export industries. Table 23 organizes imports according to economic classification, with growth rates for 1996 to 1998.

Table 23. Thailand's imports by economic classification
(billions of baht)

Economic classification	1996	1997	1998	Increase 1997 (percentage)	Increase 1998 (percentage)
Capital Goods	832.2	925.8	886.5	11	-4
Machinery and parts	459.2	474.1	411.4	3	-13
Metal manufactures	54.4	62.5	85.8	15	37
Fertilisers and pesticides	22.6	22.0	23.2	-3	5
Scientific and optical instruments	47.9	51.6	46.8	8	-9
Construction materials	0.6	0.4	0.3	-32	-35
Other	247.5	315.2	319.0	27	1
Intermediate products and raw materials	530.1	552.5	535.8	4	-3
Chiefly for consumer goods	334.6	349.3	370.2	4	6
Chiefly for capital goods	195.5	203.2	165.6	4	-19
Consumer Goods	151.1	160.7	154.5	6	-4
Non-durable goods	51.8	58.6	56.0	13	-3
Durable goods	99.3	102.1	98.5	3	-4
Fuels and lubricants	160.6	178.3	142.1	11	-20
Vehicles and parts	123.3	67.3	18.9	-45	-72
Other imports	35.6	39.6	36.2	11	-9
Total	1,832.8	1,924.3	1,774.1	5	-8

Source: Bank of Thailand
Note: Figures may not sum due to rounding.

The value of imports in 1998 was 1,774.1 billion baht, an 8 per cent decline from the previous year when the financial crisis hit Thailand. Nearly one quarter of Thai imports originated in Japan (see table 24). This reflects Japan's high level of investment in Thailand. The NAFTA, the ASEAN, and EU member countries are other major source countries.

Table 24. Thailand's major import suppliers by geographic region
(billions of baht)

Region	Value 1996	Value 1997	Value 1998	Growth 1997	Growth 1998	Share 1997	Share 1998
Japan	518.1	492.1	420.3	-5%	-15%	25%	24%
NAFTA	246.7	286.3	265.7	16%	-7%	15%	15%
ASEAN[1]	243.3	245.4	265.6	1%	8%	13%	15%
EU	276.1	268.5	221.8	-3%	-17%	14%	12%
Others	548.6	632.0	600.7	15%	-5%	33%	34%
Total	**1,832.8**	**1,924.3**	**1,774.1**	**5%**	**-8%**	**100%**	**100%**

Source: Bank of Thailand
Notes: [1] includes Myanmar, Viet Nam, and the Lao People's Democratic Republic. Figures may not sum due to rounding.

(d) *Thailand's trade figures by selected regions and countries*

This section contains a series of charts demonstrating Thailand's trade figures over the past few years with selected regions and countries. The charts show Thailand's imports and exports with the United States, Japan, ASEAN, the EU, China, and the GMS.

Figure 26. Trade between Thailand and the United States
(millions of baht)

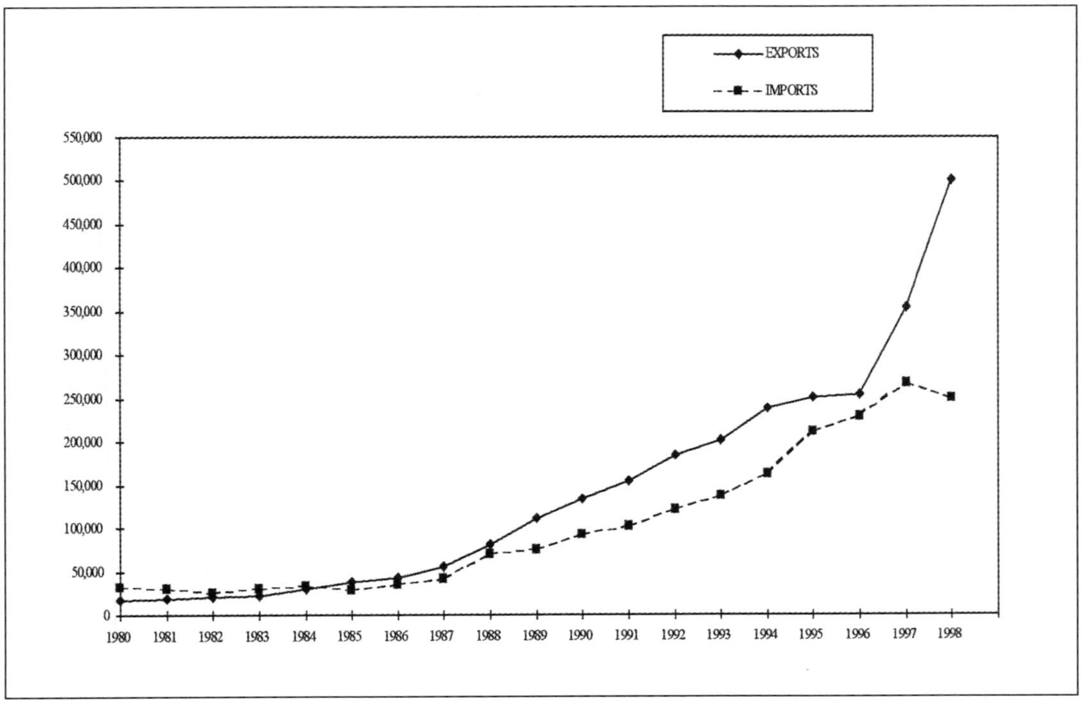

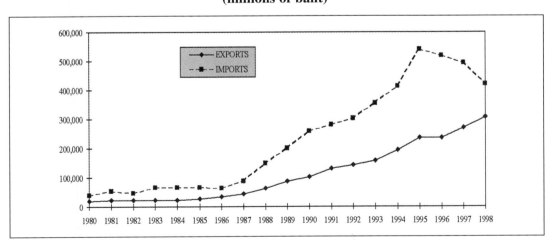

Source: Ministry of Commerce

Figure 27. Trade between Thailand and Japan
(millions of baht)

Source: Ministry of Commerce

Figure 28. Trade between Thailand and ASEAN
(millions of baht)

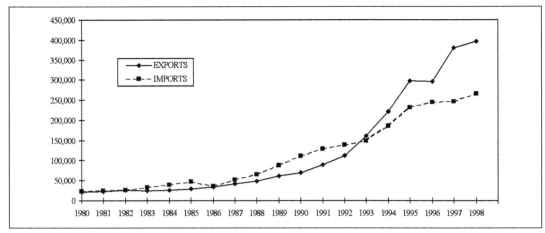

Source: Ministry of Commerce

Figure 29. Trade between Thailand and the European Union
(millions of baht)

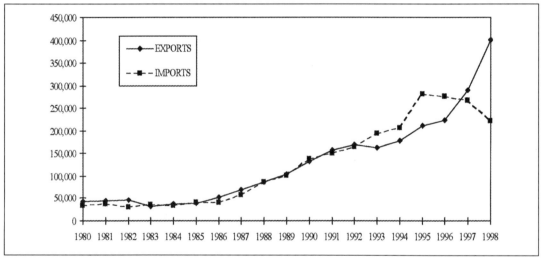

Source: Ministry of Commerce

Figure 30. Trade between Thailand and China
(millions of baht)

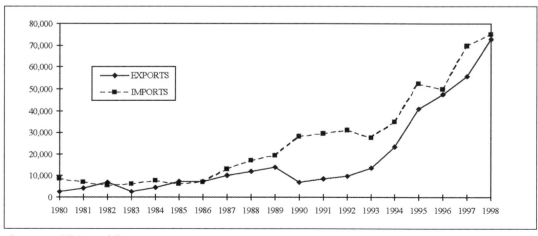

Source: Ministry of Commerce

Figure 31. Trade between Thailand and the GMS
(millions of baht)

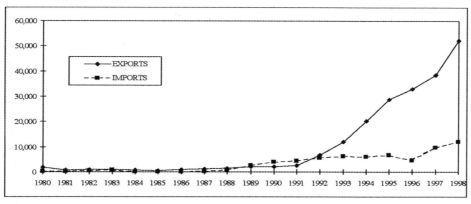

Source: Ministry of Commerce

Thailand's major exports to the GMS countries include basic industrial goods and raw materials, and agro-processing products (see table 25). Meanwhile, Thailand imports light consumer goods, raw materials, and agricultural commodities from those countries.

Table 25. Thailand's leading exports and imports with the GMS
(millions of baht)

Exports to GMS	Value in 1997	Value in 1998	Imports from GMS	Value in 1997	Value in 1998
Motor vehicles and parts	5,375.8	10,051.7	Electrical machines and parts	4,160.4	7,306.5
Polymers in primary forms	2,125.4	3,402.0	Wood	2,981.9	1,978.8
Refine fuels	3,570.0	3,312.6	Wooden products	346.4	261.9
Chemical products	2,283.3	3,272.6	Raw hide and leather	205.3	254.6
Iron or steel products	2,007.8	2,860.6	Jewellery including silver bars and gold	114.6	224.6
Cement	1,725.3	2,183.6	Metal manufactures	14.6	193.8
Machinery and parts	1,243.6	1,923.7	Shrimps and prawns	118.3	183.3
Woven fabrics	1,453.0	1,814.3	Fish and crustaceans	148.7	171.7
Rubber products	1,283.5	1,751.4	Crude oil	253.0	166.0
Beverages	1,215.7	1,086.5	Textile fibres	61.0	146.2

Source: Ministry of Commerce

4. Investment

(a)   *Foreign investment in Thailand*

For many years now Thailand has capitalized on the large amounts of foreign direct investment (FDI) that have flowed across borders throughout the world. The combination of its favorable investment climate, resources, and labour force has attracted foreign investors from all over the world. Net foreign direct investment soared in 1988, when it multiplied three-fold over the previous year, and then doubled in 1990 to US$ 2.5 billion. FDI in Thailand continues to grow despite the economic crisis. For 1998, Thailand's net FDI amounted to US$ 5 billion (US$ 6.9 billion if the financial institutions are included) compared to US$ 3.7 billion in 1997. In 1999, net FDI slowed a little to US$ 3.6 billion (see figure 32).

Figure 32. Net foreign direct investment
(millions of US dollars)

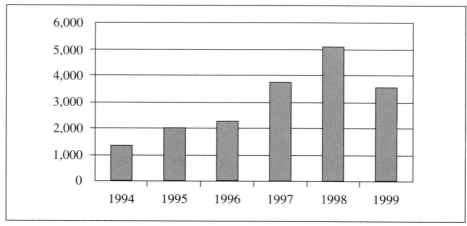

Source: Bank of Thailand
Note: Figure for 1999 is preliminary

The main sources of FDI are Japan, the United States, Singapore, and Hong Kong, China, which accounted for approximately 70 per cent of Thailand's total FDI in 1998 (see table 26). In recent years the sectors attracting the most foreign investment are chemicals and paper, minerals and ceramics, electronics, trade and services, automobiles, agro-industries, and machinery (see table 27). The large-scale manufacturing projects are stimulating investment in various support industries, such as parts and component manufacturers for the auto industry and electronics.

Table 26. Net flows of foreign direct investment in Thailand, by major countries/areas, 1990-1999
(millions of US dollars)

Country	1990	1991	1992	1993	1994	1995	1996	1997	1998	1999 (Jan.-Oct.)
Japan	1,117	624	343	305	123	556	523	1,351	1,528	778
United States	246	237	472	286	155	260	429	824	913	749
United Kingdom	45	10	129	161	44	55	57	118	134	230
Hong Kong, China	281	463	582	193	318	279	215	472	460	420
Singapore	245	259	269	61	184	136	275	314	530	1,151

Sources: Bank of Thailand and Board of Investment

Table 27. Foreign direct investment by sector, 1998-1999

Sector	1998		1999 (Jan.-Oct.)	
	US$ million	% share	US$ million	% share
Financial institutions	2,618	37.5	2,165	45
Trade	849	12	868	18
Construction	146	2	-125	-2.6
Mining and quarrying	64	1	-51	-1.1
Agriculture	0	0	2	0
Industry	2,054	29	1,275	26.5
Services	295	4	452	9.4
Investment	314	5	n.a.	n.a.
Real estate	493	7	88	1.8
Other businesses	135	2	134	2.8

Source: Bank of Thailand

(b) *Thailand's outward investment flows*

Prior to 1993, Thai outward flows were lower than US$ 200 million. Thailand's outward investment began to surge from that time and reached a peak in 1996. Even in 1996, the outward flows started to increase slightly. In 1997, Thai outward investment dropped suddenly, primarily due to the drastic slowdown in economic activity and liquidity problems faced by the private sector (see figure 33).

Figure 33. Thailand's outward investment flows, 1988-1997
(millions of US dollars)

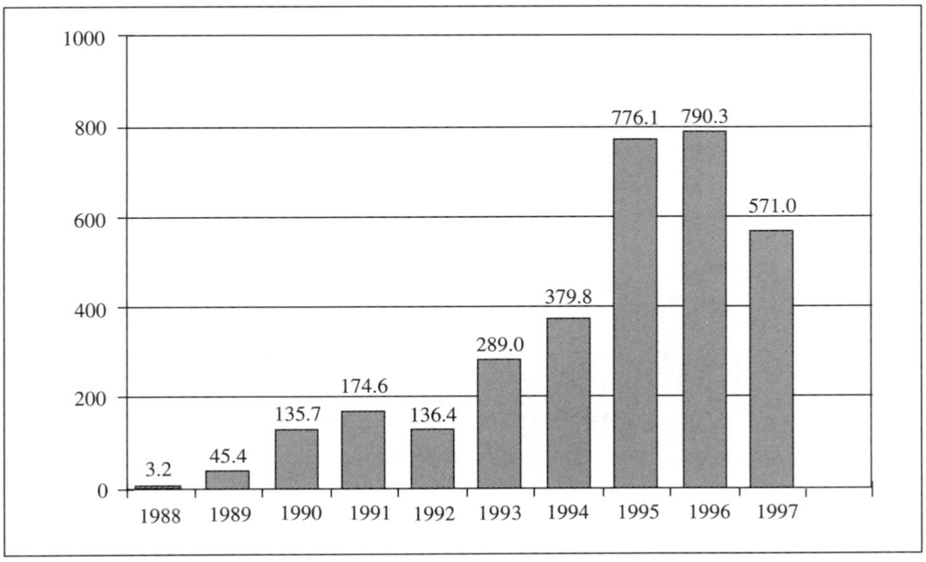

Source: Bank of Thailand

Major destinations for outward investment include the ASEAN countries, the GMS, and China. These investments were channelled mostly into the manufacturing industry and services sector (see table 28).

Table 28. Thailand's outward investment by sector, 1990-1997
(millions of US dollars)

Sector	1990	1991	1992	1993	1994	1995	1996	1997
Trade	2.7	9.7	13.8	10.1	23.7	27.9	26.1	92.4
Manufacturing	119.9	66.5	49.4	90.3	138.9	190.3	304.3	185.9
Financial Institutions	9.9	23.7	17.2	14.0	30.3	34.5	27.3	19.0
Services	0.8	28.1	12.9	87.1	85.6	294.3	232.8	118.3
Other	2.4	46.6	43.1	87.5	101.4	229.1	199.8	155.4

Source: Bank of Thailand

(c) *Thailand's investment figures with selected regions and countries*

This section contains a series of charts showing Thailand's investment figures with selected regions and countries. Like in the section on trade, the charts cover Thailand's investment with the United States, Japan, ASEAN, the EU, China, and the GMS.

The United States receives the large portion of overseas Thai investment funds. Thai business people have invested over 100 million US$ in the United States in 1997. This is equivalent to approximately 18 per cent of total Thai overseas direct investments.

Figure 34. BOI-approved American investment in Thailand, projects and investment value, 1993-1998 (millions of baht)

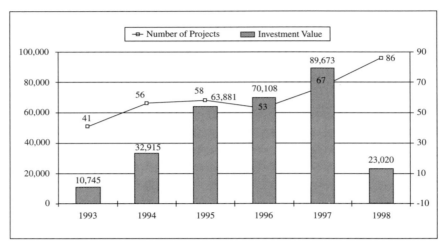

Source: Board of Investment

Figure 35. Thailand's investment in the United States (millions of US dollars)

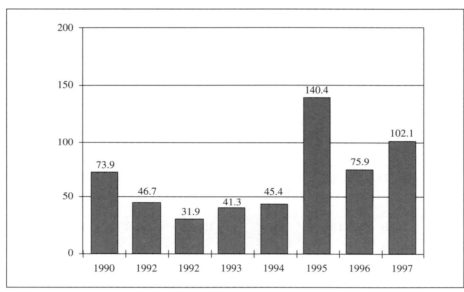

Source: Bank of Thailand

Thailand had been an active investor in the neighbouring countries of the GMS. As figure 41 indicates, significant outflows began only after 1992, with total outward flows roughly doubling in 1995, and again in 1996. Nevertheless, the economic downturn has virtually stopped Thai overseas investment, including in the GMS countries.

Lao People's Democratic Republic: From January 1988 to early 1998, Lao officials reported that 36 countries had invested nearly US$ 7 billion in the country, with Thailand ranked first (38 per cent of total investment, US$ 2,657 million). Thai business people are investing in the hotel and tourism industries, processing industry and handicrafts, banking and insurance, and telecommunication and transportation.

**Figure 36. BOI-approved Japanese investment in Thailand, projects
and investment value, 1993-1998
(millions of baht)**

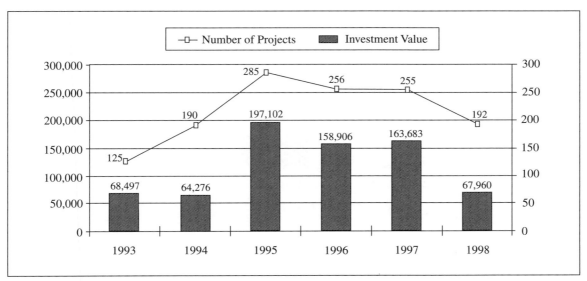

Source: Board of Investment

**Figure 37. Foreign direct investment from ASEAN countries, 1990-1998
(millions of baht)**

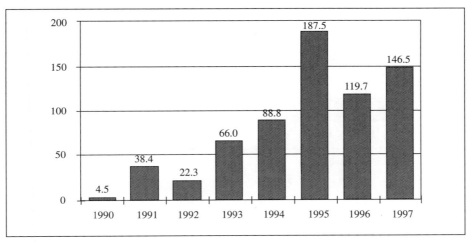

Source: Board of Investment

Myanmar: As of December 1997, Thailand ranked third in terms of the amount of capital investment in Myanmar (US$ 1,165 million). Thai investors have put money into hotels, fishery products, transportation, and agriculture in addition to industry projects.

Cambodia: In 1997, Thailand had a capital investment in Cambodia of US$ 21 million. The main industries attracting Thai investment include wood production, restaurants and hotels and tourism.

Viet Nam: In 1997, Thai companies had invested approximately US$ 53 million in Viet Nam. The main areas of Thai investment include agro-businesses such as agricultural production, feed production, as well as industrial production of ready-to-wear clothes, jewellery, mining, and the hotel and tourism services industries.

133

**Figure 38. Thailand's investment in ASEAN countries
(millions of US dollars)**

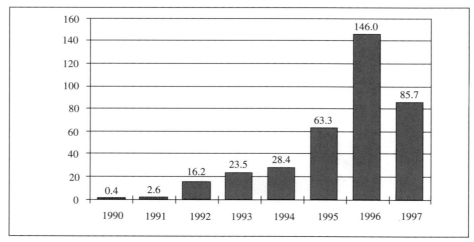

Source: Bank of Thailand

**Figure 39. Investment flows between Thailand and the EU, 1990-1997
(millions of US dollars)**

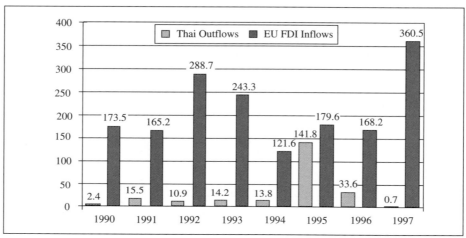

Source: Bank of Thailand

**Figure 40. Thailand's investment in China
(millions of US dollars)**

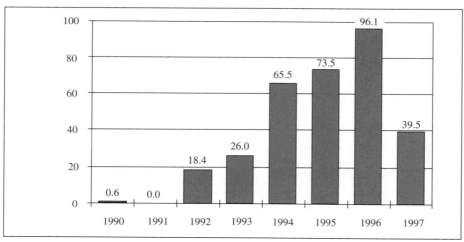

Source: Bank of Thailand

Figure 41. Thailand's outward investment in GMS
(millions of US dollars)

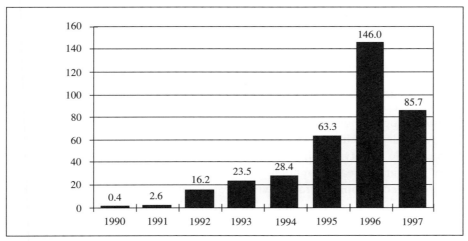

Source: Bank of Thailand

5. Currency

One of the harshest impacts of the economic crisis has been the sharp drop in the value of the Thai the baht. After remaining pegged to the United States dollar for a number of years at 25 baht to US$ 1, pressure on the baht led to the government implementing a managed float of the currency, which precipitated a huge depreciation of the baht. The baht bottomed out in early 1998 at around 56 baht to US$ 1 before gradually recovering. Figure 42 shows the exchange rate for the baht for selected months between January 1999 and December 2000.

Figure 42. Exchange rate (number of baht per US$ 1)

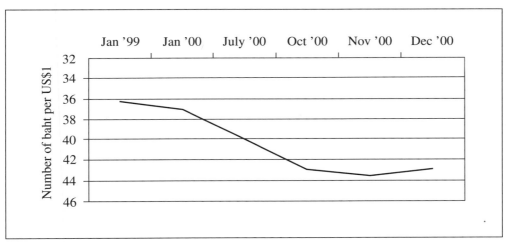

Source: Bank of Thailand

6. National economic policies and priorities

In 1959 the Government of Thailand established the National Economic Development Board (NEDB), but its name was changed to the National Economic and Social Development Board (NESDB) in 1972 to emphasize the significant role of social development in the country's development process. NESDB is the central planning agency, responsible for drawing up the National Development Plans, along with undertaking continuous studies on the social and economic situation of the country.

To date, NESDB has formulated eight Development Plans, with the Eighth Plan (1997-2001) in its final year.

In March 1996, the Cabinet approved the final draft of the Eighth Plan which is more directly focused on increasing the potential of human resources across the board to improve conditions and alternatives, increasing participation in the sustainable development of the country, strengthening economic capability and efficiency, and identifying guidelines for improving the State's administrative management.

The key objectives laid out in the Eighth Plan were the following:

- Increase the people's potential in terms of physical well-being, intellect, health, vocational skills, and ability to adapt to changes in the economy, society, and political administration.
- Develop a stable society, strengthen family and community, support human development, increase quality of life, and increase community participation in national development.
- Achieve balanced economic growth with greater stability and open up opportunities for people to participate in fostering and receiving a fair share of the benefits of growth.
- Utilize, preserve, and rehabilitate the natural resources and environment so that they can advance economic and social development and quality of life.
- Reform the administrative system in order to increase the opportunity for non-governmental organizations, the private sector, community, and individuals to participate in national development.

Due to the changing economy and current needs of the country since the economic crisis in 1997, it was required to revise the Eighth National Plan. On September 9, 1997, the Cabinet approved a proposal submitted by the NESDB, recommending a revision of the Eighth Plan according to the following guidelines:

- Maintain the Eighth Plan's objective to develop human resource to full potential in order to achieve sustainable development.
- Revise macroeconomic target, taking into account the current economic situation and the agreement between the Government of Thailand and the IMF.
- Revise the investment plan.
- Set up criteria to scale down and re-phase public investment projects.
- Revise the economic structural adjustment part of the Eighth Plan to accommodate the IMF agreement and the structural adjustment loans from the World Bank and the Asian Development Bank.

According to the above guidelines, the main objective to increase people's potential remains unchanged. The committee took into account the agreement between the Government and the IMF; the new Constitution; free trade and investment agreements; and economic cooperation at various levels. The revision mainly focused on (a) economic and financial stability leading to confidence in the country; (b) economic restructuring for self-sufficient production bases to be competitive in world markets; (c) ease the adverse economic and social effects of the crisis; and (d) give more importance to the poor and underprivileged groups.

C. Institutional and support network: public and private sector organizations

1. Government organizations and agencies

Board of Investment (BOI)

The BOI is the Government's investment promotion and policy agency. It grants a wide range of fiscal and non-fiscal incentives and guarantees to investment projects that meet national economic development goals. The BOI offers comprehensive business-related services to investors and potential investors ranging from assistance in obtaining required licences and permits, to the identification of promising investment projects and joint venture partners. It also provides support to both foreign and Thai businesses that are either planning to invest, or have already committed to invest in Thailand.

Contact address:
555 Vipavadee Rangsit Rd.
Bangkhen, Bangkok 10900
Tel: (662) 537-8111, 537-8155
Fax: (662) 537-8177

Ministry of Industry (MOI)

The MOI performs several duties, including:

- Issuing industrial policies, plans, and industrial development projects
- Monitoring and inspecting industrial factories nationwide
- Administering and managing the supply of key mineral resources
- Promoting productivity upgrading for existing industries
- Issuing industrial products standards and certifies product quality
- Playing a role in the development of industrial estates throughout the country

Contact address:
Rama VI Rd.
Ratchathewi, Bangkok 10400
Tel: (662) 202-3000
Fax: (662) 202-3048

Ministry of Finance (MOF)

The Ministry of Finance is responsible for managing public finances, setting fiscal policy, drafting the Government's annual budget, monitoring financial institutions and capital markets (along with the Bank of Thailand), collecting taxes, managing government revenues, monitoring state enterprises, and other activities.

Contact address:
Rama VI Rd.
Bangkok 10400
Tel: (662) 273-9021
Fax: (662) 273-9480

Department of Customs (under the Ministry of Finance)

Contact address:
Sunthornkosa Rd.
Klongtoey, Bangkok 10110
Tel: (662) 249-0431-40, 671-7294-8
Fax: (662) 249-2874

Bank of Thailand (BOT)

The Bank of Thailand is the country's central bank. It formulates monetary policy, supervises financial institutions, and manages the country's international reserves. The BOT also acts as the banker to the Government and financial institutions, and recommends economic policy to the Government.

Contact address:
273 Samsen Rd., Bangkok 10200
Tel: (662) 283-5353
Fax: (662) 280-0449, 280-0626, 280-0137

The Securities and Exchange Commission

In March 1992, the Securities and Exchange Act established a Securities and Exchange Commission (SEC) in Thailand. The SEC plays a supervisory and policy formulation role in the Thai capital market. However, it does not directly regulate the SET's operations, other than to give approval to the day-to-day operations.

Contact address:
14th-16th Diethelm Towers B
93/1 Wireless Rd.
Pathumwan, Bangkok 10330
Tel: (662) 252-3223
Fax: (662) 256-7711

Ministry of Commerce

The Ministry of Commerce performs several duties for the country in general and the private sector in particular. Among its functions and responsibilities are:

- Inspects, monitors, and provides services on trading registration, accounting, measuring, and fuel trading
- Issues regulations and promotion plans for major export and import products and identifies standards for exported products
- Promotes trading and marketing domestically and internationally
- Promotes the protection of intellectual property rights
- Collects, processes, and distributes commercial and statistical information as the central information base on commercial activity for public and private agencies
- Coordinates export promotion activities, including trade and marketing
- Promotes Thai products overseas, and collects and provides trading information services for Thai producers and exporters and foreign importers

Contact address:
Sanamchai Rd.
Bangkok 10200
Tel: (662) 225-8411-27
Fax: (662) 226-3319, 226-3318

Department of Commercial Registration (under the Ministry of Commerce)

The Department of Commercial Registration performs several functions for local and foreign firms, including:

- Providing registration services, and inspection and application services for corporate names
- Processing applications for the establishment of alien businesses, agencies of foreign corporations and offices of overseas companies
- Providing business information: record searches, certificates of registration, statistical data on commercial registrations, corporate status, and financial statements

Contact address:
Sanamchai Rd.
Bangkok 10200
Tel: (662) 222-9851, 226-1126
Fax: (662) 255-8493

Department of Export Promotion (DEP) (under the Ministry of Commerce)

DEP conducts research and planning for export development and promotion, provides trade information, promotes products made in Thailand, and assists foreign buyers who want to trade with Thai manufacturers and exporters.

Contact address:
22/77 Ratchadaphisek Rd., Lad Yao
Chatuchak, Bangkok 10900
Tel: (662) 511-5066-77, 512-0093
Fax: (662) 512-1079, 513-1917

Ministry of Foreign Affairs (MFA)

The MFA is responsible for foreign policy on issues of international diplomacy and economic relations. Its role for business entails providing information on trade and investment opportunities abroad to local companies and providing information on Thailand to foreign investors and traders. Additionally, the MFA assists Thai firms investing and trading abroad by providing information on the enforcement of international agreements and new trade regulations.

Contact address:
443 Sri Ayudhya Road
Bangkok 10400
Tel: (662) 643-5000

2. Chambers of commerce and other business associations

Thailand has numerous business associations, but the three main umbrella associations are the Federation of Thai Industries, the Thai Chamber of Commerce, and the Thai Board of Trade. Additionally, several foreign chambers of commerce operate in Thailand, as well as dozens of industry specific business associations. Contact information is provided below for many of the major private sector business associations.

Major umbrella associations:

The Federation of Thai Industries	**Thai Chamber of Commerce**	**Thai Board of Trade**
Queen Sirikit National Convention Centre Zone C, 4th Floor New Ratchadaphisek Road Klongtoey, Bangkok 10110 Tel: (662) 229-4255 Fax: (662) 229-4941-2	150 Rajbopit Road Bangkok 10200 Tel: (662) 622-1860-76 Fax: (662) 225-3372	Rajbopit Road Bangkok 10200 Tel: (662) 222-9031 223-2069

Foreign chambers of commerce established in Thailand:

American Chamber of Commerce	**Australian-Thai Chamber of Commerce**	**Belgian-Luxembourg- Thai Chamber of Commerce**
7th Floor Kian Gwan Building 1 140 Wireless Road Bangkok 10330 Tel: (66-2) 251-9266-7 251-1605 Fax: (66-2) 651-4474 651-4472 Email: amcham@samart.co.th	20th Floor Unit 202 Thai CC Tower 889 South Sathorn Road Yannawa Bangkok 10120 Tel: (66-2) 210-0217-8 Fax: (66-2) 210-0218 http://www.atcc.or.th	83-85 Soi Anuman Rajdhon Off Decho Road, Bangkok 10500 Tel: (66-2) 266-7871 266-8217-8 Fax: (66-2) 266-8097

**British Chamber
of Commerce**
B.B. Building, 18th Floor
Unit 1809-10
54 Sukhumvit 21 (Asoke Rd.)
Bangkok 10110
Tel: (66-2) 260-7288-9
Fax: (66-2) 260-7287
http://www.bccthai.com

**German-Thai Chamber
of Commerce**
4th Floor Kongboonma
Building
699 Silom Road
Bangkok 10110
Tel: (66-2) 236-2396
       235-3510-3
Fax: (66-2) 236-4711

**Netherlands-Thai Chamber
of Commerce**
3rd Floor Shinawatra Building
94 Sukhumvit Road
Bangkok 10110
Tel: (66-2) 258-4077
Fax: (66-2) 258-8017

**Thai-Chinese Chamber
of Commerce**
9th Floor Thai CC Tower
889 South Sathorn Road
Bangkok 10120
Tel: (66-2) 675-8574-84
Fax: (66-2) 212-3916

**Thai-Italian Chamber
of Commerce**
12th Floor Room
1208 Vanich Building
1126/1 New Petchburi Road
Bangkok 10400
Tel: (66-2) 253-9909
Fax: (66-2) 253-9896
Email: angelo@loxinfo.co.th
http://www.thaitch.org

**Danish Chamber
of Commerce**
19/121 Sukhumvit Suite
19 Soi 13 Sukhumvit Road
Bangkok 10110
Tel: (66-2) 651-5805
Fax: (66-2) 651-2652

**India-Thai Chamber
of Commerce**
13 Attakarnprasit Lane
South Sathorn Road
Bangkok 10120
Tel: (66-2) 287-3001-2
Fax: (66-2) 679-7720

**Singapore-Thai Chamber
of Commerce**
18th Floor Room
1812 B, B. Building
54 Sukhumvit 21
Bangkok 10110
Tel: (66-2) 260-8020-41
Ext. 1113
Fax: (66-2) 260-8018

**Thai-Finnish Chamber
of Commerce**
4th Floor Apt.
19/27, Ruen Rudee
Condominium
Sukhumvit Soi 1
Bangkok 10110
Tel: (66-2) 255-3251
Fax: (66-2) 255-3251

**Thai-Korean Chamber
of Commerce**
7th Floor
Kongboonma Building
699 Silom Road
Bangkok 10500
Tel: (66-2) 635-3329
Fax: (66-2) 237-1956

**Franco-Thai Chamber
of Commerce**
10th Floor Richmond Tower
75/20 Soi Sukhumvit 26
Klongtoey Bangkok 10110
Tel: (66-2) 261-8276-7
       260-8254
Fax: (66-2) 261-8278

**Japanese Chamber
of Commerce**
15th Floor Amarin Tower
500 Ploenchit Road
Bangkok 10330
Tel: (66-2) 256-9170-3
Fax: (66-2) 256-9621

**Thai-Canadian Chamber
of Commerce**
19th Floor CP Tower
313 Silom Road
Bangkok 10500
Tel: (66-2) 231-0891-2
Fax: (66-2) 231-0893
http://www.thai-canadian-
chamber.org

**Thai-Israel Chamber
of Commerce**
14th Floor Manorom
Building
3354/46-47 Rama IV Road
Bangkok 10110
Tel: (66-2) 672-7021
Fax: (66-2) 249-8632
       672-7021
Email: thaisrael@bkka-net.net.th

**Thai-Swedish Chamber
of Commerce**
19/121 Sukhumvit Suite
19 Soi 13 Sukhumvit Road
Bangkok 10110
Tel: (66-2) 651-2727
Fax: (66-2) 651-2652

Other business associations:

Association of Finance Companies
16th Fl., 29 Vanisa Building
Soi Chidlom
Ploenchit Rd., Pathumwan
Bangkok 10330
Tel: (66-2) 655-0240-5
Fax: (66-2) 655-0246-7
Email: asco@asco.or.th
http://www.asco.or.th

Association of Securities Companies
5th Fl.,195/6 Lake Ratchada
Office Complex 2
New Ratchadaphisek Rd.
Klongtoey, Bangkok 10110
Tel: (66-2) 264-0909
Fax: (66-2) 661-8505-6

Association of Thai Steel Industry
11th Fl., 990 AbdulrahimI
Building
Rama IV Rd.
Bangrak, Bangkok 10500
Tel: (66-2) 636-1645-9
Fax: (66-2) 636-1650

Chemical Business Association (N.I.M. Co., Ltd.)
8th Fl., 205 United Flourmill
Building
Samphanthawong
Bangkok 10100
Tel: (66-2) 222-7352
Fax: (66-2) 224-5616

Consulting Engineer Association of Thailand
7th Fl., SPC Building
Klongton
Bangkok 10110
Tel: (66-2) 381-7223
Fax: (66-2) 381-0857

Thai Agricultural Merchants Association
1113-5 Songwad Road
Bangkok 10100
Tel: (66-2) 235-9326

Thai Auto-Parts Manufactures Association
32-33 Moo 17, Bangna-Trad
Km. 11.65
Bangplee Yai, Bangplee
Samutprakarn 10540
Tel: (66-2) 316-8800-7
     Ext. 206
Fax: (66-2) 316-5629

Thai Bankers Association
4th Fl., 195/5
Lake Ratchada Office
Complex 2
New Ratchadaphisek Road
Klongtoey, Bangkok 10110
Tel: (66-2) 264-0083-7
Fax: (66-2) 264-0888

Thai Fertilizer Producers Trade Association
99/196-197 Prachanives 1 Rd.
Lad Yao, Chatuchak
Bangkok 10900
Tel: (66-2) 589-7111
Fax: (66-2) 589-5239

Thai Frozen Foods Association
13th Fl., ITF Silom Palace Bldg.
160/194-7 Silom Road Bangrak
Bangkok 10500
Tel: (66-2) 235-5622-4
Fax: (66-2) 235-5625
Email: thaiffa@ksc.th.com
http://thai-frozen.or.th

Thai Garment Manufacturers Association
31th Fl., Panjathani Tower
127/36 Nonsi Road
Chongnonsi
Yannawa, Bangkok 10120
Tel: (66-2) 681-2222
Fax: (66-2) 681-2223

Thai Hotel Association
203-209/3 Bavornnives
Pranakorn, Bangkok 10200
Tel: (66-2) 281-9496
     629-1931-2
Fax: (66-2) 281-4188
Email: reserve@thaihotel.org
http://www.thaihotel.org

Thai Pharmaceutical Manufacturers Association
5/97 Soi Udomsup
Boromratchachonnanee Road
Bangkok Noi, Bangkok 10700
Tel: (66-2) 433-6547
     424-8588
Fax: (66-2) 433-6547

The Thai Textile Manufacturing Association
454-460 Sukhumvit 22 Road
Klongtoey, Prakanong
Bangkok 10110
Tel: (66-2) 258-2023
     258-2044
Fax: (66-2) 260-1525

The Thai Tool and Die Industry Association (TDIA)
2nd Floor, The Bureau of
Supporting
Industries Development
Soi Kluaynamthai
Rama IV Road
Bangkok 10110
Tel: (66-2) 381-0551-1

3. Consulting, accounting, and law firms

There are many local and international consulting, accounting, and law firms in Thailand, particularly in Bangkok. The following list of names and addresses contains some of the more well-known firms, but this does not imply endorsement or certify their credibility. All the firms in the list are Bangkok offices.

(a) Consulting firms in Thailand

Accenture
989 Rama I
Tel: (662) 658-0658

Booz-Allen & Hamilton
26th Floor Capital Tower
All Seasons Place
87/1 Wireless
Tel: (662) 654-3001

Boston Consulting Group (Thailand) Ltd.
5A Floor Le Promenande
2/4 Wireless
Tel: (662) 655-0404
Fax: (662) 655-0381

Boyden Associates (Thailand) Ltd.
Sinn Sathorn Tower
Krungthonburi Road
Tel: (662) 440-0144-7

The Brooker Group Public Company Limited
16th Floor, Harindhorn Building
54 North Sathorn Road
Silom, Bangrak
Tel: (662) 267-9222, 632-1711
Fax: (662) 632-2606, 632-2607
E-mail: info@brookergroup.com
Web site: www.brookergroup.com

Ernst &Young Ltd.
33rd Floor
Lake Ratchada Building
New Ratchadaphisek Road
Tel: (662) 264-0777
Fax: (662) 264-0789-90

McKinsey & Company Inc. Thailand
M Thai Tower
All Season Place Bldg.
Wireless Road
Tel: (662) 654-0166
Fax: (662) 654-0177

Price Waterhouse Management Consultant Ltd.
175 South Sathorn
Tel: (662) 679-5161-75
Fax: (662) 679-5180

Thailand Management Association
276 Ramkhamhaeng Rd., Soi 39, Bangkapi
Tel: (662) 319-7675-8
Fax: (662) 319-5665-6

(b) Law firms in Thailand

Allen & Overy
22nd Floor, Sindhorn Building III
130 Wireless Road
Tel: (662) 263-7600
Fax: (662) 263-7699
E-mail: information@allenovery.com
Web site: www.allenovery.com

Baker & McKenzie
25th Floor, 990 Rama IV Rd.
Tel: (662) 636-2000
Fax: (662) 636-2111
Web site: www.bakernet.com

Chandler & Thong-Ek Law Office Limited
Bubhajit Building, 7th Floor
20 North Sathorn Rd.
Tel: (662) 266-6485/6510
Fax: (662) 266-6483/6484
E-mail: chandler@ctlo.com
Web site: http://ctlo.com

DEACONS
16/F Q House Sathorn, 11 South Sathorn Rd.
Tel: (662) 679-1844
Fax: (662) 679-1864
E-mail: deacons@loxinfo.co.th
Web site: www.deaconslaw.com

Domnern Somgiat & Boonma
719 Si Phya Road
Tel: (662) 639-1955
Fax: (662) 639-1956-58
E-mail: mail@dsb.co.th
Web site: www.dsb.co.th

Herbert Smith
1401 Abdulrahim Place, 990 Rama IV Road
Tel: (662) 636-0656
Fax: (662) 636-0657
E-mail: enguiries-asia@berbertsmith.com
Web site: www.herbertsmith.com

Johnson, Strokes & Master
12th Floor, TISCO Tower
48/20 North Sathorn Road
Tel: (662) 638-0880
Fax: (662) 638-0870
E-mail: jsmbkk@jsm.com.hk
Web site: www.jsm.com.hk

Miyake & Yamazaki
Suite 1903 Wall Street Tower
33-96 Surawong Road, Bangrak
Tel: (662) 266-2840
Fax: (662) 238-0858
E-mail: Kobayasi@loxinfo.co.th

Tillekie & Gibbins International Ltd.
Tillekie & Gibbins Building
64/1 Soi Tonson, Ploenchit Road
Tel: (662) 263-7700
Fax: (662) 621-0172
E-mail: postmaster@tillekieandgibbins.com
Web site: www.tillekieandgibbins.com

Vickery & Worachai Ltd.
6th Floor, Diethelm Tower A
93/1 Wireless Road
Tel: (662) 256-6311/4
Fax: (662) 256-6317/8
E-mail: vwlaw@loxinfo.co.th

Siam Premier
24th-26th Floor, Thai Wah Tower II,
No. 21/147-150, South Sathorn Rd.
Tel: (662) 679-1333
Fax: (662) 679-1314
E-mail: siamlaw@loxinfo.co.th

Freshfields Bruckkhaus Deringer
Sathorn City Tower, 10th Floor
175 South Sathorn Road
Tel: (662) 344-9200
Fax: (662) 344-9300
E-mail: james.lawden@fresfields.com
Web site: www.freshfields.com

Hunton & Williams (Thailand) Limited
34th Floor, Abdulrahim Place, 990 Rama IV Road,
Tel: (662) 636-2366
Fax: (662) 636-2377
E-mail: bbradley.th@hunton.com
Web site: www.hunton.com

Linklaters (Thailand) Ltd.
20th Floor, Capital Tower, All Seasons Place
87/1 Wireless Road
Tel: (662) 305-8000
Fax: (662) 305-8010
Web site: www.linklaters-alliance.com

Norton Rose (Thailand) Limited
130-132 Wireless Road, Sindhorn Building
Tower 2, 14th Floor
Tel: (662) 263-2811
Fax: (662) 256-6703
Web site: www.nortonrose.com

White & Case (Thailand) Limited
5th Floor, Gaysorn Place (Gaysorn Plaza)
999 Ploenchit Road, Lumpini
Tel: (662) 656-1721
Fax: (662) 656-1733
E-mail: bangkok@whitecase.com
Web site: www.whitecase.com

Pramuanchai Law Office Co., Ltd.
2038-2042 Rama 6 Road, Pathumwan
Tel: (662) 219-2031/2
Fax: (662) 219-2155/60
E-mail: pmclaw@cscoms.com

(c) *Accounting firms in Thailand*

BDO Richfield Ltd.
CTI Tower Ratchadaphisek Rd.
Tel: (662) 261-1251

Chaiyostrai Management Consultants Co., Ltd.
142/40 North Sathorn Rd.
Tel: (662) 234-6427
Fax: (662) 235-2532

D I A Accounting
316/32 Soi 22 Sukhumvit
Tel: (662) 259-5300

Deloitte Touche Tohmatsu Co., Ltd.
25th-26th Floor Rajanakarn Office Building
183 South Sathorn
Tel: (662) 676-5700
Fax: (662) 676-5757-8

Dharmniti Auditing Co., Ltd.
267/1 Pracharaj Soi 1
Tel: (662) 587-8080

Ernst & Young Ltd.
33rd Floor Lake Ratchada Building
New Ratchadaphisek Road
Tel: (662) 264-0777/661-9190/
         661-8336/661-8799
Fax: (662) 264-0789-90

KPMG Peat Marwick Suthee Ltd.
9/F Sathornthani Bldg. 2
92/18 North Sathorn
Tel: (662) 236-6161-4
Fax: (662) 236-6165

PriceWaterhouseCoopers
15th Floor, Bangkok City Tower
179 South Sathorn
Tel: (662) 286-9999
Fax: (662) 286-5050

SGV Na Thalang & Co., Ltd.
989 Rama I Rd.
Tel: (662) 658-0658

4. Financial institutions

(a)   *Commercial banks*

The commercial banking sector has undergone a significant restructuring and consolidation following the outbreak of the economic crisis. There are now only 13 commercial banks operating in Thailand, several of which were rescued by the Government and came under its control, at least temporarily, during the crisis. Some of these banks have been sold off to foreign banks, while the sale of others is still pending.

The list of commercial banks operating in Thailand is as follows:

Bangkok Bank, Thai Farmers' Bank, Krung Thai Bank, DBS Thai Danu Bank, Thai Military Bank, Siam Commercial Bank, Standard Chartered-Nakornthon Bank, Bank of Asia, Bank of Ayudhya, UOB Radhanasin Bank, Bankthai, Siam City Bank, and Bangkok Metropolitan Bank.

There are 20 foreign bank branches located in Thailand. These are:

ABN-Amro	Bank of America	Bank of China
Bank of Tokyo-Mitsubishi	Bank of Nova Scotia	Bharat Overseas Bank
BNP Paribas	Chase Manhattan Bank	Citibank
Dai-Ichi Kangyo Bank	Deutsche Bank AG	Dresdner Bank AG
Hong Kong and Shanghai Banking Corp., Ltd.	Industrial Bank of Japan	International Commercial Bank of China

Overseas Chinese Banking Corp., Ltd.	RHB Bank Berhad	The Sakura Bank
Standard Chartered Bank	Sumitomo Bank Ltd.	

(b) *Stock markets*

The Stock Exchange of Thailand (SET) is Thailand's primary stock exchange. It was established in 1974, and is supervised by a Board of Governors. The Board consists of 11 Governors, with five appointed by the Securities and Exchange Commission (SEC), five elected by the SET member companies, and a full time president, who is appointed by the Board and serves as an ex-officio Board member.

The SET considers applications from companies requesting listing on the Exchange, including ensuring applicants meet requirements as well as submit the correct documentation. It has also established information disclosure requirements for listed companies and monitors all trading activities involving listed securities.

Currently, the SET has 50 broker seats, and there are 27 active members at the Exchange. Member companies must be securities companies permitted by the Ministry of Finance to conduct securities business in the category of securities brokerage.

All listed companies are public limited firms. Becoming a listed company not only allows a firm to gain access to development capital, but also allows shareholders to benefit from investment liquidity and enjoy dividend income as a result of revenue or profit growth at the companies they invest in.

Figure 43 shows the SET's performance for 1998 and 1999, along with selected months in 2000.

Figure 43. Activity on the SET

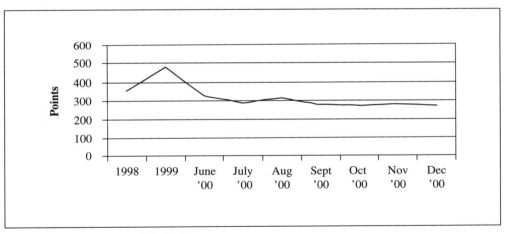

Source: Stock Exchange of Thailand

In line with the Government of Thailand's policy to support the development of small and medium-sized enterprises, in June 1999, the SET established a new secondary market for trading SME shares, called the Market for Alternative Investment. As of the end of 2000, no firms have listed on the MAI yet, but several are expected to list in 2001.

5. Infrastructure

Thailand's infrastructure clearly lagged behind its economic development during the boom years, and perhaps Thailand's growth could have been even higher had it not been for the bottlenecks created by a lack of infrastructure. Bangkok has the unenviable distinction as one of the most grid-locked cities in the world. In recognition of these problems, the Government formulated a long-term infrastructure plan to meet the demands and requirements for a modern industrial economy. Concerted efforts are being made to put in place an

145

extensive infrastructure system that can keep pace with and facilitate the country's industrialization and development.

Thailand's Eight National Economic Plan (1997-2001) continues from the previous ones in devoting increasing budgetary allowances for infrastructure investment and expansion. The Eighth Plan allots US$ 75 billion for infrastructure development, which is 47 per cent more funds than the previous plan. Among the major infrastructure projects under way are expressways, rapid mass transportation, port development, water supply, and telecommunications. Several legal reforms are ongoing to facilitate the private sector's participation in infrastructure development and to make government agencies more transparent in their procurement practices.

(a)   *Land transportation*

Thailand has one of the region's most developed road networks, covering over 170,000 kilometres. Despite the extensive road network, Bangkok became notorious for its traffic jams. Significant improvements have been made in alleviating the capital's traffic problem because of the expanding expressway system, which connects Bangkok with most of the surrounding provinces, and by new rail rapid transportation projects. An elevated train system in Bangkok opened in December 1999, and extensions are already planned. Additionally, an underground subway system is under construction and should be complete in 2003.

Thailand is spending US$ 700 million on these light train projects. Its rail network spans 4,000 kilometres and connects with all the major regions of the country. The State Railway of Thailand plans to spend US$ 4.2 billion between 1997 and 2001 to expand its double-track system to 70 per cent of its rail network.

(b)   *Air transportation*

To accommodate the flourishing tourism industry and the increasing number of business travellers, Thailand is expanding its existing international airport to accommodate 36 million people by 2003 and building a second international airport 30 kilometres east of Bangkok. Altogether Thailand has 6 international airports (although only 4 are functioning as international airports) and 29 domestic airports, with several more provincial airports pending. Thailand aims to become the region's air transportation central due to its central location in South-East Asia.

(c)   *Water transportation*

Thailand has eight international deep seaports, with the main ones in Bangkok, Laem Chabang, Phuket, and Songkhla. More ports are planned for construction, particularly in the southern region, in order to reduce the burden of the over-stretched main port in Bangkok's Klongtoey district.

Upgrading the country's sea transportation infrastructure is concentrated along the Gulf of Thailand and the Andaman Sea. The Government seeks to disperse industrial activity throughout the country by promoting the Eastern Seaboard region and the southern ports. The Eastern Seaboard is now an important centre of industry in Thailand because of the industrial parks and export processing zones that sprung up around the deep sea port in Laem Chabang. The government expects equal success in the near future for the rapidly developing port areas in the South.

(d)   *Industrial estates*

Over 60 industrial estates or special export zones are in operation throughout Thailand, and several more are planned for the southern region. Many of these are a combination of public and private sector joint ventures, while others are entirely run by the government's Industrial Estates Authority of Thailand. Several industrial areas receive special designation as export processing zones, which entitles producers in the zones to favourable treatment in the form of incentives.

(e) *Telecommunications*

A telecommunications Master Plan for 1997-2006 intends to modernize and privatize Thailand's telecommunications sector. The Master Plan envisages an increase in the number of telephones per 100 people from four in 1993 to 18.2 by 2001. To help achieve this goal and other telecom requirements, Thailand's Eighth National Plan earmarks US$ 7.5 billion for upgrading and expanding the telecommunications infrastructure.

(f) *Social infrastructure*

Thailand has a well-developed social infrastructure covering education, health, recreation, and entertainment. Excellent hospitals, world class recreational facilities, and a nation-wide educational system are easily accessible throughout the country to all citizens and foreign guests. Thailand has over 1,300 hospitals, including advanced, specialized service hospitals. Primary and secondary schools are found throughout the country. Several international schools are located in Bangkok and the major industrial areas of the country. The higher educational system contains 23 public universities and 17 private universities or colleges.

D. Legal and regulatory frameworks for trade and investment

1. Foreign investment

(a) *Overview*

Foreigners in Thailand derive their legal rights primarily from the domestic laws of Thailand. In general, foreigners enjoy the same basic rights as Thai nationals, but there are some restrictions on ownership in certain sectors, land ownership, and jobs open to foreigners. Restrictions on foreign ownership are in place for commercial banks, insurance companies, commercial fishing, aviation businesses, commercial transportation, commodity export, mining, and other enterprises. In addition, Thai participation may be required in certain circumstances.

(b) *The Foreign Business Act*

The primary piece of legislation governing foreign participation in the Thai economy is the Foreign Business Act (FBA), which came into effect in March 2000. The FBA repeals and replaces the 1972 National Executive Council Announcement No. 281 (otherwise known as the Alien Business Law, ABL). As with the Alien Business Law, the businesses noted in the Act are still divided into three categories – now termed List 1, List 2, and List 3.

However, the business categories in the FBA have been substantially changed from those of the ABL. Under the FBA, a Foreign Business Board will review the businesses listed at least once a year, and present it to the Commerce Minister. The Commerce Minister, acting in terms of the recommendations of the Foreign Business Board, is empowered to issue Ministerial Regulations. The Foreign Business Board will consist of 19 committee members from both government and private agencies. The latter will include the Thai Chamber of Commerce and the Federation of Thai Industries. A maximum of five experts can also sit on the committee.

List 1 activities are strictly prohibited to aliens. List 2 is prohibited to aliens unless permission is granted by the Commerce Minister and with an appropriate Cabinet resolution. Alien juristic entities allowed to engage in the businesses in List 2 must meet the following two conditions:

- At least 40 per cent of all of the shares are held by Thai persons or non-alien juristic entities
- Two fifths of the members of the Board of Directors are Thai

List 3 is prohibited to aliens unless permission is granted by the Director-General of the Department of Commercial Registration, Ministry of Commerce, and with the approval of the Foreign Business Board.

An alien can engage in businesses in List 2 and/or List 3 if he is a promoted investor in accordance with the Investment Promotion Act, Industrial Estate Authority of Thailand Act, or other laws.

Major features of the Foreign Business Act

Definition of "Alien":

1. A natural person who is not of Thai nationality;
2. A juristic entity which is not registered in Thailand;
3. A juristic entity incorporated in Thailand with foreign shareholding accounting for one-half or more of the total number or value of shares;
4. A limited partnership or registered ordinary partnership whose managing partner or manager is a foreigner.

Shareholding limit in other business:

None

Minimum capital:

The minimum capital is 3 million baht for businesses listed in the FBA and 2 million baht for businesses not listed in the FBA. However, the minimum capital requirement shall not be imposed in cases of re-investment.

List of business activities in the FBA:

List 1

*   Business that aliens are not permitted to do for special reasons:
*   Newspaper undertakings and radio and television station undertakings
*   Lowland farming/upland farming, or horticulture
*   Raising animals
*   Forestry and timber conversions from natural forests
*   Fishing for aquatic animals in Thai waters and Thailand's exclusive economic zones
*   Extraction of Thai medical herbs
*   Trade in and auctioning of Thai ancient objects or ancient objects of national historical value
*   Making or casting Buddha images and making monk's bowls
*   Dealing in land

List 2

*   Businesses concerning national security or safety with an adverse effect on art and culture, customs or native manufacture/handicrafts, or with an impact on natural resources and the environment.
*   Businesses concerning national security or safety
*   Production, disposal (sale) and overhaul of:
*   Fire arms, ammunition gunpowder, and explosives
*   Components of fire arms, gunpowder, and explosives
*   Armaments, and military vessels, aircraft, or conveyances
*   All kinds of war equipment or their components
*   Domestic transport by land, water or air inclusive of the undertaking of domestic aviation
*   Businesses with an adverse effect on art and culture, customs or native manufacture/handicrafts
*   Dealing in antiques or objects of art and works of art, and Thai handicrafts
*   Production of wood carvings
*   Raising silkworms, producing Thai silk thread and weaving or printing patterns on Thai silk textiles
*   Production of Thai musical instruments
*   Production of articles of gold or silver, nickel-bronze ware, or lacquerware
*   Production of crockery and terra cotta ware that is Thai art or culture
*   Businesses concerning natural resources and the environment
*   Production of sugar from sugarcane
*   Salt farming, inclusive of making salt from salty earth
*   Making rock salt

- Mining, inclusive of stone blasting or crushing
- Timber conversions to make furniture and articles of wood

List 3

- Businesses which Thais are not ready to compete in undertakings with aliens
- Rice milling and production of flour from rice and farm crops
- Fishery, limited to propagation of aquatic animals
- Forestry from replanted forests
- Production of plywood, wood veneer, chipboard or hardboard
- Production of natural lime
- Accounting service undertakings
- Legal service undertakings
- Architectural service undertakings
- Engineering service undertakings
- Construction (although there are a few exceptions)
- Brokerage or agency undertakings (although there are several exceptions, in particular trading in securities or services concerning futures trading in agricultural commodities, financial instruments or securities)
- Advertising undertakings
- Hotel undertakings, except for hotel management services
- Sale of food or beverages
- Plant breeding and propagating, or plant improvement undertakings
- Doing other service businesses except for service businesses prescribed in ministerial regulations

(c) *Types of business organization*

(i) *Sole proprietorships*

A sole proprietorship is a business owned by one person with unlimited liability. A proprietor's business and personal assets are subject to attachment and other forms of legal action. Foreigners, unless covered under the United States-Thailand Treaty on Amity and Economic Co-operation, are not permitted to operate sole proprietorships.

(ii) *Partnerships*

Thailand acknowledges three general types of partnerships. The main difference between them is the degree of liability of the partners under each type of organization. Partnerships are not promoted by the Board of Investment, and thus are rarely used by foreign investors in Thailand. The three types are:

- Unregistered ordinary partnerships, in which all partners are jointly and wholly liable for all obligations of the partnership
- Registered ordinary partnerships. If registered, the partnership becomes a legal entity, separate and distinct from the individual partners
- Limited partnerships. Individual partner liability is restricted to the amount of capital contributed to the partnership. Limited partnerships must be registered.

(iii) *Limited companies*

There are two types of limited companies – private or closely held companies, and public companies. The first type is governed by the Civil and Commercial Code, the second by the Public Company Act.

(iv) *Private limited companies*

In Thailand, they are similar to those of Western corporations, and are the most popular vehicle used to establish a permanent business in Thailand. Although there is no established minimum level of capitalization, the private limited company's capital must be sufficient to accomplish its objectives. All of the shares must be subscribed to, and at least 25 per cent of the subscribed shares must be paid up. It should also be noted that private limited companies are required to have capitalization of two million baht, fully paid up, per each work permit the company desires.

A minimum of seven shareholders is required at all times. A private limited company may be wholly-owned by aliens. However, in those activities reserved for Thai nationals, aliens' participation is generally allowed up to 49 per cent. Meetings of shareholders and directors must conform to the requirements set forth in the Civil and Commercial Code and/or the Articles of Association of the company.

(v) *Public limited companies*

Such companies registered in Thailand may, subject to the compliance with the prospectus, approval, and other requirements, offer shares, debentures and warrants to the public and may apply to have their securities listed on the Stock Exchange of Thailand (SET).

A public limited company must:

- Have a minimum of 15 promoters for the formation and registration of the Memorandum of Association
- Have not less than half of the promoters domiciled in Thailand
- Have the promoters' subscribed shares, which will be paid up in money, equal to not less than 0.05 per cent of the registered capital. These prescribed shares cannot be transferred within two years of the date of registration of the company, except with the consent of a general meeting of shareholders
- Have a statutory meeting within two months from the date when the shares have been fully subscribed, as specified in the prospectus, but not more than six months from the date of approval of the memorandum by the registrar
- Have a minimum of five directors, at least half of whom must be domiciled in Thailand
- Ensure that the directors are 20 years of age or older, and they must have clean legal records
- Have subscribers pay the full amount of each share
- Not stipulate any provisions that would prevent shareholders from becoming directors of the company
- Hold a meeting of the Board of Directors at least once every three months where a directors' certificate must be obtained and the minutes must be recorded
- Have an auditor present at all times when the balance sheet is submitted for adoption by general meeting of the shareholders

(vi) *Joint ventures*

There are various forms of joint ventures permitted in Thailand.

a. *Incorporated joint ventures*

A Thai private limited company that is owned by two or more companies or groups of shareholders is often referred to as a joint venture (although there is no language governing incorporated joint ventures in Thailand's legal code). There are no specific restrictions on joint ventures, except that companies that are majority foreign-owned are treated as "foreign." Joint ventures that receive promotional incentives from the BOI can be exempted from restrictions that would be imposed on a "foreign" venture.

b. *Unincorporated joint ventures*

The partners have joint liability to third parties dealing with the joint venture. A foreign company which participates in an unincorporated joint venture is required to obtain an Alien Business Permit and create a branch office in Thailand to engage in business as a partner of the joint venture. Such foreign partners do not need to register for their own taxpayer identification card, because merely acting as a partner is not considered "doing business." However, the joint venture itself must register.

c. *BOI joint venture criteria*

For investment projects in agriculture, animal husbandry, fisheries, mineral exploration and mining, or service sectors, Thai nationals must hold no less than 51 per cent of the registered capital. However, for projects with investment of over one billion baht, foreigners may initially hold the majority or all of the shares, but Thai nationals must acquire at least 51 per cent of the shares within five years of operation.

For manufacturing activities, majority or total foreign ownership of projects is permitted, and there is no foreign export requirement for any project. Existing projects that were subjected to export requirements as a result of previous joint venture criteria may request the removal of the export requirement from their investment promotion certificate.

d. *Other types of collaborative ventures*

- Agency/distribution agreements
- Licensing agreements
- Manufacturing agreements

(vii) *Other types of corporate presence*

There are three types of offices that may be set up by a foreign or multinational company in Thailand – representative, regional, and branch.

a. *Branches*

There is no special requirement for foreign companies to register their branches in order to do business in Thailand. However, most business activities fall within the scope of one or more laws or regulations, which require special registration, either before or after the commencement of activities. Foreign business establishments must, therefore, follow generally acceptable procedures. It is important to clarify beforehand what constitutes income subject to Thai tax because the Revenue Department may consider revenues directly earned by the foreign head office from sources within Thailand as subject to Thai taxes.

As a condition for approval of an Alien Business License to a branch of a foreign corporation, working capital amounting to a total of five million baht in foreign exchange must be brought into Thailand within certain intervals over a five-year period.

b. *Representative offices*

Trading representative offices may carry out the following activities:

- Finding suppliers of goods or services in Thailand for the overseas head office
- Checking and controlling the quality and quantity of goods purchased or hired by the head office for manufacturing purposes in Thailand
- Providing advice on various aspects of goods sold by its head office to agents, distributors and/or customers in Thailand
- Providing information to interested persons in Thailand concerning goods or services of the head office; and
- Reporting to the head office on movements of business in Thailand

The definition of a representative office excludes regional offices and other business-related trading activities. A representative office in Thailand is considered a liaison office and may not engage in any profit-seeking or profit-making enterprise. Representative offices do not generate income and therefore pay no tax.

c. *Regional offices*

A regional office is allowed to coordinate and supervise the company's branches and its affiliated companies in the region on behalf of the head office. Companies establishing regional offices are not required to register or incorporate as juristic persons in Thailand, and do not have to submit any financial statements to the Department of Commercial Registration.

However, a regional office must not:

- Derive any income from its activities. Expenditures incurred by the regional office shall be borne by the head office
- Have the power to accept a purchase order or make a sales offer
- Negotiate or enter into business arrangements with any natural or juristic person within the Kingdom

(d) *Investment incentives and performance requirements*

In August 2000, the Board of Investment replaced its 1993 Announcement No. 1/2536 Re: Policies and Criteria for Investment Promotion with a new set of policies. The major new policies are as follows:

- Tax privileges shall be granted to projects that actually benefit the economy, and good governance shall be used for managing and supervising the application of tax and duty privileges. Promoted entities shall report the operating results of their promoted projects to the BOI for review prior to the application of tax and duty privileges for that year
- Every promoted project that has investment capital of 10 million baht or more (excluding land and working capital) must obtain ISO 9000 certification or similar international certification
- Previous conditions on exports and use of local material are repealed so that the criteria for promotion will be in line with international trade and investment agreements
- Special promotion shall be given to regions or areas with low income and inadequate investment facilities. Maximum tax and duty privileges shall be given to these regions or areas
- Importance is given to small and medium industries by applying a minimum level of investment capital of one million baht (excluding cost of land and working capital) for projects eligible for promotion

The BOI also announced that it places priority on promoting the follow types of projects:

- Agriculture and agricultural products
- Direct involvement in technological and human resource development
- Public utilities and infrastructure
- Environmental protection and conservation
- Targeted industries

These projects are entitled to certain privileges. First, they are exempt from import duty on machinery regardless of where they are located. Second, the projects receive a corporate income tax exemption for eight years regardless of location. Third, they receive all other privileges entitled in each Zone.

(i) *Investment zones*

Under the new policies in August 2000, BOI made slight modifications to the three investment zones.

Zone 1: Six central provinces with high income and good infrastructure: Bangkok, Samutprakarn, Samut Sakhon, Pathum Thani, Nonthaburi, and Nakhon Pathom.

Tax and duty privileges in Zone 1 include:

- 50 per cent reduction of import duty on machinery that is subject to import duty of not less than 10 per cent
- Corporate income tax exemption for three years for projects within industrial estates or promoted industrial zones, provided that the project has a capital investment of 10 million baht or more and obtains ISO 9000 (or similar international certification) within two years of start-up date. Otherwise, the corporate income tax exemption will be reduced by one year
- Exemption of import duty on raw or essential materials used in the manufacturing of export products for one year

Zone 2: 12 provinces: Kanchanaburi, Chachoengsao, Chonburi, Nakhon Nayok, Ayudhya, Phuket, Rayong, Ratchaburi, Samut Songkhram, Saraburi, Suphanburi, and Ang Thong.

Tax and duty privileges in Zone 2 include:

- 50 per cent reduction of import duty on machinery that is subject to import duty of not less than 10 per cent.
- Corporate income tax exemption for three years, increased to five years for projects within industrial estates or promoted industrial zones, provided that the project has a capital investment of 10 million baht or more and obtains ISO 9000 (or similar international certification) within two years of start-up date. Otherwise, the corporate income tax exemption will be reduced by one year.
- Exemption of import duty on raw or essential materials used in the manufacturing of export products for one year.

Zone 3: The remaining 58 provinces with low income and less developed infrastructure.

Tax and duty privileges in Zone 3 include:

- Exemption of import duty on machinery
- Corporate income tax exemption for eight years provided that the project has a capital investment of 10 million baht or more and obtains ISO 9000 (or similar international certification) within two years of start-up date. Otherwise, the corporate income tax exemption will be reduced by one year
- Exemption of import duty on raw or essential materials used in the manufacturing of export products for five years
- Projects in a selected list of 40 of the 58 provinces in Zone 3 receive the above privileges but also additional ones such as:
  - Projects located within industrial estates or promoted industrial zones are entitled to a 50 per cent reduction of corporate income tax for five years after the exemption period, and also double deduction from taxable income of transportation, electricity, and water costs for 10 years from the date of first revenue derived from promoted activity
  - For projects located outside industrial estates or promoted industrial zones, a deduction can be made from net profit of 25 per cent of the project's infrastructure installation or construction cost for 10 years from the date of first sales, and net profit for one or more years of any year can be chosen for such deduction
- Projects in the remaining 18 provinces of Zone 3 receive additional privileges such as:
  - 50 per cent reduction of corporate income tax for five years after the exemption period
  - Double deduction from taxable income of transportation, electricity, and water costs for 10 years from the date of first revenue derived from promoted activity
  - Deduction can be made from net profit of 25 per cent of the project's infrastructure installation or construction cost for 10 years from the date of first sales, and net profit for one or more years of any year can be chosen for such deduction

(ii)   *Additional incentives*

The BOI also grants special tax and non-tax incentives to projects submitted prior to the new policies of August 2000 that relocate from Zone 1 to Zone 2, or from Zone 1 or 2 to Zone 3. However, certain conditions apply such as moving into an industrial estate or promoted industrial zone, be included in the List of Activities Eligible for Promotion, and other criteria.

(e)   *Taxation*

The Revenue Code outlines regulations for the imposition of taxes on income, with income tax divided into three categories: corporate income tax, value added taxes (or specific business taxes), and personal income tax.

(i) *Corporate income tax*

Incorporated firms operating in Thailand pay income tax at a rate of 30 per cent of net profits. Foundations and Associations pay income taxes at a rate of two to 10 per cent of gross business income, depending upon the activity. International transport companies face a rate of three per cent of gross ticket receipts and three per cent of gross freight charges.

Normal business expenses and depreciation allowances, at rates ranging from five to 100 per cent, depending on the item, or at rates under any other acceptable depreciation method, are allowed as deductions from gross income. Inventory must be valued at cost or at market price, whichever is lower. Net losses can be carried forward for up to five consecutive years. Interest payments on some foreign loans may be exempt from a firm's income tax.

Depreciation of assets of limited companies and partnerships is based on cost. The rates of annual depreciation permitted by the law generally vary from five to 20 years.

Entertainment and representation expenses are deductible up to maximum limits as a percentage of gross sales, or of paid-up capital at the closing date of the accounting period, whichever is greater.

Taxes are due on a semi-annual basis within 150 days of the close of a six-month accounting period, and employers are required to withhold personal income tax from their employees. Except for newly-incorporated companies, an accounting period is defined as a duration of 12 months. Returns must be accompanied by audited financial statements.

(ii) *Value added tax*

Value added at every stage of the production process is subject to a seven per cent tax rate. Those who are affected by this tax are producers, providers of services, wholesalers, retailers, exporters and importers. VAT must be paid on a monthly basis.

Operators whose gross earnings from the domestic sale of goods and services exceed 600,000 baht but are less than 1,200,000 baht per year can choose between paying a gross turnover tax of 1.5 per cent or the normal VAT. However, operators paying the gross turnover tax may not offset this tax by charging VAT to their customers in any step of production.

Special exemptions from VAT:

- Operators earning less than 600,000 baht a year
- Sale or import of agricultural products, livestock, and agricultural inputs, such as fertilizer, and feed
- Sale or import of published materials and books
- Auditing, legal services, health services and other professional services
- Cultural and religious services
- Educational services
- Services provided by employees under employment contracts
- The sale of goods as specified by Royal Decree
- Goods exempt from import duties under the Industrial Estate Authority of Thailand Act
- Domestic transport (excluding airlines) and international transport (excluding air and sea lines)

(iii) *Specific business tax (SBT)*

A specific business tax of between 2.5 and 3 per cent is imposed, in lieu of VAT, on the following businesses:

- Commercial banks and similar businesses
- Insurance companies
- Financial securities firms and credit financiers
- Sales on the stock exchange
- Sales of non-movable properties

(iv) *Remittance tax*

Remittance tax applies only to profits transferred or deemed transferred from a Thailand branch to its head office overseas. It is levied at the rate of 10 per cent of the amount to be remitted before tax, and must be paid by the remitting office of the offshore company within seven days of the date of remittance.

However, outward remittances for the purchase of goods, certain business expenses, principal on loans to different entities and returns on capital investment, are not subject to an outward remittance tax. The tax does not apply to dividends or interest payments remitted out of Thailand by a company or partnership; these are taxed at the time of payment.

(v) *Personal income tax*

Personal income tax is applied on a graduated scale as follows:

Net annual income (in baht)	Tax rate (per cent)
0-100,000	5
100,001-500,000	10
500,001-1,000,000	20
1,000,001-4,000,000	30
>4,000,001	37

Individuals residing for 180 days or more in Thailand for any calendar year are also subject to income tax on income from foreign sources if that income is brought into Thailand during the same taxable year that they are a resident.

(vi) *Other taxes*

Other taxes include the Petroleum Income Tax, Stamp Tax, Excise Tax, and Property Tax.

(f) *Labour issues*

In August 1998, the Labour Protection Act (1998) went into effect. It applies to all businesses with at least one employee. The features of the legislation are:

Work hours and holidays: The maximum number of hours for non-hazardous work is eight hours a day or 48 hours a week in total. Hazardous work may not exceed seven hours a day, or 42 hours per week. Employees are entitled to no fewer than 13 national holidays a year, and a minimum of six days of annual vacation after working consecutively for one full year. A female employee is entitled to maternity leave for a period of 90 days including holidays, but paid leave shall not exceed 45 days. A weekly holiday of at least one day a week at intervals of a six-day period must be arranged by the employer. The rates for overtime vary and range from 1-1/2 times to three times the normal hourly wage rate for the actual overtime worked. The maximum number of overtime working hours is limited to not more than 36 hours a week.

Minimum age: The minimum age for employment is 15 years, and workers below the age of 18 are banned from dangerous and hazardous jobs. They are also prohibited from working overtime, on holidays, or between the hours of 10 p.m. and six a.m.

Sick leave: Employees can take as many days of sick leave as necessary, but if an employee takes three months of sick leave, the employer is required to pay only one month's wages

Severance pay: Employees who have worked more than 120 days, but less than one year, are entitled to 30 days severance pay. For personnel employed between one and three years, the severance pay is not less than 90 days. Employees with three to six years of service will receive six months salary, those with more than six to 10 years service will receive eight months salary, and employees with more than 10 years service will receive 10 months salary.

Regarding workmen's compensation, the Compensation Act prescribes that an employer must provide the necessary compensation benefits for employees who suffer injury or illness or who die as a result or in the performance of their work at the rates prescribed by law.

Minimum wage depends largely on the location of the workplace. The daily minimum wages effective January 1, 1998 are:

162 baht for Bangkok, Nakhon Pathom, Nonthaburi, Pathum Thani, Phuket, Samutprakarn and Samut Sakhon.

140 baht for Chonburi, Chiang Mai, Nakhon Ratchasima, Phangnga and Ranong.

130 baht for all other areas.

The Social Security Act requires that all employers with 10 or more employees withhold social security contributions from the monthly wages of each employee. The prescribed rates to the monthly wages are:

From Jan. 1, 1999 to Dec. 31, 1999: two per cent

From Jan. 1, 2000 to Dec. 31, 2000: three per cent

From Jan. 1, 2001 onwards: 4.5 per cent

The maximum monthly wage base on which the rates are applied must not exceed 15,000 baht. The employer is required to match the contribution from the employee. Both contributions must be remitted to the Social Security Office within the 15th day of the following month.

(g)   *Land*

Non-Thai businesses and citizens are not permitted to own land in Thailand unless given permission by the Board of Investment, or unless the land is on government-approved industrial estates. Petroleum concessionaires may own land necessary for their activities. Many foreign businesses instead sign long-term leases and then construct buildings on the leased land.

On August 4, 1998, the Cabinet approved the amendments of Land Code and Condominium Act to eliminate restrictions on foreign ownership of property. The amendments are:

- Allow individual foreign investors investing specified amounts (in the region of 40 million baht) in activities of productive interest for Thailand to own up to one rai [400 square meters] of residential land. The land must be in Bangkok, Pattaya or other residential areas as provided for by law
- Allow Thai citizens married to foreigners to own land
- Permit foreigners to purchase 100 per cent of condominium buildings of five rai or less during the next five years. The previous ceiling on ownership in a condominium building had been 40 per cent
- Amend the lease provisions of the Civil and Commercial Code to provide personal rights pertaining to real estate property instead of real rights, and the period of lease of selected real estate property has been limited to no less than 15 years but no more than 30 years, and may be renewable for an additional 30 years

(h)   *Intellectual property rights*

Thailand recognizes three broad categories of property rights: patents, copyrights, and trademarks.

(i)   *Patents*

Thailand promulgated its first patent law, the Patent Act, in 1979, with significant amendments added in 1992. The Act protects both inventions and product designs and pharmaceuticals. Thailand has numerous bilateral agreements enabling citizens of other countries to file patent applications in Thailand. However, Thailand is not a signatory to the Paris Convention for the Protection of Industrial Property or a signatory of any other international conventions for reciprocal protection of patents.

In December 1997 a new intellectual property and international trade court began operations, which has significantly improved enforcement. Appeals procedures at the trademark and patent offices have also been streamlined.

A foreign patent that has not been granted a separate patent in Thailand receives no protection under the Patent Act. However, foreign patent holders or owners of rights to inventions or designs in foreign countries may enter into business transactions with parties in Thailand and seek equivalent protection through contractual obligations in the form of a licensing agreement.

(ii) *Copyrights*

The Copyright Act of 1994 protects literary, artistic works, and performance rights by making it unlawful to reproduce or publish such works without the owner's permission. The Copyright Act protects works in the categories of literary work, including computer programmes; dramatic, artistic and musical work; audiovisual material, cinematic film, recorded material; disseminated pictures or disseminated sound; or any other works in the fields of literature, science or fine arts. The Copyright Act protects computer software against reproduction or adaptation, publicity and rental of such software. Algorithms are not, however, protected.

(iii) *Trademarks*

The Trademark Act of Thailand of 1991 governs registration of and provides protection for trademarks. The Act defines a trademark as a symbol used in connection with goods for the purpose of indicating that they are the goods of the owner of the trademark. The trademark must be "distinctive" and not identical or similar to those registered by others, and must not be prohibited by section 8 of the Trademark Act of 1991.

2. Trade regulations

There are various regulations governing the import and export of goods into and out of Thailand. However, trade in certain items is restricted through outright prohibition, the imposition of duties, or licensing requirements. Thus, the export of unmilled rice and rice bran is expressly prohibited. Other goods, such as rubber, timber, rice, hides and skins, silk yarn, and iron scrap may be sold to foreign buyers, but duties must be paid on them. To export certain items, such as gold, cattle, or sugar, one must secure a license from the relevant government authorities.

(a) *Exporting*

The Act Controlling the Importation and Exportation of Goods authorizes the Ministry of Commerce to subject products to export control. At present, close to 50 items are under such control. Certain goods require export licenses under other laws, such as seeds, trees, and leaves of tobacco. Certain goods, such as sugar and rice, are subject to export licenses under the Export Standard Act, which aims to ensure that such exports are of a set quality.

In addition, the exporters of agricultural commodities may find that membership to trade associations is mandatory. These associations may in turn impose their own regulations for membership.

(b) *Importing*

The Ministry of Commerce designates classes of goods that are subject to import controls, which usually take the form of permission and licensing. Although these controls are being liberalized, at present more than 50 classes of goods require import licenses from the Ministry of Commerce. These categories frequently change through notifications from the ministry. A license to import any of the specified items must be secured from the Ministry of Commerce. Application for the license must be accompanied by a supplier's order, confirmation, invoice, and other pertinent documents.

In addition to the Act imposing the above controls, a number of goods are subject to import controls under other laws. These include:

- The import of modern drugs requires prior licensing from the Food and Drug Administration under the Ministry of Health
- The Minerals Act stipulates that without appropriate permission, an importer is prohibited from importing tungstic oxide and tin ores and metallic tin in quantities exceeding two kilograms
- The Ancient Monuments, Antiques, Objects of Art and National Museum Act provides that antiques or objects of art, whether registered or not, must not be delivered without permission from the Director General of Fine Arts
- The Armation, Ammunition, Explosives, Fireworks and Imitation Firearms Act bars people from producing, buying, using, ordering or importing arms or ammunition or explosive devices unless they have the appropriate license from the Ministry of Interior
- The Cosmetics Act stipulates that for the purpose of protection of public health, any importer of controlled cosmetics must provide the name and location of the office and the place of manufacture or storage of the cosmetics, the name, category, or kind of cosmetics to be imported, and the major components of the cosmetics

E. Main opportunities for investment

1. Agriculture and agro-industries

Thailand is blessed with land and labour resources used to produce a wide variety of agricultural products (rice, tapioca, sugar cane, rubber and canned fruits), aquacultural products (shrimp, fish), and animal husbandry products (pork products, chickens).

Given the competitive world food market, the Government of Thailand is concentrating on targeting specific markets, in particular halal food. Demand is driven by 1.5 billion Muslim consumers worldwide, generating US$ 80 billion per year.

The Government plans to promote the southern province of Pattani as the centre of world Islamic/halal food production. The project is currently in its early stages. The Government has provided funds for infrastructure, arranged tax incentives and soft loans, assisted in promotions, such as trade shows, and brought together potential investors to study opportunities to open markets in Arab countries and South Africa.

In addition, Thailand cooperates with other ASEAN countries in the Indonesia-Malaysia-Thailand Growth Triangle. These nations have adopted halal food guidelines, and as a rule Thailand produces under an ASEAN halal logo. It also provides training on halal food preparation, regulation on food control and safety and endorsement.

The bulk of investment in agriculture and agricultural products is concentrated on the production of rubber and rubber products, and the production of canned/processed seafood and refrigerated/frozen seafood.

Most promoted investment projects in this industry are family businesses that have adopted advanced technology and management. This has helped Thailand earn a sound reputation on world markets for the quality of its goods. Thailand is a world leader in pineapple, shrimp and canned tuna exports. The latter in 1998 were worth US$ 611.1 million. Continued efforts are being made to improve shrimp production, such as the development of black tiger prawn breeds, and the establishment of a tiger prawn estate.

2. Automotive and auto parts industry

With twelve local assemblers, Thailand has the largest and most dynamic automotive industry in South-East Asia. The industry employs some 15,000 to 20,000 direct (manufacturing) workers and 1.5 million indirect workers (automotive services, sales, supporting industries and suppliers).

The strength of its automotive assembly business, combined with the Government's liberalization efforts and enticing BOI investment policies, has attracted major industry players and hundreds of firms which produce automotive parts and components. The prominent auto producers in Thailand include Mitsubishi, Toyota, Honda, Ford and Mazda.

Thailand's key export markets for passenger cars are the United Kingdom, Singapore, New Zealand, Australia and Hong Kong, China. The commercial vehicles market is directed towards Australia, Portugal, Germany, Spain and Italy. New Zealand and Australia have also recently become attractive markets.

Thailand remains the world's second largest one-ton pick-up market, the world's fourth-largest market for motorcycles, and is the main automotive hub of South-East Asia.

3. Electronics and electrical equipment

The combined electronics and electrical appliance industry is by far the largest export industry in Thailand. The loss in value in the baht since 1997 has favoured the industry, allowing it to be more competitive in global terms. It is one of the few industries that survived the crisis with minimal impact. As well as being the number one export product, the domestic demand has also risen significantly over the years.

Thailand is one of the top production bases for hard disk drives in the region, second only to Singapore among ASEAN member countries.

Initially an import substitution industry, it is now regarded as a middle-level technology export-oriented industry with nearly 2,000 companies in operation producing a wide variety of products. Thailand's electronics and electrical equipment industry has registered spectacular yearly double-digit growth in recent years, consistently surpassing the overall economic growth.

4. Regional offices

In 1992, the Prime Minister's office passed a regulation facilitating the formation of regional offices of multinational corporations in Thailand in order to promote the country as a commercial centre in the region.

Despite some constraints, Thailand has a lot to offer in terms of potential market opportunities to foreign investors wishing to establish regional offices, particularly those with operations in the Greater Mekong Subregion, to which Thailand serves as a convenient gateway.

5. Computer software

Thailand's software industry is considered an exciting emerging industry and a main driver on the road to increased competitiveness in world markets.

In total there are about 300 local software firms, and 90 per cent of them are small and medium enterprises. Most of the software sold in the market is limited to localization of existing overseas packaged software. Packaged software held 19 per cent of the IT market in 1998, with growing demand for new software, specifically games and educational software.

In line with the trend towards network servers and data services, the pattern of software use is likely to shift to application servers. Internet nodes are forecasted to rise to 100 million baht by 2000.

6. Education

In an effort to improve the quality of the education system in Thailand, the Government has been encouraging the participation of the private sector through a number of means, including providing support funds such as the Human Resource Development Loan Fund and tax exemptions on educational materials by the BOI.

Also in 1998, the Cabinet eased the regulations on private sector education institutions for loan applications under government loan programmes. All levels of institutions can apply for loans, but priority is given to secondary education institutions and all institutions located outside of Bangkok. State subsidies for private sector institutions are given to existing institutions on a per capita cost basis, but subsidies are no longer available for new education institutions.

Enrolments in private sector education institutions are increasing at all levels except pre-primary, and according to the Office of the National Education Commission (ONEC), enrolments in upper secondary vocational schools will increase 80 per cent between 1997 and 2000. These forecasts imply that excellent investment opportunities exist in the private education realm.

F. Tips for visitors

1. Getting there

By air: Thailand has four international airports (in Bangkok, Chiang Mai, Phuket, and Hat Yai). Over 80 airlines fly into and out of Bangkok, including most major international carriers in the United States, Europe, the Middle East, and Asia and the Pacific.

By land: Trains are available between Bangkok and Malaysia, and for the latter the normal route to and from Thailand is Penang. There are four international border crossings between Thailand and Malaysia.

Thailand shares five international border crossings with the Lao People's Democratic Republic, including three ferry points across the Mekong River. Cambodia and Thailand have one international land border crossing between Aranyaprathet and Poipet, but others are expected to open in the coming years.

The opening of land border crossings with Myanmar tends to fluctuate depending on the circumstances at the time. As these tend to close frequently, it is advisable to check in advance. Furthermore, the land crossings with Myanmar are often only for day-trippers.

By sea: It is possible to travel between Thailand and Malaysia, and Thailand and Myanmar by boat at selected points.

2. Visas and passports

A passport is required for all foreigners entering Thailand, but not all nationalities require a visa. Foreign nationals who intend to remain in Thailand to work or conduct business must comply with visa requirements in addition to obtaining a work permit.

Visa categories:

Tourist: Tourist visas are initially valid for 60 days and are renewable at the discretion of the Immigration Department. Renewals are normally granted for periods of up to 30 days at a time.

Visitor transit: Aliens who have obtained a transit visa from a Thai embassy or consulate will be granted a 30-day stay in the Kingdom. Extensions of stay are normally granted for periods of 7-10 days. Transit, visitor transit, and tourist visa holders are not authorized to work in Thailand.

Non-quota immigrant: This category includes former residents who have lost their resident status but who have reapplied to resume their residency and who have been able to demonstrate a convincing reason to support the granting of this type of visa.

Non-immigrant visa: Foreigners seeking a prolonged stay, or those coming to work in Thailand, should obtain non-immigrant visas for all family members prior to entering the Kingdom. There are several categories of non-immigrant visas which include, among others, business visa category (B); dependent visa category (O); investment subject to the provision of the laws on investment promotion (BOI IB); diplomatic and consular visa category (D); performance of duties with the mass media (M); performance of skilled or expert work (EX); investment (with concurrence of ministries and departments concerned)-(capital investment IM); study or observation (ED).

Non-quota immigrant visas: These visas are issued to foreigners who have applied for a residence permit under a special case quota or under Non-Quota Immigrant status.

Official visas: These visas are issued to foreigners who are assigned to perform their official duties in the Kingdom and for holders of official passports of other countries or a United Nations Passport or its equivalent. They are valid for 90 days.

Immigrant visas: Immigrant visas are for those who wish to take up permanent residence in Thailand.

Diplomatic visas: These visas are issued to foreigners who perform their duties as foreign diplomatic officials or who carry out official business by holding a diplomatic passport. Foreigners who enter the Kingdom with this category of visa will be permitted to stay for 90 days.

In addition, foreigners residing in Thailand for more than 90 consecutive days are required to register their address with the Immigration Bureau every 90 days. This requirement applies to all foreigners, including holders of work permits and long-term visas. Failure to do so can result in substantial penalties.

In response to feedback from investors, the Board of Investment coordinated the establishment of a One-Stop Service Centre for Visas and Work Permits. Through joint cooperation with the Immigration Bureau and the Ministry of Labour, the centre can process applications or renewals of visas and work permits within three hours, upon receipt of proper and complete documentation.

In addition, the centre handles other transactions, including the issuance of multiple re-entry stamps, changes in class of visa (to non-immigrant from tourist or transit), and payment of fines. The One-Stop Service Centre is located at 207 Ratchadaphisek Road, 3rd Floor, Bangkok, and they may be reached by phone at (662) 693-9333-9.

3. Health

No inoculations or vaccinations are required unless one is coming from or has passed through contaminated areas. Yellow fever certificates are required for those who are coming from endemic or infected areas.

Medical care and hospitals are found throughout the country, and world class standard hospitals are located in Bangkok.

4. Currency

The currency is the baht, which consists of 100 satang. Copper coins are valued 25 and 50 satang. Silver coins are in denominations of 1, 5 and 10 baht. Bank notes are valued at 10, 20, 50, 100, 500 and 1,000 baht.

The exchange rate of foreign currencies against the Thai baht may change daily as the baht floats freely on international money markets. It is advisable to exchange foreign currencies only at commercial banks, currency exchange services or authorised money changers.

Foreign visitors are welcome to open foreign currency accounts with authorized banks in Thailand. No restrictions are imposed on the maintenance of and withdrawal from the account as long as the funds originate from abroad. Non-residents can also open baht accounts at local banks.

5. Embassies

The list of embassies in Bangkok is as follows:

Argentina
20/85 Soi 49, Sukhumvit Rd.
Tel: 662-259-0401/2

Australia
37 South Sathorn Rd.
Tel: 662-287-2680

Austria
14 Soi Nantha, South Sathorn Rd.
Tel: 662-254-6970

Bangladesh
727 Soi 55, Sukhumvit Rd.
Tel: 662-392-9437

Belgium
44 Soi Phiphat, Silom Rd.
Tel: 662-233-9370

Brazil
239 Soi Sarasin, Lumpini
Tel: 662-262-6043/23

Brunei Darussalam
19 Soi 26, Sukhumvit Rd.
Tel: 662-260-5884

China
57 Ratchadaphisek Rd.
Tel: 662-245-7032/49

Denmark
10 Soi Attakanprasit
South Sathorn Rd.
Tel: 662-213-2021

France
35 Customs House Lana
Charoen Krung Rd.
South Sathorn Rd.
Tel: 662-213-2181/4

Hungary
28 Soi Sukchai, Sukhumvit Rd.
Tel: 662-391-2002/3

Iraq
47 Pradipat Rd.
Tel: 662-278-5335/8

Israel
31 Soi Lang Suan, Ploenchit Rd.
Tel: 662-252-3131/4

Kenya
568 Soi Panit Anan
Sukhumvit Rd.
Klongton
Tel: 662-391-8294

Mexico
44/7-8 Convent Rd.
Tel: 662-235-6367

Netherlands
106 Withayu Rd.
Tel: 662-254-7701

Pakistan
31 Soi North Nana (Soi 3)
Sukhumvit Rd.
Tel: 662-253-0288/9

Canada
Boonmitr Bldg., 138 Silom Rd.
Tel: 662-234-1561/8
     237-4126

Colombia-c/o TTMC Ltd.
Than Settakij Bldg.
222 Vibdhavadi Rangsit Rd.
Tel: 662-278-4386

Egypt
49 Soi Ruam Rudi
Ploenchit Rd.
Tel: 662-252-6139, 253-0161

Germany
9 South Sathorn Rd.
Tel: 662-213-2331/6

India
46 Soi Prasanmit (Soi 23)
Sukhumvit Rd.
Tel: 662-258-0300/6

Ireland
205 United Flour Mill Bldg.
Ratchawong Rd.
Tel: 662-223-0976

Italy
399 Nang Linchi Rd.
Tel: 662-286-4844/6

Lao People's
Democratic Republic
520, 502/1-3
Soi Ramkhamhaeng 39
Bangkapi
Tel: 662-539-6667

Myanmar
132 North Sathorn Rd.
Tel: 662-233-2237
     234-4698

New Zealand
93 Withayu Rd.
Tel: 662-254-7701
     252-6103/5

Peru
10 Soi 3, Seri 2 Rd.
Soi Ramkhamhaeng 24
Hua Mak
Tel: 662-314-1054

Chile
18th Floor, Bangkok Bank Bldg.
333 Silom Rd.
Tel: 662-233-2177

Democratic People's
Republic of Korea
81 Soi Ari 7, Phahonyothin Rd.
Tel: 662-278-5118

Finland
16th Floor, Amarin Tower
500 Ploenchit Rd.
Tel: 662-256-9306/9

Greece
3rd Floor, Thanakul Bldg.
Rama IX Rd.
Tel: 662-251-5111

Indonesia
600-602 Petchburi Rd.
Tel: 662-252-3135/40

Islamic Republic of Iran
602 Sukhumvit Rd.
(between Sois 22 and 24)
Tel: 662-259-0611/3

Japan
1674 New Petchburi Rd.
Tel: 662-252-6151/9

Malaysia
35 South Sathorn Rd.
Tel: 662-286-1390/2

Nepal
189 Soi Phuengsuk (Soi 71)
Sukhumvit Rd.
Tel: 662-917240

Norway
11th Floor
Bank of America Bldg.
Withayu Rd.
Tel: 662-253-0390

Philippines
760 Sukhumvit Rd.
Tel: 662-259-0139

Poland 61 Soi 23, Sukhumvit Rd. Tel: 662-258-4112/3	Portugal 26 Captain Bush Lane Si Phraya Rd. Tel: 662-234-0372, 233-7160	Republic of Korea 23 Thiam-Ruammit Rd. Huay Khwang, Samsen Nok Tel: 662-247-7537
Russian Federation 108 North Sathorn Rd. Tel: 662-234-9824/2102	Saudi Arabia Sathorn Thani Bldg. North Sathorn Rd. Tel: 662-237-1938, 235-0875/8	Singapore 129 South Sathorn Rd. Tel: 662-286-2111/1434
South Africa 6th Floor, Park Place 231, Soi Sarasin Tel: 662-253-8473	Spain 93 Withayu Rd. Tel: 662-252-6112	Sri Lanka 48/3 Soi 1, Sukhumvit Rd. Tel: 662-251-2789
Sweden 20th Floor, Pacific Place 140 Sukhumvit Rd. Tel: 662-254-4954/55	Switzerland 35 Withayu Rd. Tel: 662-252-8992/4	Turkey 153/2 Soi Mahatlekluang 1 Ratchadamri Rd. Tel: 662-251-2987/8
United Kingdom 1031 Ploenchit Rd. Tel: 662-253-0191/9	United States of America 95 Withayu Rd. Tel: 662-252-5040/9	Viet Nam 83/1 Withayu Rd. Tel: 662-251-7201/3

6. Hotels

Thailand has become world famous for its outstanding hotels and service. Some of its hotels rank among the best in the world year after year. Business standard hotels in Thailand are also remarkable for their relative affordability, and there is certainly no shortage of suitable hotels throughout the country. Many of the major international hotel chains are found in Thailand, particularly in Bangkok and other popular tourist locations.

G. Learning more

1. Related web sites

Office of the Board of Investment
www.boi.go.th

Bank of Thailand
www.bot.or.th

Ministry of Finance
www.mof.go.th

Ministry of Commerce
www.moc.go.th

Royal Thai Government
www.thaigov.go.th

Ministry of Foreign Affairs
www.mfa.go.th

Stock Exchange of Thailand
www.set.or.th

Department of Customs
www.customs.go.th

Tourism Authority of Thailand
www.tat.or.th

Thai Airways International
www.thaiairways.com

Bangkok Post
www.bangkokpost.com

National Electronics and Computer
Technology Centre (NECTEC)
www.nectec.or.th

2. Useful reading

The Balancing Act: A History of Modern Thailand. Joseph Wright

Behind the Smile: Voices of Thailand. Sanitsuda Ekachai

Corruption and Democracy in Thailand. Pasuk Phongpaichit and Sungsidh Piriyarngsan

Culture Shock! Thailand & How to Survive It. Robert and Nanthapa Cooper

Lonely Planet: Thailand. Joe Cummings

Siam Mapped: A History of the Geo-Body of a Nation. Thongchai Winichakul

Thailand: A Short History. David Wyatt

Thailand's Boom and Bust. Pasuk Phongpaichit and Chris Baker

Thailand's Turn: Profile of a New Dragon. Elliot Kulick and Dick Wilson

Working with the Thais. Henry Holmes and Suchada Tangtongtavy

VI. VIET NAM

A. Basic operating environment

1. Geography and climate

Located on the eastern Indo-Chinese peninsula in South-East Asia, Viet Nam is for the most part a tropical country. It has over 3,000 kilometres of coastline on the Gulf of Tonkin and South China Sea, and borders China to the north, the Lao People's Democratic Republic to the west, and Cambodia in the south-west. Viet Nam has a total land area of 329,560 square kilometres.

The terrain varies from mountainous to coastal delta. In the southern and northern regions the terrain is low and flat, particularly in the delta areas, but there are also some mountainous areas in the north and north-west. The central region features highlands, hills, and mountains. The Mekong River is a prominent feature of southern Viet Nam, where it enters the South China Sea. The other major river is the Red River, which passes near Hanoi and empties into the Gulf of Tonkin.

The climate is generally humid due to Viet Nam's location between the Tropic of Cancer and the Equator, but it can vary from region to region. Northern Viet Nam has two main seasons. The relatively cool and humid season runs from November to April, and the temperatures can dip to 0 degrees Celsius in the mountain areas. The hot rainy season is from May to October.

Southern Viet Nam has a relatively constant temperature but has three distinct seasons. The rainy season runs from May to October, followed by the relatively dry season from November to February. The driest season lasts from February until April. Central Viet Nam's climate varies, with the south-central provinces following a pattern similar to southern Viet Nam and the north-central provinces more like the northern portion of the country.

2. History

In 111 B.C., ancestors of the present-day Vietnamese, inhabiting part of what is now southern China and northern Viet Nam, were conquered by China's Han Dynasty. Chinese rule lasted more than 1,000 years when the Vietnamese ousted the Chinese in 939 A.D. and began a southward expansion that, by the mid-18th century, reached the Gulf of Siam.

However, even after freeing themselves from the Chinese, Viet Nam has not always been united. Viet Nam was finally unified in its present borders in 1802, when Emperor Gia Long's armies consolidated control. In 1858 the French conquest of Viet Nam began with an attack on what is now the city of Danang, and by 1884 Viet Nam was officially incorporated into the French Empire.

The Vietnamese never truly accepted French rule, and by 1930 the Vietnamese Nationalist Party had staged the first significant armed uprising against the French. On September 2, 1945 the Viet Minh, an alliance of nationalist and communist groups led by Ho Chi Minh, announced the formation of a Democratic Republic of Viet Nam and proclaimed Viet Nam's independence. The French were determined to regain control of their former colony, and thus an eight-year war commenced.

A prolonged struggle ensued among the Vietnamese communists (led by Ho Chi Minh), the French, and the Vietnamese nationalists (nominally led by Emperor Bao Dai). Ho Chi Minh's Viet Minh forces fought a highly successful guerrilla campaign and eventually controlled much of rural Viet Nam, particularly in the North.

The French military disaster at Dien Bien Phu in May 1954 led to negotiations called the Geneva Agreements, whereby the Viet Minh and French forces were separated at the temporary military demarcation line at the 17th parallel, marking the end of the eight-year war and of French colonial rule in Indo-China. The Geneva Agreements also called for an eventual national election to unify the country.

In the southern half of the country, an anti-Viet Minh administration took hold, initially led by the former Annamese emperor Bao Dai and subsequently by the anti-communist Ngo Dinh Diem. In October 1955, Ngo Dinh Diem proclaimed the Republic of Viet Nam with himself as president, setting the stage for the devastating war that took place during the late 1950s until 1975 between the communist North led by Ho Chi Minh and the anti-communist South, which received massive military assistance from the United States.

The United States began a troop withdrawal programme in 1969, concurrent with the assumption by South Vietnamese armed forces of a larger role in the defense of their country. While the United States withdrew from ground combat by 1971, it still provided air and sea support to the South Vietnamese until the signing of the ceasefire agreement. The peace agreement was concluded on January 27, 1973.

Despite the withdrawal of the United States, the civil war continued until the communists captured Saigon in April 1975. In mid-November 1975, the decision to reunify the country was announced despite the vast social and economic differences remaining between the two sections. Elections were held in April 1976 for the National Assembly, which was convened the following June. The Assembly ratified the reunification of the country and on July 2 renamed it the Socialist Republic of Viet Nam. In Dec. 1976, Secretary General Le Duan who in effect had led the party since Ho Chi Minh's death in 1969 was elected as party leader. The National Assembly appointed a committee to draft a new constitution for the entire country. The party Central Committee approved the constitution in September 1980 and new National Assembly elections were held in April 1981.

In 1986, the death of Secretary General Le Duan, as well as alarm over the economy's downward spiral, set the stage for the watershed sixth Party Congress in December 1986. Spearheaded by Nguyen Van Linh, who was named the new party leader, the Party Congress endorsed the need for sweeping economic reform, or "doi moi" (renovation), as well as a policy of "openness" patterned to a degree on the policies being promoted in the former Soviet Union.

In the mid-1990s Viet Nam adopted a new course in foreign affairs, particularly because of the major changes that occurred earlier in Eastern Europe and the former Soviet Union. The realignment in international affairs and the economic reform programme attracted numerous European and Asian companies, which perceived Viet Nam as the last great frontier in South-East Asia.

3. Population

The April 1999 census indicated that Viet Nam has a population of over 76 million people, an increase of about 12 million, or 17 per cent, over the past decade. The birth rate is under two per cent. Population density is 231 per square kilometre, making the country the third most densely populated South-East Asian country behind Singapore and the Philippines. The urban population is 23.5 per cent.

The literacy rate of people over 10 years old is 91 per cent. The labour force is 38 million strong, of which 10 per cent work for the State.

Ethnic Vietnamese comprise 85-90 per cent of the population, but several ethnic groups are also present such as the Chinese, Hmong, Tai, Khmer, Cham, and several mountain groups.

The major religions are Buddhism, Hoa Hao, Cao Dai, Christianity (predominantly Roman Catholicism but also some Protestantism), animism, and Islam.

4. Language and culture

(a)   *Language*

The Vietnamese language is a mix of Austro-Asiatic languages and Mon-Khmer languages. Although it is distinct from Chinese, much of the language incorporates thousands of Chinese words. Vietnamese is a tonal language. The script was phonetically romanized in 1548 by a French missionary and called *quoc ngu*. The most widely spoken foreign languages in Viet Nam are Chinese (Cantonese and Mandarin), English, French, and Russian.

The numerous hilltribes have their own languages, but overall these are a small minority of the total population.

(b) *Culture*

Viet Nam has been subject to the powerful influences of Confucianism, Taoism, Buddhism and Christianity. Over the centuries the former three have merged with popular Chinese beliefs and ancient Vietnamese animism to form what is known as Tam Giao (or "Triple Religion").

Popular artistic forms include traditional painting produced on frame-mounted silk; a diverse range of theatre, puppetry, music and dance; religious sculpture; and lacquer ware.

Vietnamese food comes in many varieties. However, staple Vietnamese food comprises white rice taken with vegetables, meat, fish, spices and sauces, and *pho*, which is a rice noodle soup.

5. Economy

Upon unifying the country in 1975, the Vietnamese Communist Party leaders embarked on developing a socialist economy featuring the nationalization of the industrial and agricultural sectors. However, as early as 1978 the Party realized that production and employment were not growing as targeted. Moreover, Viet Nam's subsequent military occupation of Cambodia in 1979 drained many of the country's resources until they withdrew in 1989.

In 1979 the Communist Party initiated new economic policies that loosened some of the socialist controls over the economy. Another set of more substantive changes occurred in 1986 with the launch of the *doi moi* reforms. Among the changes was the new contract system to encourage Vietnamese farmers to cultivate their land. Rice production increased almost immediately. The reforms also boosted production in the manufacturing sector.

The Vietnamese economy is not fully liberalized as a true market economy, however. The structural economic reforms are progressing, albeit slowly, creating a mix of the heavy state-owned sector and the newer private sector. Relaxation of the Enterprise Law stimulated thousands of new small and medium sized enterprises, but the state sector still dominates the economy. The advent of the Law on Foreign Investment in 1987 (and a new law in 1996) allowed foreign investors to enter the Vietnamese market and diversify the economy.

Reform of the SOEs continues with equitization, diversification of ownership, and the liquidation of non-viable enterprises. The government formulated a three-year plan to equitize one-third of all the SOEs, but as of August 2000 only 451 had been transformed.

Foreign assistance is officially being sought to help Viet Nam pay the US$ 750 million cost of shedding around 400,000 state workers. The Ministry of Finance is drafting a proposal to seek offshore funds that would greatly help ease the burden caused by so many redundancies.

The World Bank believes that current targets should see SOEs releasing 600,000 workers by 2005. Planned equitizations, mergers, dissolutions, and bankruptcies should produce this figure, according to the World Bank.

The financial sector is also undergoing reform, with plans to create a government Asset Management Company to subsume bad debts from commercial banks. Also there are plans to privatize some state banks and to adopt international classification standards for non-performing loans.

6. Government

Head of State: President Tran Duc Luong (since September 1997)
Head of Government: Prime Minister Phan Van Khai (since September 1997)

Viet Nam is a one-party state ruled by the Vietnamese Communist Party (VCP). The VCP's constitutionally mandated role and the occupancy of all senior government positions by Party members ensure the primacy of the Politburo's guidelines and enable the Party to set the broad parameters of national policy. However, the Party is slowly reducing its formal involvement in government operations and allowing the government to exercise significant discretion in implementing policy.

The Party selects candidates in elections for the National Assembly (the main legislative body), the President, the Prime Minister, and local government. The VCP Central Committee is the supreme decision-making body in the nation, with the Politburo as the centre of policy-making.

A standing board consisting of the five most senior members of the Politburo oversees day-to-day implementation of leadership directives.

The executive branch is headed by the President (head of state and chair of the National Defense and Security Council) and the Prime Minister, who heads the cabinet of ministries and commissions. The President, on the proposal of the Prime Minister and ratification of the National Assembly, appoints the cabinet. The National Assembly elects the president from among its members for a five-year term.

The President appoints the Prime Minister from among the members of the National Assembly and the Deputy Prime Ministers are then appointed by the Prime Minister. At the grassroots level, People's Committees govern in local jurisdictions and are run by local party members.

The legislative branch comprises the National Assembly, or Quoc-Hoi (450 seats; members elected by popular vote to serve five-year terms). The last National Assembly elections were held in July 1997 with the next due in 2002. At the local level the People's Councils play a significant role in administration.

The judicial power resides in the Supreme People's Court. The National Assembly, on the recommendation of the President, elects the chief justice for a five-year term.

In terms of administrative subdivisions, there are 61 provinces; three municipalities under central government control; one special zone; urban quarters and rural districts; and urban precincts and rural communes.

B. Macroeconomic business climate

1. Gross domestic product and other macro-indicators

After rapid growth in the mid-1990s, the Asian economic crisis and other factors slowed the Vietnamese economy's growth rates in 1998 and 1999 to 4.4 per cent and 4.8 per cent, respectively. Figure 44 shows GDP growth rates for 1992-1998. According to the Asian Development Bank, the economy grew 4.8 per cent and is expected to grow at 6 per cent in 2000 and 6.5 per cent in 2001.

Figure 44. GDP growth rates, 1992-1998

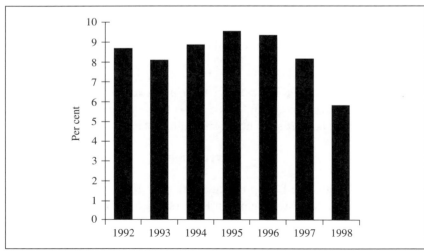

Source: World Bank

168

The GDP per capita has risen from US$ 1,111 in 1992 to US$ 1,689 in 1998.

The manufacturing sector has experienced the highest growth rates of the three main sectors, with an average of 11.8 per cent annual growth between 1995 and 1999. For the same time series, the services sector averaged 6.4 per cent annual growth and the agriculture sector averaged 4.2 per cent. Figure 45 shows the annual sector growth rates.

Figure 45. Sector growth rates and CPI inflation, 1995-1999
(percentage)

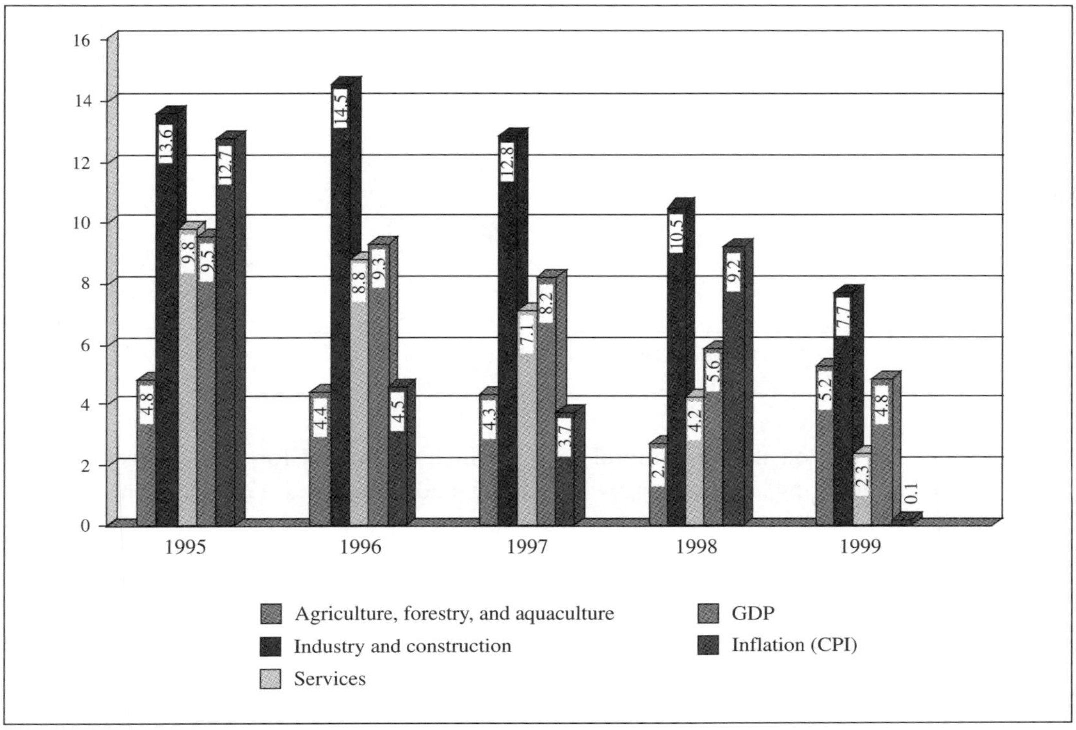

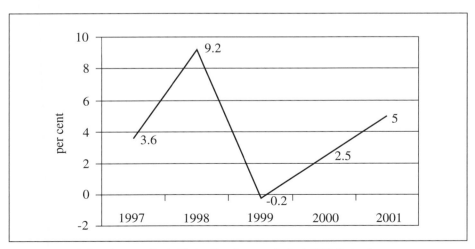

Source: *Viet Nam National Administration of Tourism* (www.vietnamtourism.com)

The inflation rate for 2000 was expected to remain below three per cent. However, inflation is likely to increase slightly to about 5 per cent in 2001 (see figure 46).

Figure 46. Annual inflation rate, 1998-2001*

Source: Asia Development Bank, "Asian Development Outlook 2000 Update"

* Forecasted growth for 2000 and 2001

The Vietnamese economy still has a large state-owned economic sector that accounted for 39.5 per cent of GDP in 1999 (see figure 47). The economic reforms have increased the private sector's share of GDP, but it only comprises a small portion of the total GDP.

Figure 47. Structure of GDP by ownership, 1999

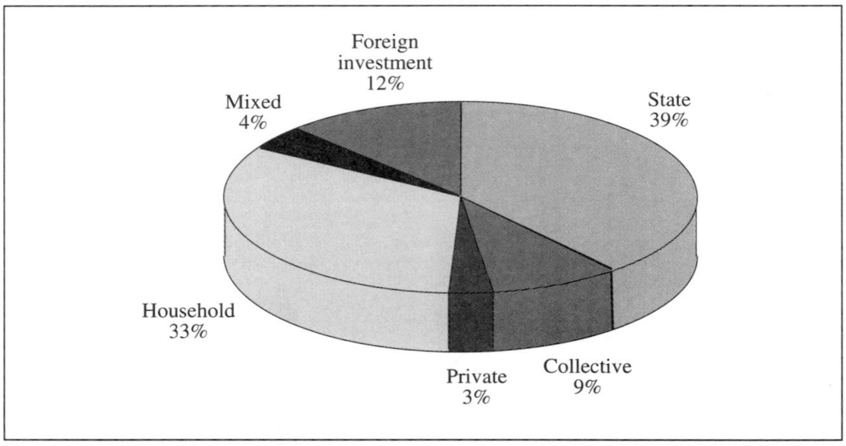

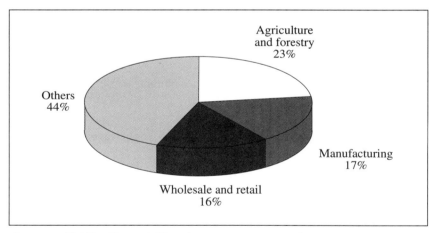

Source: Viet Nam Economic Times (www.vneconomy.com.vn)

Viet Nam relies heavily on the agricultural sector, which accounted for 22.5 per cent of the country's GDP in 1998. The manufacturing sector is growing strong and comprised 17.3 per cent of GDP in 1998, followed by wholesale and retail activities at 15.5 per cent (see figure 48).

Figure 48. Breakdown of GDP by main economic sector, 1998

Source: Viet Nam Economic Times (www.vneconomy.com.vn)

2. Main economic sectors

(a)   *Agriculture, forestry, and fisheries*

Agriculture, forestry, and fisheries combined are the dominant economic sector, accounting for nearly 26 per cent of GDP and employing 70 per cent of the work force. Viet Nam is undertaking a concentrated upgrading of the agro-industry which has raised the country from struggling to achieve self-sufficiency to being a major exporter of rice and coffee in just a few years. Viet Nam is now the world's second largest exporter of rice, behind only Thailand.

Figure 49. Agriculture sector annual growth rates

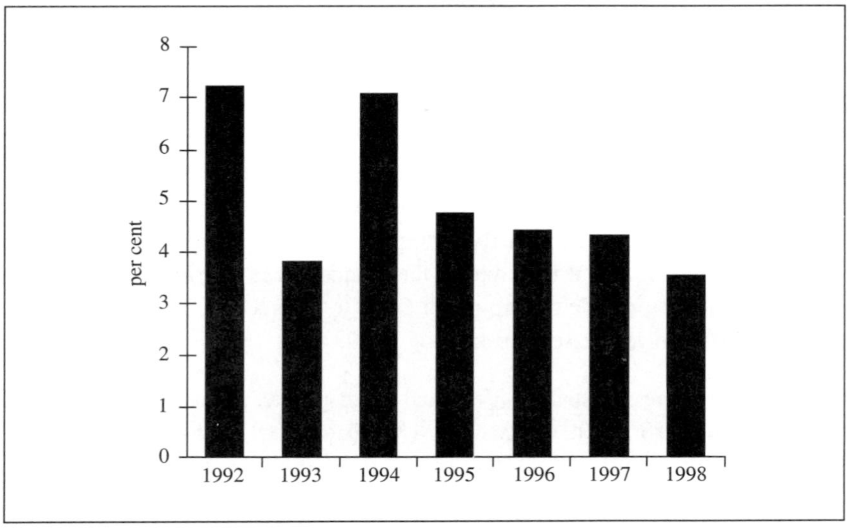

Source: World Bank

Viet Nam has a coastline of 3,260 kilometres with 3,000 large and small islands and an exclusive economic zone (EEZ) of more than 1 million square kilometres. The country has an additional 1.4 million hectares of inland fishing waters. The fisheries sector employs more than three million people.

(b)   *Oil, gas, and mining*

Viet Nam has the potential to become a regional oil and natural gas supplier. Ongoing exploration has led to several oil and gas discoveries in recent years.

(i)   *Oil*

Viet Nam has 600 million barrels of proven oil reserves and further discoveries are likely. Viet Nam has no major oil refineries and therefore almost all of its oil production is exported. Export markets include Japan (the largest importer of Vietnamese oil), Singapore, the United States, and the Republic of Korea. Viet Nam exported an estimated US$ 2 billion worth of oil in 1999 and oil exports are one of the country's largest foreign currency earners.

Most oil exploration and production activities occur offshore in the Cuu Long and Nam Con Son Basin. The Government of Viet Nam controls both the oil and gas upstream and downstream. For upstream activities, Viet Nam Oil and Gas Corporation (Petro Viet Nam), a government-owned company, is the only firm authorized to conduct petroleum operations in Viet Nam on an individual basis. Any petroleum exploration and production activities by foreign investors must be conducted in cooperation with Petro Viet Nam.

For downstream activities, several government-owned companies such as Petrolimex and Petec, under the Ministry of Trade, Petro Viet Nam Trading Company (Petechim), under Petro Viet Nam, SaigonPetro under Ho Chi Minh City People's Committee, and Vinapco, under Viet Nam Airlines have been licensed to import oil and gas. Petrolimex imports most of the total value of imported petroleum products.

Viet Nam has issued 37 investment licenses for oil and gas exploration since industry development began in 1998. About 30 companies, many of which are American or European, now operate offshore.

(ii)   *Natural gas and liquefied petroleum gas*

Viet Nam's natural gas consumption is rising, with further increases expected as gas fields come on stream. Natural gas reserves are approximately 6.8 trillion cubic feet. However, after major gas discoveries in 1996, production has moved more slowly than expected.

171

Viet Nam is a growing consumer and exporter of liquefied petroleum gas (LPG). Japan is the major consumer of Vietnamese LPG exports, receiving the country's first export shipment in May 1999. Domestic consumption is increasing rapidly and is expected to reach up to 50 per cent annual growth over the next few years. Vietnamese consumed an estimated 190,000 tons of LPG in 1999.

(iii)   *Coal and mining*

Viet Nam contains coal reserves estimated at 165 million short tons, the majority of which are anthracite. Production has increased dramatically in recent years as seen in the doubling of output between 1994 and 1998. This has resulted in an increase in exports (primarily to Japan) and an increase in coal stockpiles. Unfortunately Viet Nam's export markets have been shrinking, which has exacerbated an over supply problem. The state coal company, Vinacoal, considered a nationwide halt in production to reduce the estimated four-million-ton stockpile, but instead it cut back on production in the second half of 1999.

The country is promoting the construction of coal-fired power plants. Vinacoal plans to build as many as 11 new power plants, ranging from 100 megawatts (MW) to 300 MW each. Two 100-MW plants in Na Duong and Cao Ngan are already under construction, and nine more are under consideration. Viet Nam previously focused more on hydropower and the shift to coal marks an important change in its energy sector.

Viet Nam is endowed with an abundance of other mineral resources such as coal (3-3.5 billion tons), bauxite (3 billion tons), iron ore (700 million tons), copper (600,000 tons), tin (70,000 tons) and chromate (10 million tons).

The country is also rich in granite, marble, clay and silica sand. Almost all of these resources remain largely untapped. Foreign investment in the extraction and processing of these minerals, particularly the mining and processing of those minerals used in infrastructure projects such as steel, is strongly encouraged by the government.

(c)   *Manufacturing*

The manufacturing sector employs about 12 per cent of the country's workforce and generates about 17 per cent of GDP. Light manufacturing, particularly in food processing, textiles, and footwear comprises the bulk of manufacturing activities.

The textile and garment industry presently accounts for around 16 per cent of industrial output but is a key source of employment and one of the country's major export industries.

Heavy industry makes up a small portion of output, and like light industry it currently suffers from the prevalence of old, obsolete machinery and technology.

(d)   *Tourism*

Viet Nam's natural beauty, coupled with its open-door policy, has propelled the tourism industry into a high rate of growth. Viet Nam has 62,000 tourist hotel rooms with 116,300 beds. The occupancy rate in 1999 was 55 per cent. Visitor arrivals in 1999 were 1,781,754, up 17 per cent from 1998. However, the rapid increase in tourist arrivals has exposed the inadequacies of the sector in terms of infrastructure and services. As a result, major investment is required in the areas of transportation, training and tourism service industries.

In the first quarter of 2000, there were 530,000 visitors, an increase of 14.2 per cent over the same period of the previous year. Turnover in the public tourism sector in 1999 was 7,400 billion dong.

Viet Nam forecasts that the country will receive 8.7 million foreign and 15-18 million local tourists in 2010. The sector's share of GDP is expected to increase to 15.4 per cent in 2010 from 4 per cent in 1984.

For services in general, the sector achieved some impressive growth rates in 1995 and 1996, followed by a decline in the subsequent years. Figure 50 shows the growth rates for the services sector.

Figure 50. Services sector annual growth rates

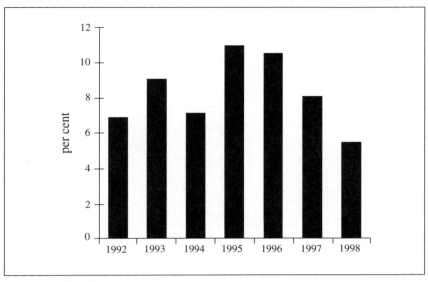

Source: World Bank

3. International trade

(a) *Overview*

Viet Nam has integrated itself into the global trading system since its economic reform movement took hold and as the government sought to expand its trading partners. Viet Nam's trade patterns have shifted from the former Eastern Bloc countries to Asia, Western Europe, and even the United States.

After five years of negotiations, Viet Nam signed a Bilateral Trade Agreement (BTA) with the United States in July 2000, to be implemented over the next few years.

The BTA will operate on two main fronts: first, each country will grant the other Most Favoured Nation (MFN) status with respect to trade in goods, services, and investment. This means, for instance, that the average United States rate of duty on imports from Viet Nam will drop from 40 per cent to 3 per cent. Second, the BTA obliges Viet Nam to phase in a wide range of market-oriented reforms designed to open Viet Nam's domestic market to foreign investment and competition.

The signing of the BTA should also bring Viet Nam closer to receiving additional trade benefits offered by the United States to developing countries under its Generalized System of Preferences (GSP). The process of negotiating and implementing the BTA, and gaining some measure of support from the United States should also bolster Viet Nam's prospects of joining the World Trade Organization (WTO) within the next few years.

Once the BTA comes into effect, it will remain in effect for only three years, but will automatically be extended for successive terms of three years unless terminated by either party at least 30 days before the end of a term.

Viet Nam's exports rose between 15 and 35 per cent throughout much of the 1990s until the effect of the Asian economic crisis was felt in 1998, when exports grew only 1.9 per cent. Table 29 shows trade data for the 1990s.

Table 29. Exports, imports, and trade deficits, 1990-1999

Year	Export (US$ million)	Increased, Decreased (%)	Import (US$ million)	Increased, Decreased (%)	Trade Deficit (US$ million)	Rate of Trade Deficit (%)
1990	2,404.0	23.5	2,752.4	7.3	348.4	14.5
1991	2,087.1	-13.2	2,338.1	-15.1	251.0	12.0
1992	2,580.7	23.7	2,540.7	8.7	-40.0	–
1993	2,985.2	15.7	3,924.0	54.4	938.8	31.4
1994	4,054.3	35.8	5,825.8	48.5	1,771.5	43.7
1995	5,448.9	34.4	8,155.4	40.0	2,706.5	49.7
1996	7,255.9	33.2	11,143.6	36.6	3,887.7	53.6
1997	9,185.0	26.6	11,592.3	4.0	2,407.3	26.2
1998	9,361.0	1.9	11,495.0	-0.5	2,134.0	22.8
est. 1999	11,523.0	23.1	11,636.0	0.9	113.0	1.0

Source: Viet Nam National Administration of Tourism (www.vietnamtourism.com)

While the country's exports grew at impressive rates in the 1990s, its imports rose rapidly as well until the Asian economic crisis struck. As seen in table 2, Viet Nam experienced a trade deficit throughout the decade except for 1992. Overall the export sector performed strongly in 1999, helping to shrink the trade deficit to US$ 113 million from US$ 2.1 billion in 1998. However, the trade deficit will likely worsen for 2000 because of the dramatic rise in prices of imported petroleum and related products. Viet Nam paid about US$ 746 million for imported petroleum products in the first five months of 2000, an increase of 129.5 per cent from the previous year.

(b)   *Exports*

Exports were expected to rise 23 per cent in 1999 over 1998. Much of the increase can be attributed to the depreciation of the Vietnamese currency, the *dong*. The export turnover for 2000 was expected to reach US$ 10.7 billion.

The main export items, as seen in figure 51 include crude oil, rice, garments and footwear, computers and parts, coffee, rubber, and marine products, especially frozen shrimp.

Figure 51. Major Viet Nam exports by commodity, 1999
(millions of US dollars)

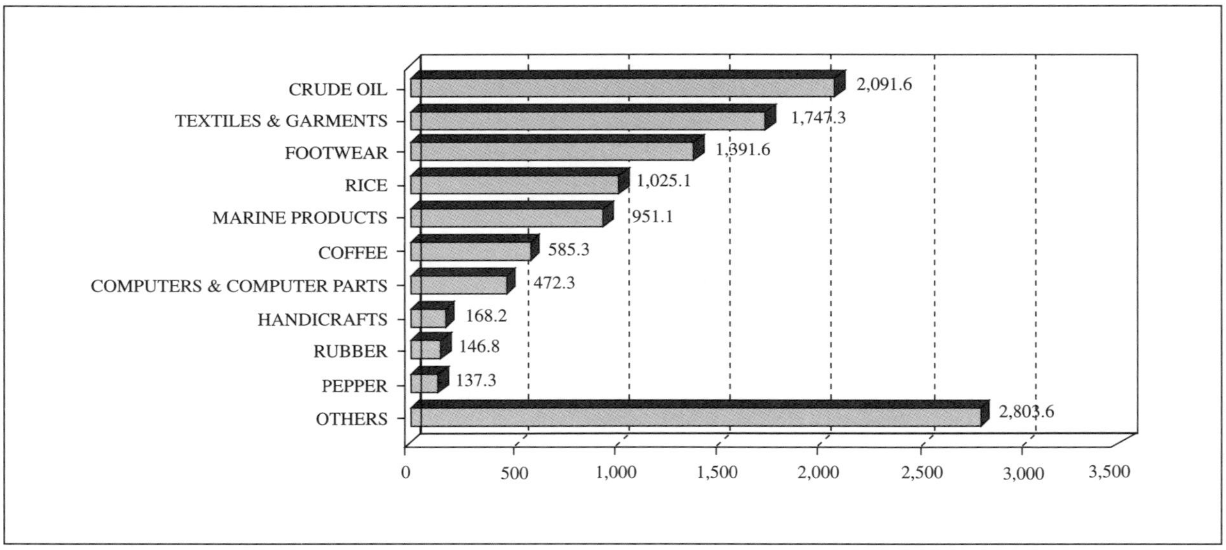

Source: EXIM Bank of Thailand

174

Footwear companies earned nearly US$ 1.4 billion in exports in 1999, up 30 per cent over 1998, making them one of the top foreign exchange sectors. The United States is the largest footwear export target following the recent signing of a trade pact between Hanoi and Washington. In 2000, Viet Nam's footwear industry was expected to export US$ 1.45-1.50 billion worth of products. Currently the EU remains the largest importer, accounting for 80 per cent of the volume.

Viet Nam's 1999 rice exports amounted to 4.5 million tons and exceeded US$ 1 billion. In 2000, total exports of 4.3 million tons of rice were projected. Of this total, 2.9 million tons will be exported from Ho Chi Minh City and the Mekong Delta, 1.2 million tons by state-owned companies and foreign investment enterprises, and the rest by large businesses in all economic sectors. The Asian market accounts for 54.5 per cent of Viet Nam's rice exports, with Africa taking 22.8 per cent and the Middle East around 12 per cent.

Viet Nam exported 378,872 tons of coffee beans in 1999, an increase of 41 per cent over the previous year. The United States tops the list with imports of 78,546 tons, followed by Germany with 51,150 tons; Italy with 40,909 tons; Belgium with 33,329 tons; and Spain with 30,642 tons.

In the nine months prior to July 2000, Viet Nam exported 508,970 tons of coffee, an increase of 54.43 per cent. However, due to world market prices, export earnings during the same period dropped 4.73 per cent to US$ 446.86 million. With an expected coffee output of between 450,000 tons to 500,000 tons in the 2000 crop season, Viet Nam will take over from Indonesia as the biggest coffee producer in the world. Currently Viet Nam has 350,000 hectares under cultivation for coffee.

Viet Nam's major trade partners are in East Asia, demonstrating the importance attributed to regional trade (see figure 52). While the United States only comprised 4.4 per cent in 1999, the normalization of trade relations should benefit Viet Nam's exports immensely over the next couple of years. The World Bank has estimated that Viet Nam's exports to the United States (mostly footwear, coffee, seafood, and oil) will increase to US$ 800 million (more than double 1999 levels) in the first year the BTA comes into effect. Most of the growth will come from footwear and textile exports, since coffee and seafood are already exempt from United States import duties.

Figure 52. Major Viet Nam export markets, 1999

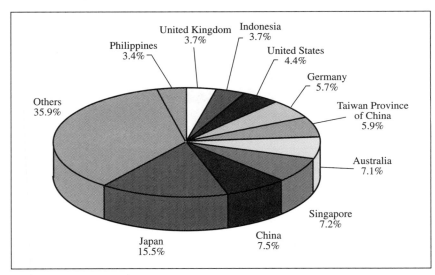

Source: EXIM Bank of Thailand

(c)   *Imports*

Major import items are petroleum products, machinery, tractors, tires, steel and iron products, electronic goods, cotton, textiles, and fertilizers. Figure 53 shows the key imports for 1999.

Figure 53. Major Viet Nam imports by commodity, 1999
(millions of US dollars)

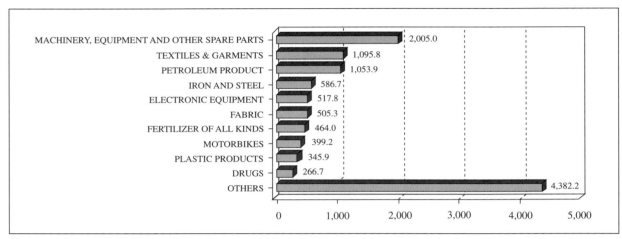

Source: EXIM Bank of Thailand

As with exports, Viet Nam imports most of its goods from East Asia (see figure 54). From outside the region, the United States sends the most goods to Viet Nam.

Figure 54. Major Viet Nam import markets, 1999

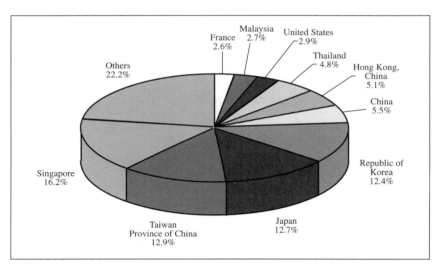

Source: EXIM Bank of Thailand

4. Investment

Foreign direct investment (FDI) grew rapidly from 1991-1996 as many of the economic reforms and implementation of the Foreign Investment Law (1987) took shape. However, FDI has fallen sharply over the past few years from US$ 8.6 billion in 1996 to an estimate of US$ 1.6 billion in 1999 (see figure 55). The main causes of the decline are the fallout from the regional economic crisis, intense worldwide competition for attracting investment, and slow implementation of further structural reforms of the Vietnamese economy.

Figure 55. Foreign direct investment in Viet Nam

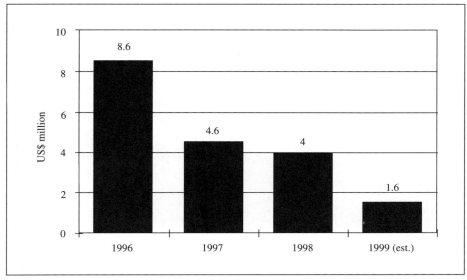

Source: ASEAN Secretariat

Table 30 shows a breakdown of total investment (foreign and domestic) in Viet Nam from 1995 to 1999. Although the FDI appears to be fairly stable over between 1995 and 1998, the depreciation of the dong actually meant a decline in investment.

Table 30. Investment capital in Viet Nam, 1995-1999
(billions of Vietnamese dong)

	1995	1996	1997	1998	est. 1999
1. State-owned capital	26,047.8	35,894.4	46,570.4	51,600.0	64,000.0
a. State budget	13,575.0	16,544.2	20,570.4	20,700.0	26,000.0
b. Credit budget	3,064.0	8,280.2	12,700.0	14,800.0	19,000.0
c. Budget from owner companies	9,408.8	11,070.3	13,300.0	16,100.0	19,000.0
2. Other sector's capital	20,000.0	20,773.0	20,000.0	20,500.0	21,000.0
3. Foreign direct investment	22,000.0	22,700.0	22,700.0	24,300.0	18,900.0
Total	**68,047.8**	**79,367.4**	**96,870.4**	**96,400.0**	**103,900.0**

Source: Viet Nam National Administration of Tourism (www.vietnamtourism.com)

The major sources of FDI are shown in table 31. In terms of dollar value, Singapore heads the list with US$ 5.8 billion. For the number of projects, Taiwan Province of China leads with 634. Nearly 3,000 foreign investment projects have been approved in Viet Nam. According to the ASEAN Secretariat, by the end of August 1999 US$ 15.2 billion worth of foreign investment projects had been implemented, representing 42 per cent of the total registered capital.

Ho Chi Minh City attracts the most investment both in terms of the number of projects and the amount of capital. The capital city, Hanoi, ranks second in these categories (see table 32).

In the initial few years after the Law on Foreign Investment came into effect, much of the FDI in Viet Nam was aimed at oil and gas exploration and exploitation, and construction of hotels and office buildings. The pattern has changed to where manufacturing industries are now attracting a great deal of the FDI. Table 33 shows a breakdown of FDI according to sectors.

Table 31. Capital investment in Viet Nam by different countries/areas
(1 January 1998 to 31 July 2000)

Country	No. of projects	Capital Investment (US$ billion)
Singapore	249	5.8
Russian Federation	61	5.0
Taiwan Province of China	634	4.9
Japan	324	3.6
Hong Kong, China	323	3.4
France	157	2.1
British Virgin Islands	94	2.0
United States of America	116	1.3
United Kingdom	39	1.1
Malaysia	86	1.1
Republic of Korea	292	1.0
Australia	97	1.0
Thailand	125	1.0
Panama	9	0.675
Netherlands	40	0.626

Source: Viet Nam Ministry of Planning and Investment (MPI)

Table 32. Capital investment by provinces in Viet Nam
(1 January 1988 to 31 July 2000)

Province	No. of projects	Capital (US$ million)
Ho Chi Minh City	1,053	11,000
Hanoi	445	7,500
Dong Nai	294	3,200
Ba Ria - Vung Tau	99	2,500
Binh Duong	319	2,000
Hai Phong	112	1,400
Quang Ngai	8	1,300
Quang Ninh	52	870
Lam Dong	50	866
Da Nang	61	786
Hai Duong	27	493
Ha Tay	31	444
Thanh Hoa	8	425
Vinh Phuc	26	318
Khanh Hoa)	52	290

Source: Viet Nam Ministry of Planning and Investment (MPI)

**Table 33. Capital investment in the different industrial sectors in Viet Nam
(1 January 1988 to 31 July 2000)**

Sector	No. of projects	Capital (US$ billion)
Heavy Industry	578	6.2
Hotels/Tourism	199	5.0
Light Industry	866	4.0
Construction	272	3.5
Urban Construction	3	3.3
Post & Telecommunications	136	3.2
Oil & Gas	62	3.0
Offices for lease	105	3.0
Food	191	2.2
Agriculture/Forestry	267	1.1
Other services	160	0.838
Culture/Health/Education	91	0.525
Sea-products	95	0.344
EPZ/Industrial Zone	5	0.302
Banking-Finance	35	0.243
Other sectors	4	0.27
Total	**3,069**	**37**

Source: Viet Nam Ministry of Planning and Investment (MPI)

The number of workers employed by foreign-investment businesses increased from 267,000 in 1997 to 296,000 in 1999, which indicates that the foreign-funded sector has undergone significant production expansion. Furthermore, the foreign-funded sector's export value rose to nearly US$ 2.6 billion in 1999, representing an increase of 30 per cent over 1998. The sector now contributes 10.3 per cent of the country's GDP.

A significant amount of investment emanates from the overseas Vietnamese, known as the Viet Kieu. A surge in Viet Kieu investments could follow some key rule changes. Inter-ministerial Circular 10/2000/TTLT has removed some major obstacles faced by Viet Kieu and expatriates who possess certificates of permanent residence in Viet Nam. Viet Kieu have traditionally preferred to invest under the name of relatives in order to avoid dual pricing and to access better tax rates.

Officially, 50 Viet Kieu projects worth US$ 200 million operate under the FIL. Additionally, there are 370 businesses with a registered capital of US$ 28.6 million established under the Law on Encouraging Domestic Investment. However, some observers believe that, taking into account unofficial investments, Viet Kieu have invested at least US$ 1.2 billion in the homeland, mainly in property, software, aquaculture and fishery-processing.

The latest circular stipulates that Viet Kieu and resident expatriates can now invest through Amended Decree 51 on Encouraging Domestic Investment. The circular is effective from September 1, 2000 and will allow these investors to receive the same land tax rate and land rent incentives as domestic investors.

The circular also applies the one price mechanism for land rents, raw materials, fuel, and a number of other services. Viet Kieu and resident foreign investors will pay the same price for accommodation, travel, water, electricity, medical treatment, telecom, education, and training as Vietnamese.

As for outward investment, in the fiscal year ending April 2000 Viet Nam carried out 11 projects abroad with a total investment capital of US$ 4.9 million, the highest figure ever recorded by the country. Also in the past year, overseas projects expanded to include financial and banking joint ventures, software industry, wooden products, and handicrafts.

In order to put the recent achievements in their proper perspective, from August 1989 when Viet Nam started to make investments abroad until early 1999 the country had only 18 projects licensed by other countries with a combined investment capital of nearly US$ 8 million. Of these earlier overseas investments, 12 projects with 70 per cent of the total investment capital were involved in aquatic products processing and sea transport.

The increased investment abroad is due to the government Decision 22/1999/ND-CP on investment outside of Viet Nam that took effect on April 29, 1999. The decision not only creates a legal framework for investment abroad but also encourages Vietnamese businesses to integrate into the regional and world markets.

5. Currency

The Vietnamese dong, like so many currencies in East Asia, depreciated in relation to the United States dollar over the past few years. In January 1998, the exchange rate was US$ 1 for 12,293 dong, but by January 17, 2001 the exchange rate stood at 14,578. Table 34 contains a summary of the dong's depreciation since January 1998.

Table 34. Selected exchange rates for the dong (based on US$ 1)

Date	Exchange rate	Trends, 1/98 to 1/17/01
1 January 1998	12,293	Average rate: 13,808
31 December 1998	13,894	High: 14,578
31 December 1999	14,030	Low: 12,280
31 December 2000	14,566	
17 January 2001	14,578	

Source: www.oanda.com

6. National economic policies and priorities

Before the Asian economic crisis began in mid-1997, Viet Nam's economy had been growing rapidly. Between 1990 and 1997, it experienced an average annual GDP growth rate of eight per cent. The financial crisis had a negative impact on the economy, which is not predicted to resume high growth rates without continuing reforms.

The Government's "2000 Socioeconomic Development Masterplan" highlights key areas for attention. The country should "gear itself to overcome the current economic growth slow-down" and create sustainable development. This strategy should also increase production efficiency and competitiveness, improve investment usage, stabilize the macro-economic environment and make financial operations more transparent.

The Government is committed to "tackling important social issues and popularizing educational, medical, cultural, sports and games facilities and it will gradually improve the salary system". To reach these goals, the master plan focuses on the following areas:

First, concentration on agricultural production and the rural economy with priority for irrigation work, anti-natural disaster projects, and the application of advanced technology, such as high-yield plant seeds and animal strains. Measures will be taken to settle outstanding legal issues that might hinder agricultural production or the marketing of products. State management should be united in the whole production process as well as the export of farm, forest, and aquatic produce. Differences between supply and demand will also be tackled.

Second, the Government will tackle difficulties in industrial production and services, encourage in-depth investment projects, technical renewal and management reform or restructuring to minimize production costs and improve product quality. This will increase competitiveness as well as boost enterprises' production, marketing, and export capacities.

Third, domestic markets need to expand, especially in remote rural and mountainous areas. Farmers require greater assistance in selling their goods domestically. Measures that might increase purchasing power in production, construction, and consumption so as to increase domestic sales are also necessary.

Fourth, there is a strong need to stimulate national investment as well as increase the efficiency of capital, especially capital investments from the State budget.

A fifth area of attention is to implement the national financial policy in line with the orientation to promote demand in construction, production, and consumption.

Sixth, Viet Nam needs to conduct scientific research to apply new technology to production and the service industry.

The National Assembly set the following targets for 2000:

- GDP growth: 5-5.6 per cent
- Industrial growth: 10.5 per cent
- Agricultural growth: 3.5-4 per cent
- Food output in rice equivalent: 33.5-34 million tons
- Growth in industrial output value: 10.5-11 per cent
- Growth in services: 5-5.5 per cent
- Growth in exports: 11-12 per cent
- Inflation rate: to be held at six per cent
- Budget deficit: not exceeding five per cent
- Employment: for 1.2-1.3 million people
- Vocational training: for 780,000 people
- Reduction in poor households: to 11 per cent
- Reduction of birth rate: by 0.5 per cent

C. Institutional and support network: public and private sector organizations

1. Government organizations and agencies

Ministry of Planning and Investment

There are four main departments under the Ministry:

- Department of Investment Legislation and promotion
- Department of Foreign Investment
- Department of Industrial Zones, Export Processing Zone Management
- Department of FDI Project Monitoring

Contact address:
56 Quoc Tu Giam, Hanoi
Tel: (844) 823-5606/823-2890
Fax: (844) 747-4142/845-9271

Ministry of Industry

The Ministry of Industry's goal is to encourage local and foreign firms to establish factories in the country. It also oversees most matters concerning the industrial sector.

Contact address:
54 Hai Ba Trung Street, Hoan Kiem, Hanoi
Tel: (844) 825-2852, 826-7870
Fax: (844) 826-9033

Ministry of Trade

The Ministry of Trade promotes the country's products and plays a major role in regulating business.

Contact address:
31 Trang Tien, Hanoi
Tel: (844) 824-2124, 825-3881
Fax: (844) 826-4696

Ministry of Agriculture and Rural Development

Contact address:
2 Ngoc Ha, Hanoi
Tel: (844) 845-9617, 846-8160
Fax: (844) 845-4319

2. Viet Nam Chamber of Commerce and Industry (VCCI)

Founded in 1963, VCCI is an independent and non-governmental organization serving the needs and representing the interests of the business community in Viet Nam. With members throughout the country, including all of the largest Vietnamese business groups and corporations, as well as many foreign companies, the VCCI provides a useful access to the country's business community.

Its main activities are:

- Maintaining dialogue with the Government aimed at creating a more favourable business and investment environment
- Assisting overseas business delegations in exploring the business environment and opportunities in Viet Nam
- Providing trade and investment information through a series of software and printed publications
- Providing consulting services to foreign companies seeking trade and investment opportunities in Viet Nam
- Organizing trade and investment missions to foreign countries to look for trade opportunities and investment partners
- Organizing Vietnamese trade shows and assisting local manufacturers and companies to participate in international trade fairs and exhibitions abroad. It also organizes international trade fairs and exhibitions
- Issuing certificates of origin for Vietnamese exports
- Assisting and providing services in industrial and intellectual property protection

Contact addresses:

Head Office	*Branch Offices*	
Hanoi	Ho Chi Minh City	Danang City
33 Ba Trieu Street	171 Vo Thi Sau	256 Tran Phu
Tel: (844) 825-3023	Tel: (848) 823-0301	Tel: (8451) 822-1719
Fax: (844) 825-6446	Fax: (848) 829-4472	Fax: (8451) 822-930
Haiphong City	Vungtau City	Cantho City
10 Dinh Tien Hoan Street	36/6 Vo Thi Sau Street	29 Cach Mang Thang Tam Street
Tel: (8431) 842-894	Tel: (8464) 852-710	Tel: (8471) 824-918
Fax: (8431) 842-243	Fax: (8464) 859-651	Fax: (8471) 824-169

3. Accounting, law, and consulting firms

There are several firms to provide accounting, legal, and business consulting services. The list of firms below does not imply endorsement or vouch for their capabilities.

(a) *Accounting firms*

Arthur Andersen

Ho Chi Minh City	Hanoi
Level 10, Sun Wah Tower	17 Bis Pham Dinh Ho 115 Nguyen Hue
Street, District 1	Hai Ba Trung District
Tel: (848) 821-9269	Tel: (844) 821-9780
Fax: (848) 821-9268	Fax: (844) 821-9775

PriceWaterhouseCoopers

Ho Chi Minh City	Hanoi	Danang
4 Floor Saigon Tower	4 Floor, International Centre	68 Nguyen Chi Thanh 29
Le Duan Street	17 Ngo Quyen Street	Tel: (84 0511) 834-362
Tel: (848) 823-0796	Tel: (844) 825-1215	Fax: (84 0511) 832-243
Fax: (848) 823-0796	Fax: (844) 825-1737	

Auditing & Consulting Company (A & C Co.)
Head office

138 Nguyen Thi Minh Khai Street	Khanh Hoa
District 3, Ho Chi Minh City	100 Quang Trung Street
Tel: (848) 829-1791, 824-3136	Tel: (8458) 811-591
Fax: (848) 825-8199	Fax: (8458) 811-593

Accounting & Auditing Financial Consultancy Service Co. (AASC)
Le Phung Hieu Street, Hoan Kiem District, Hanoi
Tel: (8404) 8262775
Fax: (8404) 825-3973

Auditing & Informatic Service Co. (AISC)
42 Nguyen Thi Minh Khai Street, District 3
Ho Chi Minh City
Tel: (848) 829-5163
Fax: (848) 829-4281

BHP Auditing
111 Nguyen CongTru Street, District
Ho Chi Minh City
Tel: (848) 821-5014
Fax: (848) 821-5015

Bourne Griffiths Viet Nam Ltd.
3rd Floor, 27 Ly Thai To Street, Hoan Kiem District
Hanoi
Tel: (844) 824-2733
Fax: (844) 826-4380

Ernst & Young Co. (Hanoi)
15th Floor, Deaha Business Centre
360 Kimma Street
Tel: (844) 831-5100, 814-5152
Fax: (844) 831-5090

Hanoi Profession of Auditing & Accounting Co., Ltd.
21 Phuong Mai Street
Dong Da District
Hanoi
Tel: (844) 576-0737
Fax: (844) 576-0713

(b) *Legal firms*

Baker & McKenzie
Ho Chi Minh City
12th Floor, Saigon Tower
29 Le Duan Street, District 1
Tel: (848) 829-5585
Fax: (848) 829-5618

Hanoi
3rd Floor, 63 Ly Thai To Street
Hoan Kiem District
Tel: (844) 825-1428
Fax: (844) 825-1432

Gide Loyrette Nouel Co.
Hanoi
4th Floor, 56 Ly Thai To Street
Hoan Kiem District
Tel: (844) 826-2060, 825-1958
Fax: (844) 825-7919

Helen Yeo & Partners Co.
Ho Chi Minh City
2 Ngo Duc Ke Street, Me Linh Blg
District 1
Tel: (848) 822-9362, 833-9363
Fax: (848) 824-4981

Hoan Kiem Law Consultancy & Services
Hanoi City
28 B17 Nam Thanh Cong Area
Tel: (844) 851-5712
Fax: (844) 831-0482

Hung Vuong Law Firm
Hanoi City
47 Le Hong Phong Street
Tel: (844) 823-1949, 843-5801
Fax: (844) 843-5801

Johnson Stokes & Master Co.
Ho Chi Minh City
6th Floor, Saigon Tower
29 Le Duan Street, District 1
Tel: (848) 822-8860
Fax: (848) 822-8864

Kelvin Chia Partnership
Hanoi City
Rm 201, 43 Tran Xuan Soan Street
Hai Ba Trung District, Ha
Tel: (844) 822-8787, 822-8788
Fax: (844) 825-1875

Viet Law Economic & Consultancy Co. Ltd.
Hanoi City
57 Nguyen Du Street
Tel: (844) 822-8298
Fax: (844) 822-2478

Viet Law Firm Ltd.
Ho Chi Minh City
57B Tu Xuong Street, District 3
Tel: (848) 820-2138, 822-3507
Fax: (848) 822-8298

(c) *Consulting firms*

Investment & Trade Service Consultant
Ho Chi Minh City
287 Phan Dinh Phung
Phu Nhuan District
Tel: (848) 845-7148
Fax: (848) 842-1106

Javidec International Co.
Hanoi
61 Hang Chuoi Street
Hai Ba Trung District
Tel: (844) 821-1554
Fax: (844) 971-3093

Linh Nhat Co., Ltd.
Hanoi City
25A An Duong Street, Tay Ho District
Tel: (844) 829-3853
Fax: (844) 823-9848

Thanh Ha Co., Ltd.
Hanoi City
21 Nguyen Chi Thanh Road
Ngoc Khanh Ward, Dong Da
Tel: (844) 771-5655
Fax: (844) 771-5661

Thaoly Consultants Ltd.
Ho Chi Minh City
223 Huynh Van Banh Street
Phu Nhuan District
Tel: (848) 844-4748
Fax: (848) 845-4378

4. Financial institutions

In 1990, the State Bank of Viet Nam (SBV) became Viet Nam's central bank. The transformation made it necessary to turn over its credit functions to four newly reorganized banks:

- Bank for Agriculture & Rural Development
- Bank for Investment & Development
- Foreign Trade Bank of Viet Nam (Vietcombank)
- Industrial & Commercial Bank of Viet Nam (Incombank)

(a) *Bank for Agriculture & Rural Development*

Established in November 1990, its main role is financing the agricultural and rural sector. The bank mobilizes funds from urban areas and lends to the farming communities throughout the country.

(b) *Bank for Investment & Development of Viet Nam*

Established in November 1990, the Bank for Investment & Development acts as a commercial bank by issuing long-term credit for financing development projects. It receives funds from institutional organizations such as the Asian Development Bank (ADB), World Bank, and the International Monetary Fund (IMF) for the sole purpose of financing infrastructure development.

(c) *Bank for Foreign Trade of Viet Nam (Vietcombank)*

Vietcombank is the largest state-owned commercial bank in Viet Nam, accounting for an estimated 70 per cent of the country's import-export trade financing. Its main objectives are to grant long-term credits for financing state infrastructure and telecommunication projects, and medium-term credit, usually to state-owned companies for state economic and development projects such as exporting, importing raw materials and machinery, and manufacturing equipment projects.

(d) *Industrial Trade Bank of Viet Nam (Incombank)*

Incombank was also established in November 1990 and focuses on domestic banking activities, such as issuing short-term credit, mainly to state-owned companies.

In addition to these major state banks there are over 90 other commercial banks, joint stock banks, foreign banks, and other private banks.

(e) *Stock market*

The Securities Trading Centre (STC) officially opened its doors in Ho Chi Minh City on 21 July 2000. Preparations for the first stock market date back to the early 1990s. More than 400 Vietnamese state-owned enterprises and joint stock companies have equity, with roughly 50 of them meeting the basic criteria to list on the exchange. As of 2000, four companies had listed on the STC:

- Refrigeration Electrical Engineering Corporation
- Cable and Telecommunications Materials Company
- Foreign Forwarding and Warehousing Company
- Hai Phong Paper Joint-Stock Company

The STC is open on Monday, Wednesday, and Friday from 08:00 to 11:00.

The Ministry of Finance plans to issue government bonds on the bourse with the first batch valued at US$ 21.4 million. The ministry is discussing with the State Securities Commission, the supervisor and regulator of Viet Nam's stock market, a plan to auction government bonds. This activity could become normal practice for mobilizing capital.

As of 2000, there were six securities companies licensed to provide brokerage services:

- Saigon Securities Company
- First Securities Company
- Bao Viet Securities Company
- Asia Commercial Bank Securities
- Thang Long Securities Company
- Bank for Investment and Development of Viet Nam Securities

United Kingdom-based investment fund Dragon Capital was the first foreign entity given permission to trade in securities on Viet Nam's stock market, after receiving a code from the Hong Kong and Shanghai Banking Corporation (HSBC), the only foreign-invested institution licensed to provide a stock custody service in Viet Nam.

Foreign investors can purchase no more than 20 per cent of the shares in any one company's shares or investment certificates listed by an investment fund.

The sale of shares issued by state-owned enterprises and joint stock companies to foreigners cannot exceed 30 per cent of the company's total registered capital. Where the number of shares wanted by foreigners exceeds 30 per cent, a share auction must be opened. Foreign investor shares can be converted or sold after one year. This is limited to three years if the foreign investor is a part of the issuing company's management board. Decision No. 228/QDNH5 issued by the governor of the State Bank of Viet Nam in December 1993 was the first regulation allowing foreigners to invest in the country in the form of stock purchases.

Under this decision, stocks owned by foreign shareholders were fixed at a maximum of 30 per cent, while individual foreign shareholders could buy 10 per cent of a company's total shares. It also stipulated that foreign investor shares could only be sold after five years.

5. Transportation

Viet Nam's transportation system consists of an estimated 105,000 kilometres of roads (including 47,000 kilometres of rural roads), 2,600 kilometres of railway, 11,000 kilometres of navigable inland waterways, eight national seaports, 20 provincial seaports, several inland river ports, three international airports, and an additional number of smaller domestic airports.

(a) *Airports*

International airports: Noi Bai (Hanoi), Tan Son Nhat (Ho Chi Minh City), Danang (Danang city).

Domestic airports: Gia Lam (Hanoi), Cat Bi (Haiphong), Dien Bien (Lai Chau), Na San (Son La), Vinh (Nghe An), Phu Bai (Hue), Pleiku (Gia Lai), Phu Cat (Qui Nhon), Nha Trang (Khanh Hoa), Buon Ma Thuot (Darklak), Lien Khuong (Da Lat), Vung Tau (Ba Ria -Vung Tau), Phu Quoc, Rach Gia (Kien Giang).

(b) *Road network*

There are a number of major highways and bridges linking Viet Nam to its neighbouring countries. The main one is National Highway 18 and 18B, which extends 118 kilometres from an industrial complex at Cai Lan to the border between Viet Nam and China. More links to Viet Nam's neighbouring countries are being planned or constructed, such as with the Lao People's Democratic Republic. The road links with the Lao People's Democratic Republic will extend to Thailand and form the ADB's "East-West Corridor".

National highway routes are as follows:

National Highway No. 1: Hanoi – Bac Ninh – Lang Son; Hanoi – Nam Dinh – Ninh Binh – Thanh Hoa – Vinh – Ha Tinh – Song Hoi – Song Ha – Hue – Danang – Tam Ky – Quang Ngai – Qui Nhon – Tuy Hoa – Ninh Hoa – Nha Trang – Cam Ranh – Phan Rang – Phan Thiet – Bien Hoa – Ho Chi Minh – Tan An – My Tho – Sa Dec – Long Xuyen – Vinh Long – Can Tho – Soc Trang – Bac Lieu – Ca Mau.

National Highway No. 2: Hanoi – Viet Tri – Tuyen Quang – Ha Giang
National Highway No. 3: Hanoi – Thai Nguyen – Cao Bang
National Highway No. 5: Hanoi – Hai Duong – Hai Phong
National Highway No. 6: Hanoi – Ha Dong – Hoa Binh – Son La
National Highway No. 32: Hanoi – Son Tay
National Highway No. 18: Hai Phong – Quang Ninh
National Highway No. 9: Dong Ha – Lao Bao
National Highway No. 14: Danang – Kon Tum – Pleiku – Buon Ma Thuot – Song Be
National Highway No. 19: Qui Nhon – Pleiku
National Highway No. 26: Ninh Hoa – Buon Ma Thuot
National Highway No. 20: Phan Rang – Dalat – Bao Loc – Dong Nai
National Highway No. 13: Ho Chi Minh – Song Be
National Highway No. 22: Ho Chi Minh – Tay Ninh

(c)   *Inland waterways*

Transportation of freight and passengers by waterways has evolved over many centuries in nearly all the cities and provincial towns in Viet Nam. With an estimated 39,000 kilometres of waterways, Viet Nam's river transportation accounts for about 36 per cent of the total national freight volume. There are two major inland waterways: the first situated in the Red River area with five main ports and the other extending along the Mekong River.

(d)   *Rail*

There are approximately 2,600 kilometres of rail network covering over 260 stations, the most important being the Hanoi-Ho Chi Minh City line, also known as the "Unification Express Route," which stretches over 1,730 kilometres and forms the key north-south rail axis.

6. Communications

Between 1991-1995, over US$ 1 billion was invested in upgrading Viet Nam's telecommunication systems. In 1998 there were approximately two telephones for every 100 people. The telecommunication network in Viet Nam has eight earth satellite stations with direct communications channels to over 40 countries and indirect communications with nearly every country in the world.

Additional cable lines are being installed to link Viet Nam to China, the Lao People's Democratic Republic, Thailand, Malaysia, and Singapore. With future plans to install more networks, including all villages in rural and remote areas in the country, it is estimated that there will be six telephones for every 100 people by 2000.

7. Other infrastructure

(a)   *Energy and electricity*

There has been a dramatic surge of demand for electricity over the past 15 years in both the industrial and household sectors in Viet Nam. The completion of the Hoa Binh hydroelectric project in 1994 has helped to generate a total capacity of 4,400 MW.

In 1997, electricity output increased to over 19,000 million kilowatts. Other sources of electricity are hydro stations (45 per cent of the total), coal powered plants (16 per cent) and natural gas (36 per cent).

In 1995, the Government of Viet Nam embarked on a five-year plan to modernize existing power plants and construct new ones in the central and northern areas as part of a national effort to boost power generation to 30-33 billion kilowatts by 2000.

In 1998, Viet Nam had a total electric generating capacity of 4.9 gigawatts (GW). For that same year, hydropower accounted for roughly 87 per cent of electricity generation, while thermal power accounted for about 13 per cent. The state power company, Electricity of Viet Nam (EVN), is working on developing a national electricity network by 2020, including the construction of Viet Nam's first nuclear power plant by 2020.

Foreign companies are becoming involved in the growing Vietnamese power market. In July 1999, EVN and a consortium including Tokyo Electric (Japan), Lahmeyer International (Germany), and Pacific Power International (Australia) signed a contract to construct a 600-MW plant in the Mekong Delta. The plant will be oil-fired but could switch to natural gas. Electricite de France (EdF) is leading a consortium that aims to build a 700 MW gas-fired plant to be part of the Phu My power complex.

(b)   *Ports*

Viet Nam has eight national seaports, but Ho Chi Minh City and Haiphong handle the vast majority of traffic. The former serves most of the southern region, whilst the northern region is served by Haiphong. Another important port is Danang at the mouth of the Song Han River, which serves the central highlands and much of the transit traffic to and from the Lao People's Democratic Republic. As the East-West Corridor develops, Danang will become an increasingly important transit point for goods originating from as far away as Myanmar.

Saigon Port in Ho Chi Minh City has the capacity to handle an estimated 4 million tons of cargo yearly and can handle 15,000 deadweight ton ships. Haiphong Port with 11 berths and a total length of 1,800 metres can handle about 4.5 million metric tons yearly.

D.   Legal and regulatory frameworks for trade and investment

1.   Foreign investment

(a)   *Overall investment climate and the law on foreign investment*

The major laws governing foreign investment are the Law on Foreign Investment in Viet Nam, Decree 18, and Regulations on Foreign Investment in Viet Nam, often referred to collectively as "FIL" for foreign investment legislation. FIL provisions detail the form and organization for four types of investment vehicles, investment guarantees, taxation, banking and foreign exchange, and other pertinent issues. The Law on Foreign Investment, promulgated in 1987, has been amended several times with the most recent version of the law occurring in May 2000.

The amended Law on Foreign Investment now contains 21 fresh additions and 20 changed articles. Major changes include alterations to investment forms and voting procedures in joint ventures.

Investors will now be allowed to open offshore accounts and can expect investment procedures to be simplified. A number of import tariffs and tax exemptions have been changed while land use rights concerning mortgages and clearance have been improved.

Joint venture boards will be required to reach mutual agreement when making appointments and dismissals of general and deputy general directors. Mutual agreement will still also be required for changes to business functions. Other important issues like the voting procedures requiring mutual agreement when making annual final accounting reports, loans, and appointment and dismissal of chief accounts were noticeably missing in the amendments.

One change now allows companies that suffer monetary losses from changing regulations to offset those losses against their income to lower their tax bill.

The amendments will reduce some of the current and fixed expenses for investors that were already too high compared to other countries in the region. For example, electricity is 25 per cent higher than throughout the region, while postal and telecommunications charges are four to five times higher.

Investors are now allowed to open offshore accounts, assuming approval from the central bank. The taxes on profits reimbursed overseas were lowered to 3, 5 and 7 per cent from the previous 5, 7 and 10 per cent brackets.

Foreign investors are allowed to invest in Viet Nam in various areas of the economy. Viet Nam encourages investment in economic sectors and localities as follows:

(i) *Sectors:*

    a. *Production of exports;*

    b. *Cultivating, growing, and processing agricultural, forestry, and aquatic products;*

    c. *High technology, advanced know-how industries, with a view to protecting the ecological environment, investment in research and development;*

    d. *Labour-intensive industries; processing materials and using domestic natural resources efficiently;*

    e. *Construction of infrastructure and other important industrial production facilities;*

(ii) *Localities:*

    a. *Mountainous and remote regions;*

    b. *Areas underdeveloped in terms of socio-economic factors;*

    c. *Foreign investment licenses are not granted in sectors and areas where foreign investment may hamper national security and defense, cultural and historical heritage, custom, and the ecological environment.*

In accordance with planning and development guidelines, the government specifies which localities are suitable for foreign investment, issues lists of priority and prime priority investment projects, lists of conditional investment sectors, and lists of prohibited investment sectors. Private economic organizations are allowed to engage in investment cooperation with foreign investors in most sectors and under conditions regulated by the government.

(iii) *Perceived problems*

Following a Ministry of Planning and Investment (MPI) survey of 64 foreign-investment enterprises, officials identified the three most pressing problems in Viet Nam's investment climate: dual pricing, discrimination against private firms in favor of state-owned enterprises, and difficulties in accessing land. Other problems the MPI pollsters found were related to the business approval and labour recruitment processes. The lowest ranked complaint related to difficulties in choosing which form of investment would be most suitable to conduct business.

(iv) *Investment guarantees*

The Government of Viet Nam guarantees that capital and other lawful assets of investors will not be expropriated or confiscated by administrative measures and that businesses with foreign invested capital will not be nationalized. Additionally, laws and regulations will not be applied retroactively if they adversely affect investors' interests.

(v) *Remittances and conversion policies*

Subject to foreign exchange availability and after payment of all tax obligations, foreign investors may repatriate their share of legal after-tax profits (only during the year in which the profits were actually made), principal and interest due on loans, royalties or fees paid, invested capital and any other legally owned money and assets.

This guarantee is valid if the activities are supported by an underlying contract that has been approved by the relevant government authorities.

Expatriates working for businesses with foreign invested capital are allowed to remit their income abroad.

Under the FIL, foreign parties to a BCC and foreign investment enterprises are generally required to be self-sufficient in foreign currency requirements to pay expenses, repatriate profits, and repay loans and other foreign currency expenditure requirements.

Foreign investment enterprises may apply to the State Bank to purchase foreign currency. However, it distributes available foreign currency according to official priorities with favored projects, such as infrastructure construction and import-substitution, having priority.

(vi) *Land ownership*

The principle of private ownership of land does not yet exist in Viet Nam. Foreign investment under the FIL permits foreign investors to use land by leasing it directly or through a joint venture relationship with a local partner who has been allocated land use rights by the State.

Land leases to foreign entities may be granted for up to 50 years or in special circumstances 70 years with the approval of the Prime Minister.

In the case of a joint venture, the State grants the land lease to the Vietnamese partner (invariably state-owned) who usually contributes the land as legal capital worth the value of the land use right.

(b) **Investment procedures**

All foreign investment must have a license issued by the Ministry of Planning and Investment in Hanoi, except branches of certain types of foreign companies, such as banks, which require the approval of the relevant ministries. From July 1, 1999 foreign investors no longer had to pay local licensers to register business applications. The ruling is applicable to all forms of foreign direct investment in Viet Nam.

Previous Ministry of Finance rules said that foreign investors had to pay 0.01 per cent of the project's total amount as a registration fee at a minimum of US$ 50 and maximum of US$ 10,000 per project.

The MPI is designed as a "one-stop" licensing body responsible for coordinating with other government authorities to evaluate and approve an investment license application. Once a license has been approved, the MPI monitors and regulates the performance of licensed projects.

To direct foreign investment into priority areas, the MPI publishes an investment priority list that provides information regarding projects, industries, and locations identified by various Vietnamese authorities as those appropriate for foreign investment.

For evaluation purposes, investment projects are classified as Group A or Group B, with mandated approval periods of 47 days and 40 days, respectively.

Group A requires the approval of the Prime Minister and includes projects in industrial zones, export processing zones and BOT; projects with investment capital of US$ 40 million or more; projects in the areas of culture, press, and publishing; projects related to national defense and security; and projects that use five hectares or more of urban land and 40 hectares or more of other types of land.

Group B includes all other projects and is approved solely by MPI, except for certain kinds of projects that can be approved by the provincial People's Committees and Industrial Zone Authorities. Investors can expedite the licensing process by informing and consulting with the relevant State and local authorities about the investor's purpose and progress before formal submission of the application.

Group B projects that can be licensed by the People's Committees and Industrial Zone Authorities entail projects with a legal capital of US$ 10 million or less in Hanoi and Ho Chi Minh City; projects with a legal capital of US$ 5 million or less in other provinces; and projects in industrial zones. However, local authorities may be required at times to consult with the MPI before issuing an investment license.

Several elements of an application carry weight in MPI's evaluation criteria: (1) legal status and financial capabilities of the project's foreign and Vietnamese partners; (2) tangible and equitable benefits to the Vietnamese people; and (3) compatibility with the Government's policy goals and priorities in terms promoting economic and social development, jobs creation, greater production capability, and technology transfer.

The application process is summarized below:

Group A projects

Stage 1: Investor submits application to MPI.
Stage 2: Application forward by MPI to concerned ministries.
Stage 3: Relevant ministries render a written opinion to MPI. (Failure to reply means automatic consent.)
Stage 4: MPI establishes advisory committee, if necessary.
Stage 5: MPI submits opinion to the Prime Minister.
Stage 6: Prime Minister issues decision to grant or deny license.
Stage 7: MPI notifies applicant.
Stage 8: MPI issues investment license.

Group B projects

Stage 1: Investor submits application to MPI or People's Committee (if applicable for the latter).
Stage 2: MPI forwards application to concerned ministries.
Stage 3: If the application is under MPI jurisdiction, the provincial People's Committee issues a written opinion to MPI. (Failure to reply means automatic consent.) If under the jurisdiction of the People's Committee, then it evaluates the project itself.
Stage 4: MPI issues a decision to grant or deny license. Or, if relevant, the People's Committee issues a decision on the project.
Stage 5: MPI notifies applicant.
Stage 6: MPI issues investment license.

The application package must include the following:

- *Application form*, which includes names of the parties involved, name of the company, address, legal capital, amount of each party's contribution to capital, information on the Board of Management, profit and loss distribution ratios, insurance information, dispute resolution procedures, and anticipated tax treatment
- *Joint venture contract*, if applicable
- *Charter* of the foreign invested enterprise
- *Feasibility study and environmental impact assessment*, if required
- *Corporate documents* related to the legal and financial status of the parties in the project
- Additional documents, if relevant to the project: *technology license contract, trademark license contract, and memorandum of understanding for a land lease*

(c)   *Types of investment forms*

   (i)   *Business cooperation contracts (BCC)*

A BCC is a contractual arrangement between the foreign and Vietnamese party and no separate legal entity is created. It is considered the most flexible arrangement in some respects but has other limitations with respect to the other investment types.

A BCC receives a business license as opposed to an investment license and is not entitled to many tax holidays and other concessions given to foreign investment projects. In practice, the duration granted rarely exceeds 15 years and is commonly five years.

To secure Ministry of Planning and Investment (MPI) approval, the parties involved must show that a high degree of commercial involvement on both sides will occur, and that it is not merely a subcontracting arrangement (processing contracts are regulated by the Ministry of Trade).

BCCs are common in the petroleum and telecommunications sectors, where foreign investors are prohibited from having operational involvement or management control.

    (ii)   *Joint venture enterprise (JV)*

A JV is the most common form of establishment, accounting for about 70 per cent of total foreign investment. A joint venture creates a private limited liability company through shared ownership by Vietnamese and foreign partners. The minimum legal capital requirement for the foreign party is 30 per cent and there is no statutory ceiling limit.

In practice, JVs are usually structured as a 70 per cent contribution by the foreign party, and 30 per cent by the Vietnamese party. Legal capital contribution by the foreign party may be in the form of cash, plant, equipment, technology, and know-how.

The Vietnamese party's contribution is usually land-use rights. Under the FIL, valuation of all capital contributions is based on international market prices.

Licenses are issued for a maximum duration of 50 years, although in special cases, they may be granted up to 70 years.

JVs are required to form a board of directors, referred to as the Board of Management in Viet Nam, the membership of which reflects the proportion of each party's capital contribution.

However, the guiding principle for the management of foreign investment projects in Viet Nam is equality between both parties. As such, at least two members on the board must be from the Vietnamese party, and certain major decisions affecting the JV require a unanimous vote of the board. Other decisions require a two-thirds majority. Perhaps most important is that Vietnamese partners benefit from a right to veto in joint venture enterprises.

    (iii)   *100 per cent foreign owned enterprise (FOE)*

The FOE is established as a limited liability company incorporated with 100 per cent foreign capital. Like JVs, FOEs can only be established for specific investment purposes. The FOE accounts for about 17 per cent of foreign investment.

The duration of operation of an FOE is stated in the investment license but normally does not exceed 50 years. Foreign investors are not entitled to ownership of land under an FOE, but it can lease land from the government, institutions, and special industrial/export zones.

    (iv)   *Build-Operate-Transfer (BOT)*

The BOT investment form is designed to attract private foreign investment in public infrastructure projects. Under a BOT license, investors build the infrastructure, operate the project for a reasonable time period to recover their initial investment and earn a reasonable profit, and at the end of the contractual period, transfer the project without compensation to the Vietnamese government.

(d)   *Performance requirements/incentives*

Viet Nam has certain requirements, such as localization of production and export commitment for specific industries and projects. Requirements are usually discussed during contractual negotiations with the Vietnamese partner or during the investment licensing process. Subsequently, the negotiated terms are set forth in contracts establishing the joint venture or may be expressly stated in the foreign investment license.

In general, a licensed foreign investment is eligible for the incentives specified below:

Corporate income tax: The standard rate is 25 per cent, which compares favorably with rates of 25 per cent, 35 per cent, or 45 per cent specified for Vietnamese-owned enterprises. Preferential rates of 10 per cent, 15 per cent, and 20 per cent may be applied to investment projects meeting certain criteria or identified as projects of special importance prescribed by the MPI.

Rates of 20 per cent, 15 per cent, and 10 per cent have specific eligibility requirements and duration. The eligibility requirements depend on such factors as the percentage of production exported, the number of workers employed, and the type of business activity. The duration schedules are as follows:

- 20 per cent: 10 years
- 15 per cent: 12 years
- 10 per cent: 15 years

Import duty: A joint venture company, 100 per cent foreign-owned enterprise, and the foreign party to a BCC are exempt from paying duty on the import of equipment and materials which form part of the capital contribution of the foreign investment.

Technology transferred as part of a foreign party's capital contribution is also exempt from import duty.

Export manufacturers receive reimbursement of import duties paid on materials used in production once the finished products are exported.

Other incentives: Tax refunds are available on profits reinvested for at least three years. Joint ventures and 100 per cent foreign-owned enterprises may carry forward their losses for up to five years.

Foreign investors may also enjoy tax concessions and holidays for investments in Export Processing Zones (EPZ) and Industrial Zones (IZ).

Projects located in EPZs enjoy the following investment incentives, among others:

- Exemption from export tax on finished products exported from the EPZ to foreign markets
- Tax rates of 10 per cent for production enterprises and 15 per cent for service enterprises
- Exemption from tax on profits for the first four profitable years for production enterprises and first two profitable years for service enterprises
- A tax rate on profit remitted abroad of five per cent

Projects located in an IZ enjoy the following investment incentives, among others:

- Profit tax rates of 18 per cent for production enterprises and 22 per cent for service enterprises; those firms that export at least 80 per cent of their production enjoy a lower rate of 12 per cent;
- Exemption from profits tax for the first two profitable years for production enterprises and one year for service enterprises;
- Export processing enterprises located in an IZ are still entitled to enjoy EPZ tax incentives.

(e)   ***Taxation***

Viet Nam imposes various taxes on foreign business activity.

- *Corporate income tax*: The corporate income tax was described in section 4 above.

- *Value added tax (VAT)*: On 1 January 1999, Vietnam introduced a VAT regime. The scheme has two calculation methods and a four-tiered rate structure that includes rates of zero per cent, 5 per cent, 10 per cent and 20 per cent, with 10 per cent being the standard rate. Twenty-six categories of goods and services are exempt from VAT. Foreign-owned enterprises and BCCs can temporarily defer VAT payment on raw materials and materials imported for manufacturing exported goods.

- *Income remittance tax (IRT)*: IRT is a withholding tax imposed on income remitted abroad. IRT is imposed at rates of 3 per cent, 5 per cent and 7 per cent with the lowest rate reserved for encouraged categories of investment.

- *Special sales tax (SST)*: The SST is an excise tax imposed on goods and services that are considered to be luxurious. SST is imposed on automobiles, tobacco, alcohol, and golf for example.

- *Personal income tax*: Viet Nam's income tax for foreigners and Vietnamese citizens/permanent residents ranges from 0 to 50 per cent. The scale is as follows:

For Vietnamese citizens and permanent residents of Viet Nam, the income tax rates range from 0 to 60 per cent. The scale is as follows:

Individual's income per month (in dong)	Tax rate (in per cent)
Up to 5 million	0
Over 5 million to 12 million	10
Over 12 million to 30 million	20
Over 30 million to 50 million	30
Over 50 million to 70 million	40
Over 70 million	50

Source: KPMG Ltd. (Viet Nam)

Individual's income per month (in dong)	Tax rate (in per cent)
Up to 2 million	0
Over 2 million to 3 million	10
Over 3 million to 4 million	20
Over 4 million to 6 million	30
Over 6 million to 8 million	40
Over 8 million to 10 million	50
Over 10 million	60

Source: KPMG Ltd. (Viet Nam)

Foreigners working in Viet Nam are not subject to social security or an insurance levy, but employed Vietnamese citizens must contribute 5 per cent and 1 per cent of their base salary to the State Social Insurance and Health Insurance funds, respectively. These contributions are deducted by the employer, who is also required to contribute 15 per cent and 2 per cent, respectively, of their employees' base salary to these two funds.

(f)   *Labour issues*

In October 1999 the Government introduced a five-day working week. If a holiday coincides with a Saturday or Sunday, administrative employees have the following working day off. Beneficiaries are cadres, civil servants, and people working in administrative offices and socio-political organizations of the State.

The Ministry of Labour, War Invalids, and Social Affairs provides state-owned businesses with guidelines on how to implement the five-day working week system. Their owners decide working and leisure time in line with the Labour Code of businesses of other economic sectors. However, the State encourages these businesses to implement a 40-hour working week. The official monthly minimum wage for foreign-investment joint ventures is US$ 40.

(i) *Workers' rights*

Unions are controlled by the Vietnamese Communist Party and have only nominal independence. However, union leaders influence some key decisions, such as those on health and safety issues, and on minimum wage standards.

Workers who wish to join or form unions must receive approval from the local office of the Party-controlled Vietnam General Confederation of Labour (VGCL).

The VGCL is the umbrella organization under which all local trade unions must operate, and it claims four million members in branches in each of the major cities and provinces. VGCL officers report that the VGCL represents 95 per cent of public sector workers, 90 per cent of workers in state-owned enterprises, and 50 per cent of private sector workers.

The Labour Law requires provincial trade union organizations to establish unions within six months at all new enterprises with more than 10 employees as well as at existing enterprises that operate without trade unions. Management of those companies is required by law to accept and co-operate with those unions.

The Labour Law provides for the right to strike under certain circumstances. The law requires that management and labour resolve labour disputes through the enterprise's own labour conciliation council. If that fails, the matter goes to the provincial labour arbitration council.

Labour courts, which were established in 1996 within the people's court system, have heard a small number of cases but still are in the early stages of development and lack sufficient personnel because of government budget constraints.

The government-controlled labour unions stipulate written procedures for managing labour disputes that permit unresolved disputes to be arbitrated before a court. Unions have the right to appeal a council decision to the provincial people's court and to strike. However, the law prohibits strikes in 54 occupational categories, including enterprises that serve the public and those that are important to the national economy or national security and defense. These functions are defined by the government and include electrical production, posts and telecommunications, railway, maritime and air transportation, banking, public works, and the oil and gas industry.

(ii) *Collective bargaining*

Workers must have the approval of the provincial or metropolitan branch of the VGCL to organize unions in their enterprises, but they also can bargain collectively through the party-approved unions at their enterprises. In the past the State generally set wages since most employees worked for state companies.

With the growth of the private sector and the increased autonomy of state firms, a growing percentage of companies are setting wages through collective bargaining with the relevant unions.

2. Customs and trade procedures

(a) *Tariff code*

Import and export duties are based on the Law on Export and Import Duties, issued in December 1991, with subsequent amendments. In 1994, the Ministry of Trade assumed the responsibility for initiating changes in tariffs, which are then considered by the Ministry of Finance as to whether proposed changes should be submitted for the Prime Minister's approval. As the government reviews revenue sources on a quarterly basis, tariff rates are often adjusted to accommodate the current balance of payments situation.

(b) *Formal tariffs*

Import duties are levied on most items. Rates are specified in the "Export and Import Tariff for Commercial Goods," which is subject to frequent revisions. In January 1996, rates on a list of goods under the

Common Effective Preferential Tariffs (CEPT) scheme were lowered to below 60 per cent. The highest rates are levied on consumer goods, especially products considered as luxury items (e.g., liquor, cigarettes, and cars).

Capital goods and materials are granted low or zero duties. Tariffs on 857 imports from ASEAN are five per cent or below, of which over half are commodities, machinery and equipment. Exemptions are granted for certain goods, including non-refundable aid, goods in transit and temporary imports, and re-exports for exhibitions.

Goods brought in for foreign-investment projects may qualify for exemption if they fall under three categories: (1) Goods and technology transfer considered as capital contribution by the foreign partner; (2) Goods and materials for use in export production; and (3) Goods used for capital construction or as fixed assets for business co-operation contracts.

(c)   *Excise taxes*

Other taxes include the special sales tax on the import of cigarettes, alcohol and spirits, firecrackers, automobiles, and all kinds of gasoline. Importers pay the special sales tax on importation, ranging from 15 per cent to 100 per cent. The tax is calculated on the basis of applying the applicable tax rate to the CIF value of the goods.

(d)   *Import quotas*

The Ministry of Trade, in consultation with the Government Price Board (GPB) and the relevant ministries (e.g., Ministry of Agriculture and Food Industry and Ministry of Construction), set formal import quotas on cement, fertilizers, petroleum products, steel, sugar, and various other materials and commodities.

Some products are also subject to less formal and temporary "quantitative targets" that the MOT regulates to complement economic goals. For example, import quotas on motorcycles and automobiles (finished and CKD kits) in an effort to encourage a long-term strategy for the "localization" of automobile parts production. Import quotas are often administered through the import licensing system managed by MOT and are mainly granted to state-owned enterprises.

Streamlining the tariff structure is one remaining key trade liberalization issue. However, some of the government's major obstacles stem from pressures to protect domestic industries and the potential loss of significant tax revenues.

Nevertheless Viet Nam is committed to reducing or eliminating tariffs and other trade restrictions since it is a requirement of its membership in the ASEAN Free Trade Area (AFTA) and if it is to realize its hopes for membership in the WTO.

(e)   *Customs procedures*

The General Customs Department, with local offices throughout the provinces, is responsible for inspecting and supervising goods and collecting export and import taxes.

Customs valuation of imported products may be based on CIF prices declared by the importers or on reference prices established by the administration authorities. Although in principle reference prices are used to counteract the practice of under-invoicing, the system is not always responsive to world market price fluctuations.

The formal rules on customs declaration require that an application be lodged at the local office of the General Department of Customs for each permitted consignment of imported or exported goods. For imports, a declaration must be made within 30 days of the arrival of the goods in Viet Nam. Customs is required to respond within one day, and any duty must be paid within 30 days of receiving the custom's notification. In the case of exports, duty must be paid within 15 days of receiving notification.

(f)   *Import licenses*

The Ministry of Trade issues import licenses, which are required for all imports. However, only certain enterprises are authorized by the MOT to engage in direct import and export activities. Although once reserved for a small number of state-owned enterprises, direct import rights are now accessible to a larger number of companies. As part of the foreign investment license, joint ventures and 100 per cent foreign-owned enterprises are granted import rights for materials or goods as specified in their licenses.

In general, authorized enterprises will have an import allocation, which is typically valid for a period of six to 12 months, and an import license, which may cover several shipments. For those companies, including foreign firms, that do not have import or export rights, they must do so through an authorized import-export company. The average transaction cost for the service is about 2-3 per cent of the value of the consignment of goods.

The import of firearms, ammunition, explosives and military equipment; drugs and toxic chemicals, dangerous and unhealthy cultural products; materials for making cigarettes; second-hand consumer goods (except motorcycles and cars under 12 seats) and used equipment are prohibited, with certain exceptions. As certain products are often placed on temporary bans, current advice should be sought.

(g)   *Export procedures*

Companies with prospects for receiving an export order will be granted the permits or licenses to export the goods as well as import the inputs required for export production.

Export duties are levied on mostly natural resources and commodities, with a maximum rate of 45 per cent. Manufactured goods for exports are exempt from export duty.

Prohibited exports include antiques of high value, logs, timber, rattan canes, and precious or rare plants and animals. Three commodities – rice, oil and wood products – are subject to government imposed quantitative restrictions or targets and are administered through export quotas.

(h)   *Other relevant regulations for import/export*

Generally, the Vietnamese importer (agent, distributor, import-export company or joint venture partner) handles the preparation of documentation and licenses. Shipping documents include commercial invoices, pro forma invoices, bills of lading, packing lists, certificates of origin, insurance certificates, and import licenses.

Goods exported or imported as samples or for the purpose of advertising are subject to export or import duty. Exemption from duty is granted to goods permitted to be temporarily exported or imported for exhibitions.

At the end of the exhibition, they must be re-imported into Viet Nam in the case of temporary exports, or re-exported from Viet Nam in the case of temporary imports. Documents required for exemption for exhibitions include a notification of, or invitation to, the exhibition and an export or import license from the Ministry of Trade.

Since 1 January 1997, all products distributed in Viet Nam have to have labels with the following information on the name of the product, name and addresses of manufacturer, quantity, composition, quality, instructions for use or maintenance, date of manufacture and expiration dates.

Specific information by product or by standard may be provided by the importing organization or sought from the relevant ministry or the government's management body with overall responsibility, i.e., General Department of Standards, Weights, Measures and Quality (STAMEQ) of the Ministry of Science, Technology, and Environment (MOSTE).

The operation of customs warehouses was approved in 1994. Entities permitted to lease customs bonded warehouses are foreign enterprises; individuals and overseas Vietnamese; Vietnamese import-export licenses companies; and foreign investment enterprises licensed to carry import-export activities. Most goods pending import and domestic goods pending export can be deposited in bonded warehouse under the supervision of the provincial customs office.

The exceptions are goods prohibited from import or export, Vietnamese-made goods with fraudulent trademarks or labels, goods of unknown origin, and goods dangerous or harmful to the public or environment. The lease contract must be registered with the customs bond unit at least 24 hours prior to the arrival of the goods at the port.

Documents required are a notarized copy of authorization of the holder to receive the goods; a notarized copy of the warehouse lease contract; the bill of landing; a certificate of origin; a packing list, and customs declaration forms.

Owners of the goods pay import or export tax when the goods are removed from bonded warehouse.

E. Main opportunities for investment

1. Oil and gas

Amendments to the Oil Law in May 2000 offer further financial incentives to foreign investors. Investors will be allowed to earmark up to 70 per cent of the output value to recover their investment capital, compared to the 30-35 per cent range previously applied.

Moreover, foreign investors can open bank accounts and raise funds abroad to finance their oil and gas projects in Viet Nam.

Under the previous law, an across-the-board 50 per cent corporate income tax applied to oil projects. Deep-sea oil exploration projects now enjoy a 32 per cent tax.

Article 3 of the law defines encouraged oil and gas projects as those carrying out oil and gas operations in deep water areas, offshore waters, and areas that have especially difficult geographic and geologic conditions according to the block list decided by the Prime Minister.

2. Insurance

Until June 1999, the life insurance industry was closed to foreign investment. The Viet Nam Ministry of Planning and Investment effectively opened the market by granting licenses to two foreign companies to sell insurance in Viet Nam. In the past, foreign companies were limited to minority participation in joint ventures with Viet Nam's two largest state-owned companies, and to "representative offices," a device used by over 30 foreign insurance companies.

The MPI issued a life insurance license to a joint venture between Taiwan's Chinfon Global Corporation and Canada's Manulife Financial, allowing the joint venture to be the first foreign company to sell life insurance in Viet Nam.

A license was also issued by MPI to Allianz-AGF, thereby creating the first 100 per cent foreign-owned non-life insurance operation in Viet Nam. The newly formed company is only authorized, however, to sell insurance to non-Vietnamese clients.

In January 1998 the Government issued the Decree on the Encouragement of Foreign Investment. Numerous business operations were listed, including the following:

3. Agro-business

- Processing of agricultural, forestry, and fishery products for export
- Technology for preserving food; post-harvest technology, and related bio-technology and biological measures in agriculture, fisheries, and forestry
- Production of materials for safe insecticides

- Manufacturing of equipment, spare parts, and agricultural machinery
- Raising international standard livestock

4. Industry

- Exploration, exploitation, and down-stream processing of minerals
- Production of petrochemicals
- Production of steel, alloy, non-ferrous metals, and sponge iron
- Manufacturing of machine tools for metal machining
- Manufacturing of spare parts for vehicles and motorbikes
- Ship building and production of equipment and spare parts
- Precision mechanical equipment
- Manufacturing of wastewater treatment equipment
- Production of cement and other building materials
- Pharmaceuticals
- Production of high quality packaging for export
- Production of chemicals and dyes

F. Tips for visitors

The most temperate months of the year in the south are November through to January. Tet (Lunar New Year, which is also celebrated as Chinese New Year in many parts of the world) is always a peak travel time. While the exact date changes each year, Tet is normally celebrated in February.

Local guides are available through Viet Nam Tourism, a state-operated tour operator. Virtually all hotels can arrange for these guides, who charge about US$ 25 a day, not including transportation or meals. Most guides are trained at the government tour guide school and are worth the fees.

1. Getting there

International flights are available to Hanoi and Ho Chi Minh City from numerous cities, including Bankok, Hong Kong, Singapore, Guangzhou, Moscow, Paris, Jakarta, Kuala Lumpur, and others. Several airlines operate to and from these cities, such as Thai International Airways, Singapore Airlines, China Southern Airlines, Cathay Pacific, Aeroflot, Qantas, Malaysian Airlines, and Garuda.

Viet Nam Airlines serves the following international flights:

Bangkok, Singapore, Paris, Hong Kong, Seoul, Sydney, Berlin, Jakarta, Manila, Taipei, Guangzhou, Vientiane, Amsterdam, Moscow, Frankfurt, Kuala Lumpur, Los Angeles, Melbourne, Dubai, Osaka, Kaohsiung, and Phnom Penh.

Cruise ships stop in Viet Nam at Ho Chi Minh City and Danang, but arriving by sea on a freighter or private vessel is not recommended without prior authorization from the Immigration Office in Hanoi.

Land vehicles are permitted to enter Viet Nam from certain border points with China, Lao People's Democratic Republic, and Cambodia with the proper authorization.

2. Passports and visas

A valid passport and visa are required of all foreigners visiting Viet Nam. Vietnamese embassies and consulates issue visas, and some travel agencies, particularly in Bangkok, and overseas offices of Viet Nam Tourism are able to issue tourist visas. Tourist visas are good for 30 days and may be extended after your arrival in Viet Nam. Fees vary from embassy to embassy, and are about US$ 50 in Bangkok.

A double entry visa is also available for tourists making side trips from Viet Nam to destinations in Thailand, Cambodia and the Lao People's Democratic Republic. You are required to state your intended ports of arrival and departure, changing either of these upon or after your arrival will result in much red tape.

Business visas are good for six months and allow for multiple entries. Sponsorship by a licensed Vietnamese enterprise is required.

3. Travel within Viet Nam

While there is an extensive network of train and bus services within Viet Nam, it is easier and more comfortable to fly. Viet Nam Airlines and Pacific Air serve most major cities between Ho Chi Minh City and Hanoi, including Nha Trang, Dalat, and Hue. It is cheaper to buy domestic air tickets once you arrive in Viet Nam.

From Hanoi:
Daily flights to Ho Chi Minh City, Hue, Danang, Nha Trang. There are periodic flights to Na San and Vinh.

From Ho Chi Minh City:
Daily flights to Hanoi and Danang. There are also periodic flights to Qui Nhon, Nha Trang, Dalat, Buon Ma Thuot, Pleiku, and Phu Quoc.

Additionally, Northern Airport Flight Service Company has flights to Halong Bay by helicopter. There are two flights per week, Saturday at 0800 and 1530, departing from Gia Lam Airport. Tickets can be purchased at the Metropole Hotel.

For those travelling by rail, tickets can be purchased at stations in Hanoi, Ho Chi Minh City, Nha Trang, Hue, and Danang.

There are inter-province and inner-province bus stations in each province with convenient passenger services. Taxi services are available in many big cities and provinces. In addition to public transport services, using motorbikes, cyclos, bicycles, and other vehicles is common in Viet Nam.

4. Health

Vaccinations are not required to enter Viet Nam, unless you are coming from an infected area. However, it is wise to ask your own physician about prudent health precautions before you travel as vaccinations for cholera, typhoid fever, and tetanus may be in order. If you plan to travel outside major cities you may also want to consider taking an anti-malaria drug.

5. Money

Viet Nam's official currency is the dong. Viet Nam's unofficial currency is the US dollar and in major shopping areas, hotels and restaurants in Ho Chi Minh City and Hanoi, you can use dollars and dong interchangeably and in practically any combination.

You can exchange foreign currency and travelers' cheques at banks throughout Viet Nam, although some banks charge a commission of as much as four per cent. Most merchants and hotels will not accept travellers' cheques.

6. Embassies and consulates

There are 16 foreign embassies in Viet Nam and dozens of consulates, with the latter in Hanoi and Ho Chi Minh City.

The embassies' addresses are as follows:

Algeria
13 Phan Chu Trinh St.
Hoan Kiem District
Hanoi
Tel: 825-3865
Fax: 826-0830

Australia
Van Phuc Compound
Badinh District
Hanoi
Tel: 831-7755
Fax: 831-7711, 831-7733
www.ambadane@hn.vnn.vn

Belgium
48-50 Nguyen Thai Hoc St.
Hanoi
Tel: 845-2263, 823-5005
Fax: 845-7165

Brunei Darussalam
4 Thien Quang Street
Hoan Kiem District
Hanoi
Tel: 826-4816, 826-4818
Fax: 822-2092

Cambodia
71 Tran Hung Dao Street
Hoan Kiem District Hanoi
Tel: 825-3788, 825-6473
Fax: 826-5225

Canada
31 Hung Vuong Street
Hanoi
Tel: 823-5500
Fax: 823-5333

Czech Republic
13 Chu Van An St.
Hanoi
Tel: 845-4131-2
Fax: 823-3996

Denmark
19, Dien Bien Phu Street
Hanoi
Tel: 823-1888
Fax: 823-1999

Egypt
26 Phan Boi Chau Street
Hoan Kiem District Hanoi
Tel: 846-0220
Fax: 846-0218

France
57, rue Tran Hung Dao Hanoi
Tel: 825-2719
Fax: 826-4236

Germany
29 Tran Phu Street Hanoi
Tel: 840-245
Fax: 845-3838

Hungary
43-47 Dien Bien Phu Street
Badinh District Hanoi
Tel: 845-2858
Fax: 845-2748

India
58-60 Tran Hung Dao Street
Hoan Kiem District Hanoi
Tel: 824-4989
Fax: 824-4998

Indonesia
50 Ngo Quyen Street
Hoan Kiem District Hanoi
Tel: 825-3084
Fax: 825-9274

Lao People's
Democratic Republic
22 Tran Dinh Truong

United Kingdom
5th Floor, Central Building
31 Hai Ba Trung Street
Hoan Kiem District Hanoi
Tel: 825-2510, 825-2349
      825-2350
Fax: 826-5762

United States
7 Lang Ha Street Hanoi
Tel: 831-4580, 843-1500
Fax: 831-4601

7. Hotels

There are several business quality hotels in the country, but most are in Hanoi and Ho Chi Minh City. Hotel rates are charged in United States dollars, although some smaller hotels outside of the main cities may accept payment in dong.

Some of the main business hotels include:

In Hanoi

Hilton Hanoi Opera
1 Le Thanh Tong Street

Hotel Nikko Hanoi
84 Tran Nhan Tong Street
Tel: (844) 822-3535
Fax: (844) 822-3555
Web site:
www.hotelnikko.com.vn

Melia Hanoi
44 Bly Thuong Kiet Street
Tel: (844) 934-3343
Fax: (844) 934-3344

Sedona Suites Hanoi
96 To Ngoc Van Street Quang
Ba Tay Ho District
Tel: (848) 718-0888
Fax: (848) 718-0666
E-mail: sedonahanoi@fpt.vn

Sofitel Metropole Hanoi
15 Ngo Quyen Street
Tel: (844) 826-6919
Fax: (844) 826-6920
E-mail:
sofitel@sofitelhanoi.vnn.vn

Sunway Hanoi Hotel
19 Pham Dinh Ho Street
Hai Ba Trung District
Hanoi
Tel: (844) 971-3888
Fax: (844) 971-3555

In Ho Chi Minh City

The Caravelle Hotel
19 Lam Son Square, District 1
Tel: (848) 823-4999
Fax: (848) 824-3999
E-mail:
caravellehotel@hcm.vnn.vn
Web site:
http://www.caravellehotel.com

Hotel Sofitel Plaza
17 Le Duan Blvd., District 1
http://www.accor-
hotel-vietnam.
com/sofitel-plazasaigon

Majestic Hotel
01 Dong Khoi St., District 1
Tel: (848) 829-5514/829-5517
Reservations: (848) 822-8750
Fax: (848) 829-5510
E-mail:
hotelmajestic@sgtourist.com.vn
Web site:
www.majesticsaigon.com

Omni Hotel
251 Nguyen Van Troi Street
Phu Nhuan District
Telephone: (848) 844-9222
/9333
Fax: (848) 844-9198
E-mail:
omnires@marcopolohotels.com
Web site:
http://www.marcopolohotels.
com/saigon/index.html

Rex Hotel
141 Nguyen Hue Blvd.
District 1
Tel: (848) 829-2185/829-3115
Fax: (848) 829-6536
E-mail:
rexhotel@hcm.vnn.vn
or
rexhotel@sgtourist.com.vn
Web site:
http://www.rexhotelvietnam.com

Sedona Suites Ho Chi Minh City
65 Le Loi Boulevard
Saigon Centre, District One
Tel: (848) 922-9666
Fax: (848) 822-9229
E-mail:
sedona@hcmc.netnam.vn

G. Learning more

1. Related web sites

www.vietnamavenue.com
www.vinaone.com
www.vietnam.tdb.gov.sg
www.aboutviet.net
www.vietnamaccess.com/
invest/invest.htm
www.vietnamembassy-usa.org

www.vneconomy.com.vn
www.vir-vietnam.com
www.searchasiaco.com/vietnam
www.vietnamglobe.com
www.viam.com

www.viam.com

www.business-in-vietnam.com
www.govietnam.com
www.vietnamonline.net
www.vnn.vn
www.vietnamtourism.com

www.vnagency.com.vn

VII. YUNNAN PROVINCE, CHINA

A. Basic operating environment

1. Geography and climate

Yunnan Province is located in southwestern China and is its eighth largest province with a total area of 394,000 square kilometres or 4.1 per cent of the country's landmass. Yunnan shares 4,060 kilometres of border with Myanmar, the Lao People's Democratic Republic, and Viet Nam. The border with Myanmar spans nearly 2,000 kilometres, while the Yunnan-Lao border covers 710 kilometres and the portion with Viet Nam extends 1,350 kilometres. Overland connections with these countries are well developed with 20 roads connecting Yunnan with its three neighbours.

Yunnan's terrain is basically mountainous, with 84 per cent of the country covered by mountains and 10 per cent consisting of highlands. River valleys comprise only 6 per cent of the total land area. The subregion's major river, the Mekong, is called the Lancang River in China.

The climate in Yunnan is characterized by two main seasons: the dry monsoon in winter and a hot, humid monsoon during the summer months. However, climatic variations are found throughout the province because of the differences in elevation and latitude. Tropical, sub-tropical, and temperate conditions are found in various parts of Yunnan.

2. Population

Yunnan has a diverse population of over 42 million people. Fifty-one ethnic minority groups inhabit Yunnan, 15 of these are indigenous to Yunnan. Ethnic minorities comprise around 14 million of the province's total population. Some of the main ethnic groups are the Bai, Hani, Dai, Lisu, Wa, Lahu, Naxi, Jingpo, Bulang, Pumi, Nu, De'ang, Dulong, and Jinuo. The various languages, traditional dress, and customs create a fascinating microcosm of cultural diversity.

3. Languages

With numerous ethnic groups in Yunnan, dozens of languages can be heard throughout the province. However, Mandarin Chinese is used for official purposes and in business. English is not widely spoken in Yunnan, and foreigners will usually require an interpreter.

4. Administrative structure

Yunnan has 16 prefectures and 126 countries. Eight of the prefectures have the status of ethnic minority autonomous prefectures. The three main cities, Kunming, Qujing, and Yuxi, are also classified as prefectures and fall under the jurisdiction of the provincial government. Yunnan contains three national development zones: Kunming Dianchi National Tourism and Vacation Zone, Kunming Economic and Technological Development Zone, and Kunming Hi-tech Zone. Additionally, there are 22 development and holiday zones at the provincial level.

B. Macroeconomic business climate

1. Yunnan's economy

The economy of Yunnan grew rapidly throughout the 1990s, as seen in figure 56. With growth rates reaching 10 per cent for ten consecutive years, Yunnan's GDP is now the seventeenth largest in China. Much of the progress has been facilitated by rapid industrialization. Between 1991 and 1995, Yunnan's industrial output increased annually at an average of 13.7 per cent. The core industries are tobacco, machinery, metallurgy, agricultural products, chemicals and building materials.

**Figure 56. Yunnan GDP growth, 1990-1998
(in 100 million yuan)**

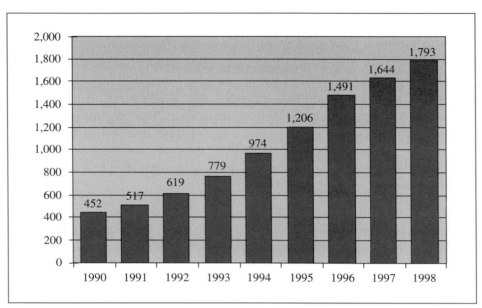

Source: Office of Foreign Investment Affairs, General Information of Yunnan Province

Agriculture is still the base of the provincial economy, however, producing nearly 30 billion yuan in 1996. In 1998, agricultural output surpassed 13 million tons. Major crops include rice, corn, wheat, beans, tobacco, tea, sugar cane, rubber, vegetables, and fruit.

2. International trade

Yunnan, like the rest of China, has gradually liberalized its economy and has reaped substantial benefits from opening up to the outside world. Through its policy of open border cities, international trade has flourished in Yunnan, especially with neighbouring countries. International trade reached US$ 1.66 billion in 1999, with US$ 1.03 billion in exports from Yunnan and US$ 625 million in imports.

Major import items include agricultural products, tobacco, technology, and equipment. Most imported goods originate from Myanmar (its largest trade partner), the United States, Germany, Hong Kong, China, the United Kingdom, and Japan. Yunnan trades actively with its border neighbours, the Lao People's Democratic Republic and Viet Nam, but Myanmar is the main border trade partner, accounting for 80 per cent of border trade, while Viet Nam and the Lao People's Democratic Republic each make up 10 per cent.

3. Foreign investment

At the end of 1999, foreign investment in Yunnan totalled US$ 2.54 billion in approved projects and US$ 1.22 billion in contracted and actual investments. Over 1,850 foreign investment enterprises from 41 countries and territories were in operation in 1999. Yunnan's main foreign investors include the United States, Singapore, Thailand, Japan, France, and Canada. It also receives substantial investment from Hong Kong, China, and Taiwan Province of China.

Figure 57 shows the breakdown of foreign investment projects according to sector.

Most foreign firms enter into equity joint ventures in Yunnan. Only 28 per cent of the foreign firms in the province are 100 per cent foreign-owned (see figure 58).

Figure 57. Main sectors of foreign investment, 1999

Figure 58. Forms of foreign enterprises in Yunnan

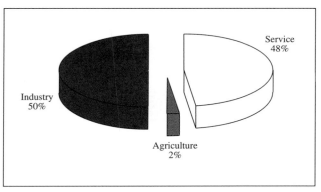

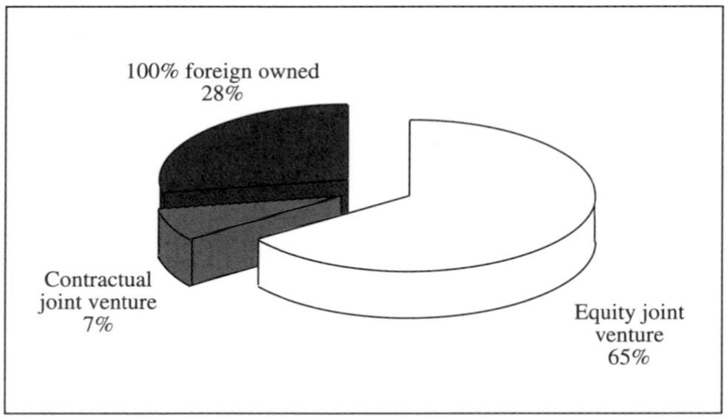

Source: Foreign Investment Office of Yunnan

Source: Office of Foreign Investment Affairs of Yunnan Province

4. Natural resources

Yunnan is well endowed with natural resources. Over 24 per cent of the province is covered with forests, and 39 per cent of this is pine. As a result, Yunnan has an estimated 1.2 million tons of pine resin available for various industrial uses.

Yunnan contains six major river systems comprised of over 600 rivers. The extensive river systems and variations in elevation offer Yunnan massive hydropower potential with an estimated potential of 90 million kilowatts of power. The Manwan Hydropower Station has an installed capacity of 1.25 million kilowatts.

Another major natural resource in Yunnan is coal, which serves as the leading form of energy used in the province. Yunnan's estimated coal reserves amount to 67 billion tons, with 23 billion tons already proven. Seventy six per cent of the reserves are brown coal, and 21.6 per cent are bituminous.

Several other forms of energy such as wind and solar power have great potential in Yunnan because of the topography.

5. Human resources

Yunnan's population of over 42 million is well educated and skilled and provides a reliable and competent workforce.

C. Institutional and support network: public and private sector organizations

1. Government organizations and agencies

The administrative structure of the Yunnan Provincial Government is rather elaborate, therefore, only the government agencies that investors are likely to deal with are presented below.

The Office of Foreign Investment Affairs (OFIA) of the Yunnan Provincial Government was established in 1997 to enhance and facilitate foreign investment in the province. Its main functions include:

- Implementing foreign investment policies and measures determined by the Yunnan Provincial Party Committee and the Provincial Government.
- Coordinating relations between the province and the external environment.
- Serving as the leading coordinating agency for provincial and local government agencies and administration with foreign funded enterprises.
- Scrutinizing and approving foreign investment applications.

- Conducting research related to foreign investment in Yunnan and making policy recommendations to the Yunnan Provincial Government.

Contact information:
Office of Foreign Investment Affairs
465 Beijing Road
Kunming 650011
Tel: 86-871-313-5012; 313-3875
Fax: 86-871-313-9143
E-mail: web@ns.tenway.com.cn

The Yunnan Provincial Foreign Investment Service Centre provides numerous services to foreign investors. Its services cover three broad areas: legal advice for businesses, investor services, and information supply.

1. *Legal advice for businesses*: The centre assists Chinese and foreign investors in understanding the laws, regulations, and policies of the Yunnan Government. It also provides advisory support on investment guidelines and related procedures for establishing a business.

2. *Investor services*: The Foreign Investment Service Centre assists throughout the entire investment process, starting with inspection tours for prospective investors. Once an investor decides to invest, the centre assists with negotiations and the preparation of application documents, including submitting the application for the approval process on behalf of the customer. Customers can utilize the centre for negotiations. Their services also extend to the construction phase and actual operation of the business. Additional services include briefings for foreign investors and information about Yunnan and its policies.

3. *Project Data Bank*: The Foreign Investment Centre maintains a database that contains information on investment projects, networks and contacts, and experts in various fields. The data bank also facilities matchmaking for joint ventures and cooperative business activities.

Contact information:
Foreign Investment Service Centre
13th Floor, Yunnan Foreign Trade Building
175 Beijing Road, Kunming 650011
Tel: 871-318-5013; 318-4980
Fax: 871-314-9574
E-mail: ynfisc@public.km.yn.cn

Yunnan Provincial Complaint Centre for Foreign Funded Enterprises: The Centre seeks to uphold the rights of foreign investors and to facilitate the set up and smooth operations of their businesses. Should foreign funded enterprises consider their legitimate rights and interests to be infringed upon by the conduct of any government department or staff, they may lodge a complaint with the Complaint Centre for Foreign Funded Enterprises. Any violations of laws or regulations will then forwarded to the appropriate administrative and judiciary bodies by the Centre. The Centre can also serve as an arbitrator between the disputing parties.

Contact information:
Yunnan Provincial Complaint Centre for Foreign Funded Enterprises
1st Floor, Building of Yunnan Provincial Discipline Inspection Committee
2 Xichang Road, Kunming 650032
Tel: 871-419-5806, 417-2578
Fax: 871-419-5806

2. Chamber of commerce

The Yunnan Chamber of Commerce is a non-government organization for industrial and commercial entrepreneurs. Despite its NGO status, it is a part of the Yunnan Committee of the Chinese People's Political Consultative Conference. The Yunnan Province Chamber of Commerce has 34,000 members in more than 20,000 private enterprises. The Yunnan Chamber of Commerce performs several functions to enhance the business climate throughout the province and the region. Firstly, it participates in economic and social decision-making that affects the province through its involvement in policy formulation and regulations. Secondly, the Yunnan Chamber of Commerce protects the legal interests and rights of its members and acts as a channel of communication to the government authorities. A third area of activities is services for its members, such as information, technology assistance, training, and advisory assistance in various facets of business. Fourthly, the Yunnan Chamber of Commerce promotes cooperation between foreign and local companies and fosters relations with other chambers of commerce in South-East Asia, particularly those in the Greater Mekong Subregion.

3. Transportation

As a part of its policy of opening to the outside world, Yunnan has invested heavily in developing its infrastructure. Being landlocked, Yunnan has had to rely on developing extensive land connections with its neighbours in order to conduct trade and facilitate communications. There are ten national land ports in Yunnan, ten provincial land ports, and 80 outlets for cross-border trade.

Traveling by road is made easy in Yunnan by a vast network of roads that span over 76,900 kilometres. There are over 1,500 kilometres of grade 2 highways or better. The highway system links Yunnan with the surrounding provinces of Sichuan, Guizhou, Guangxi, and Tibet, along with neighbours, Myanmar, the Lao People's Democratic Republic, Viet Nam, and indirectly, Thailand. Under the current Five-Year Plan, which ends in 2001, the province has been busy upgrading and extending six trunk highways that link Yunnan to neighbouring provinces and countries. By 2005, a complete highway system will connect Yunnan to Bangkok, Thailand and Yangon, Myanmar.

Yunnan has 2,076 kilometres of railroad and a new rail link is under construction between Neijiang and Kunming. Yunnan will eventually be a part of the proposed Pan-Asia railroad, a project that is currently being studied and is intended to link all the countries of South-East Asia by rail. In 1998, the railways in Yunnan carried 31 million tons of freight and nearly 13 million passengers.

Currently there are 10 airports in Yunnan, the major one being Kunming International Airport with an annual passenger capacity of 10 million passengers. The other nine airports are domestic ones throughout the province. A new airport, Lincang, is expected to open soon.

Rivers are also an important means of transportation in Yunnan. Over 1,300 kilometres of rivers are currently used for transportation, and altogether there are over 8,000 kilometres of navigable waterways. The main water ports are in Shuifu, Suijiang, Jinghong, Simao, and Dali.

A key development to increased access to the region is an agreement signed by four countries to open up the Lancang-Mekong River for commercial purposes. In April 2000, China, the Lao People's Democratic Republic, Myanmar, and Thailand signed an "Agreement on Commercial Navigation on the Lancang-Mekong River". This agreement, which takes effect in 2001, is intended to develop the river as a major means of international passenger and cargo transportation in the Greater Mekong Subregion. Yunnan and Myanmar are also working on land and water transportation on the Ayeyarwady River.

4. Communications

Telecommunications in Yunnan are continually improving and expanding. The telecommunication network utilizes advanced digitalized fiber optics and other high-tech components such as satellites. As of 1998, there were over 3 million telephone lines and nearly 2 million users. Mobile telecommunications are also widely available through the GSM system. Currently the GSM system has 520,000 lines and 420,000 users.

D. Legal and regulatory frameworks for trade and investment

1. Foreign investment

(a) *Overall investment climate*

As noted earlier, Yunnan has opened up its economy to the outside world and readily accepts foreign investment in numerous business sectors. Yunnan is also committed to closer economic cooperation with the other Greater Mekong Subregion countries. Many of the province's investment policies and related regulations are relatively new (i.e. within the last three years) and therefore still evolving. Some earlier difficulties with government agencies imposing numerous charges on foreign firms have been removed, due to a firm commitment by the Province to wipe out corruption. The Complaint Centre for Foreign-funded Enterprises is evidence of Yunnan's efforts to attract investors and ensure that their businesses function as smoothly as possible.

China's forthcoming entry into the World Trade Organization (WTO) is expected to be a boon for businesses operating in China, and the recent passage by the United States of permanent most favored nation trading status for China should also bring immense benefits.

(b) *Foreign investment law*

Selected articles from the foreign investment code of Yunnan Province are offered below. Some of the key topics in the provisions are highlighted for easy searching. For the full text see the Yunnan Investment Affairs Office web site: www.invest-yunnan.com.

Chapter 1: General Provisions

Article 1: On the basis of the state laws and regulations and particularities of the province, these regulations are hereby set forth for the purpose of encouraging foreign investment in the province, protecting the legal rights and interests of foreign-funded enterprises, regulating the actions of the administrative organizations thus promoting foreign investment in the province.

Article 2: All the organizations and individuals falling under the jurisdiction of the province which are involved in foreign investment and its administration are subject to these regulations.

Article 3: The *Foreign Investment Office of the Provincial Government* is responsible for organizing and coordinating foreign investment in the province. The Provincial Government Departments for planning economic and trade, foreign trade and economic cooperation, foreign affairs, construction, environmental protection and administration for industry and commerce are obliged to provide their services to foreign investors in line with their respective areas of responsibility.

Article 4: Foreign investors should propose their investment projects in accordance with the *Investment Guide and Guidelines for Foreign Investment* published by the province and the state respectively. *Foreign investment is encouraged in the following fields*: infrastructure, agriculture, bio-industry, mining, new-technology, tourism, dormitory housing projects, and environmental protection.

Article 5: Foreign investment is encouraged in various forms including equity joint ventures, contractual ventures and solely funded enterprises. Other forms are also possible such as joint shareholdings, majority shareholdings, joint operations, mergers, outright purchases, leasing, trusteeships, contracting out, renovations, restructuring and mixed ownership of state owned, collectively owned, or private enterprises. Build-Operate-Transfer, purchase of operation rights and utility fee collecting rights are also options for infrastructure projects.

Article 6: Foreign-funded enterprises are under the jurisdiction of the state laws and regulations and must not endanger national security or public interests. The contractual obligations of all parties will be overseen by the relevant government departments.

Chapter 2: Establishing, Adapting and Terminating Foreign-Funded Enterprises

Article 8: For the convenience of foreign investors, there will be a highly efficient *one-stop assessment, approval and registration procedure* to be used when establishing foreign-funded enterprises.

Article 9: For projects which are in line with the guiding policy, the relevant government offices at various levels should finish all the formalities relating to the approval of project proposal, feasibility study, contract and articles of association followed by the *issue of the business license within 15 working days* after receipt of all the required documents.

Article 10: Those projects which are in line with the guiding policy and whose total investment is within provincial approval limits falling into the following categories will be registered directly: (1) solely foreign funded enterprises; (2) equity joint ventures and contractual joint venture enterprises with no state contribution; and (3) scientific enterprises encouraged by the state, export-oriented enterprises whose production and construction requires no provincial input. For the above-mentioned enterprises, the industrial and commercial administration should finish all the registration formalities within five working days after receipt of all required documents.

Article 11: The above-mentioned enterprises whose business requires *operating permits* will obtain their business license before applying for any permits.

Article 12: Any *alterations to the major terms of contracts* will be handled by the original approval departments, and must be finished within 15 working days after receiving all required documents. Those enterprises that are registered directly will have their alterations approved by directly approaching the original registration organization.

Article 13: Upon *termination*, foreign funded enterprises will go through liquidation procedures before submitting the termination for approval to the original departments. Those enterprises that are registered directly will have their termination approved by directly approaching the original registration organization.

Chapter 3: Protection of Rights and Interests of Foreign Funded Enterprises

Article 14: Within their scope of business, foreign funded enterprises are entitled to conduct their business activities independently. *Personal rights and property of foreign investors* and employees are protected under state laws.

Article 15: The *patents, copyrights, trademarks, knowledge,* confidential technology and business information, computer software and brand names of foreign investors are protected under state laws.

Article 16: Foreign funded enterprises must enjoy *equal treatment* in use of water, electricity, gas and telecommunications as well as from financial, insurance, legal, employment, consultancy, design and advertising services.

Article 17: Foreign funded enterprises may reserve in their bank account foreign exchange from their operational income. They may also sell their *foreign exchange income* to the bank or buy from the foreign exchange pool in case of need. Foreign investors may remit their legitimate income abroad directly from their foreign exchange account or by buying foreign exchange from designated banks.

Article 21: Should foreign funded enterprises consider their legitimate rights and interests to be infringed by the conduct of any government department or staff, they may lodge a complaint with the *Complaint Centre for Foreign Funded Enterprises*. They may also apply for re-examination or file a lawsuit in the courts.

Chapter 4: Preferential Treatment for Foreign Funded Enterprises

Article 22: Foreign Funded Enterprises concerned with energy, communication, water conservancy, environmental protection, agriculture, forestry and animal husbandry and other related industries with terms of operation longer than 10 years will be *exempt from corporate tax* for two years starting from the first profit-making year. These enterprises will receive a full tax rebate from the financial bureau for the third, fourth and fifth years of operation.

Article 23: Those foreign funded enterprises which have been approved as technologically advanced enterprises with terms of operation longer than 10 years will be *exempt from corporate tax* from the first profit-making year. They will receive a full corporate tax rebate from the financial bureau for the third to the seventh years of operation. For the first three years of operation the proportion of V.A.T designated to the local financial departments will be rebated by these departments. Upon expiry of the above-mentioned preferential terms, favorable tax rates may still be obtained for enterprises that fulfill requirements from the provincial tax department.

Article 24: Foreign funded enterprises involved in energy, communication, environmental protection and urban public utilities whose actual investment exceeds 10 million dollars will have the proportion of their *V.A.T. designated for the local financial departments rebated* for the first three years of operation upon approval.

Article 25: Foreign funded enterprises *re-investing their profits in the province* and with terms of operation longer than five years, the local financial bureau will rebate corporate tax according to the amount re-invested.

Article 26: Foreign funded enterprises involved in agricultural projects that do not encroach on farming land will be *exempt from agriculture tax for the first three years*. For the fourth and fifth years, the above taxes paid will be rebated by the local financial bureau.

Article 27: Foreign funded enterprises will be given priority in the allocation of *land use rights*. Allocation of these rights will be at the same price level for all enterprises (domestic or foreign). Arrangements can be made to pay by installments if necessary. When foreign funded enterprises invest in Dormitory Housing Projects, they may sell 30 per cent of the floor area at a higher profit margin.

Chapter 5: Regulations for Administrative Departments

Article 29: When foreign funded enterprises go through formalities for *land use rights, city planning permission, design, provision of water, electricity and gas, telecommunications and fire prevention, the local construction administration bureau* will be responsible for co-ordination. The following time limits apply: a) if the area of land required be within the approval limit of the province, the land use administration bureau will issue the Certificate of Approval of Land for Construction or Certificate of Land Use Rights within five working days; b) the City Planning Bureaus will issue planning permission for the land and the license to begin construction within 10 working days; and c) departments for provision of water, electricity and gas, telecommunications and fire prevention will approve and issue certificates within five working days.

Article 30: The *Economic and Trade Commission* at various levels will be responsible for co-ordination to resolve the difficulties arising from the operation of foreign funded enterprises.

Article 31: The *Provincial Foreign Affairs Office* will be responsible for certifying the status of foreign experts working in foreign funded enterprises. The office should complete these formalities within two working days after receipt of required documents. Upon certification, *Confirmation for Employing Foreign Experts and Foreign Expert Certificates* will be issued.

Article 32: *Government departments at various levels will strictly abide by the following stipulations*: (a) no inspections or penalties and punishment of foreign funded enterprises are allowed unless clearly stipulated by law and regulations; (b) it is not permitted for law enforcement departments to order banks to transfer money or freeze bank accounts of foreign funded enterprises and foreign investors unless stipulated by law; (c) not to use their privileges to appoint enterprises of institutional departments to monopolize operation or promote hidden monopolies and unethical competition; and (d) no infringement on the legal rights and interests of foreign funded enterprises is permitted.

Article 34: The *annual monitoring of foreign funded enterprises* will be carried out by the departments in charge of foreign investment at various levels.

Article 35: *The fees charged to foreign funded enterprises* by administrative departments will be collected in accordance with relevant laws and regulations.

Article 37: The government regulatory bodies at various levels are responsible for overseeing the practices of the administrative departments. The complaint *Centre for Foreign Funded Enterprises* should carry out its duty in accordance with the law to safeguard the legal rights and interests of foreign funded enterprises.

Chapter 6: Legal Obligations

Article 39: Any *violation of the regulations* herewith, in particular the case set out below, will result in the individual responsible and their superior receiving administrative punishment according to the severity of the consequences.

(a) Illegal inspection of any foreign enterprise
(b) Illegally appropriating money from foreign funded enterprises
(c) Forcing foreign funded enterprises to buy particular products
(d) Forcing foreign funded enterprises to pay to participate in training courses in order to reap a financial benefit
(e) Appointing or covertly appointing intermediary agencies to foreign funded enterprises
(f) Forcing foreign funded enterprises to contract out construction projects to particular corporations
(g) Leaking business secrets and confidential information of foreign funded enterprises
(h) Infringing on the personal or propriety rights of foreign investors, their employees and dependents
(i) Other actions infringing on the rights and interests of foreign funded enterprises. Any losses incurred by foreign funded enterprises will be compensated. Should the violation break the law, the individuals responsible will be prosecuted.

Article 40: Should a *foreign funded enterprise suffer losses due to false or undue services* provided by the intermediary agencies, these agencies will compensate such losses. In serious cases, the responsible persons will be punished and their credentials revoked. Legal proceedings will follow should the behavior break the law.

Chapter 7: Appendix

Article 42: These regulations also apply to investment from enterprises and individuals of Hong Kong Special Administrative Region, Macao and Taiwan.

Article 43: The Yunnan Provincial People's Government is responsible for the interpretation of these regulations.

(c) *Procedures for foreign investment in Yunnan*

The requirements and procedures for foreign investment in Yunnan are detailed below. The text is extracted from the Yunnan Investment Affairs Office web site.

"Procedures for the Examination and Approval of Foreign-Funded Projects at Provincial Level"

In accordance with the "Regulations of Yunnan Province on the Improvement of Foreign Investment Administration," the present "Procedures of the Examination and Approval for Foreign-Funded Projects at Provincial Level" are enacted under the scenario of "one-window-for-all, one-stop and one-stamp-for-all services" and on the principles of openness, standardization and efficiency.

(i) *Acceptance of applications*

1. The Office for Foreign Investment Affairs of the Yunnan Provincial Government (hereinafter referred to as the Office) is responsible for accepting and handling all applications from foreign investors for establishing enterprises in Yunnan, and has the task of deciding whether or not to approve the said applications or to pass them on to the state authorities for examination and approval.

2. In order to facilitate the examination and approval work, the organizations and individuals that apply to set up foreign-funded enterprises (hereinafter referred to as the applicants) should submit to the Office six copies of one complete set of genuine and qualified documents.

3. Application documents include:

    a) Application letter for the establishment of the proposed enterprise.
    b) Feasibility study (concurrent with the project proposal).
    c) Contracts and articles of association.
    d) List of equipment that will form part of the total investment.
    e) Application letter for Industry and Commerce registration and relevant material.

The Office has the responsibility for assessing whether or not the applications and their appendices submitted by the applicants are qualified. In cases where received applications are found to be unqualified, the Office should immediately notify the relevant applicants to make the necessary supplements and amendments.

4. If the application is required to contain an assessment of environmental impact, evaluation of assets and land, selection of sites and registration of project name, the applicant shall apply to the departments concerned for the said assessments and evaluations prior to the submission of the project application. At the request of the applicant, the Office may notify the departments concerned with making such assessments and evaluations.

5. The applicant can obtain the forms for Industry and Commerce registration from the office after the name of the proposed project is preliminarily approved by the relevant administrative authorities for industry and commerce. These forms should be submitted to the Office as part of the qualified application documents.

6. Once the documents submitted by the applicant are confirmed acceptable, they will be formally handled by the Office, and an acceptance notice will be issued to the applicant by the Office. The Office shall finish all examination and approval work within 15 working days after acceptance of the application.

(ii) *Comments solicitation*

1. Within two days after the acceptance, copies of the application documents should be circulated by the Office to the relevant departments of the Provincial Government (hereafter referred to as the competent departments) to seek their comments.

2. The documents circulated by the Office for soliciting comments should be dealt with as a matter of urgency by the competent departments who should make comments on the said documents within eight days after they are received. The documents shall be assumed to be agreed on by any departments who fail to present their comments within the period stipulated above.

3. The comments presented by the competent departments shall be deemed as their official opinion concerning the proposed project. The following comments should be solicited:

    a) Comments of the Provincial Planning Commission and the Economic and Trade Commission on the feasibility study.
    b) Comments of the Provincial Bureau of Foreign Trade and Economic Cooperation on contracts and articles of association.
    c) Comments of the Provincial Administration for Industry and Commerce with regard to the registration and business scope of the proposed project.

d)   Comments of the Provincial Land Administration regarding to the use of land for the proposed project.

e)   Comments of the Provincial Bureau of Environmental protection concerning the environmental impact of the proposed project.

f)   Comments of the departments governing the particular sector trade to which the proposed project belongs.

4.   In the process of making comments, the competent departments should inform the Office to notify the relevant applicant to make any necessary supplements and amendments to the application.

5.   The comments of the competent departments should be submitted in writing to the Office with the signature of the leader in charge and the official stamp of the department.

(iii)   *Project assessment*

1.   As a requirement for some large and important projects, a meeting should be convened to assess the feasibility study by the Office or its authorized government departments such as the Provincial Planning Commission, the Economic and Trade Commission, and other concerned departments. The assessment done by the authorized government department should be reported to the Office.

2.   This assessment should be completed within 15 working days.

(iv)   *Synthesizing comments*

1.   The office will oblige the competent departments to make their comments on the application documents within the aforementioned period.

2.   The office will oblige the [relevant authority] from the competent departments immediately after they become available, and carry out relevant analysis and evaluation based on the resulting information. If there is a difference of opinion, the relevant departments shall be consulted. Any major problems with projects are subject to the decision of the provincial government.

3.   For any projects in sectors that are restricted by the government or where there is a marked difference of opinion by relevant departments, the Office will convene a meeting to discuss the project. This meeting will be presided over by the director general of the Office or his authorized deputy. Representatives from relevant departments will attend the meeting as required.

(v)   *Issue of certificates and feedback*

1.   The Office should issue the applicant with an approval paper if an application has passed the general examination. Along with the approval paper, the applicant can also obtain his or her certificate of approval and business license from the Office.

2.   If an application fails to pass the examination, the Office shall officially inform the applicant of the reasons for the failure.

3.   If amendments and supplements are necessary for the application, the Office shall inform the applicant in writing of the contents of the amendments and supplements.

(vi)   *Miscellaneous*

1.   The Office for Foreign Investment Affairs of the Yunnan Provincial Government is responsible for implementing and interpreting these procedures.

2.   These procedures come into effect from the date of release.

(d) *Taxation*

For taxation matters, foreign investors should acquire a copy of "The Income Tax Law for Foreign-Funded and Foreign Enterprises". The following extract on taxation in Yunnan is drawn from the Yunnan Investment Affairs Office web site (www.invest-yunnan.com) but contains minor editing.

(i) *Preferential Policies for Foreign-Funded Enterprises in Accordance with Relevant Taxation Laws and Regulations*

According to Article 8 of the Income Tax Law for Foreign-Funded and Foreign Enterprises, any foreign-funded enterprise involved in production, scheduled to operate for a period of not less than 10 years shall, from the year in which it begins to make profits, be exempt from income tax for the next two years and allowed a 50 per cent reduction in the third to fifth years.

Any foreign investment enterprise which is engaged in agriculture, forestry, or animal husbandry, and any enterprise with foreign investment which is established in underdeveloped border and remote areas may, upon approval from the competent department for tax affairs under the State Council for an application filed by the enterprise, be allowed a 15 per cent to 30 per cent reduction in the amount of corporate income tax payable for a period of 10 years following the end of the tax exemption and reduction period outlined in the preceding paragraph (Article 8 of the "Income Tax Law for Foreign-Funded and Foreign Enterprises").

Export-oriented enterprises invested in and operated by foreign businesses for which the output value of export products amounts to 70 per cent or more of the total product output value of the enterprise for that year may pay enterprise income tax at a 50 per cent reduced rate after the period of enterprise income tax exemptions or reductions has expired according to the provisions of the Tax Law (Clause 7, Article 75, "Rules for the Implementation of the Income Tax Law for Foreign-Funded and Foreign Enterprises").

Advanced technology enterprises invested in and operated by foreign businesses which still remain technologically-advanced after the period of enterprise income tax exemptions or reductions has expired may continue to pay enterprise income tax at 50 per cent of the rate specified in the Tax Law for an additional three years (Clause 8, Article 75, "Rules for the Implementation of the Income Tax Law for Foreign-Funded and Foreign Enterprises").

Foreign-funded enterprises established within the territory of Yunnan are exempt from the 3 per cent local corporate income tax (Clause 1, Article 10, "Regulations of Yunnan Province for Encouraging Foreign Investment").

Any foreign investor of an enterprise with foreign investment who re-invests profits obtained from the enterprise directly into that enterprise by increasing its registered capital, or uses the profit as capital investment to establish other enterprises with an operation term of not less than 5 years shall, upon approval from the tax authorities of an application filed by the investor, be refunded 40 per cent of the income tax paid on the reinvested profits (Article 10, "Income Tax Law for Foreign-Funded and Foreign Enterprises").

Foreign investors of enterprises with foreign investment who directly re-invest their profits derived from the said enterprise into the establishment or expansion of an export-oriented enterprise or an enterprise with advanced technology shall have the entire portion of the corporate income tax that has already been paid on the re-investment refunded (Clause 1, Article 81, "Rules for Implementation of the Income Tax Law for Foreign-funded or Foreign Enterprises").

Chinese-foreign equity joint ventures engaged in port and dock construction where the period of operations is 15 years or more, shall, following application by the enterprise and approval thereof by the national tax authorities at provincial-level, from the first profit-making year, be exempt from corporate income tax for five years and subject to corporate income tax at a 50 per cent reduced rate for the next 5 years (Clause 1, Article 75, "Rules for Implementation of the Income Tax Law for Foreign-funded or Foreign Enterprises").

Where, for special reasons, it is necessary to shorten the useful life of fixed assets of any foreign-funded enterprise, the accelerated depreciation method may be adopted, following approval of the enterprise's application by the State Taxation Administration (Article 40, "Rules for Implementation of the Income Tax Law for Foreign-funded or Foreign Enterprises").

If a foreign-funded enterprise or an organization established in China by a foreign enterprise is engaged in production or business operation and makes a loss in a certain year, the said loss may be made up by their earnings from the following year or years if the said loss could not be covered by the one year's earnings. However, the maximum term for making up the loss must not exceed 5 years.

(ii) *Preferential Tax Policies of the State for Encouraging Foreign Investment in Central and Western China*

For foreign-funded enterprises established in Shanxi, Inner Mongolia, Jilin, Helongjiang, Anhui, Jiangxi, Henan, Hunan, Sichuan, Yunnan, Tibet, Shaanxi, Gansu, Nixia and Xinjiang provinces or autonomous regions, which are engaged in projects within either the encouraged category or restricted category B, corporate income tax is reduced to 15 per cent for a further three years after the expiry of the preferential tax period in accordance with the current preferential tax policies. In addition, if the foreign-funded enterprise is certified as an export-oriented enterprise with over 70 per cent of its output for export, its applicable corporate income tax rate may be further reduced to 10 per cent (Document: Guoshuifa No. 172, 1992).

Foreign-funded enterprises engaged in energy and transport infrastructure are entitled to corporate income tax reduced to 15 per cent, subject to approval by the State Taxation Administration (Guoshuifa No. 13, 1999).

Foreign-funded enterprises, which carry out technological development and whose expenditure for the current year in the said technological development increases by 10 per cent or more, compared with the previous year, are entitled to use their income tax payable for the current year to offset up to 50 per cent of their actual expenditure for technological development in the current year. If the income tax payable for the current year is inadequate to offset 50 per cent of the enterprise's expenditure on technological development that year, then the offset amount shall not exceed the enterprise's income tax payable in the current year and the excess part may not be left for offsetting in the coming years (Guoshuifa No. 173, 1997).

Foreign-funded enterprises established within the territory of Kunming and engaged in production are eligible for the reduced corporate income tax rate of 24 per cent, and 15 per cent for foreign-funded high-tech enterprises set up in the Kunming New and High-Technology Industrial Development Zone (Clause 4, Article 10, "Provisions of Yunnan Province for Encouraging Foreign Investment").

Corporate income tax at the reduced rate of 24 per cent is applicable to foreign-funded enterprises of a production nature established in the three opening-up border cities of Hekou, Wanding and Ruili (Clause 5, Article 15, "Provisions of Yunnan Province for Encouraging Foreign Investment").

Foreign-funded enterprises within Kunming Dianchi Tourism and Vacation Zone are entitled to 24 per cent corporate income tax rate ("Announcement by the State Taxation Administration on Tax Issues for National Tourism and Vacation Zones", Guoshuifa No. 248, 1992).

A reduced corporate income tax rate of 24 per cent is applicable to Chinese-foreign equity joint ventures engaged in port and dock construction and financial institutions such as foreign capital banks and Chinese-foreign banks established in Kunming, where the capital contribution of the foreign investor or the funds for business activities allocated by the bank's head office to the branch exceeds US$ 10 million, and where the period of operations is ten years or more (Clause 2 and 3, Article 73, "Rules for Implementation of the Income Tax Law for Foreign-funded or Foreign Enterprises").

Financial institutions such as foreign capital banks and Chinese-foreign banks established in Kunming with a capital contribution from the foreign investor or funds for business activities allocated by the bank's head office to the branch exceeds US$ 10 million and the period of their operation is ten years or more shall, following application by the enterprise and approval thereof by the local tax authorities and commencing with the first profit-making year, be exempt from corporate income tax in the first year and subject to corporate income tax at a 50 per cent reduced rate for the second and third years (Clause 5, Article 75, "Rules for Implementation of the Income Tax Law for Foreign-funded or Foreign Enterprises").

(iii) *General Taxation Issues*

Foreign enterprises in China pay taxes in the following categories: corporate income tax, value added tax, business tax, consumption tax, urban house tax, and vehicle and vessel license tax. Customs duties, value added tax, and consumption tax are levied on the goods entering and leaving the country according to related customs duty regulations. Both foreign and Chinese personnel in a foreign-funded enterprise shall pay individual income tax.

a. *Taxation rates on the income of foreign-funded enterprises*

Since July 1991, the government has levied a business income tax. The categories and rates are as follows:

Additional tax preferences can be obtained for the following:

a) With government approval, a preferential tax rate of 15 per cent will be applied to construction projects in transportation, energy and port facilities; and technology-intensive projects or projects with a total foreign investment of more than US$ 30 million and with a lengthy investment recovery period;

b) Foreign-funded productive enterprises whose operation period is more than ten years shall be exempted from income tax for two years starting from the first profit making year, and shall be exempted from half of the above tax for the following three years. All the foreign funded enterprises in Yunnan Province are exempt from the local income tax.

b. *Value added tax*

Organizations and individuals that sell goods or provide services of processing and repair on the territory of China and import goods into China shall pay value added tax.

Table 35. Foreign business tax rates
(percentage)

	Kunming Area	Kunming National Hi-tech Industrial Dev. Zone	Dianchi Lake Tourism and Vacation Zone	Border Economic Operation Zones in Hokou Ruili and Wangding	Other Areas
Production enterprises	24	Hi-tech: 15 Others: 24	24	24	30
Non-production enterprises	30	30	24	24	30
Enterprises w/annual exports over 70% of annual total output value	12	Hi-tech: 10 Others: 12	12	12	15

Source: Office of Foreign Investment Affairs of Yunnan Province

Except in cases stipulated below, sellers or importers shall pay value added tax at the rate of 17 per cent. Sellers or importers of the following commodities shall pay value added tax at the rate of 13 per cent: grain, vegetable cooking oil; running water, air conditioning, hot air, gas, liquefied gas, natural gas, biomarsh gas, coal products for domestic use; pictures, newspapers, magazines; feed, chemical fertilizers, farm machinery, and agricultural film; and other items regulated by the State Council such as mining and ore-dressing products of metallic and non-metallic ores, and agricultural products).

Exporters are exempt from value added tax unless stipulated otherwise by the State Council.

c. *Consumption tax*

A consumption tax is imposed on the processing and import of cigarettes, alcoholic drinks, alcohol, cosmetics, skin creams and moisturizers, hair care articles, costly ornaments and jewelry, firecrackers and fireworks, gasoline, diesel fuel, tires, motorcycles, automobiles (cars, cross-country cars, minibuses with fewer than 22 seats) and those who deal in the retailing of gold and silver ornaments. In these cases, enterprises should refer to the "Provisional Regulations of the People's Republic of China on Consumption Tax" and the "Detailed Rules for the Implementation Rates of Taxation on the Income of Foreign-Funded Enterprises".

d. *Business tax*

The business tax varies according to the type of business activity. The categories and their respective rates are as follows:

a) transportation, construction, post and telecommunications, construction, post and telecommunications services, cultural and sports undertakings: 3 per cent;

b) services (including agent service, hotel industry, catering industry, warehousing and storage business, leasing industry, advertising industry); transferring intangible assets (right to land use, patents, technology without patent, trademark privileges, copyright, goodwill); and selling real estate: 5 per cent;

c) financial and insurance activities: 8 per cent;

d) entertainment (discos, karaoke bars, music saloons, billiard rooms, golf courses, bowling alleys, and amusement parks): 5 per cent if they are in rural areas and townships, 10 per cent if they are in other places.

e. *Urban house tax*

Tax rates for urban houses (owned and rented) are as follows:

a) Owned: the house's value the tax rate is 1.2 per cent, and it is calculated on the basis of the value acquired by the method of the house's original value minus depreciation;

b) Rental: 12 per cent.

f. *License tax*

Foreign-funded enterprises shall pay a license tax on the motor vehicles they own and use according to the "Provisional Regulations on License Tax," and the "List of Yunnan Provincial License Tax".

g. *Individual income tax*

People who have lived in China for one year or longer shall pay income tax on the income derived both inside and outside of China. People living in the country for less than one year shall pay income tax on the income derived inside China.

h. *Other taxes*

Additional taxes include the increment tax on land value, the tax on natural resources, the stamp tax, and animal slaughter tax.

(e)   *Land issues*

As noted earlier, foreign invested enterprises have equal rights to land use in Yunnan as local firms and at prices equal to those offered to domestic firms.

Other matters related to land use rights are extracted from the Yunnan Investment Affairs Office web site:

(i)   *Fees for the transfer of land use rights*

Foreign-funded enterprises may obtain the right to use land by means of transfer. The land use right can be transferred by means of negotiation, bid invitation, or auction according to the different purposes of land use. If an enterprise is unable to pay the transfer fee in a lump sum, it can negotiate a concession in the transfer contract that allows for payment by installments or shortens the tenure of the transfer so as to reduce the fee.

(ii)   *Charges for the use of sites*

Foreign enterprises can acquire land use rights through allocation. Firms will pay the Chinese government for site preparation costs (including expenses for land requisition, dismantling old buildings, the relocation of residents, and installation of public utilities), and land rental. Foreign firms that acquire land use rights through allocation and pay the entire land preparation costs in a lump or at its own expense are exempted from land rentals for the first five years after establishment. From the sixth to tenth years, the firm will be exempt from half the land rental.

For foreign firms investing in promoted industries for non-profit projects, namely education, culture, health, and scientific research projects, and pay the land preparation costs in a lump sum are exempt from land rental.

Domestic firms seeking to form a joint venture with a foreign company that has been allotted land use rights must apply to the appropriate land management department and pay the transfer fee. Another option is for the Chinese partner in the joint venture to pay the land rental costs.

(iii)   *Leasing*

Foreign funded enterprises can acquire land use rights by leasing. Under this option, the firm pays rent to the land management department of the local government.

2. Customs duties and procedures

Exemptions on customs duties for imports are available for foreign investment projects if the imported equipment, accessories, and spare parts are for use within the importing firm. Also, they are exempt from value added tax except for certain goods such as cars, computers, and others.

Import licenses are not required for importing raw materials, fuel, bulk cargo, spare parts, auxiliary equipment and materials, and packaging materials used in the production of exported goods. However, the imported goods are held until the documents pass through the clearance procedures.

E. Main opportunities for investment

Investment is welcome in most sectors of the economy and it is open to all nationalities. A major source of investment in China is from overseas Chinese and from Taiwan Province of China, Hong Kong, China and Macao, China. Potential investors should consult the provincial "Regulations on the Guidance of Foreign Investment" and the "Guiding Catalogue of Industries for Foreign Investment" produced by the State Council.

However, the Yunnan government promotes the following selected sectors and activities for foreign investment:

1. Infrastructure

1. Development and operation of local railways and related bridges and tunnels (however, 100 per cent foreign ownership and operation is not permitted).
2. Construction of highways, bridges, and tunnels.
3. Development and operation of civil aviation airports (again, 100 per cent foreign ownership is not allowed and the Chinese partner must have a controlling stake in the venture).
4. Development and operation of hydropower stations and thermal power stations with a capacity of 300 MW or more.

2. Agriculture and biological resources

1. Cultivation and processing of tropical cash crops.
2. New varieties of commercial plants and fruit trees.
3. Investment in nurseries, plantations and processing plants.
4. Developing post-harvest technology.
5. Livestock rearing and processing.

3. Minerals

1. High density phosphorous compound fertilizers, food and feed additives, and other refined chemicals.
2. Iron and steel activities
3. Nonferrous metals

   Mono-crystalline silicon and polycrystalline silicon
   Hard alloys, tin compounds, antimony compounds
   Nonferrous composites and new alloys
   Mining of copper, lead and zinc ores
   Mining of aluminum ore (but 100 per cent foreign operations are not permitted)
   Risk exploration for mineral resources
   Manufacture of building materials and nonmetal products

4. Tourism

1. Development of national and provincial tourist destinations and scenic spots.
2. Construction of recreational facilities in vacation zones.

5. Technology

1. Development of new high technology.
2. Upgrading of conventional industries through applied high technology.

6. Environmental protection

1. Recycling industrial waste products.
2. Equipment for urban sanitation.
3. Pollution control and equipment.

F. Learning more

1. Related web sites

Office of Foreign Investment Affairs of Yunnan Province: http://www.invest-yunnan.com

Mekong Express: http://www.mekongexpress.com: Contains information on foreign investment, maps, visa policies and more.

2. Recommended readings

Kunming Planning Commission, Foreign Investment Approval Office of the Kunming Municipal People's Government (1998). *Investment Guide to Key Projects in Kunming*.

Kunming Planning Commission, Foreign Investment Approval Office of the Kunming Municipal People's Government (undated). *Projects for Foreign Investment in Yunnan*.

Office of Foreign Investment Affairs of Yunnan Province. *Guide to Investment in Yunnan* (contains a series of booklets and information leaflets on Yunnan).

United Nations ESCAP (1999). *Guidebook on Trading with China*, 5th edition.

VIII. REGIONAL RATIONALE AND A CORRESPONDING STRATEGY FOR GMS FIRMS

A. Introduction

In much the same way that the countries of the GMS recognized the benefits of a regional strategy, companies operating in the GMS should adopt a similar regional approach in their business activities. Taken individually, some of the GMS members are less than ideal investment markets because of their underdeveloped status and shortages of vital input for the economy such as human resources, capital, technology, infrastructure, and other factors. Moreover, some of the domestic markets cannot provide sufficient economies of scale. Despite these disadvantages, the GMS is still a viable business environment, particularly if firms begin to think in terms of cross-border activities and apply strategies that help to develop the regional private sector. This last chapter of the GMS Business Handbook is designed to encourage firms to think broader than the typical single country focus and apply some strategic tools to enhance the competitiveness of the GMS.

B. The rationale behind regional economic cooperation

Economic strategies have transformed greatly over the past 20 years. The former policies of autarky and import substitution industrialization have been abandoned in most instances in favor of integration with the world markets. The reasons for the shift in development strategy were obvious: most States lacked the necessary input factors to supply a solid foundation for the economy; protected domestic industries typically lacked efficiency; and domestic markets often lacked economies of scale. All of these were instrumental factors in the economic reforms made throughout the GMS since the late 1980s.

Producing for the global market brought its own set of challenges, however. First, intense competition for overseas markets meant that industries had to become more productive, efficient, and increase the quality of products and services. Limited individual capacities of some states, namely in terms of technology, human resources, and ingenuity, compelled States to work together. Second, each State's economy requires certain production inputs that could not be provided domestically or least not very efficiently and in adequate quantities, and thus it became imperative to harness the comparative advantages found in other economies.

Various market failures have prevented many countries from fulfilling their economic potential. Markets are not perfect, and many States face similar problems and needs which make coordination and cooperation more desirable. Salient market failures include the breakdown or lack of information flows, the inability to provide public goods, and the indivisibility of certain goals. All three failures, along with a desire to exploit potential spillover benefits, induce multilateral cooperation. In the GMS, these problems are compounded by the incompleteness of the economic reforms.

Looking specifically at regional economic development areas (REDAs) such as the GMS and their connection with the emerging global trends, the overall rationale for REDAs is that greater benefits can be obtained through subregional cooperation than would be possible through independent action. To understand the desire to create a REDA, the specific rationales are discussed below in terms of economic, political, and social justifications.

1. Economic rationale

In theory a REDA will generate economic growth by making maximum use of the inherent but underutilized economic potential in the proposed development area. The rationale for a REDA is predicated on the assumption that natural complementarities, such as labour, natural resources, finance capital, and technology are distributed irrespective of national boundaries, and by means of transnational production they can be utilized in the most efficient way possible. Efforts are made to increase the flow of goods, labour, and capital across boundaries for transnational production to occur, thereby making the REDA a more attractive trade and investment opportunity.

Hence, the driving force behind the creation of a REDA is the recognition that *greater benefits can be obtained through subregional cooperation than would be possible through independent action*. REDAs enable States to overcome deficiencies in labour, technology, resources, land, and infrastructure by facilitating access to the required inputs found in the subregion.

In addition to the individual interests of each country, REDAs can facilitate overall regional economic cooperation. In instances where regionwide integration is difficult to achieve, bilateral and subregional economic arrangements can be forerunners to broader cooperation because of the relative ease with which agreements can be made with only a few members. Subregional arrangements, then, are often much more feasible than regional attempts at economic cooperation, but through their aggregation help achieve broader regional goals.

An additional economic rationale for the creation of a REDA is that it encourages greater liberalization of the economy. Taking advantage of the factor endowments lying across the border necessitates granting reciprocal access to one's own economy so that efficiency can be maximized and other benefits of a subregional growth area realized.

In a related justification for REDAs, they can also encourage greater decentralization to the local level. Subregional growth areas tend to alter the vertical relationship between the central government and the local governments, especially when it comes to dealing with local counterparts across the border. Rather than having the central government direct and handle all of the communication with their neighbours, local officials are often given increased leeway in dealing with local officials over local issues.

2. Political rationale

REDAs also have implications for peace and security in the region. They promote greater cooperation and harmonization of policies, such as customs, tariffs, and possibly banking and finance as well, in order to free up the flow of goods, capital, and labour across national boundaries. This applies not only at the national level as Governments try to cooperate to enable the REDA to materialize, but it also brings the local governments into more formalized relationships or at the very least greater contact with one another. By creating more linkages of interdependence among the local economies, force is less likely to be used in settling a dispute because of the disruptive effects it would have on economic activities.

Domestic security is also enhanced within REDAs because of the economic development that occurs along the frontiers. In many GMS countries, the periphery areas are inhabited by ethnic minorities or other socio-economically marginalized people who often have little contact with the Government; also these areas are often the poorest regions. The economic benefits from greater cross-border trade and investment will develop these fringe areas which are frequently neglected in national development strategies and by foreign investors. The generation of greater wealth for people in the periphery will help remove many of the economic sources of contention between people in these areas and the central government.

3. Social rationale

The social rationale for REDAs is closely related to the political and economic justifications. Increased contact through cross-border economic activities will help promote mutual understanding of cultures, which in turn enhances border security. The social rationale also parallels the economic ones in that the citizens involved in the REDA will likely gain substantial improvements in their standard of living and quality of life. Presumably economic development will bring concomitant benefits such as better education, improved health services, and a more elaborate social safety net.

C. Economic benefits of REDAs

A well-structured REDA creates a multitude of potential benefits to its members. In general, economic benefits arise from better economies of scale and more closely integrated and competitive business sectors among the members. Specific benefits include new sources of supplies, expanded markets for products and services, increased investment opportunities, new employment, technology transfer, and skills development. These benefits derive from the increased flow of goods, people, and capital, and the opportunity for combining these in transnational production.

Taking a closer look at the GMS, several benefits to businesses are evident. First, the *complementarity of production factors* across the border means that firms can gain greater access to resources, land, capital, labour and other necessary inputs as the member countries work to lower barriers to cross-border flows of goods and people. Resource endowments differ throughout the GMS, and the GMS scheme helps to bring these together. For example, the GMS contains extensive amounts of minerals and other natural resources which are enticing investment opportunities, as noted in the earlier chapters. Cambodia offers a wide variety of minerals, coal, and other valuable resources; Myanmar is rich in forests and natural minerals (gold, copper, zinc, granite, iron, nickel, and several types of gems); and Yunnan has extensive coal deposits. As the economic cooperation within the GMS deepens, investment activities designed to harness these resources across the borders will become more viable.

Second, regional economic cooperation brings about a *larger market size and potential for economies of scale*, even if one invests in the smaller economies such as Cambodia or the Lao People's Democratic Republic.

Third, the *economic corridors and other forms of cross-border infrastructure* in the GMS facilitate the transnational movement of goods, services, people, and information to a greater extent than would otherwise be possible on a unilateral or even bilateral basis. These economic corridors and the development of transportation infrastructure will stimulate nodes of economic activity, such as special production and trade zones, from the existing opportunities and endowments along the routes. In other words, they will bring the major market centres in the Mekong region together and thereby expand the market reach or open up new areas to trade and investment.

Trade and investment activities in each member of a REDA are likely to increase substantially for a number of reasons. First, businesses gain greater access to the comparative advantages dispersed among the participating units of the REDA, particularly in regard to inputs to production. This lowers their costs and makes their goods more competitive in the global market – thus attracting additional investment and increasing exports. Second, by reducing the barriers to trade among members, goods from one country can be marketed more easily and cheaply in the other REDA members. Third, many REDAs contain an important outlet to global markets such as a port or international airport. Landlocked countries such as the Lao People's Democratic Republic and Yunnan Province of China lack a strategic outlet to distribute goods, and subregional initiatives such as the economic corridors help alleviate these disadvantages. Fourth, new or expanded infrastructure is likely to result from the establishment of a cross-border economic growth area. REDAs provide supply side incentives to encourage investment through the provision of new infrastructure or optimizing the existing infrastructure for financial and industrial cooperation.

Additional benefits include: (1) improved networking and information exchange arising from cross-border cooperation; (2) pooling of resources from donor agencies and other sources of assistance (as opposed to competing for scarce funding and assistance); and (3) preparing for liberalization and entry into world markets in a more manageable scope.

Other benefits of a regional approach are specific to the level of development of the various members. For more developed states such as Thailand, regional economic cooperation offers solutions to rising labour costs and the challenges of economic restructuring. Transborder economic arrangements provide outlets for relocating sunset industries to lesser developed countries like Myanmar, Cambodia, and the Lao People's Democratic Republic. Labour intensive industries can be transplanted across the border to an area which has lower labour costs, and thereby free up resources and capital in the more advanced country for high-tech and higher value added industries.

A likely benefit of REDAs that has not been explored extensively is the potential for stimulating "clusters" in a particular industrial sector. An industrial cluster is an agglomeration of linked or related business activities comprising industries, suppliers, and support services in a limited area. The contributions that clusters make to economic development are increasingly recognized, and the conditions in most REDAs would be ideal for the growth of industrial clusters across borders. Industrial clusters often arise naturally without any government-initiated planning, although well-planned public sector efforts to develop the broad infrastructure to support clusters can play an important role. (Clusters will be discussed further in section E.3.).

D. The roles of the state and the business sector in regional economic cooperation

Despite the predominant market orientation of REDAs, they are still subject to the limitations of state sovereignty and controls, particularly in regard to cross-border activities. Regional economic cooperation arrangements are generally government-initiated and require a certain level of government involvement to expand commercial and investment activities within the area. In general the role of the government in a REDA is to provide a policy environment conducive for the development of the REDA, namely in regard to the necessary legal and regulatory frameworks. More specifically, the Government determines the investment incentives, controls the tariff and customs schedules for imports and exports, and regulates the flow of people into and out of the country. Additionally, the State is expected to provide the initial infrastructure for a growth area to emerge, including electricity, transportation networks, water supply, and more.

Another core function of the state is to develop the linkages with its counterparts and reach agreement on the basic form of the regional economic arrangement and the general policy requirements. Local governments will also develop closer linkages with each other, but their level of autonomy and decision-making authority will depend on the central authorities.

The role of the business sector in a REDA encompasses both the foreign and local business communities. The business sector's contributions consist primarily of providing the capital investment and employment opportunities, while also performing the production and export activities within the REDA. Since the business sector is the real engine of growth, the success of the GMS hinges on the business sector taking the lead role once the Governments fulfill their duties in creating a positive business environment.

However, the business sector's willingness and desire to take advantage of the transnational business opportunities are contingent upon the Governments providing the appropriate policies, incentives, infrastructure, and other basic public goods in the initial stages. Hence, the business sector performs the actual implementation of the REDA. Equally important is the expectation that the business sector will take up an increasing share of the responsibility for expanding or upgrading the basic infrastructure. The GMS programme is at this critical juncture where the business sector needs to be more involved in the overall planning and direction of the GMS and take advantage of the current opportunities provided by the GMS for greater cross-border economic activity.

As noted in an earlier chapter, one of the fundamental weaknesses with the GMS up to now is the minimal role given to the private sector by the Governments. One of the key determinants in how the GMS will fare in the coming years is the extent to which public-private sector dialogue and partnerships are utilized in the planning and policy-making of the next phase of the GMS.

Public-private sector partnership is the key to producing an effective transnational growth area. There is a strong need for close collaboration between the public and business sectors in planning and implementing the GMS. Without a high level of interface between the two realms, their goals and expectations might not converge. For instance, if the Government does not fully support regional economic cooperation, a willing business sector is unable to pursue transnational economic activities because of the preliminary functions that must be performed by the State. If the Government misjudges the kinds of opportunities desired by the business sector and the policy requirements of businesspeople, then the business sector will not take advantage of the REDA's activities.

E. Firm strategies in the GMS context

How should foreign and domestic firms respond to what the GMS is attempting to accomplish, and how can they make the most of the opportunities presented in this regional setting? All across the world firms are reacting to several global trends: (1) the shortening of product lifecycles; (2) the importance of global production networks; (3) a shift from mere product-based transactions to knowledge-based transactions; and (4) lower barriers to market entry. In response to these and other changes, more emphasis is being placed on increasing the competitiveness of firms, countries, and even subregions; the microeconomic foundations of businesses; and building industry clusters. All three of these are highly interrelated but are often unknown or neglected by domestic GMS firms and in some cases by foreign firms that are simply looking for raw materials and cheaper labour.

1. Competitiveness

Competitiveness is an often talked about concept in economics and business but one that is hard to define and understand. There are almost as many definitions as there are authors on the subject, which leads to confusion and uncertainties as to whether people are discussing the same concept. At the heart of competitiveness is the idea that continuous increases in productivity give firms, sectors, and even countries strategic market advantages. These advantages lead to rising incomes, an improved quality of life, and stable, long-term economic growth. Competitiveness arises from higher productivity, better quality goods and services, and innovation.

The well-known Harvard Business School professor Michael Porter points out that competitiveness of the country depends broadly on three factors:

1. political, legal, and macroeconomic context;
2. quality of the microeconomic business environment; and
3. sophistication of company operations and strategy.

The macroeconomic context refers to three main areas: economic foundations, legal system, and the political system. The economic foundations entail the investment and trade policies, liberalization, fiscal and monetary policies, and others. The legal system is critical in terms of the commercial codes and enforcement of laws and regulations. Lastly, the political system needs to be stable, have effective regulatory agencies and institutions, and be supportive of the business community.

The microeconomic conditions refer to infrastructure (namely the quality and supply of telecommunications, water, electricity, transportation network, education, and social services), capital availability, science and technology, the quantity and quality of suppliers, the sophistication of buyers, and the level firm rivalry.

The sophistication of company operations and strategy means the choices made by firms about competing in certain industries, their strategies for positioning themselves in that sector, and the quality of the plans and decisions.

2. Focus on micro-factors

Macroeconomic policies are a necessary but not sufficient contributor to economic growth and development. An improved macro-environment will not necessarily generate sustained growth unless the underlying micro-foundation is sound. And eventually, the key determinant of sustained productivity growth will be the extent to which the "innovation terrain" is conducive to activities that deepen and strengthen the microeconomic foundations of competitiveness (see figure 59).

Figure 59. The innovation terrain

Political, legal, and macroeconomic context

The Innovation Terrain

Framework Conditions

Transfer Factors

Innovation Dynamo

Science and Engineering Base

Quality of the microeconomic business environment

Sophistication of company operations and strategy

The Microeconomic Foundations

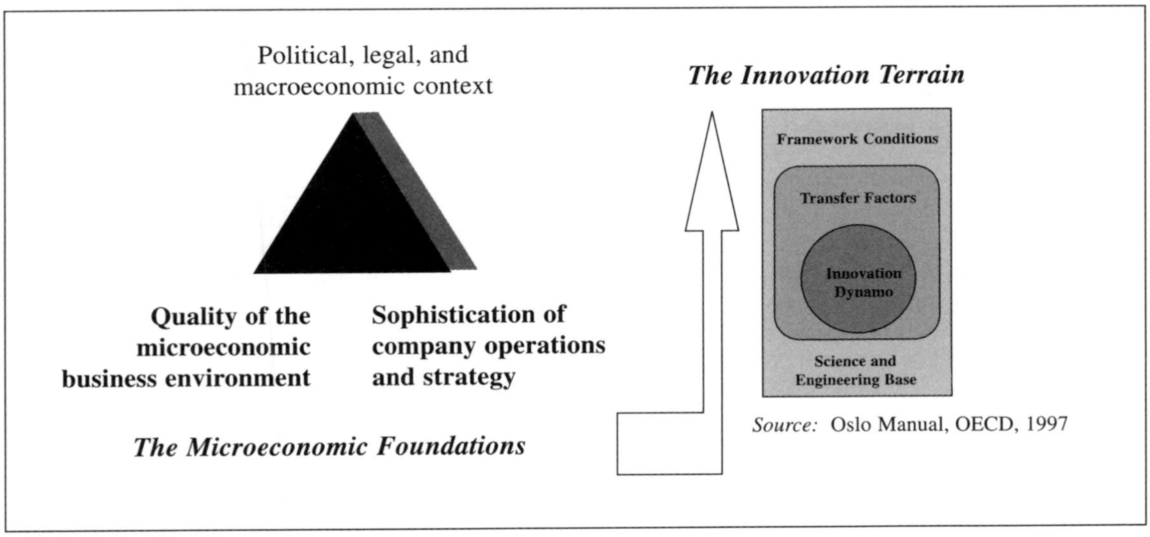

Source: Oslo Manual, OECD, 1997

Macro-factors are clearly important concerns for businesses, as they shape the context in which firms operate; however, firms often neglect to address the microeconomic factors that can enable them to perform better and become more competitive. Much of the attention, and subsequently the majority of complaints, by businesses in the GMS is directed at the macro-level, particularly in terms of the legal and regulatory frameworks. Without trying to minimize the importance of the macro-environment, firms in the GMS need to take a closer look at their micro-level foundations and apply many of the business tools and concepts in use in the more developed economies around the world.

The microeconomic foundation is considered vital because it reflects much more closely the actual operating units that generate wealth in the economy. We can examine in detail the micro-factors that need to be considered to support the operations of the business community, in particular the infrastructure, advanced institutions, and human resources needed for companies to develop more sophisticated operational strategies.

Michael Porter characterizes the business micro-environment in terms of four interrelated influences (see figure 60):

1. *Factor (input) conditions*: The quality and specialization of underlying inputs that firms draw on in competing.

2. *Demand conditions*: The sophistication of home demand and the pressure from local buyers to upgrade.

3. *Related and supporting industries*: The availability and quality of local suppliers and related industries.

4. *Context for firm strategy and rivalry*: The context shaping corporate investment, the types of strategies employed, and the intensity of local rivalry.

Each of these elements needs to be considered in order to understand (and influence) the microeconomic business environment in such a way as to enhance competitiveness and sustainability.

Figure 60. Microeconomic environment

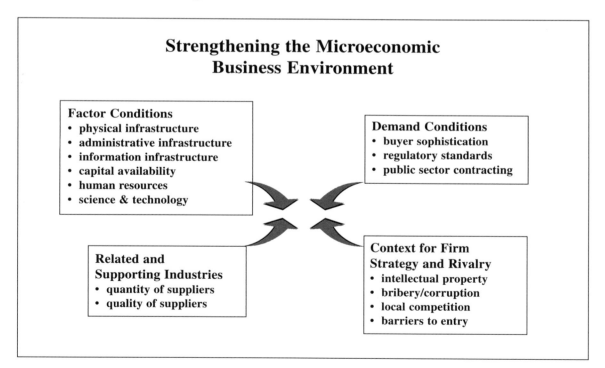

226

In his 1998 article in the Global Competitiveness Report, Michael Porter writes:

Overall, the process of economic development requires a transformation of the types of competitive advantages a nation's companies enjoy in international markets. Advantage must shift from comparative advantage (low-cost labour or natural resources) to competitive advantages due to unique products and processes. What were strengths in traditional ways of competing become weaknesses. Changes are often resisted, because past approaches were profitable and because old habits are deeply engrained in institutions.

What are some of the adaptations that more competitive firms (and even sectors) are making to improve the microeconomic foundation? Firms in the more developed economies have shifted their focus over the past several years to acquire more sophisticated company operations and strategies. Some of the key developments and new directions for firms include:

- Moving from assembly-based operations to *value chain-based operations*.
- Shifting from sector-based to *cluster-based linkages*.
- Becoming *market-driven* instead of supply-driven, and looking at regional and global markets as opposed to serving only domestic markets or single export destinations.
- Emphasizing *competitive advantage* instead of merely comparative advantage.

Many of these strategic changes adopted by firms around the world relate to some of the problems facing the private sector in the GMS. Firms in this region, including many of the foreign firms, are still using the old strategies noted above. The GMS and other developing countries are usually seen as offering comparative advantages for low cost labour and primary commodities, and firms often assume these are sufficient factors for success. However, comparative advantages do not necessarily translate into competitive advantage in the world market. Likewise, the foreign and domestic private sector in the GMS has not progressed far in creating value chains and clusters. Local firms are typically not linked into global supply chains and have few, if any, linkages with firms outside their specific sector. Foreign companies in the GMS often take advantage of labour and raw materials with the intention of exporting goods outside the region instead of building supply chains and outsourcing activities with local firms. Also, many firms in the GMS do not adequately analyze what customers and suppliers really want, and instead produce goods without responding to changes in consumers' tastes, differences among markets, the needs and quality standards of firms higher up the value chain, and other market-driven factors.

Firms in the GMS, both foreign and indigenous, need to consciously consider these issues and explore modalities for increasing their firm level, industry, and regional competitiveness. What, then, are some of the key micro-level strategies that GMS firms should consider?

1. Focus on changing market conditions, trends, and opportunities in the regional and global economies. Apply new production technology and information technology (IT); determine preferences of markets.
2. Increase one's competitiveness in world markets on the basis of product differentiation through research and development (R&D), improved logistics, and more focused marketing activities instead of relying only on low costs.
3. Devote more attention and resources to improving human resources of firms, especially in uses of technology and higher value skills development.
4. Promote the concept and benefits of clusters (see next section) and explore possible initiatives for building clusters and networking.
5. Work more closely with related firms in developing benchmarks for that industry and using the benchmarks to determine the necessary changes to increase the industry's global competitiveness.

3. Clusters

Clusters are increasingly recognized around the world as vital elements of economic growth because of the contributions they can make in enhancing competitiveness within countries as well as across borders. Michael Porter defines clusters as:

"...geographic concentrations of interconnected companies and institutions in a particular field. Clusters encompass an array of linked industries and other entities important to competition. They include, for example, suppliers of specialized inputs such as components, machinery, and services, and providers of specialized infrastructure. Clusters also often extend downstream to channels and customers and laterally to manufacturers of complementary products and to companies in industries related by skills, technologies, or common inputs. Finally, many clusters include governmental and other institutions – such as universities, standards-setting agencies, think tanks, vocational training providers, and trade associations – that provide specialized training, education, information, research, and technical support."

Clusters help bring collective benefits and solutions to problems faced by individual firms. Among the ways clusters help are:

1. Collective efficiency as a result of cooperation helping to improve performance.
2. Technological spillovers and upgrading.
3. Sharing scarce resources.
4. Achieving international standards.
5. Improved product quality and response time (arising from cooperation and competition within the cluster).
6. Joint action and articulating the cluster's needs to policy makers.
7. Help small enterprises overcome growth constraints and promote learning.

Industrial clusters tend to arise somewhat naturally rather than result from a specific decision by firms or policy makers to consciously "create" a cluster. Nevertheless, numerous countries have initiated various activities between the public and private sectors to promote clusters and the corresponding value chain linkages. Key activities include:

1. Bringing in specialists to run workshops on competitiveness and clusters for private sector, government officials, universities, and others.
2. Setting up strategy meetings between government officials and potential industry clusters, especially for identifying key obstacles and needs.
3. Embarking on benchmarking exercises for the industry.
4. Building linkages and value chains between:
   a. Big and small firms
   b. Foreign and domestic firms
   c. Firms in neighbouring countries
   d. Higher education institutions and industry

Clusters will not suddenly emerge even if the aforementioned activities are conducted. Instead, the conditions for clustering and the requisite linkages will build up gradually, as shown in figure 61.

Figure 61. Stages of cluster evolution

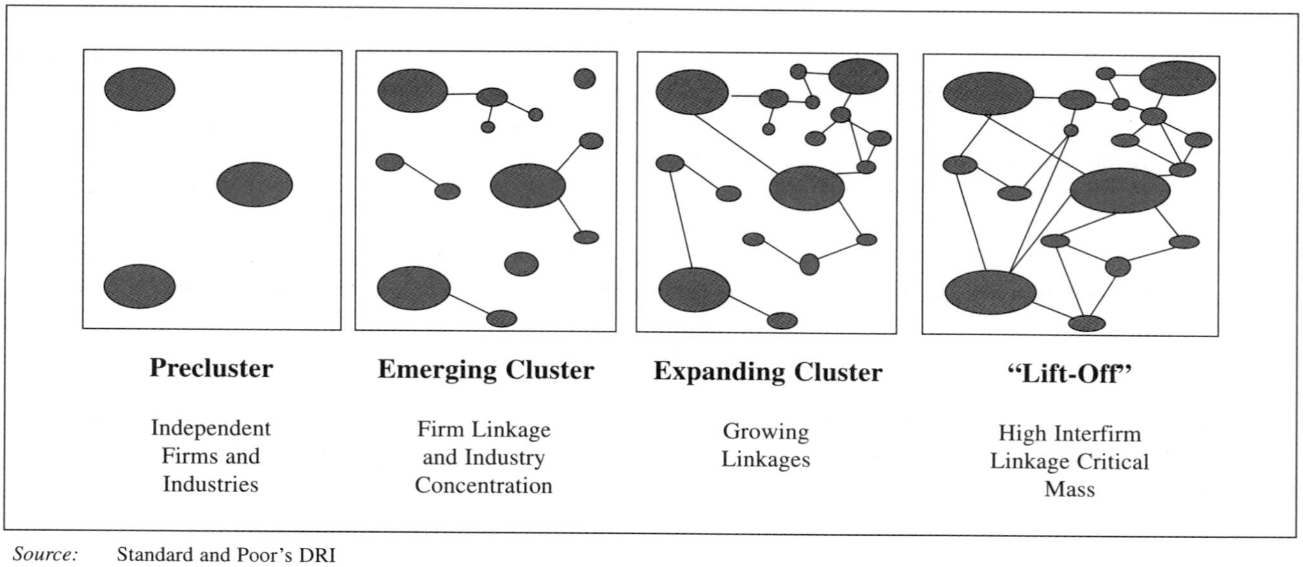

Precluster	**Emerging Cluster**	**Expanding Cluster**	**"Lift-Off"**
Independent Firms and Industries	Firm Linkage and Industry Concentration	Growing Linkages	High Interfirm Linkage Critical Mass

Source: Standard and Poor's DRI

Will the development of clusters help make the GMS globally competitive? Clusters are not necessarily a panacea for the all of the GMS's ills, nor will they be effective under all circumstances. Successful clusters require several conditions to become competitive. First, the appropriate technology must be accessible to the cluster firms. As noted earlier, one of the benefits of clustering is the spillover of technology and upgrading. Once one or more firms within in the cluster adopt improved technology, the others are exposed to it through their proximity and ongoing contacts within the cluster. To maintain their individual competitiveness, the other firms will have to adopt the newest technology that is giving other cluster firms an advantage.

Second, successful clusters must have adequate skilled labour that is adaptable to changing technology and processes. However, firms in the cluster will also need to invest in human resources development to provide for the appropriate training opportunities.

The availability of capital is a third requirement for successful clustering. If the firms within a cluster are unable to acquire finance and other forms of capital, especially for technology development and procurement, then they unlikely to become competitive.

Fourth, the Government is expected to provide the proper legal and regulatory frameworks to allow the private sector to operate efficiently and effectively. The development of strong legal and regulatory frameworks requires open and regular channels of public-private sector dialogue so that Government understands the needs of the private sector and can promulgate laws and regulations that help the private sector become globally competitive. In addition to the investment codes, taxation policies, court systems, and other key elements of the legal and regulatory setting, the ability to form industry associations can also facilitate the rise and success of clusters. Although clusters are broader than industry associations, the linkages and networking activities of business associations can be instrumental in the development of clusters.

Fifth is adequate physical infrastructure. Governments and the private sector share responsibility in the provision of infrastructure. The Government is obligated to provide certain public goods for infrastructure development, while the private sector also undertakes for-profit infrastructure projects. Clusters need decent infrastructure to facilitate communication among firms, to be able to receive and utilize technology, and to move goods to and from markets.

Are these prerequisites fully in place in the GMS for clusters to emerge and flourish? Clearly not all of them, but the above discussion intends to offer firms in the GMS a basic roadmap for building up the competitive foundation for the region. Some of the issues and strategies can be undertaken by the private sector itself, such as fostering better linkages between foreign and local firms, human resource development, and improving the micro-foundations of firms. For other matters the private sector must encourage the governments of the GMS to engage in open discussion about the key policy issues.

F. GMS company profiles: experiences and lessons learned

Having focused on the micro-environment where firms operate in the first half of this chapter, it is useful to take a look at how some GMS companies are conducting their business activities. Six GMS firms related their experiences and offered advice for investors looking to start up in the GMS.

1. Myanmar Nyunt Co., Ltd., Myanmar

Myanmar Nyunt Co., Ltd. is one of Myanmar's leading private exporters of beans and pulses. Beans and pulses are Myanmar's second largest agricultural export earner behind rice. The company was established in 1989 when Myanmar moved towards a market-oriented economy, but its origins date back as far as 1946. Myanmar Nyunt specializes in supplying premium and handpicked selected beans to foreign markets. The major products include black matpe, green mung beans, black-eyed beans, red kidney beans, butter beans, pigeon peas, konnyaku (a wild potato product), and niger seeds. All of its products are cleaned, sorted, and graded with the company's own modern machinery, which ensures that the product quality and packaging meet international standards. Myanmar Nyunt's major export markets are Japan (which accounts for 70 per cent of the company's exports), the European Union, and the United States (combining for 25 per cent of sales), but it also sells to Malaysia, Singapore, and India. Annual exports are over US$ 1 million.

Myanmar Nyunt does not sell its products to other GMS countries because of the high level of competition from local companies in the GMS that supply beans and pulses. Moreover, government regulations in Myanmar impose a 10 per cent export tax that reduces profit margins and renders the company's products less competitive than some of its GMS competitors. Therefore, Myanmar Nyunt has sought ways to diversify its products and cater to specialized markets to compensate for the disadvantages it faces. For example, konnyaku is a specialty item sold exclusively to Japan, where it is used in unique dishes such as sukiyaki.

Myanmar Nyunt relies on other strategies as well to ensure its success in Myanmar. It focuses on beans more than oil seeds because of some export restrictions on oil seeds, whereas beans do not have any limits and can be sold directly to the overseas clients. But perhaps the most important strategy for the company's success is to import products and resell them in the local market. Importing is necessitated by the relatively low profit margins offered by exporting due to the 10 per cent tax. U Tun Aung, the company's executive director, explains that he imports construction materials because the profit margins are much higher when goods are re-sold domestically, but he cannot rely on import activities alone. Exporting is required in order to acquire foreign exchange, which is in short supply in Myanmar. The hard currency he receives from exporting beans and pulses is then used to finance the import of construction materials.

Two additional success factors noted by U Tun Aung are his trust with established customers and his strategic use of trade fairs throughout the world. Myanmar Nyunt's customers in the United States and European Union are willing to pay in advance of the delivery of containers. Customers send their payment by means of telegraphic transfer one or two days in advance of the shipment, which enables Myanmar Nyunt to cover the costs of delivery. U Tun Aung says this kind of transaction would not be possible without the trust his company has developed with long-term customers. In regard to trade fairs, he uses them in particular for networking and identifying new potential clients, but also to keep abreast of the latest technology in equipment and seeds and to generate new business ideas.

When asked what advice he would offer to companies looking to start up in Myanmar, U Tun Aung stressed the importance of engaging in both export and import activities. Companies looking solely to export goods will likely not be as competitive because of the export tax and exchange rate differences, but they can be very profitable if they also import goods for re-sale in Myanmar.

Contact information:
Myanmar Nyunt Co., Ltd.
106/108 93rd Street
Kandawgalay P.O.
Yangon, Myanmar
Tel: 951-280-099
Fax: 951-280-632
E-mail: myanmarnyunt@mptmail.net.mm

2. Royal Group of Companies, Cambodia

The Royal Group of Companies was established in 1989 by the late Chairman and CEO Mr. Sophan Kith as a general trading company in Australia for import and export activities. In 1990, Royal Group began supplying office equipment to the United Nations Transitional Authority in Cambodia (UNTAC). Royal Group currently serves as an exclusive distributor for world-renowned brands in several product lines.

Its main business activities are in the fields of telecommunications, trading, agriculture, genetic engineering, cattle breeding, and fish farming. Royal Group operates through a number of joint ventures and wholly owned subsidiaries that employ 800-900 people in administration, sales, finance, logistics, and service. Some of its specific business activities include:

- Royal Cambodia Co., Ltd., which is a sales and marketing company and engages in import and export.
- Exclusive distributorship of Canon office equipment, Motorola radio communications, and Bell helicopters.
- Royal Biotech Aqua Farm Ltd., which is involved in fish farming.

- Royal Cryogenics conducts genetic engineering, animal husbandry, and cattle breeding.
- Millicomm International Cellular S.A. (joint venture) for mobile cellular communication.
- Cam-GSM Mobitel, which will operate the second international gateway for Cambodia (Royal Telecam TELE 2).

Oknha Thieng Kith, Royal Group's Vice Chairman and Managing Director, attributes much of the company's success to its pioneering spirit. For instance, Royal Cambodia Co., Ltd. was the first company to introduce modern office equipment to Cambodia. A second success factor is the company's knowledge about the market. Royal Group conducts extensive market research to understand trends and customers' needs and preferences. Oknha Thieng Kith himself spent two months travelling throughout Cambodia immediately after returning from living in Australia for 10 years to understand how Cambodians live, what their needs are, people's capabilities, and other issues related to market research. By going around and talking to people and seeing how they live, he was better able to plan the company's strategy.

When asked what advice he would give to firms looking to start up in the GMS, Oknha Thieng emphasized the importance of cultivating the right contacts within the government. He said it is imperative in the GMS for new investors to explain thoroughly to the Government what the firm intends to do, how it will accomplish these activities and, most importantly, how the government and general public will benefit from the investment project. According to Oknha Thieng, too often firms fail to convey clearly to the Government the benefits of the investment project and explain why the Government should support it. Investment projects are often delayed or not approved if the host country's Government does not immediately see the anticipated benefits of an investment project.

A second piece of advice offered by Oknha Thieng for new investors is to take a medium to long-term perspective on a start up business. He emphasized the importance of having a sound financial capital reserve, because one should expect to suffer losses in the first five years or so until recovering the investment costs. Also, the financial sector in much of the GMS is extremely weak and loans are not easy to acquire. Thus, new firms must have sufficient working capital of their own to get through the initial stages of the investment.

Third, Oknha Thieng emphasized the importance of conducting extensive market research before commencing with an investment project. Consumer needs and preferences, purchasing power, and the availability of local suppliers are some of the critical issues that investors should know about before preparing a business plan for the GMS.

Contact information:
Royal Group of Companies
Royal Group Building
246 Preah Monivong Blvd.
Phnom Penh, Kingdom of Cambodia
Tel: 855-23-426-414; 426-419
Fax: 855-23-426-415
E-mail: royalgroup@bigpond.com.kh
Web site: http://www.bigpond.com.kh/users/royalgroup

3. GMS Power Public Co., Ltd., Thailand

GMS Power Public Company Limited is the private power development subsidiary of MDX Public Company Limited. Since its inception in 1993, GMS Power has experienced rapid growth in terms of business activities, new projects under development, and the number of employees. GMS Power has or is planning projects in each of the GMS countries, leading towards its vision of an integrated power grid for the region.

GMS Power has positioned itself to become a leading regional independent power developer. The company has entered into joint ventures with various Governments in the GMS to bring power generation closer to consumers as well as to ensure a stable income for the countries concerned. At present, GMS Power operates or is developing the following projects in the region:

- *Theun-Hinboun Power Project (Lao People's Democratic Republic)*: This US$ 240 million, 210-megawatt electricity plant became operational in 1998, and is a joint venture between Electricite du Laos, MDX Lao (a joint venture of GMS Power), and Nordic Hydropower. The plant is the first privately-owned foreign power plant to sell power to Thailand.
- *Nam Ngum 3 Hydropower Project (Lao People's Democratic Republic)*: Through its joint venture, MDX Lao, GMS Power is preparing to implement a second power project with the Government of the Lao People's Democratic Republic. Negotiations are continuing with the government for the 440-megawatt hydropower plant to be constructed, and GMS Power has also entered negotiations with the Electricity Generating Authority of Thailand for the plant to sell its electricity to Thailand.
- *Jinghong Hydropower Project (Yunnan, China)*: In the first of three planned power stations in Yunnan, GMS Power will hold a 70 per cent stake in the Jinghong Hydropower Plant. GMS Power, the State Power Corporation of China, and the Yunnan Electric Power Group Co., Ltd. signed an agreement in September 2000 for the 1,500-megawatt power station.
- *Bang Bo Power Project (Thailand)*: Through another of its joint venture companies, GMS Power began construction on a 350-megawatt gas-fired power plant in mid-2000. The US$ 250 million project, scheduled for completion in mid-2002, also involves one of the world's largest energy companies and a leading Taiwanese industrial bank.

Mr. Robert Kay, GMS Power's Executive Vice President, offered valuable advice on successfully operating in the GMS. He urged foreign firms to always involve a local company as a way of strengthening the capabilities of these developing firms. Furthermore, such capacity building measures will benefit your future operations in that country by having trained local counterparts, and it also helps build a positive relationship with the Government.

Mr. Kay also recommends that foreign firms carefully consider the full realm of needs for the labour force. While training is typically required, foreign employers must also be aware of other needs typically not required in developed countries, such as housing for the workers and transportation from their residences to the firm. Another important success factor related to operating in the local community is to provide community assistance such as model farms and schools. GMS Power factors these costs into its budget, but in the long run these measures help improve the company's operations and relationship with the community.

When asked about the issue of corruption in the GMS and how firms can minimize its occurrence, Mr. Kay suggested that foreign firms attempt to get as many people and institutions involved in the project as is practical. The involvement of multilateral agencies and others creates greater awareness of the project and helps lessen the chances of corruption.

Lastly, he noted the benefits of going "the extra mile" to demonstrate the foreign firm's commitment and sincerity to develop the host country. For instance, GMS Power went beyond the contractual terms and constructed a road for one of the government ministries in the Lao People's Democratic Republic, which likely paved the way for future benefits for the company.

Contact information:
GMS Power Public Company Limited
7th Floor, Nai Lert Tower
2/4 Wireless Road
Lumpini, Pathumwan
Bangkok 10330 Thailand
Tel: 662-253-0428
Fax: 662-267-9094

4. Euro Asian Seeds Co., Ltd., Thailand and Yunnan Province

Euro Asian Seeds Co., Ltd., established in 1991, operates in Thailand and Yunnan Province of China. The company's main line of business is buying and selling potato seeds and tubers, but it includes other vegetable and flower seeds as well. Euro Asian Seeds imports its seeds from the Netherlands, Germany, and the United Kingdom and sells on average about 100 metric tones per year to companies and farmers in Thailand. It then purchases an annual average of 1,500-2,000 metric tons of potato tubers from the farmers and re-sells them to processing factories and wholesalers.

Euro Asian Seeds formed a joint venture in 1997 in Yunnan with the Food Processing Co., Ltd. and the Kunming Agriculture Technology Bureau called the Kunming Luyuan Agriculture Development Co., Ltd. The joint venture company aims to develop and produce potato seeds in Yunnan to eliminate the need to import seeds from Europe. Also, Kunming Luyuan Agriculture Development Co. will eventually produce approximately 50,000 metric tons per year of potato tubers from the seeds.

Euro Asian Seeds' joint venture in Yunnan is still in the tissue culture phase of producing seeds, but soon it expects the seeds to be planted by farmers in Luliang. The company's Managing Director, Mr. Somchai Upara, intends to import the potato seeds from the joint venture into Thailand as a lower cost replacement for the imported European seeds.

Mr. Somchai selected Yunnan for the site of the joint venture for several reasons. First, the production costs in Yunnan are cheaper than importing seeds from Europe. Second, the production costs in Yunnan are more cost effective than in Thailand. Third, the Chinese market is extremely vast, and the population consumes a high quantity of fresh produce. Fourth, the climate and soil conditions in Yunnan are ideal for potato seed production.

Mr. Somchai emphasizes the importance of offering his farmer clients high quality potato seeds that produce high yields. Otherwise, the farmers, who are simultaneously his customers (for seeds) and suppliers (for tubers) will not have much incentive to buy his seeds or be able to offer a sufficient quantity and quality of potato tubers for him to re-sell to wholesalers and processing factories. Two of the keys to his effective relationship with the farmer clients are the contract system and technology support. He also noted the importance of regularly utilizing information technology such as the Internet to assess trends in his line of business, such as consumer preferences and changes in production and processing techniques.

Contact information:
Euro Asian Seeds Co., Ltd.
1314-1322 Srinakarin Road
Suanluang, Bangkok 10250 Thailand
Tel: 662-322-4330; 321-6869
Fax: 662-726-3394; 322-4329

5. AA Company Limited, Viet Nam

AA Company Limited is a Vietnamese interior design and furniture manufacturing company that was established in 1990 and became a private limited company in 1993. AA Co., Ltd., based in Ho Chi Minh City, started out refurbishing and manufacturing furniture for the local market, including foreign investor clients. Gradually the company expanded it services and markets to include overseas customers in Sri Lanka, Japan, Singapore, France, and the United States.

AA Co., Ltd. provides interior design services to international standard office buildings and hotels in Asia, and is currently Viet Nam's leading company in the field. AA also produces wooden furniture, fire-rated doors, stained glass, and soft furnishings for the domestic and international markets. Over the past four years, AA's annual sales have averaged approximately 20 per cent growth.

Much of the company's success is attributed to its good reputation for quality products and services, and its positive relationships with international construction firms and consultants. One of the keys to developing AA's reputation was the successful completion of its first overseas contract with the Colombo Hilton Hotel in Sri Lanka in which AA supplied the furniture for renovating the rooms. Soon afterwards, AA won several high-profile contracts around the world, including the Angkor Century Hotel (Cambodia), the Micasa Apartments (Cambodia), the Kanuhura Hotel (the Maldives), and the Shangri-La in Singapore.

A second success factor is the company's quality products. AA has its own manufacturing plant and utilizes the high quality and abundant local timber. A third factor, according to Mr. Nguyen Quoc Khanh, AA's Director, is that AA developed a capable team of project coordinators who have a strong capacity to work on overseas projects. The capabilities of the project coordinators enable AA to respond to the clients' needs and demands.

Contact information:
AA Co., Ltd.
117 Ly Chinh Thang, District 3
Ho Chi Minh City, Viet Nam
Tel: 848-846-8828
Fax: 848-846-8829
E-mail: aa-company.ltd@hcm.vnn.vn
Web site: http://www.aacompanyvn.com

G. Measures for facilitating cross-national flows of goods, people, and services

The success of the GMS hinges on the members' willingness and ability to facilitate the flow of goods, people, and services across borders. One of the main concerns of the GMS programme is to pursue measures for increasing cross-border exchanges. Below are a few suggested activities that can be conducted in the GMS to help foster cross-border flows. One of the most effective ways of achieving these goals is to fast-track the implementation of various elements of ASEAN economic cooperation and extend these in a formal way to Yunnan Province of China.

Investment promotion: Explore ways to attract local and foreign investment into the GMS by marketing the complementary endowments in the area, the flow of production factors across borders, and possibly offer special economic zones with incentives. Possible activities for the growth triangle include: coordinating marketing strategies; institutional capacity building for local investment bodies; inter-agency cooperation measures; harmonized approval and regulatory procedures for cross-border investment projects; acceleration of the ASEAN Investment Area (AIA); and an investment information exchange system.

Trade facilitation: Consider approaches to improving the efficiency and effectiveness of trade procedures, documentation, and data exchange within the GMS. Possible activities include: harmonization of customs and inspections procedures and documentation requirements, developing a consistent classification system of goods; trade related information systems; joint export promotion activities; accelerating the ASEAN Free Trade Area (AFTA); and establishing export quality standards for agriculture goods.

Business sector collaboration: Putting in place cooperation mechanisms between the business sectors in the GMS to support other activities and create a sustainable dynamic to create economic activity.

Value chains and cluster development: Taking the previous point one step further, develop networking within and among economic sectors throughout the GMS in order to foster supply and value added chains. Also explore policy and regulatory frameworks that will stimulate industrial cluster development in the GMS.

Industrial planning: Coordinate industrial planning among the members based on the potential complementarities and resource endowments. Promote the ASEAN Industrial Cooperation scheme (AICO) among firms in the GMS to take advantage of the preferential tariff rates and non-tariff privileges. This will stimulate transnational production and value chains.

SME development: Pool resources and experience for special SME programmes within the GMS. These could include special financing packages for SMEs, joint training, joint marketing efforts, and linkages with selected export destinations and foreign firms needing suppliers (i.e., matchmaking).

Human resource development: Embark on cross-national human resource development programmes for farmers, labourers, and entrepreneurs.

Rural development: Explore modalities for integrated rural development. The GMS is comprised of mostly rural areas that are deficient in basic infrastructure needs such as electricity, water, transportation networks, sanitation systems, education, and health.

In closing, critical success factors are summarized here to help guide the policy makers and private sector in the development of the GMS:

Involvement of the private sector: The private sector must be the key player in the implementation of the GMS. Several attempts at fostering regional economic cooperation have failed because of the lack of attention to and involvement of the private sector. The business community is the engine of economic growth, and policy makers who are leading this initiative must make them equal partners in the planning and implementation of the GMS.

The appropriate role of government in the GMS: The governments of the GMS should see their role as providing an environment conducive to business and economic growth within the subregion. This includes improving the legal and regulatory frameworks for business, allocating sufficient resources for the development of the border areas, and demonstrating a clear commitment to the deepening of the GMS programme.

Continued economic liberalization: The full benefits of the GMS will be unobtainable if economic liberalization does not continue. To varying degrees, all of the GMS economies are undergoing reform in response to the inefficiencies and market distortions that became manifest the over past few years, especially during the Asian economic crisis. Moreover, they are facing contradictory pressures from home and abroad to protect domestic markets (including labour) or to further liberalization, respectively. Although the pace of liberalization is a matter for the individual governments to decide, regional cooperation cannot occur in an environment characterized by restricted markets, cronyism, and other unfair advantages to rent-seekers.

Set tangible goals and realistic expectations: Regional economic cooperation will not bring immediate benefits to everyone, nor will it quickly make the GMS globally competitive. Instead, it is a process that evolves over time and requires patience and nurturing. Members will need to prioritize activities and set forth goals that are practical and stand a good chance at being achieved. Unrealistic expectations and overly ambitious goals, which were clearly evident in the early years of the GMS, will only lead to slippage in implementation and disappointment with regional economic cooperation.